The *Parents*™ Magazine Baby and Childcare Series combines the most up-to-date medical findings, the advice of doctors and child psychologists, and the actual day-to-day experiences of parents like you. Covering a wide variety of subjects, these books answer all your questions, step by important step, and provide the confidence of knowing you're doing the best for your child—with help from *Parents*™ Magazine.

Other *Parents*™ Childcare Books
Published by Ballantine Books:

PARENTS™ BOOK OF TOILET TEACHING

PARENTS™ BOOK FOR YOUR BABY'S FIRST YEAR

PARENTS™ BOOK OF CHILDHOOD ALLERGIES

PARENTS™ BOOK OF BABY NAMES

PARENTS™ BOOK OF BREASTFEEDING

PARENTS™ BOOK OF PREGNANCY AND BIRTH

PARENTS™ BOOK FOR THE TODDLER YEARS

PARENTS™ BOOK FOR RAISING A HEALTHY CHILD

PARENTS™ BOOK OF INFANT COLIC

PARENTS™ BOOK OF CHILD SAFETY

Parents™
Book for
New Fathers

DAVID LASKIN

BALLANTINE BOOKS • NEW YORK

For Kathleen and Emily
who made me a father

Sale of this book without a front cover may be unauthorized. If this book is coverless, it may have been reported to the publisher as "unsold or destroyed" and neither the author nor the publisher may have received payment for it.

Copyright © 1988 by Gruner + Jahr, U.S.A., Publishing

All rights reserved under International and Pan-American Copyright Conventions. Published in the United States of America by Ballantine Books, a division of Random House, Inc., New York, and simultaneously in Canada by Random House of Canada Limited, Toronto.

Library of Congress Catalog Card Number: 87-91850

ISBN 0-345-33707-7

Manufactured in the United States of America

First Edition: June 1988
Fourth Printing: November 1991

Contents

	Acknowledgments	vii
CHAPTER 1	Introduction: Fatherhood New and Old	1
CHAPTER 2	Deciding to Have a Child	7
CHAPTER 3	Knowing About the Pregnancy—Conception and Fetal Development	20
CHAPTER 4	Feeling About the Pregnancy	54
CHAPTER 5	Problems in Pregnancy	94
CHAPTER 6	Preparing for the Birth	117
CHAPTER 7	Labor and Birth: The Father's Role	158
CHAPTER 8	The First Weeks of Your Baby's Life	207
CHAPTER 9	Now What Do We Do? Mastering the Practical Routines	235
CHAPTER 10	Coping with the Inevitable	265
CHAPTER 11	Feeling Like a Family	287
CHAPTER 12	Caregiving: Who, How and When?	297
CHAPTER 13	Fathers in Special Situations: Adoptive and Single Fathers	324
CHAPTER 14	The Growth of a Relationship	339
Appendix A	Infant Development Chart	363
Appendix B	Resources for Fathers	376
	Index	393
	About the Author	408

Acknowledgments

My first and biggest thank-you goes to all the fathers all over the country who shared their experiences with me in interviews. Some are friends, some are relatives, most are perfect strangers—all were terrifically open, generous, thoughtful, and eager. Without them this book would never have gotten off the ground.

Thanks also to the professionals in the fields of childbirth education, nursing and midwifery, psychology, child development, and fathering who shed light, offered guidance, and provided me with books, resources, and names of fathers to interview: Diana Simkin of Family Focus in New York, Lois Fink of the Long Island Jewish Medical Center, Robert Scherb, family psychologist Jerry Sachs of Father Focus in New York, Rick Bell of St. John's Hospital in St. Paul, Jenny Whitman, midwife Lorenzo Martinez of the Fatherhood Project, Robert McCall, Stephanie Farrow of Childcraft of New Mexico, Martha Griffin, Suzanne Wilson of New York's Childbearing Center, Kitty Ernst of the National Association of Childbearing Centers, Melanie Brand of Aims Community College in Greeley, Colorado, JoAnne Fisher of the Franklin Maternity Hospital and Family Center in Philadelphia, Dr. Ken Lewis of the Child Custody Evaluation Service in Glenside, Pennsylvania, and New York University Medical Center for providing illustration models.

I'm grateful to my editors, Elizabeth Crow at *Parents* for her enthusiasm and support, and Joëlle Delbourgo at Ballantine for her unflagging dedication and for her friendship and thanks to Karen HWA for seeing the book through.

I learned most about fatherhood from being a father. Many thanks to my wife, Kathleen O'Neill, for sharing the adventure of parenthood with me, as well as for reading, listening, suggesting, and calming. And a giant thank-you to our daughter Emily for teaching me about fatherhood, babyhood, and all the amazing things that fathers and children have together.

1. Introduction: Fatherhood New and Old

After millennia of being revered, feared, ridiculed, rejected, yearned for, and simply taken for granted, fathers seem suddenly to be in fashion. The media can't get enough of us. We're featured cuddling our young ones in heartwarming ads for insurance, film, fast food, and high tech equipment; in more and more sit-coms we're in the kitchen, the nursery, and right smack in the middle of our kids' emotional and social lives; we're celebrated in bestselling books of humor, anecdote, and self-congratulation; we're the subject of surveys, studies, feature stories, and celebrity gossip columns; we're on the cover of glossy magazines grinning with our gorgeous babies. We don't bumble anymore! When our sit-com wives go away for the day (or forever), we don't succumb to domestic nervous breakdowns. We're not remote anymore! We don't bury ourselves in our pipes and our slippers and our newspapers, only surfacing in times of family crisis or when someone needs a "talking-to." We're warm and competent (at least most of the time), concerned and involved. We nurture. We've taken the giant step from "Father Knows Best" to "The Bill Cosby Show." We're the New Fathers actively practicing the New Fatherhood.

Or at least that's what television writers, advertising executives, moviemakers, and journalists would have us think.

What do *we*, the so-called New Fathers, think? And more important, what do we *do*? The truth, as so often with media-reported trends, is a little grayer, a little more complicated, a little less flashy, and a lot more stubbornly rooted in difficult issues and hard work than *People* magazine or "Punky Brewster" would have us believe. But change, whether one views it as gray or glitzy, has occurred—there is no doubt about that. Long after media trend-spotters have forgotten all about the New Fatherhood, we New Fathers will be up to our elbows in it, changing diapers, dropping our kids off at day-care centers, coaching our partners through their labors, negotiating over chores, slicing time out of our work schedules to be with our families. A real, quantifiable shift has occurred in American fatherhood during the past two decades. As James Levine, director of the Fatherhood Project at New York's Bank Street College and author of *Who Will Raise the Children?* (Lippincott, 1976), has written: "The redefinition of fatherhood has been going on in virtually every arena of American life for well over ten years—even before Dustin Hoffman learned to make French toast in *Kramer versus Kramer*" (*Across the Board*, March 1986).

It's a redefinition that we see in the fact that fathers now expect (and are expected) to attend the births of their children. We see it in the fathers' groups that are springing up around the country. We see it in the sharp rise in the numbers of single fathers who are raising their children under age three by themselves (more than twice as many now as in 1970). And perhaps most importantly, we see it in our own lives and our desires to be with our babies, to participate in their upbringing, to experience their developments, not through anecdotes told by our partners but through our own daily involvement in their care. Yale psychiatry professor and doctor, Kyle D. Pruett, puts his finger on it in his book *The Nurturing Father* (Warner Books, 1987): "All of us in the myriad disciplines that comprise the field of child development have noticed that fathers and their babies are finding themselves in increasing physical and emotional contact with one another, though for many different reasons."

To witness this increasing father-baby contact in action, we don't have to go any farther than our own homes, the homes of our friends and relatives, the streets and parks and shops of the communities we live in. Fathers are *in there* with their children in a way they were not a generation ago. Who among

Introduction: Fatherhood New and Old

us gets praised for changing a diaper nowadays—and yet how many of the diapers *we* wore did our fathers take off and put on? The sight of fathers pushing strollers on weekday mornings is becoming increasingly common in our larger cities—and even in some of our smaller cities and suburbs—as the ranks of full-time fathers, job-sharing fathers, and fathers who work part-time or on flex-time schedules swell.

Change has a variety of sources. It comes from internal forces bound up with our feelings about our sex roles, about our relationships, about our own fathers, and from such external forces as the economy and the women's movement. One very powerful external force emanates from changes in our partners' lives. As the mothers of our children go off to full-time, out-of-the-home work in increasing numbers, more child-care responsibility falls to our lot. There are intricately connected issues of time, money, work, and love. Who can, who should, who wants to make the time and the sacrifices to raise the children? Both desire and necessity are at work here. Together they are pushing fathers and their children together. Whether we want to be New Fathers or not, we are.

Change is here. We can measure it, observe it, celebrate or bemoan it. But we shouldn't exaggerate it. Yes, we New Fathers are different from the old fathers, but when you get down to the nuts and bolts, we're often not *that* different. A survey of over 14,000 fathers conducted by *Parents* magazine (results published in the September 1985 issue) found that 51 percent of fathers said they do a quarter of the child care and about one-third said they do half; this means, concludes the survey analyst, that "despite this effort by husbands to pitch in, the wives are still shouldering most of the child-care and household responsibilities.... Wives are more likely than their husbands to do every task listed, with the single exception of putting the kids to bed, which couples do about equally."

The plain truth of the matter is that we New Fathers often think we're doing more than we really are—or more than our partners think we are. One expecting father I talked to gave a perfect (and perfectly unconscious) illustration of this attitude. "When the baby's born, I want to be totally involved in child care," he said, "*at least* 50 percent." Then I asked how much time he and his wife were planning to take off when the baby was born. He wasn't planning to take any time—too busy; his wife would take three months and then go back to work part-time. I wondered how he would manage to do 50 percent of the child care without a break in his heavy work schedule—but I didn't say so. As a new father myself, I wasn't about to undermine his good intentions or punch holes in his ideals.

Maybe we're deceiving ourselves at times, but we're trying. Maybe we have a long way to go, but at least we're on our way.

This is a book for all fathers who are on their way toward greater involvement with their children or who want to be. It's also a book *of* these fathers, for the core of the book is based on interviews with fathers of different ages, professions, levels of education, and degrees of involvement from all over the country. I've asked truckdrivers from the Midwest, lawyers from New York, clerical workers from Colorado, doctors from Arizona, teachers from Pennsylvania, and psychologists from California about their feelings and experiences as fathers. How did they react when they found out their partners were pregnant? What was the birth like? What role did they play in the first weeks? How do they handle child care? How did they survive the crisis period of early infancy? What are their special activities and routines with their babies? What aspects of fatherhood do they like best? What part of it has been most trying? These are a few of the questions I put to this group of fathers.

The book begins with the time that the fathers-to-be and their partners contemplate having a child and ends with their baby's first birthday. For nearly all the men I talked to, this was an incredible journey on which the highs far outnumbered the lows. The journeys were all different, but each one passed the same landmarks: hearing the fetal heartbeat for the first time, witnessing the birth, changing the first diaper, being with the baby alone for the first time, watching the baby learn to sit and stand and talk. I learned, in hearing these men describe their experiences and responses, that there are many different styles of involvement, many different ways of caring for our children. And the more I learned, the less I judged.

This is also a book of practical information, a "how-to"

Introduction: Fatherhood New and Old

book on everything from how to make a baby to how to hire a baby-sitter, from how to choose a birth method to how to change a diaper. In the early months of our contact with our babies, the practical and the emotional are inextricable. Being with our babies means caring for them; emotional involvement at this age means physical involvement. As one father put it, "Just being with my daughter when she was very young was a form of connection. Any activity—be it carrying, changing her, putting on her clothes—is as good as any other. The important thing to me and my wife was to share. We knew that if we had kids, we'd do it together." Fathers who want to share but are not sure how can ground themselves in the basics here. In Appendix A, there is a chart on infant development that new fathers can consult to find out what the coming months have in store.

If this book has an underlying message, it's this: If you want to be involved, if you want to feel connected to your child, nothing beats rolling up your sleeves and doing it. A hands-on approach, not only to the actual routines of child care but to the responsibility for planning and anticipating those routines, bonds you to your child in a way that nothing else can. The more you do, the closer that bond becomes. So much of love for a small child is simply participation. It's not always fun; in fact, a lot of it is downright boring, and it never lets up. But it gives you and your child a common ground that you'll never lose.

This is also a book of self-discovery for me. In talking to other fathers, in reading about pregnancy, childbirth, father-infant bonding, child development, childcare, full-time fathers, adoptive and single fathers, I learned a lot about myself as a father, as a husband, as a caregiver and a child-raiser. When I began work on the project, my daughter was ten months old and I considered myself a very involved New Father, although I balked at the prospect of spending an entire day alone with her, giving her dinner by myself, or altering my work schedule to suit her (or my wife's) needs. In the year that has passed, I've assumed a very nearly equal role in her care and upbringing. I not only do it, but in some small yet important way, I'm proud of it. I think it's right. And I've discovered that though I don't always like what equal involvement entails (I *still* don't like giving her dinner alone), I very much like what it has done to our relationships—mine and my daughter's, mine and my wife's, my wife's and my daughter's.

I can only hope that in reading and using this book, other fathers will discover as much joy as I have in writing and living it.

2. Deciding to Have a Child

Why do we have children? It's a question so basic that it seems at once profoundly mysterious and innately obvious. When we consider ourselves as a species of animal, the answer is simple: we have children to perpetuate our kind. But switch the focus to your own life as an individual, and you immediately run into complications. Having a child is not like buying a new house, finding a new job, taking up a new sport, joining a new church. In fact, it's not really like any other decision you'll ever make. Logic, practical benefits, self-improvement enter in little if at all. You don't have a child because it makes you richer or healthier or more challenged mentally or physically or more attractive or more comfortable (though your children may make some of these things happen in time). Presumably you have a child because you—and presumably your partner—want to have a child.

For some, having a child is a way of completing the bond of marriage, of deepening the relationship, or expressing the depth that already exists; for others, a child fulfills some deep, intimate need—it marks a passage into adulthood, a completion of one major aspect of the human life cycle. Many people experience a mysterious urge to perpetuate their family line, to leave someone behind them to grow up with their love, and to pass it down to yet another generation. Bringing a child into the world is the most powerful creative act of which we are capable, an act whose power we feel both drawn to and often somewhat frightened of. And yet for many, it's an act made with no reflection, no doubt, no wonderment: it's simply inconceivable that they *wouldn't* have a child. For still others, the act is a mistake that they have chosen not to correct: the decision is not based on choice but acceptance.

The reasons are beyond reason: they are fundamentally emotional—and they may be fundamentally different for you and your partner. But for both of you, the reasons behind your joint decision to have a child involve the most basic and important things in your life: your relationship, your sense of self, your feelings about the future, your values. Again, the mysterious and the obvious coming together.

For many of us, the decision to have a child is simply part of how we live our lives: the reasons and the timing are built in to the assumptions we acquire as we grow up. Graduate high school, perhaps college, get married, get a job, have kids is a scenario that lots of men more or less accept as a given; just as lots of men assume they'll go on for graduate education, live with a woman for several years before contemplating marriage, and "face" the decision about children when the time comes—that is, put off thinking about it as long as possible.

Brant, a thirty-year-old banker from a small city in Colorado, is one of those expecting fathers who always expected to have kids. "I always assumed we would have kids, ever since we got married. Without a baby, there would have been something missing from our lives."

Charles, a thirty-eight-year-old doctor from Albuquerque, had two children from his first marriage and saw no reason to have any more. But he said his second wife, ten years younger than himself, "needed to have a child and I did not have the right to deny her that biological need."

For Sam, a lawyer from New York, the need came from himself, not his wife, and it was based in psychology and events of his own childhood rather than a biological imperative. "I've known I wanted a child since I was nine years old," he said. "I was beaten as a child and my strongest memory while the beating was occurring was how awful this was and how I would never do this to my children. Wanting to have

Deciding to Have a Child

children was a way of proving that you could have children and *not* treat them this way."

Don, a thirty-eight-year-old marketing manager, always assumed he and his wife (also thirty-eight) would have children, but somehow they never got around to it. "The instinct was there," he said, "but we kept deciding to put it off for another year. We probably would have found excuses to have put it off even longer—maybe indefinitely, but then nature caught up with our planning." Don's wife discovered she was pregnant, taking them both by surprise. As of this writing, the baby is due in five days and both are delighted. Many couples I talked to, particularly couples in their midthirties, took this route: endless indecision, with nature finally stepping in and taking over.

For other expecting fathers, there was never a moment's doubt or hesitation: it was not a question of "whether" but "when" and "how many." Said Vincent, a thirty-four-year-old engineer from Albuquerque, "Both my wife and I come from large families and when we decided to get married we agreed we wanted a large family of our own. Originally we wanted five children, but after our first arrived, we decided three would be enough." (They now have two boys with a third baby on the way.)

Michael, a clerical worker in his late twenties from Greeley, Colorado, is another father who was sure all along. "I had been wanting a child longer than my wife had. In fact as long back as I can remember I wanted kids very bad and always assumed I'd have them. If we couldn't have had kids together we would have looked into adoption. I've *been* ready for a long time."

Ron, a New York attorney, came to the decision from a very different personal perspective: "Until the time I got married to Susan [his second wife], the idea of having a child was unthinkable to me. It was a major issue in my first marriage: I didn't want a baby but my first wife did. In fact, I was *repulsed* by the idea and couldn't even imagine myself in the role of father." For Ron in his first marriage, becoming a father would have been one more link in the chain binding him into a relationship he wanted out of. But once he found the right woman, then fatherhood "kind of fell into place," as he puts it. This is another fairly common pattern for men: to link fatherhood with a strong, successful marriage. Like Ron, many men consider having children to be a trap if the marriage relationship is not right. They don't think about children in the abstract as something they know they want—but rather children enter the realm of the possible only when they're happy in their marriages.

David, a thirty-four-year-old New York–based graphics designer and also in a second marriage, waited not only for the right relationship but for the right stage of his own development before embarking on parenthood. As he puts it: "I felt I had lots of growing up to do before I had a kid. I felt it was a question of taking on more responsibility not only in my job and with money, but in myself. The emotional and financial aspects really went hand-in-hand." Although he and his wife had reached a kind of philosophical agreement on the subject—"we wanted to take our relationship a step further, to make our commitment deeper"—David still felt he had to wait until the practical matters were settled. This meant not only getting the graphics design business that he and his wife own and run together with a third partner on a sure footing, but moving to a big enough apartment and having enough money in the bank.

Although sex roles have changed somewhat with the times, most men in our society continue to assume that they should support their families financially; however, perhaps fewer and fewer men assume that they must (or can) do this alone. Few of us have the luxury of deciding about children in a vacuum; like David, we link economic issues to emotional issues. Even Michael, who knew he wanted a child as far back as he can remember, felt that having the practical matters in place was essential before starting a family. Other men may feel they don't even *want* a child until they are in a position to support the family. As one father-to-be put it, "We had been moving around a lot in the first years of our marriage, but when I found a job with stability, we bought a house. Once the practical matters were settled, the baby seemed possible."

For some men, it's not only money but a desire to pursue their own interests freely that influences the timing of fatherhood. "Until the last three or four years, I was just *too self-*

Deciding to Have a Child

ish," one expectant father told me, "too into myself and my career. Now that I've really established my career and been successful at it, I want to have a child and want to enjoy my child."

Many men have this notion that fatherhood means the end of freedom—freedom to work or play in the way you want, freedom to enjoy your marriage or your self. (Whether this perception is really borne out by experience remains for later chapters to discuss.) Robert Scherb, a family psychologist and leader of discussion groups for expectant fathers, said that many of the men he has seen fear that having a child means "giving up your adolescence at last. This passage definitely needs a ritual—either to celebrate or to mourn it. Some men raise a toast to mark the passage. In my case, I bought myself new stereo equipment in a kind of tail-end-of-adolescence fling." Loss of freedom is just one of a number of anxieties that men associate with fatherhood; there is also fear that their wives will ignore them for the baby, fear that they simply won't *like* the baby, fear that the baby won't like *them*, fear that they won't be able to deal with the demands of a small child, especially the crying. Often what it boils down to is fear of the unknown.

This was certainly the case for me. I had always liked children and assumed I'd have them... when the time was right (a formula that kept things nice and vague). I loved my nephews, even on the rare occasions when I baby-sat for them solo. But, when the time seemed like it was more or less right, I hesitated. To me, the whole thing seemed a bit like jumping off a high diving board. What if you change your mind in midair? What if you land on your face—or do a belly-flop? So I rehearsed a hundred questions I (and my wife) thought I'd answered already. Were we *really* ready? Did I really like kids? How was I going to finish the book I was working on? What about traveling? Maybe I was born to be an uncle— maybe two hours was my limit of endurance when it came to babies. Like so many men, I began to think of fatherhood as the *end* of my life instead of the *beginning* of someone else's life. Suddenly, all the deep-seated emotions that had led to our decision flew out the window. I was scared. For me and lots of other men there's a big difference between *deciding* and actually *trying* to have a child. The reality of it can throw everything into disarray.

Dan, a writer who lives outside Washington, D.C., and his wife edged up gradually to the decision to have a child. They had a number of doubts and anxieties in common and others that conflicted. There were practical as well as "philosophical" issues to work out. Dan shared with me the thoughts and feelings that surrounded this decision: "We always assumed we wanted children, although early in our marriage we were thinking much more about our careers. We would talk about it in a fantasy way—and there were certainly pregnancy scares. One thing that was a real turning point in our decision was when we first started seeing our friends and relatives have children. Seeing a number of people we identified with go through the process gave a more definite shape to our assumption, made it something we could visualize more. It also made us feel more comfortable with babies. I know I had felt awkward around kids and had always admired people who seemed to have a natural way with children. My wife felt the same way. The experience of being around the babies of friends and family led to a sense of awakening. The anxiety just evaporated.

"At some point we began thinking that when my wife (a college teacher) finished her dissertation, it would be a good time to have a child. It seemed right to have kids a little later in our marriage when we felt more settled. The dissertation was a convenient watershed because it *seemed* that it would be finished when we were in our late twenties or early thirties, and finishing the thesis would settle us.

"But the thesis dragged on and we both felt that maybe the point of feeling settled never really arrives in life. As we got closer to our early thirties, we began talking about it more seriously. Still, we hesitated. I took the line that it should be more my wife's decision to give the go-ahead since her career would be more disrupted. I wanted her to feel comfortable about that. I guess underneath we both had deep-seated anxieties about the enormous changes the baby would bring. My wife saw those changes more clearly—she's more realistic. I

Deciding to Have a Child

could lapse into fantasy of what it would be like riding a bike with my son or daughter in the backseat, walking in the woods, having picnics. She appreciated more that a process would begin from which there was no turning back.

"We began to think, If only there were a computer large enough so that you could enter all the information about your life and have it figure out how you could arrange things; how to fit in quality time with a baby, time for work, and time for all the other things we wanted to do outside work. We realized instinctively that we never would succeed in arranging things scientifically so that baby, career, and personal ambitions all meshed perfectly with enough time for everything. We sort of gave up on the scientific approach and the decision to try to have a child just took on a momentum of its own."

Even after the decision began to gather momentum, they still faced the question of *when* would be the right time to try. Ultimately, Dan and his wife let the issue of timing be decided for them by external circumstances: "Being sensible Yuppies whose lives revolve around the academic calendar, we decided we would plan a child to be born early in summer so my wife would have the entire summer off during the baby's first few months." Nature, however, had different plans for them, and the baby arrived in late October—right smack in the middle of the school year. Although it was inconvenient, it's easy to understand why they let this happen. Making the decision to go ahead and start trying to conceive a child can be so difficult that once you've taken the plunge and thrown away the birth control, it's almost impossible to go back—even if it means your baby may not suit the schedules your careers demand.

The Age Factor

For many couples, age is a strong factor in determining their decision to have a child. Several fathers in their mid and late twenties told me that they were eager to start their families now because they didn't want to wait until they were too old. Some felt that it would be easier on them physically: they'd be more resilient at age twenty-five about making up the sleep their newborns would deprive them of and they'd be better playmates once their kids hit the toddler years. Others in their twenties took a more long-term approach: they figured that if they got their child-bearing "over with" now, they'd still be relatively young when the kids were grown and out of the house.

Expecting fathers in their mid to late thirties (with partners the same age) frequently find themselves in a "now or never" situation when it comes to having children. "Time was closing in" is how one expectant father age thirty-eight put it. (Technically speaking, time is closing in only for women, since most men are physically capable of becoming fathers from adolescence until death—but obviously this bit of biology has little bearing on the practical decision that a couple makes together.) These couples may have ruled children out in their twenties, wavered a bit in their early thirties, debated it endlessly as they approached the midthirties, and then, as they passed thirty-five, realized that they'd be missing out on something too important. (See the next section for more on the phenomenon of delaying children.)

Scientists have speculated whether there is some kind of "biological clock" that goes off for men (as well as women) in their thirties, triggering an instinct to produce children. For millions of us who have trouble making up our minds about this issue, time simply catches up and makes the decision for us. Suddenly, we realize that we *can* handle the practical arrangements after all, that we don't care all that much about going to Mexico next year or seeing every new movie, that pursuing two careers at break-neck speed is not the only thing in the world. And it's possible that many of us are influenced by seeing so many of our peers become parents. You see your crowd turn from spontaneous, freewheeling couples to parents locked in by the schedules of baby-sitters and early-rising babies. *Everyone* else seems to have children—so why not us?

Another phenomenon that the press has drawn attention to recently is the older father, in his forties, fifties, or even sixties. He may be starting a second family with a second (younger) wife or he may have remarried or married for the first time and decided that he would now like to have children after all. Older dads starting second families frequently comment that they want to do it differently this time around. With their first families they were old-style uninvolved fathers: now with their second families they want to be New Fathers, attending the births of their children, participating fully in infant care and child-raising. Unlike most younger dads who are still struggling up the ladders in their careers, many of these older dads have established themselves in secure positions, and thus it may be easier for them to take time off from work to be with their new families.

Beyond age, beyond peer pressure, beyond fashion or practical arrangements or life-style, there is an intimate self-assessment that goes into the decision to have a child. What it came down to for so many of the men I spoke with was a sense that their lives would somehow be incomplete—that they wouldn't have fulfilled themselves—had they never become fathers.

Mike, a geneticist, used the language of his field: "My wife and I didn't want to be a genetic death. There was this urge to pass along our genes." Rich, a quality control inspector from St. Paul, said more simply: "My wife and I had been married three years, during which we really got to know each other. We knew something was missing from our lives and we realized that it was a child. We were ready." Ron Hansen, in an *Esquire* magazine article entitled "The Male Clock" (April 1985), wrote about "that in-the-craw feeling of being incompletely a part of the human species until you've produced offspring; of not growing much beyond age twenty-one unless you begin to care greatly for one of your own." Although we may not describe it in quite this way, this is a version of what we're experiencing. At some psychological level, at some point in time, this desire for fulfillment through fathering a child overrides all the doubts, anxieties, and misgivings. We may not feel entirely ready, entirely convinced, or even entirely grown-up ourselves, but we've decided.

Delaying Children: A National Phenomenon

It doesn't just *seem* that so many people are waiting longer to have children—it really is happening all over the country. Americans as a whole are getting married later, having fewer children, and waiting longer to have those children. The nation's fertility rate is on the decline with the exception of one group: women in their thirties. Starting in the late 1970s and continuing into the present, women aged thirty to thirty-nine began to have more children, and especially more first children. Interestingly, women aged thirty-five to thirty-nine experienced an even larger increase in first births than women age thirty to thirty-four. The corresponding statistics for men show a similar pattern: in 1975, there were 81.5 births per 1,000 for men aged thirty to thirty-four, whereas in 1980, the figure jumped to 91 for this group; thirty-five- to thirty-nine-year-old-men also showed an increase in this five-year period (from 39.9 births per 1,000 in 1975 to 42.8 in 1980). On the other hand, the twenty- to twenty-four-year-old-group showed a marked decline from 96.2 births per 1,000 men in 1975 to 92 per 1,000 in 1980, and the twenty-five- to twenty-nine-year-old-group also showed a decline in births (from 123.9 to 123). It is also worth noting that women who gave birth when they were over thirty were more likely to have attended college and to hold professional jobs than mothers in their twenties or teens.

None of this comes as much of a surprise. The statistics merely corroborate what we've seen happening all around us, and happening to us. Given the social and economic conditions that prevail in America today, the delayed children phenomenon makes perfect sense. It's all part of the baby-boomer life-style that the news media so enjoys tracking. The baby-boomers, that bulge in the nation's population that occurred from 1946 to 1956, are finally getting around to having children, and they're doing it in their own characteristic way. Many baby-boomers didn't have time or interest in having kids ten, fifteen years ago; they were in their twenties then and they were busy with careers and relationships. Children

Deciding to Have a Child

were viewed as an impediment to self-fulfillment, trips to Europe, killer career paths. And besides, in the baby-boomer world view, *they* were still the kids. Baby-boomers were encouraged to prolong their adolescence, to be free, to experiment, to fulfill themselves. The short and winding road from campus radical to Yuppie consumed all of the boomers' focus and energy. Having kids meant settling down, making sacrifices, taking on responsibilities—in short, growing up.

As one thirty-eight-year-old expectant father put it, "I've always had a thing about avoiding responsibility and I never quite felt my age. There was a reluctance to commit myself. Now that the baby is due so soon, it seems like a final commitment to growing up."

And worse, having kids meant becoming like one's parents—the progenitors of the baby boom, that post–World War II generation that couldn't wait to get married, move to the suburbs, and raise big all-American families. The baby-boomers *could* wait and did wait—until they hit thirty, thirty-five, thirty-nine, and it suddenly seemed that time was running out. The now-or-never syndrome set in, and lots of boomers took the plunge. So now we're in the midst of a new phenomenon: a miniboom of the offspring of the original boom! This miniboom produced 3.75 million American babies in 1985, the highest number in twenty years.

Other reasons also enter into the decision so many people are making to delay children. One crucial factor is economic: children are expensive. (*Newsweek* estimates that the cost of raising a single child from birth to age eighteen with four years of college at a private institution is $135,000.) In more and more marriages, the partners work full-time, both because they want to and because they need to. Many two-career couples simply cannot afford to have children, or at least *think* they cannot afford it, until they are on a firm financial footing. Often what this means is waiting until substantial salary increases start coming in, which may not happen until they've been working five to seven years. So, even couples who might have wanted children earlier are waiting. There are also the practical considerations of space and time. Where are you going to fit a child in your cramped one-bedroom apartment?

Who's going to care for the child when you both return to work and resume your long and unpredictable hours? As Jane Price put it in *You're Not Too Old to Have a Baby* (Farrar, Straus & Giroux, 1977), "Children have become a luxury option."

Delaying children does have its rewards. The post-thirty-five-year-old fathers I interviewed were without exception positive about the decision to delay. "I have waited a while certainly," said one thirty-seven-year-old expectant father, "but I'm glad I waited as long as I have. More time has given me a wider perspective. I feel I know who I am, I've done what I wanted, and I'm comfortable financially. Now we're ready." A thirty-eight-year-old father (expecting when I interviewed him, but as of this moment the father of a three-day-old nine-pound baby boy) went even further: "I pity those poor twenty-two-year-old kids that were in my Lamaze class who are about to become fathers. I remember myself at that age. They're going to be losing out on so much and it will be lost to them forever. The benefit for me of waiting until I'm older is that I've gotten things out of my system and can provide a quality of life for my baby that I couldn't have given him ten years ago."

On the other hand, the dads in their twenties I talked to were all equally positive about having children young. "It's a hectic life-style," said one twenty-six-year-old father of two. "We're always doing something for or with the kids. It can be exhausting. I'm glad we had them when we're young." And when this dad turns thirty-eight and his kids are in their teens, he may be the one pitying the thirty-eight-year-old father quoted above who will be fifty!

Perhaps the moral is that becoming a father at any age has its benefits and its drawbacks. Fathers in their twenties have youth on their side. They're not fixed in their ways, they have more raw energy, they're closer to the enthusiasms of childhood. They're also likely to have less money and less secure jobs than older fathers. Fathers in their mid and late thirties have lived out their youths unencumbered by family responsibilities; they have no regrets about missing out on freedom and experimentation; they are likely to be better off financially, more advanced in their careers, and have practical matters under control. But some of these older dads worry about how a baby will fit into their settled adult life-styles, and those who look into the future may wonder how they are going to deal with rambunctious teens from the depths of middle age.

Whether you've waited until your thirties were drawing to a close or whether you've known you were ready as your twenties were dawning, the decision to have a child will have a tremendous impact on your life almost immediately. Even before a baby is conceived, the decision affects your marriage, your sex life, your feelings about work, money, time, and responsibility. And then there is the miracle and mystery of your baby's creation. When *exactly* does the embryo come into being? What is your contribution to the new life? What are the stages of growth in the womb? The next three chapters take you through the pregnant months, discussing first the facts of conception and the growth of your baby inside your wife's body and then the emotional experience that men go through as this amazing nine-month period in their lives unfolds. If you're expecting, suspecting, or trying—read on.

3. Knowing About the Pregnancy—Conception and Fetal Development

Viewed purely from the outside, a father's role in conception and fetal development is pretty limited. You make love with your wife—or, in the harsh words of science, you "deposit your sperm"—and you wait nine months. The rest is up to her: *her* egg receives the sperm, the egg implants and grows inside *her* uterus, *her* body nourishes the fetus and eventually gives birth to the baby. Undeniable and inevitable.

But when you think about what happens *inside*—inside your body all the time as you produce sperm and inside the life span of that lucky sperm as it completes its marathon race and fertilizes the egg—you realize just how amazing and dramatic your contribution is.

This chapter examines the amazing contribution that you make to the creation of the new life, exploring the process by which a man produces sperm, the journey of sperm to the egg cell, the optimal timing for conception, and whether there is anything a couple can do to influence the sex of their child. Also discussed are the most common causes of male infertility and how to treat them. In addition, this chapter charts the progress of the fetus from the moment of conception until the new life is ready to emerge into the world and become your baby.

Knowing About the Pregnancy

Life Cycle of a Sperm

Every day, every moment of every day as you go about living your life, your body is busy producing sperm—millions and millions of them. It happens all the time from the onset of puberty until death. You don't have to think about it, work at it, eat special foods, exercise, or pay: it's free, it's continuous, and it's effortless. Sperm production—or spermatogenesis—begins in the 800 seminiferous tubules that fill the inside of a man's testes. In the first stage of their life, sperm are called spermatogonia and they contain forty-six chromosomes, the number contained by all human cells except the mature sexual reproduction cells, which contain twenty-three. In the seventy-five or so days that it takes them to mature, the spermatogonia divide in half and their chromosomes drop from forty-six to twenty-three; they develop the characteristic tadpole-like shape of the mature sperm cell.

At maturity, the sperm is 1/600 of an inch in length and consists of an oval-shaped head, a short neck, and a long cylindrical middle section that ends in a long thin tail, ten times as long as the head. It is the whipping, flailing motion

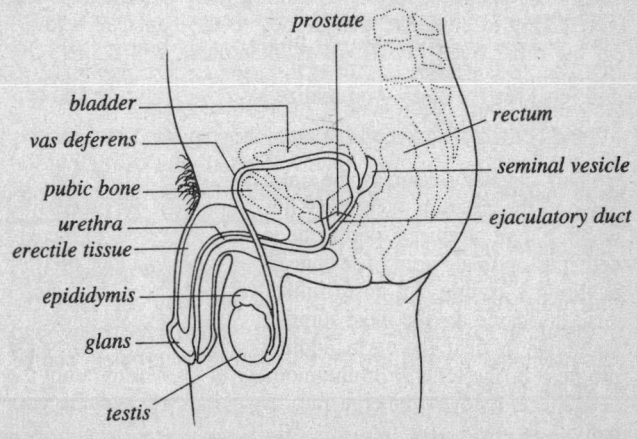

The male reproductive system

of this tail that propels the sperm, and when it's moving well, a sperm can cover an inch in four minutes. Every healthy sperm your body produces comes with all this equipment. The astounding part is that in each ejaculation you send out 200 to 400 million of them!

After the sperm hatch and grow in the seminiferous tubules, they migrate to the epididymis, an organ that consists of eighteen feet of coiled tube that sits on top of the testes. They spend several days there and then move on to the vas deferens, a duct that moves the sperm on to the seminal vesicle. There the newly produced sperm collect and wait for ejaculation to send them on their way into the urethra, which is the tube in the center of the penis that conveys both urine and semen to the outside.

Sperm accounts for only 2 percent of the substance you ejaculate, the rest being made up of fluids produced by the prostate, the seminal vesicle, and the two Cowper's glands. These fluids provide a medium in which the sperm swim and they also protect the sperm inside the vagina.

Sperm do not live forever: when they are stored for long periods in the ducts, they grow old—"senile"—and lose their motility (the ability to move). This is one reason to have intercourse fairly frequently if you want to conceive a baby: the fresher the sperm supply, the healthier they are and thus the more likely to complete the journey to the egg (see below). On the other hand, *too* frequent intercourse will deplete the sperm supply. For maximum fertility it's best to wait thirty to forty-eight hours before having intercourse again.

Another factor to keep in mind is the extreme heat sensitivity of the testes. You may have wondered why nature put the testes outside of our bodies, making them vulnerable to bumps and kicks. Part of the reason is to keep them cooler, six degrees cooler than the rest of the body. If the testes get too hot, they will cease producing sperm: a long hot bath or even tight underwear that press the testes into the body can raise the temperature sufficiently to interrupt sperm production and cause temporary infertility. A male infertility problem can be as simple as that.

Knowing About the Pregnancy

Fertilization: The Sperm's Journey to the Egg

It's just as well that nature has given men such an abundant supply of sperm, because the journey a sperm must make in order to reach an egg (or ovum, in the language of science) is right up there with the labors of Hercules. Ejaculation is the easy part: the contractions of the penis and the vas deferens send some 200 to 400 million sperm into the upper vagina, where they immediately begin swimming and swarming in every direction. The acid environment of the vagina is hostile to alkaline-loving sperm, and vast numbers of them quickly die. Only those that swim by chance to the cervix have any hope of making it farther, and even then, the sperm must make contact during the brief period when the cervix is receptive. This receptive period occurs during the three or four days before ovulation and on the day of ovulation itself.

Once they pass through the cervix (and of the hundreds of millions of sperm deposited, only several thousand complete this stage), the sperm must cross the two inches of the uterus and then enter the Fallopian tube, where the actual joining of

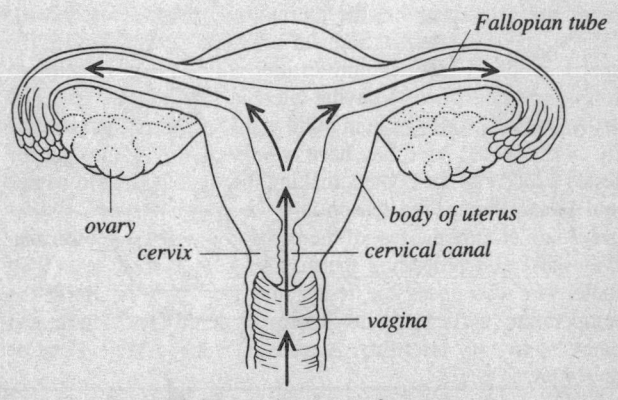

The sperm's journey to the egg

egg and sperm takes place. Chance enters in here again because the woman has two Fallopian tubes connecting her two ovaries with her uterus, and a few thousand sperm will head for the left tube, while a few thousand others will head for the right. The egg, of course, will be in one tube or the other, so those that entered the wrong one will have gone all that way for nothing.

Some authorities put the number of sperm that enter the correct tube as low as 200; others say it is several thousand. In any case, the sperm that have made it that far are only a tiny fraction of those that started out on the five-inch journey some thirty to forty minutes previously. They have traveled a distance of three thousand times their own length, the equivalent of a six-foot man swimming three miles upstream.

Of course, the sperm's journey to the Fallopian tube is paralleled by the egg's journey from the ovary, which takes place every month. At ovulation, the egg cell (which is the largest in the human body) moves from one of the two ovaries into one of the Fallopian tubes. The tube actually sweeps the tiny egg into its opening through the action of fimbriae, which are rather like waving tentacles. Once the egg enters the midsection of the tube, it is ready to be fertilized—but it is ready only for a brief period, between twelve and twenty-four hours.

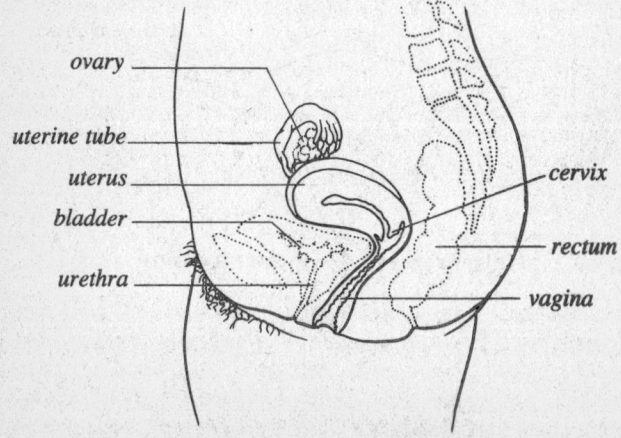

The female reproductive system

Knowing About the Pregnancy

If there are no sperm present during this period, the no longer fertile egg proceeds down the Fallopian tube to the uterus, where it will be discharged during the woman's menstrual period.

Conception

If, however, living sperm come into the presence of the egg during its period of ripeness, one of them will penetrate the exterior walls of the egg and the two nuclei will fuse. The egg, like the sperm, has only twenty-three chromosomes, half the number of the other human cells. At the moment of fertilization, the twenty-three sperm chromosomes match up with the twenty-three egg chromosomes to make one complete cell—the cell from which your baby grows.

At the moment of conception, the forty-six chromosomes in the cell of the fused sperm and egg contain all the genetic material that determines your baby's physical characteristics—hair color, eye color, head shape, size, features—it's all there from the very start. Also, the sex of your baby is determined at this instant, and it's determined by you, the father. Of a human being's twenty-three pairs of chromosomes, one pair is known as the sex chromosomes, which scientists have labeled X and Y. In women, the chromosome pair always consists of two Xs, whereas men have an XY pair. Thus, the sperm cell, which has only one-half of the twenty-three pairs, may contain either the X half or the Y half. If an X pair sperm reaches the egg, then the baby will be a girl—XX. If the sperm carries a Y chromosome, then the baby will be a boy—XY. The chances are about fifty-fifty. So all those men who feel left out by pregnancy may take heart at the knowledge that *they* were the ones who determined the baby's sex right at the start.

Once fertilization takes place, your baby begins growing rapidly. Twelve hours after the fusing of egg and sperm, the single forty-six-chromosome cell divides into two cells; sixty hours later there are sixty-four cells. And five days after fertilization, the embryo has five hundred cells—but we're getting ahead of ourselves here.

Getting Pregnant: Timing

Timing is everything in pregnancy. The egg, as already mentioned, is ripe and waiting in the Fallopian tube for only twelve to twenty-four hours, and if there are no sperm around during this time, fertilization will not happen. Sperm, however, have a slightly longer life span: some may live inside the vagina for up to seventy-two hours. So you have three or four days each month during which you and your wife could conceive a baby. The trick is knowing *which* three or four days.

Part of the problem here is the variability in the menstrual cycle of women. We know that ovulation occurs regularly at around fourteen days before the start of the next menstrual period—so, if you had a crystal ball and could discern just when that would occur, there would be no difficulty in timing a conception. But a normal menstrual cycle (the time from the beginning of one period until the beginning of the next) could be anything from eighteen to forty days, which is quite a wide range; in an eighteen-day cycle, ovulation will occur only four days after the onset of the period, whereas in a forty-day cycle, it would be twenty-six days after the start of the period. (These are the extremes: the average cycle is twenty-eight days, with ovulation occurring on day fourteen.)

Most couples don't really have to worry about this. They decide they want a child, they stop using birth control, perhaps they increase their sexual frequency a bit, and a few months later they're pregnant. (On the average, it takes most couples about six months to conceive, with variations depending on the age and health of the prospective parents.) But if you've been having trouble getting pregnant, you'll want to try to get your timing right—and there are ways of doing this without resorting to a crystal ball.

There are three primary signs of fertility in women: 1) changes in cervical mucus, 2) changes in body temperature upon waking up, and 3) changes in the cervix itself. Cervical mucus is the most important sign. During ovulation a woman discharges a small amount of wet mucus that looks rather like

Knowing About the Pregnancy

raw egg whites. A woman can check for this discharge herself with her finger. To maximize the chances of getting pregnant, you should have sex as soon as the mucus discharge begins to change from sticky to wet. Body temperature is a less useful indication since a slight dip in a woman's temperature indicates that ovulation has passed. The "feel" of the cervix is a slightly better indicator: it will soften up at the time of ovulation. If your wife presses her cervix gently with her finger, at the time of ovulation it will feel rather like a lip, whereas it feels more like the tip of one's nose during menstruation.

Some women also feel a slight twinge of pain in one ovary or the other at the time of ovulation. Known as *mittelschmerz*, this is a good sign that the time is right. Tenderness in the breasts can be another indicator of ovulation.

If your wife has been keeping track of these signs and she's pretty sure she's ovulating or about to, don't feel that you must have sex around the clock in order to conceive. In fact, too frequent sex will reduce your chances because your body won't be able to replenish your sperm supply that quickly. It's probably best to have sex every other day starting just before the time of ovulation.

To favor conception, use the missionary position (man on top) and remain inside your wife for several minutes after intercourse. Your wife should stay on her back with her hips slightly raised for a half an hour after sex. And never use any lubricants, creams, or vaselines during sex—all of these can kill off sperm.

The Sex of Your Baby: Can You Choose?

Don't get your hopes raised too high, because the answer to choosing a baby's sex is still only *maybe*. Through the ages there have been all sorts of notions about how to determine a baby's sex (Aristotle claimed that sex when the north wind was blowing produced boys, south-wind sex made girls; Hippocrates, however, insisted that it all had to do with on which side the woman reclined after intercourse: right for boys, left for girls). One of the most widely discussed theories (and let us stress *theory*) of the past fifteen or so years is one originally propounded by Landrum B. Shettles and D. M. Rorvick in a book called *Your Baby's Sex: Now You Can Choose* (Dodd, Mead, 1970).

The essence of their theory is that Y sperm (those that make boys) are faster and more numerous than X sperm (those that make girls), but that X sperm live longer. Shettles and Rorvick advise that if you want a boy you should abstain from sex in the period before ovulation and then have sex as close to ovulation as possible. Before sex, the woman is to use an alkaline douche of baking soda and water. The man should penetrate deeply and the woman should have an orgasm. This procedure favors immediate fertilization, a condition that is advantageous to those quick but short-lived Y sperm.

The procedure for a girl is the opposite: you want to create an environment that is hostile to sperm so that only the tough, slow, long-lived X sperm can make it to the egg. So the woman takes an acid douche of white vinegar and water and you have sex two or three days before ovulation with shallow penetration and no female orgasm. Then you abstain from sex until ovulation is over.

Does it work? The answer differs depending on whom you ask, but not even Shettles himself claims that it's foolproof (although he does say it has an 85 percent success rate).

Dr. Elizabeth Whelan has advanced a theory based on timing that is almost exactly opposite to that suggested by Shettles. Whelan says that if you want a girl you should have intercourse on the day of ovulation, as well as the two days before ovulation; for a boy she recommends sex on the fourth, fifth, and sixth days before ovulation is to occur. Others have come up with entirely different procedures based on what a woman eats: a diet high in sodium and low in calcium/magnesium favors boys; a sodium-free diet with lots of calcium/magnesium favors girls.

Clearly, science still has a couple of giant steps to take before it fully illuminates this mystery of Mother Nature. There is yet another theory—this one strictly nonscientific—that claims that most people who really have a strong preference get what they want. So maybe wishing very hard is the best method of all.

From Conception to Embryo: Your Baby's First Two Weeks

Several hours after sperm begin their journey inside a woman's body, the process of fertilization is complete. One single sperm penetrates the barriers surrounding the ovum, the sperm nucleus fuses with the ovum nucleus, and the fertilized cell, called a zygote, has come into existence. At this point, your wife's body takes over with no further assistance required from you. The single-celled zygote—your baby-to-be—has begun a complex and intimate relationship with his or her mother.

Still in the Fallopian tube, the zygote begins to divide—first into two identical cells called blastomeres. Then these

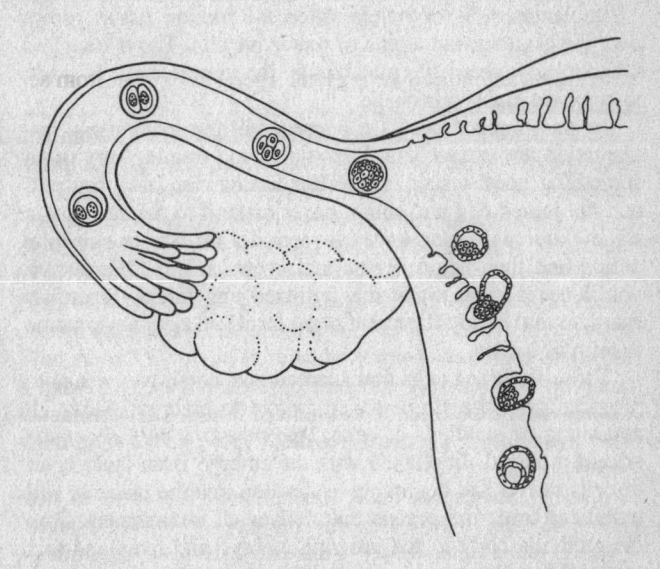

Cell divisions in the Fallopian tubes and uterus, implantation in the uterine wall

two cells each divide, producing four cells, which soon split into eight cells, and so on. By the third day after fertilization, there are sixty-four cells forming a tiny but solid ball known as a *morula* (the Latin word for mulberry). Continuing its cell divisions, the morula makes its way toward the uterus and enters it three or four days after fertilization. It has changed its shape from a solid ball to a hollow ball of cells surrounding an inner cavity filled with fluid, and it is now called a blastocyst. Growing rapidly all the while (by five days there are 500 cells), the blastocyst spends a couple days floating around the uterus, getting used to its home for the next nine months; and then, sometime between day six and day eight, the process known as implantation takes place.

Scientists describe implantation as "an invasion of the endometrium," which means that the cells of the growing blastocyst actually destroy part of the lining of the uterus (the endometrium) as they burrow in and adhere firmly.

Implantation is complete when the uterine tissue grows over the blastocyst in a kind of protective cup. The multicelled invader, now securely embedded in the uterine wall, is ready to enter the embryonic stage.

As one might expect, the processes of fertilization and implantation are extraordinarily complex and fragile. Very often something goes wrong, even after fertilization has occurred, and the joined egg and sperm never make it to the embryonic stage. Your wife may have her period a bit late or skip one period and then begin her normal cycles again. Chances are you'll never even know the fertilized egg failed. Scientists estimate that 30 to 50 percent of all fertilized eggs never come to term as babies.

Those fertilized eggs that succeed take about two weeks to progress from the single-celled zygote to embryo. Although consisting of hundreds of cells, the embryo is only about the size of a period. Implanted with the embryo is an outer layer of cells that is just beginning to develop into the placenta and umbilical cord, the organs that deliver all nourishment from the mother's body to the growing embryo and fetus and that carry off wastes.

While all of this complicated and crucial activity has been transpiring inside the Fallopian tube and uterus, you and your wife have been going blithely about your business. Because she hasn't yet completed a menstrual cycle, she hasn't missed her period, and thus the two of you still have no idea that she's pregnant. But you're about to find out.

Weeks Two Through Eight: Embryo to Fetus

No period of human growth even begins to rival the first month of embryonic development when your future baby increases 10,000 times in weight and size. But this is only one of many astonishing developments the embryo is going through in the weeks after implantation. At one month, the embryo has three distinct layers of cells—the outer layer giving rise to the skin, sensory organs, and nervous system; the middle layer producing the systems of muscles, circulation, and excretion; and the inner layer growing into the digestive and glandular systems as well as the lungs. The embryo measures one-quarter of an inch. Shaped rather like a crescent moon with swellings and folds that almost suggest facial features at one end and a long tail at the other, the embryo already has a tiny heart pumping blood through microscopic arteries and veins. All of the major systems, organs, and body parts are beginning to differentiate, including the embryonic brain.

In the next month, the embryo grows an entire inch and has enough substance to weigh in at one-thirty-eighth of an ounce. If you could peek inside at your two-month-old embryo, you'd see a recognizably human creature, about half of which is head with distinct facial features and even a tongue. There are limbs with well-formed fingers and toes. All of the organs and systems that your baby will be born with are present in the embryo eight weeks after conception, and some are already beginning to function. The bones are just starting to form—in fact, this is what divides the embryonic stage from the fetal stage. The embryo has only cartilage providing its body framework, and when real bone cells begin to replace this cartilage, the embryo is considered a fetus—and fetus he or she remains until his or her birthday, whereupon the fetus becomes your baby.

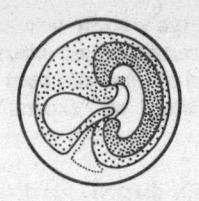

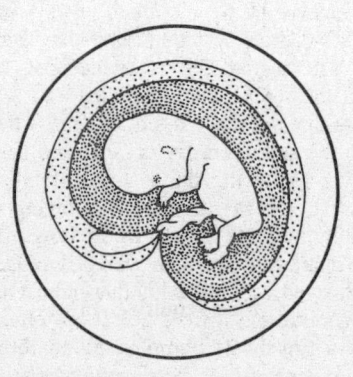

Growth from embryo to fetus

Male Infertility: Causes and Treatments

Couples who conceive and bear children with no trouble have the luxury of sailing through pregnancy in blissful ignorance. There is no need to read, to learn about the intricacies of the human reproductive system, to analyze or consult with anyone: their bodies do all the "work," leaving their minds free.

But for the estimated 15 to 20 percent of couples who do not achieve pregnancy easily—or at all—life is not so simple. True, science has made great strides in this area, but fundamental questions remain unanswered. Many infertile couples begin by reading books on the subject; then they con-

Knowing About the Pregnancy

sult a specialist and undergo a round of tests. Some will then have operations or take certain drugs; others will be told that "it's all in your head" and to relax and keep trying. Some will succeed after being informed by "experts" that there is no chance; others will never succeed even though medical science pronounces them fit. Life and its creation remain mysteries, and there is no better indication of that fact than our limited understanding of infertility.

It is estimated that 30 to 40 percent of all infertility problems originate with the man, and yet despite this statistic, research into male infertility lags far behind female infertility research. The studies and books we do have identify two broad categories of problems: 1) production problems: an inability to produce active and mature sperm in sufficient quantity or semen in the proper quantity, and 2) transport and deposit problems: an inability to move the sperm from the seminal vesicle where it collects, through the urethra, and into the vagina, either due to a blockage, an infection, or because of sexual problems. Within these two categories are a number of specific causes, ranging from easily corrected environmental factors to conditions requiring surgery.

Production Problems

An ejaculation is considered normal if 60 percent of the sperm present in it have a normal shape and motility. Problems arise when the situation is reversed and the numbers of abnormally shaped and immobile sperm top 60 percent. Or, the percentage of healthy active sperm might be normal, but the total number of sperm present in a given ejaculation could be abnormally low. (The range of normal is 20 to 200 million per cubic centimeter of ejaculate.) An additional production problem is known as aspermia—sperm production is normal but there is no semen present.

The most common cause of sperm production problems is a varicocele. Essentially, this is a varicose vein present in the scrotum, and usually on the left side. If you touch it, a varicocele feels like a small bag of spaghetti that has somehow been inserted into the scrotum; because it's usually painless, chances are you won't even know you have one. Scientists still do not know how a varicocele impairs fertility—one current theory is the back-up of blood overheats the testicle and either kills or deforms sperm—but it is known that this condition accounts for 30 to 40 percent of all male fertility problems. Fortunately, a varicocele may be corrected by surgery in which the affected veins are tied off. The procedure involves a day and a night in the hospital and about a week before all normal activities, including sex, may be resumed. About 80 percent of the men who undergo this surgery show a marked improvement in their sperm count, although it takes three months to register. If the wife has no fertility problem of her

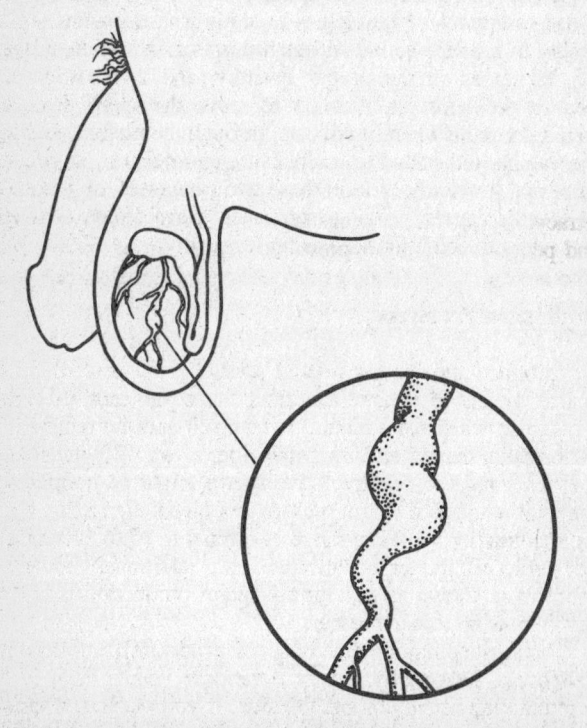

Location of a varicocele in the scrotum, with enlargement showing swollen vein

Knowing About the Pregnancy

own, pregnancy results in about 45 percent of the cases.

Other causes of production problems include malfunctioning of the endocrine system resulting in improper hormone balance, bacterial infection, and even certain drugs and alcohol.

In the case of infection, bacteria may be killing off your sperm or rendering them immobile. Some bacteria will cause a burning sensation during urination or a discharge from the penis, but some produce no symptoms whatsoever. The sperm may also transfer the infection to your wife, and if the condition is allowed to continue, you both may become infertile. Such bacteria can be detected through tests and controlled by antibiotics. When mumps is contracted by adult men, it may cause damage of the testes that results in fertility problems, although this is quite rare.

Researchers have now learned that both tobacco and marijuana hinder the production of sperm and that alcohol can temporarily alter the hormonal balance needed for optimal sperm production. Certain antibiotics, including penicillin and tetracycline, and other drugs taken for cancer, malaria, colitis, and peptic ulcers all suppress the production of sperm. Men who are exposed to high levels of certain pesticides, industrial chemicals (including lead and toluene), certain gaseous anesthetics, and radioactive substances including X-rays show marked decreases in sperm production as well as a greater risk of producing offspring with birth defects. In most cases, sperm production returns to normal in three to twelve months after the man ceases being exposed to the noxious substance; whenever possible, men should take precautions to minimize such exposure.

But even men who take no drugs or alcohol, inhale no pollutants, and stay away from X-rays may have their sperm production affected by something as common as emotional stress. *Try to relax* may not be such bad advice in such cases after all, although it's unlikely that stress *alone* will cause long-term infertility. As mentioned above, overheating of the testicles will also cause temporary infertility by killing off sperm—such overheating can arise from a serious fever, long hot bath, tight underwear, or a long hot car ride. These conditions are for the most part easily remedied. It does occasionally happen that the testes fail to descend into the scrotum: a simple operation performed during early childhood will correct this situation. But if it is allowed to continue for any length of time, the body's heat can cause permanent damage to the undescended testes and render the man infertile.

Transport and Deposit Problems

The majority of cases of male infertility arise from problems with sperm production, but problems with sperm transport and deposit can be more painful, both physically and psychologically, and more difficult to treat. A blockage of one of the ducts through which sperm pass or even a complete absence of the necessary duct will render a male infertile. The duct most commonly blocked is the epididymis, and operations have successfully reversed the blockage in about half the cases.

Untreated gonorrhea can cause an obstruction of the vas deferens, and prostatitis, more common in older men, will impair the functioning of the prostate, which produces some of the necessary fluid in semen. Another problem is retrograde ejaculation, which means that semen flows up into a man's bladder instead of out the urethra. It can be a side effect of diabetes or a complication following urinary surgery or the result of such medications as tranquilizers or antihypertensive drugs. A sign of retrograde ejaculation is an absence of sperm in the ejaculate and milky-colored urine following ejaculation. Drugs and in some cases surgery have successfully treated this condition; in other cases, the sperm is recovered from the man's bladder after ejaculation and used to artificially inseminate his wife.

Yet another deposit problem arises from a condition known as hypospadias, in which the opening normally located at the tip of the penis occurs on the underside and back from the tip. Sperm ejaculated from such a penis will be deposited in the outer section of the vagina, and thus the chances of it reaching the cervix are greatly diminished. Again, artificial insemination may be used to effect pregnancy.

Knowing About the Pregnancy

Sexual problems, particularly impotence and premature ejaculation, also account for a number of cases of male infertility. The causes are more often psychological than physical, but that may only make it more difficult for a man to bear, to talk about, or to try to solve. It's encouraging to know that sexual problems can be treated more easily and with better results than most physical or hormonal problems. Therapists report a 60 percent success rate in helping chronic impotence and even better results with premature ejaculation, which is more common.

Getting Help for Infertility Problems

Not too many years ago, fertility problems were *always* blamed on the woman. It was assumed that if the male could ejaculate, he could father children, and that was that. It thus became the woman's responsibility to "do something" about the situation. Even if a man wanted to "do something," too, there wasn't much he *could* do. Now that we know that 30 to 40 percent of fertility problems originate with men (and that an even greater number are *joint* problems), science is at last catching up with the need to help men. But slowly.

One promising sign is that a medical specialty devoted to male reproductive health has emerged in recent years. This is known as andrology (not to be confused with androgyny—the 1980s version of unisex that the media made such a deal about when Michael Jackson and Boy George reigned supreme) and it is a subspecialty of urology. Even if you are unable to consult an andrologist, there are very definite steps that both you and your wife can take if you have a fertility problem.

The first routine measure is to get a semen analysis (also known as a sperm count). When you agree to such a test, you will be asked to produce a fresh semen sample (a maximum of four hours before delivering it to the doctor) by masturbating into a clean, usually plastic container. Sperm count is something of a misnomer for this test, for the counting of the number of sperm per cubic centimeter is only part of it. The doctor will also test for the quantity of ejaculate (between 2 and 6 milliliters is normal), its alkalinity, and the shape, size, and motility of individual sperm. The doctor will also measure the proportion of seminal fluid to sperm, and test for the presence of bacteria or abnormal number of white blood cells.

Like most medical tests, a semen analysis is not foolproof, and results often vary quite widely from test to test for the same man. If the doctor finds a very low sperm count or no sperm at all, you'll be asked to produce another sample for further tests. This is irritating at best and can quickly become infuriating. But unfortunately it is the only way medical science has yet come up with to begin an investigation of the causes of male infertility.

If you're up to the stage where you are actively seeking help for a fertility problem, you've probably been living with a good deal of anxiety, frustration, and downright despair for some time. The emotional impact of infertility is tremendous on both a man and his wife. Even competent physicians can seem callous, and well-meaning friends and relatives have a strange knack for offering the most hurtful advice. For many men difficulty in producing a child seems like the equivalent of announcing to the world that you're a failure as a man, as a lover, as a person. You say "infertile," but you sense what people hear is "impotent." Very often, getting help for the emotional side of infertility becomes even more pressing than finding a treatment for the infertility problem itself. It's important to recognize the toll this is taking on you and your relationship with your wife and try to treat the emotional wounds, whether through counseling, or just by keeping the lines of communication in your marriage open.

If your sperm count is low or if you are producing an abnormally large number of malformed or immobile sperm, the next step is to determine the cause. As already mentioned, varicoceles are responsible for by far the greatest number of production problems, and this condition can be corrected surgically with fairly good results. Surgery for duct blockages is available, but the results are far less encouraging. Some doctors advocate hormone treatments of various sorts to counteract low sperm count, but again, the results have not been impressive enough to warrant general use. And in some cases, sperm numbers have actually been lowered.

Knowing About the Pregnancy

As this discussion of the causes of male infertility indicates, a great number of factors or combination of factors can be creating the problem. For some lucky men, solving an infertility problem may be a simple matter of making minor adjustments in their life-styles: changing to loose-fitting underwear, switching from hot baths to warm showers, cutting down on drinking and smoking. Others may endure years of tests and still never father a child. But although treatments remain limited, they are definitely worth pursuing. Your best course is to discuss the problem with your family doctor first and get his or her suggestion for a good urologist or andrologist. Some hospitals have infertility clinics staffed by experts in the field. Ask your family doctor for referrals or contact one of the organizations listed below to direct you to the best specialist or clinic in your area:

> American Fertility Society
> 1608 Thirteenth Avenue South
> Birmingham, AL 35205
>
> Planned Parenthood of New York City, Inc.
> Family Planning and Information Service
> 810 Seventh Avenue
> New York, NY 10019
>
> Resolve, Inc.
> P.O. Box 474
> Belmont, MA 02178
>
> The Barren Foundation
> 6 East Monroe Street
> Chicago, IL 60603
>
> United Infertility Organization
> P.O. Box 23
> Scarsdale, NY 10583

Alternative Methods of Fertilization and Conception

Although progress in treating male infertility remains limited, scientists have achieved some breakthroughs in alternative methods of depositing sperm and conceiving babies, particularly through in vitro (outside the body) fertilization. Some of these techniques are expensive and have given rise to controversy, but if you're interested, read on.

Artificial Insemination

Artificial insemination—the introduction of sperm into a woman's vagina by injecting it through a syringe or similar device—has been around for some time. The first recorded successful pregnancy achieved in this way dates back to 1790. The procedure is relatively simple, painless, and inexpensive, and it offers an excellent chance at fatherhood for men who can produce sperm but cannot deposit it effectively, either because of impotence, retrograde ejaculation, or hypospadias (see earlier discussion). It is also sometimes used for men with a low sperm count, although with less success.

If your wife is to be artificially inseminated with your sperm, the procedure is known as AIH—artificial insemination by husband. In cases in which the husband does not produce enough healthy sperm to effect a pregnancy, or if he does not want to pass on some hereditary disease to his offspring, the procedure is known as artificial insemination by donor, or AID.

For AIH, you will produce a semen sample by masturbating into a clean plastic container, and then, in most cases, the sample is frozen until needed. The insemination will be scheduled for the day before your wife is expected to ovulate and will be performed in a doctor's office.

For AID, the semen will be provided by an anonymous donor who has received a small payment for providing a semen sample, which is frozen until use or stored in a "sperm

Knowing About the Pregnancy

bank." Careful physicians will perform thorough screening of donors for diseases or genetic irregularities; however, this is not always the case and it is a good idea to screen your doctor before agreeing to AID. Shocking as it sounds, there have been cases of women contracting gonorrhea through AID. Find out what sort of screening procedure your doctor uses, and if it doesn't meet your own standards, find another doctor. In most cases, medical students, hospital residents, graduate students, or medical personnel will be selected as the donors. Many doctors will try to match up the husband and the donor's general physical characteristics, such as hair and eye color, body type, and so on. And if you're planning to have more than one child, you can use sperm from the same donor each time, so all of your children will be full brothers and sisters. The insemination is performed in the same way as for AIH.

Although AID is a painless procedure physically, it definitely takes a psychological toll, particularly on the husband. It is natural for a man to feel somewhat uneasy about his wife conceiving and bearing another man's child. Most doctors will direct a couple to some sort of counseling to help them deal with the difficult issues. Studies have shown that the majority of men eventually come to terms with their conflicts, especially once the baby is born. As most adoptive parents can testify, it doesn't take long before you begin to feel that the baby you hold, feed, care for, and love is really *yours*. And AID fathers have the definite advantage over adoptive fathers of knowing and loving the baby's mother, experiencing the pregnancy with her, hearing the baby's heartbeat, and feeling the first kicks, and, if they choose, participating in the birth.

At the Forefront of Science: High-Tech Fertilization

Until 1978, the term "test-tube baby" evoked a science fiction scenario akin to Frankenstein. But in July of that year, a living healthy test-tube baby named Louise Joy Brown was born in England, and the term instantly leapt from the realm of science fiction to incontrovertible fact. Actually, the preferred term for the procedure is "in vitro" (in glass or outside the body) fertilization. What happens is that a ripe egg is removed from the woman's body; it is exposed to active sperm in a laboratory dish; and when the fertilized egg has reached the eight to sixteen cell stage, it is inserted into the woman's uterus, where, it is hoped, it will implant and develop into a baby. That is how Louise Joy Brown came into being.

The procedure offers hope to couples with a variety of infertility problems, especially women with damaged Fallopian tubes and men with an abnormally low sperm count or poor motility. Sperm that would have been unable to complete the journey from vagina to Fallopian tube have a much better chance of fertilizing an egg when they are placed in direct contact with it in a laboratory dish. Unfortunately, the procedure is quite expensive (costs may be anywhere from $5,000 to $25,000 per pregnancy) and only 10 to 20 percent of the eggs so fertilized actually implant and go on to full term. But still, many thousands of couples are willing to try the procedure, and there are more and more facilities available to them. In 1986, there were 132 in vitro clinics around the country. Since 1978, some 2,000 children have been produced through in vitro fertilization.

In the past ten years, there have been a number of advances and refinements on in vitro fertilization.

In *embryo freezing*, usually for in vitro fertilization, numerous eggs are extracted from the woman (multiple egg production is stimulated by fertility drugs), but only a maximum of three embryos are introduced into the uterus. The remaining embryos are frozen until they may be needed. The question of how to dispose of the unneeded frozen embryos has become the subject of moral and legal controversy.

GIFT stands for gamete intrafallopian transfer, a procedure in which a ripe egg is extracted from the woman, mixed with her husband's sperm, and then reinserted into the entrance of an oviduct. This allows fertilization to take place inside the woman's body in the natural way. Twins—the first children to be conceived by this method—were born in April 1985, and since then doctors report a 30 percent success rate.

In *artificial embryonation*, a couple will essentially borrow the body of another woman for several days during which one of her eggs is artificially inseminated with the husband's sperm and allowed to begin growing. Once it has reached a

Knowing About the Pregnancy

certain stage, the embryo will be flushed out of the woman's body and implanted in the wife's uterus in the same method used for in vitro fertilization. At present, the procedure has been performed successfully only on a limited basis.

The whole area of sperm and egg donation has also opened up in the past few years. Sperm donation is what AID is all about. It is a relatively simple procedure and has been going on for some time. Now science has made egg donation possible as well, although extracting a ripe ovum from a woman's body is a more complicated and difficult procedure than producing sperm through masturbation. However, it is possible for a couple in which the man is fertile but the woman produces no eggs to obtain an egg from another woman, have it fertilized in vitro by the husband's sperm, and then inserted into the wife's uterus.

Another variation comes under the heading of surrogate mothering. A woman will agree to conceive and bear a child for another couple (the husband's sperm is introduced through artificial insemination) and then allow the couple to adopt the baby at birth. At present, the whole area of surrogate parenthood remains entangled in legal and religious controversy. Another possibility is for a woman only to *carry* the fetus for nine months. A wife who can produce eggs but is unable to achieve successful pregnancy will have one of her eggs removed from her body, fertilized by her husband's sperm, and then implanted in the body of the other woman, who carries the baby to term. A seven-pound, three-ounce girl was born through this method of surrogate parenthood in April 1986.

Described clinically, these new high-tech fertilization techniques sound frighteningly like something out of *Brave New World*. Science seems to be tampering with the very stuff of life itself, destroying our last intimacies and mysteries. Some feel we have already gone far enough down this path. And the question arises: Where will it end—with the creation of a new life from a single cell? with the "manufacture" of sperm and egg cells? with artificial everything? Quite aside from the high costs involved, these new procedures are obviously not for everyone. But for those who can accept them and afford them —and need them—the various new in vitro fertilization procedures offer hope. And when one strips away the clinical language and forgets about the possible science fiction horror scenarios of the future, one is left with the simple fact that these procedures enable couples who were childless to become parents. They offer hope.

The Pregnant Months: How Your Partner and Baby Change

The average pregnancy lasts 280 days counting from the first day of the last menstrual period to the day the baby is born. This is forty weeks, or slightly more than nine calendar months. Please keep in mind that the material here (and the infant development chart in Appendix A) reflect *averages*. Your baby will in all likelihood develop at a slightly different rate; so if your wife doesn't detect fetal movement at five months, don't panic!

Four Weeks

The fetus: Fertilized egg has implanted in the uterus. The cells, multiplying rapidly, begin to differentiate. The outer cells will become the placenta, which supplies the baby with nutrition and oxygen; the inner cells become the fetus. By day twenty-eight, the conceptus is about one-hundredth of an inch big—just visible to the human eye.

The mother: No changes yet—neither of you even knows she's pregnant.

Eight Weeks

The fetus: Length, almost one inch long. This is a critical period of development as the conceptus progresses from embryo, with rudimentary spinal cord and "buds" for limbs, to fetus, which has all essential human features and organs in an early but recognizable form. The developing fetus becomes encased in the amniotic sac. Initial development is from top to

Knowing About the Pregnancy

bottom, with head forming before chest and abdominal cavity (during weeks five and six). During the seventh week, the heart (which beats 115 to 155 times a minute) is beginning to pump blood through tiny blood vessels; rudimentary lungs are present and liver and kidneys appear. The fetus has a brain and fully formed spinal cord. All major internal organs, including brain and heart as well as limbs and skeleton, are present and beginning to develop. Toes and fingers are forming. The face begins to take on shape recognizable as human with well-defined nostrils, eyes sealed by eyelids, ears, jaw, and mouth. By the end of the eighth week, the baby's spine begins to make its first small movements, although the mother will not feel them until twenty or twenty-four weeks.

The mother: By now she has usually missed a period, although there may be a "false period" with light bleeding and some sensations of menstruation. The breasts enlarge and feel tender, and the nipples may become more prominent. The newly expecting mother may feel unusually tired, go to bed early, take naps, have trouble getting up in the morning. Some women experience morning sickness—nausea or queasiness first thing in the morning, after meals, or even from the smell of food cooking. Some develop a dislike of certain foods, particularly alcohol. Flatulence and constipation are common problems in the first trimester. Many women complain of feeling bloated and heavy. Increased levels of the hormones estrogen and progesterone may trigger emotional depression similar to the moods many women experience immediately before their periods. Increased hormones may also be responsible for lower back aches and the frequent need to urinate. Average weight gain is about one pound a month.

Twelve Weeks

The fetus: Length, about two and one-half inches; weight, about one-half ounce. This is a period of rapid growth and the completion of all initial developments. Arms and legs, fingers and toes are clearly developed; the fetus has muscles and exercises them by moving around the uterus, although your partner will still not feel it. By ten weeks, the eyes, still sealed

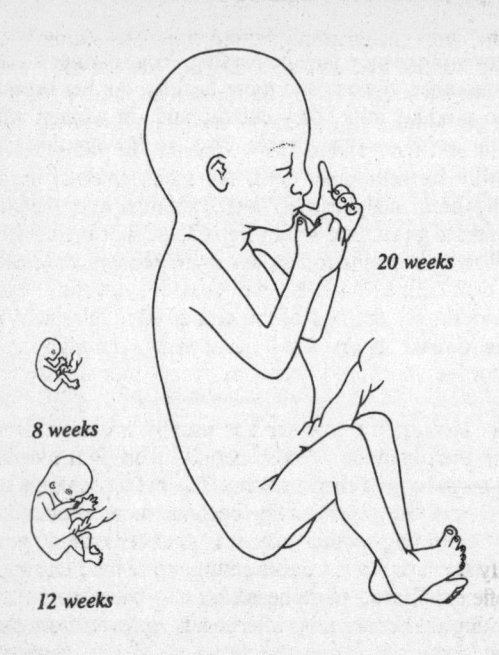

The growth of the fetus from 8 weeks to 20 weeks (relative size is correct)

beneath eyelids, can move; the inner ear has developed fully and the outer ear is progressing toward full development; the palate is forming inside the mouth. At the end of week eleven, the fetus's limbs have reached their final form, although they still appear spindly and the finger and toes are still joined by webbing. The baby's genitals have developed and all major organs are now in place: they will keep growing throughout the pregnancy, but the basic structure is there by twelve weeks. The fetus can open its mouth to drink the amniotic fluid; it can move its head; its heart and circulatory system are working well; reflexes from the spinal cord guide its movement around the amniotic sac. The risk of major abnormality in the baby's internal or external organs is much reduced after this period of development is completed.

The mother: Feelings of nausea and some of the fatigue of very early pregnancy may be passing. Your partner's skin may look smoother, tighter, and more healthy. As her breasts prepare to produce milk, they enlarge and, in women with fair skin, the veins become visible. Nipples and areolae may become darker. Vaginal discharges may increase. Although the uterus is growing, the pregnancy is still not visible. Your partner's body is producing more and more blood and will do so until ten weeks before the end of pregnancy.

Sixteen Weeks

The fetus: Length, about seven inches; weight, over four ounces. Now that the fetus is completely formed, the main thrust of development is on the maturing of the internal organs, particularly the lungs, and on weight gain (which increases seven- or eightfold during the last six months of pregnancy). The fetus begins breathing movements (it will not actually use its lungs to breathe until after birth) and swallowing reflexes. Your baby's heartbeat will show up on a sonogram. Some hair appears on head, eyebrows; finger- and toenails grow out. The fetus derives all of its nourishment from the placenta now. A fine downy hair known as lanugo is beginning to cover the baby's body.

The mother: Now in the second trimester of pregnancy, your partner feels a lot better than she did at the start—less tired, less queasy, healthier, and more like her old self in general. For most women, the second trimester is the most enjoyable period of pregnancy, marked by a feeling of well-being and a new surge of energy, as well as an increase in appetite and, for some women, a renewed (or even enhanced) interest in sex. Hormonal levels begin to stabilize, mood swings diminish. However, her figure is starting to change as the uterus grows. During this month, the top of the uterus reaches three-quarters of the way to the navel. The expecting mother may have trouble fitting into her regular clothes as her waistline gradually vanishes. Her body is producing more blood and there is a considerable amount of amniotic fluid in the uterus.

A few women experience a kind of fluttering sensation or something akin to gas bubbles in their stomachs—the very first fetal movements that she can detect. But most women, especially first-time mothers, don't feel the baby move until five months of pregnancy have been completed.

Twenty Weeks

The fetus: Length, ten inches; weight, more than one-half pound. Although your baby's facial features are now fully developed, they are quite wrinkled, and your baby's body is covered with a cheesy protective coating known as vernix caseosa. The fingers and toes have lost their webbing and are completely separated, with finger- and toenails. It is likely that the fetus hears and responds to outside sounds. Babies kick, grasp, and suck their thumbs and move around a great deal, and with vigor. Reflexes are present.

The mother: Your partner will no longer have any doubts when she feels the baby kick and move around. She is putting on weight rapidly, her stomach is starting to stick out, and she definitely looks pregnant, not fat. The top of the uterus is at the same level as the navel. Some women sweat more copiously than usual and some feel a permanent congestion in their noses; many feel a distinct rise in their body heat and complain of always being warm, even in cool weather. Your partner may get dizzy and she may have many more headaches than usual. It's important for her to drink lots of fluids.

Twenty-four weeks

The fetus: Length, thirteen inches; weight, almost one and one-half pounds. Growing rapidly, your baby is also starting to form a definite sleep and waking cycle. Kicks and movements are so definite now that you may be able to feel them if you place your hand on your partner's stomach—or, as you lie next to your partner, you may feel the baby kicking you. Lungs have developed, but they're not mature enough to sustain life outside the uterus for more than a few hours. This is a

Knowing About the Pregnancy

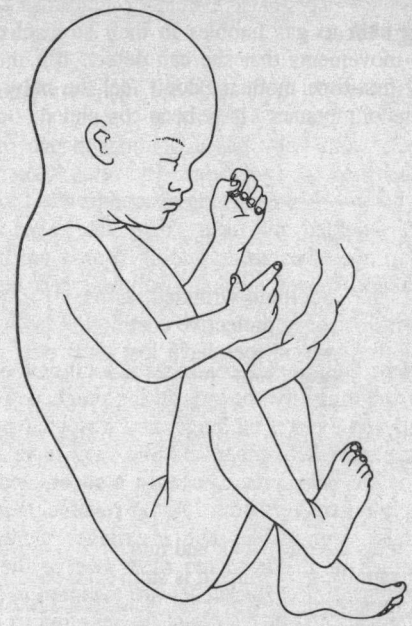

Fetus at 24 weeks

period of important and rapid development in the fetal brain, which continues to grow and develop over the next four years of your child's life. Good maternal nutrition is essential for both physical and mental growth in the fetus.

The mother: Many women begin to experience heartburn, a common side effect of pregnancy. Your partner will feel her uterus tighten and relax in the practice contractions (called Braxton Hicks contractions), a preparation for labor. Although the breasts will not produce milk until the baby is born, all the necessary bodily changes for future milk production have been completed. As a woman's body changes to accommodate the pregnancy, she produces more blood (40 to 90 percent more), breathes more quickly and less deeply, her heart beats faster, and her kidneys are subjected to greater stress.

Twenty-eight Weeks

The fetus: Length, almost fifteen inches; weight, almost two and one-half pounds. If born at the end of the twenty-seventh week, your baby has a fighting chance of survival under optimal medical conditions. The fetus looks more and more like a baby—skin is turning opaque (it was transparent), but it's still wrinkled and lacks "baby fat," eyes are open, eyebrows and eyelashes are appearing. Bones are hardening. The baby hears, moves, sucks, swallows, and responds to pain.

The mother: Weight gain continues (a total gain of between twenty-five and thirty-five pounds during pregnancy is considered normal) and there is no longer any way your partner can hide the fact that she's pregnant. She may have to urinate frequently as the baby presses against bladder, and she may feel extremely thirsty very often. As the relatively easy second trimester ends, your partner will experience increasing discomfort—much of it due to the sheer size of the load she carries around with her. Backaches are common as the uterus grows ever bigger and heavier, and the pressing of the uterus on the stomach and diaphragm may cause increasing heartburn and shortness of breath. Pregnant women often retain a lot of water, making them feel uncomfortably heavy and bloated. Sleeping on the stomach is impossible and she may need pillows to prop her up in bed.

Thirty-two Weeks

The fetus: Length, sixteen inches; weight, more than three and one-half pounds. Your baby is "all there"—everything is formed and in place, and during the duration of the pregnancy your baby is basically building up fat. The testes of a male baby descend outside the abdominal cavity. A good percentage of babies born now survive (some hospitals report a survival rate as high as 80 percent, provided the baby weighs over three pounds two ounces). The major problem for pre-

Knowing About the Pregnancy

mature babies are the lungs, which are still immature at this period, and the skull, which is very delicate and may sustain damage during delivery.

The mother: The baby now takes up so much room inside your partner's body that stomach, intestines, and bladder feel a constant pressure. Her nipples may begin to secrete colostrum, a yellowish substance that is the forerunner of breast milk. Hemorrhoids and varicose veins are common problems in the last trimester. Good nutrition, rest, and the right kind of exercise are as important now as throughout the pregnancy. The baby's kicks may be so vigorous and frequent that they cause discomfort and may keep your partner awake. Some women experience swelling of the ankles and feet. Weight gain has probably slowed somewhat. Your partner may begin to turn inward, focusing her precious energy on the life inside her.

Thirty-six Weeks

The fetus: Length, eighteen inches; weight, more than five pounds. More than 90 percent of babies born at this time in the pregnancy survive. As your baby keeps growing and building up body fat, he or she will have less room to move around in the uterus, and thus fetal movements will feel fainter than the flopping around of several weeks back, even though the baby is actually stronger. Most babies' heads drop down into the pelvis and stay down until birth.

The mother: Your partner will now feel so huge that she can't imagine keeping this up much longer. Actually, some of her discomfort may be relieved when the baby's head engages in the pelvis, and she may get a resurgence of energy in the final weeks. Doubts and anxieties are common as the due date approaches. Your partner may become depressed by her physical condition, increasingly tired as comfortable sleep positions become harder to find, irritable, and even resentful of pregnancy. Some women react to a kind of "nesting instinct" that prompts them to get everything ready for the baby. Your

52   PARENTS™ BOOK FOR NEW FATHERS

partner may be undergoing many of the same emotional shifts as you are: worries about the delivery, renewed concerns about the impact of a baby on your relationship and life-style, doubts over her abilities as a parent. Sex may become more and more difficult both physically and emotionally.

Forty Weeks

The fetus: Length, nineteen inches; weight, seven pounds. Weight gain is rapid in the last four weeks of life inside the

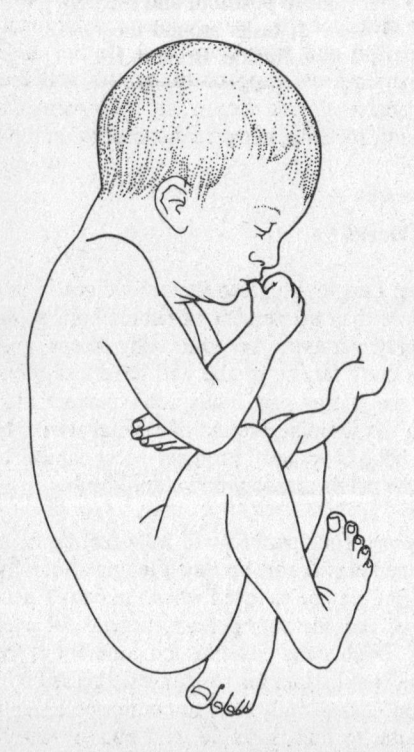

Full-term fetus at 40 weeks

Knowing About the Pregnancy

womb, with some babies putting on up to an ounce a day as they build up layers of fat. The lungs achieve full maturity. The baby's presenting part (the part of the body that comes out first—in most cases the head) presses against the cervix, and labor could begin any time now. Your baby is ready to be born and begin his or her life outside the womb.

The mother: Your partner may find the final weeks of pregnancy terribly difficult—the waiting is hard, the physical burden immense and exhausting, she may no longer be able to get into a comfortable sleep position, and she may have to depend on you for all sorts of tasks around the house. She feels all kinds of odd sensations inside: Braxton Hicks contractions can be quite intense now, fetal movements may seem more sporadic and light, and her cervix starts to soften and thin out. The pregnancy has reached full term. Any day now, she will become a mother—and you will become a father.

4. Feeling About the Pregnancy

There is a scene in Woody Allen's movie *Hannah and Her Sisters* in which the character Woody plays, an extreme hypochondriac, learns that he doesn't have the brain tumor that has terrified him for weeks. Ecstatically relieved, Woody races out of the hospital. You see him skipping joyously down the sidewalk, practically clicking his heels in the air—until about ten seconds later he suddenly stops dead. A whole new set of anxieties has just occurred to him, nipping his joy in the bud and dragging him down into worry and bewilderment.

Millions of expecting fathers play out a similar (though perhaps less comically exaggerated) scene when their wives first deliver that short but tremendously awesome sentence: "I think I might be pregnant."

"I screamed," one expecting father told me. "I was ecstatic and very excited. Then I stopped and looked at her. 'You're kidding, right?' I said."

No matter how long you've wanted a child, no matter how sure you felt about your decision, no matter how much you've read and talked and thought about it, the reality of finding out that this miracle has happened—that you're really going to *be* a father—is bound to knock you off your feet. Like Woody Allen in that movie, you may find yourself stopping in midleap as you tense up with all sorts of new anxieties. How are we going to afford this? That's the first question that crops up for many men, followed by a spectrum of worries that range from the practical (do we have enough space?) to the fantasti-

Feeling About the Pregnancy

cal (what if I can't figure out how to be a father?). And this is only the first five minutes!

Pregnant fathers go through a lot in those nine long months of pregnancy. It's more than the emotional turmoil of joy and worry chasing each other; it's a shift in the very basics of your life: your home, your marriage, your sense of self, your responsibilities. True, pregnant fathers don't go through the physical changes that their wives must endure as the fetus grows inside (many men, however, do have some physical symptoms, discussed later in this chapter), but then fathers-to-be don't get the kind of solicitous attention and consideration that pregnant women get. This is all part of the strange no-man's-land of pregnant fatherhood: you're excited but feel a little left out, you're stressed but feel you must be strong, you're changing but you're not sure how, you're somehow *different* and no one else even notices. "It's a bit of a lonely time" is the way one expecting father put it. No matter how far along the pregnancy is, the pregnant father never *shows*— but he feels a slew of new emotions, conflicts, joys, and uncertainties right from the very start.

That's what this chapter is all about: the emotional experiences of expecting fathers from the day they heard the news until the pregnancy had reached term and they were about to make that incredible transition to *actual* fatherhood.

More on First Reactions

"My wife called me up at the office and she was crying. She had just found out she was pregnant. She was happy but at the same time surprised and upset to some degree, because we hadn't really been trying. I just remember feeling very happy. There is something tremendously massaging to the male ego in the news that your wife is pregnant. I bought her flowers at lunchtime and went up to her office. We closed the door and kissed and hugged.... But I must admit I was also a little frightened about the news and having it thrust on me so suddenly. It was the idea that I had no control over my fate, because the pregnancy did come as a surprise. But basically I was elated. The feelings of responsibility closing in didn't come until a little later."

This was one of my favorite "I'm about to become a father" narratives. To me, it suggested a sensation almost of vertigo—emotions whirling, thrill and pride with a vague undertone of fear, and maybe even a bit of resentment over the loss of control. First learning about a pregnancy can do strange things to men, especially if total control is one of their things. In their book *Expectant Fathers* (Hawthorn, 1978), Sam Bittman and Sue R. Zalk tell of one father-to-be who hurled rocks at every window in his house the day he learned his wife was pregnant and another man who cried and withdrew into a sullen shell. I didn't encounter any reactions quite this extreme, but several men I interviewed made it clear that negative emotions outweighed the positive when they learned the news.

Ron and his wife, both attornies, were in the process of changing jobs when she became pregnant, and the anxiety associated with this affected his reaction to the news. "The job business made it all really complex," Ron recalls. "My wife had just left her job, taking a $15,000 pay cut, and after accepting a new job she found out she was pregnant. We went through a horrible week. One of the women partners was very upset that my wife was pregnant (even though she had explained at the interview that we were trying). This was a strain—and I had strains of my own. I got a job offer for a lot of money doing something I didn't want to do, so I turned that offer down. Learning about the pregnancy right at the time of these job changes made us both feel very divided. It came down to principle versus hard cash. The anxiety over these practical matters took a lot of the excitement out of it. However, the joy and excitement crept up on us."

For Brant, a thirty-year-old banker from Greeley, Colorado, it wasn't so much the joy that crept up on him as the *reality* of the pregnancy: "When she told me I just stood there in a state of shock. In fact, it was the furthest thing from my mind. I was wondering if it was for real. It didn't sink in for a while. I didn't really start thinking about the repercussions until later."

Vincent, an engineer from Albuquerque and the father of two with another on the way, said his reactions all three times

Feeling About the Pregnancy

were about the same: "It wasn't especially a high. I didn't bounce off the walls. With the first the awesome responsibility hit me both when I found out about the pregnancy and then right at the birth."

Pregnant fathers in real life seldom feel what they're supposed to feel—or they feel so much more than they're supposed to feel. (What *are* you supposed to feel? Probably something similar to the way John Wayne would have handled the news in one of his movies: boyish pride followed by manful control—"You run along and make our baby, little woman, and I'll take care of the Indians and rattlesnakes out there . . .") It's also probably true that the more you let yourself feel all those other things—whether it's fear, anger, or even a sense of panic—the better off you and your partner will be. Finding out that your partner is pregnant is such a highly charged situation that you may feel almost on stage, sort of watched by an imaginary audience to see if you play your role properly. The more you play that role (however you interpret it), the more likely you are to feel resentful later. Having a child is enough of a jolt to your life without adding on the alienation of role-playing. If you're not yourself at the beginning, you're probably going to feel more excluded as the pregnancy progresses.

One first reaction that several men mentioned to me was *relief*. "I was so relieved to know that we wouldn't have to go through the hell of fertility tests or the complexities of trying to adopt" is how one pregnant father put it. Of course, relief indicates that there was some fear that things wouldn't work out—another non–John Wayne emotion. And the flip side of relief is worry, even more alien to the John Wayne terrain. According to some studies, worry plagues expectant fathers even more than it does expectant mothers, and it can be the predominant emotion that men experience when they first hear the news. I remember being nearly sleepless for three nights as soon as there was any possibility that my wife might be pregnant. We had lived through a late first trimester miscarriage the previous year, and although we desperately wanted another pregnancy, we both also felt desperately anxious when we succeeded. What joy I felt I kept buried deep inside; I suppose I felt that if I let my happiness show I would be tempting fate and somehow "jinx" things. The two of us, with our haggard faces and obsessive calculations of weeks until we were "safe," were about as far as a couple could be from the standard image of exuberantly expectant parents. On the brighter side, at least I didn't have to worry about money, responsibility, loss of control, work, or any of those things: the worry about the viability of the fetus consumed my worry storehouse entirely.

Once that crucial three-month mark was passed and it looked like we were really going to make it this time, my feelings about the pregnancy opened up in an entirely new way. It hit me that there was actually a little baby growing inside there. And, looking back, I can see that this realization was the start of my relationship with my child.

No matter what stage of fatherhood we're at, we'll never forget our first reactions to "the News"—whether we jumped for joy, fretted over finances, worried about the fetus, or a combination of these. But we'll also, almost before we know it, pass on to other reactions. That's the great thing about pregnancy: so much happens to us, around us, through us, on top of us, without our doing anything to make it happen. At the center of this little storm of changes is the fetus, occupied solely with its development, growing silently at its own pace, regardless of our conflicts, terrors, and joys. How an expecting father feels about this silent, mysterious being that he has helped bring into existence is going to color his entire experience of the pregnancy. This, after all, is what it's really about.

Feelings About the Fetus

Ask a man whose wife is eight weeks pregnant about his relationship with the fetus and chances are you'll get a wry smile, a shrug, and a terse comment along the lines of, "Well, it's pretty abstract at this stage of the game." Ask the same man the same question a few weeks later after he's heard his baby's heartbeat, seen his baby on a sonogram (see Chapter 5), or later still when he feels the baby kicking, and you're more than likely to be knocked over by the force of his enthusiasm.

Feeling About the Pregnancy

Dan, a thirty-four-year-old writer and now the father of a seven-month-old boy, gave me a vivid account of this transformation in his own feelings: "I had a lot of ambivalence about the idea of having children, and the ambivalence was still very much there when my wife got pregnant. I wondered whether this was a good thing to do, whether we were getting in over our heads, whether I could handle it, whether the demands of a baby would lead to my resenting the baby, whether I wasn't being foolish about having blithely gotten myself into this. I idiotically gave way to my own fantasies about being a great dad with a perfect kid who shared my interests and would never throw up, never wake up in the middle of the night, never get into drugs—and I thought, Now look where I am, but it's too late.... My wife had come to peace with the decision, but I guess because I was less involved biologically, I didn't feel as close to the baby and thus I continued to wrestle with the kinds of issues I had before she got pregnant.

"But, as the pregnancy went on, and I could feel the baby kick and hear the baby's heartbeat, I felt more involved and the doubts and anxieties subsided. We had this nightly ritual called the 'listening post' where I'd press my ear around my wife's stomach until I could pick up the baby's heartbeat. The visceral reality of the baby—feeling him move, seeing the sonogram, hearing the heartbeat—this made all the doubts and questions and issues involving careers beside the point. The baby's presence began to take over."

Ron experienced a similar turn-around in his feelings. "I was totally ignorant about the growth of a child in the womb, so a number of things surprised me. The biggest thing was seeing the sonogram, seeing this little person with fingers, eyes, heartbeat—that was the single most important event in the pregnancy for me. It made the whole thing *real* to me, made the fetus seem like a real person. I had never really thought there was this *thing* in there that wakes and sleeps, opens and shuts its eyes, moves around. Somehow I had thought that whatever was in there really wasn't alive until it got out. So the sonogram at three months was a real shock. And it made me feel that much more part of the process."

For Michael, a clerical worker from Greeley, Colorado,

feeling the baby kick brought back the joy he experienced when he first learned about the pregnancy. "When I first felt the baby move I felt, 'Oh, it's really in there.' It brought back the excitement that I felt at the start. You get really excited at first and then nothing happens for a while; then you feel the baby move or hear the heartbeat and it brings back the excitement of the beginning."

When Ron and his wife learned later in the pregnancy that their baby was a girl, it marked for him another major milestone in his relationship with the fetus. For Don, another New York expecting father I interviewed, finding out the sex had a huge impact on his feelings about the baby: "When my wife went for the amnio (see Chapter 5) and we found out afterwards we were going to have a boy, it really made a difference to me. I was the last male in the line and I had secretly wished for a boy all along—but somehow I never felt it would make as much of a difference as it did make once it was confirmed. At periods I find myself so incredibly happy that I'm on the verge of tears. There is an element of happiness I'm experiencing that I've never known before. These are 'major league emotions'—feelings I knew I was capable of but didn't think I'd indulge myself in are surging over me at unexpected times. The sonogram and amnio were definitely turning points. I find it difficult to imagine fatherhood without that. It changes things so immeasurably. You really begin to imagine the baby as a small person."

Bob, a family therapist, echoes this feeling that the sonogram and amnio were what made the pregnancy real. "The doctors let me watch the sonogram and amnio and it was fascinating. First they locate the baby and the pockets of fluid, then you see the baby's finger go into its mouth. That for me was the realization that we were actually having a baby and this is real stuff. That's when I started reading. I realized that it's not a couple of cells, it was real. And from then on, at each step the pregnancy become more real. It was at this point that we gave the baby a name."

The first physical evidence of life—be it the sonogram, heartbeat, or baby's kick—was the turning point for all the fathers I spoke to, and I'm sure the same holds true for the majority of men. It may be that there's some deep psychologi-

Feeling About the Pregnancy

cal reason for this. Perhaps men don't really *want* to believe in the pregnancy until they absolutely must. Or perhaps it has less to do with the psyche than with the imagination. No matter how much you read about fetal development or how many photos of the human fetus you study, it's nearly impossible to fathom that a simple act of yours brought this being into existence, that it's inside your partner's stomach, which still looks as flat and normal as ever, and that it's going to come out in less than a year and be your baby. Even a lot of newly pregnant mothers have trouble with these concepts. (In fact, it doesn't stop even after the baby is born. The more of a person your baby becomes, the more difficult it is to believe that he or she was once two cells produced by you and your partner's bodies.) But with that first kick, image, heartbeat, there's nothing left to imagine: it's there, right before your eyes or ears or under your hand. To me, feeling these little eruptions from inside my wife was both thrilling and a bit unnerving, almost creepy. It was so alien to anything I had ever felt before, so unexpected and so undeniably *other*. Suddenly the baby has announced itself as an independent person, with its own limbs and heart and will to kick and turn around in there. It's amazing to realize that by spreading your palm out over your partner's abdomen you're actually holding your baby. Amazing and also a lot more complicated than when the whole business was largely a matter of abstraction and the vague and distant future. Suddenly the birth date may seem to be approaching a lot more quickly.

For a number of the men I spoke to, this turning point in their feelings toward the fetus was also a time when they began to fantasize about things they would be doing with their babies. Michael, who described himself as "a sports fanatic," said, "I fantasize about my baby being a boy all the time. I want a boy to play sports with. I'm into all sports and have been since school, and I already have little muscle shirts and baseball outfits for the baby." [As it turned out, Michael got his wish for a son about two weeks after this interview.]

One New York expecting father imagined doing "New York things" with his daughter (they had had an amnio so they knew): "I fantasize about going to the Museum of Natural History and the Metropolitan, taking her to concerts, spending time in the Park. I picture her looking just like my wife—a playful, teasing little blonde kid." Then he added that along with the pleasant fantasies, certain worries arose at this time: "I haven't thought about her future personality much, though I do worry, What if my child has major emotional problems?" Worry and fantasy are in many ways the opposite poles of the parental world. It seems only natural that they spring up together at the time when we first start to accept the reality of the baby's existence.

Don recalls a particularly vivid dream he had soon after learning that the baby was to be a boy: "I dreamed I was exposing my son to all the things missing from my own life, exposing him to a broad range of things, including art, that my dad never took much of an interest in. In the dream, my son was three or four years old." Don felt that he had made the baby older because he was worried that he wouldn't be able to relate to the baby as an infant. In this he is not alone: many men skip over the early months in their fantasies or dreams about the baby, and in fact, when expectant fathers (and mothers, too) try to visualize what their newborn will look like, they usually conjure up something along the lines of the "Gerber baby"—a plump, smiling six-month-old. I remember being shocked when we toured the hospital and saw the newborns in the nursery. They were so incredibly tiny and helpless, so utterly unlike the little person in my dreams, who could miraculously talk, shake hands, and smile at birth!

For some men, the concept of relating to a fetus remains fairly meaningless no matter how many sonograms they've seen or kicks they've felt. How can you relate to something you've never met? is one fairly common question. What, after all, is there to relate to? is another. These questions do have a point, and it's probably the rare expecting father who has *never* contemplated them. The fact is, relating to a fetus remains partly a matter of *choice* on the father's part. You can choose to remove yourself entirely or you can choose to include yourself. As Bittman and Zalk put it in *Expectant Fathers*, "The father... will be excluded from as much of the relationship [with his baby] as he is willing to be."

Including yourself can mean simply taking an interest, letting yourself daydream, or even talking with the fetus. Talking

Feeling About the Pregnancy

to a fetus is really not as strange as it sounds when you stop to consider that the baby's ears develop by the eighth week of pregnancy and the baby begins to respond to sounds by week seventeen. A number of the expectant fathers I interviewed said they talked to their babies in utero all the time, and although they may have felt silly at first, they ended up feeling that it created a real bond between them. It's a good way of overcoming the feelings of exclusion that so many of us experience during pregnancy, feelings that may make us resent both mother and baby and that may lead us to remove ourselves emotionally from the whole business. And it's just possible that your unborn baby not only hears you but becomes accustomed to your voice—hence, in a way *knows* you even before birth. I remember talking to my daughter in the delivery room just seconds after she was born and saying with wonder that she seemed to recognize me. I was startled when the nurse commented, "She probably does—she's been listening to your voice for several months now."

The real issue here is making contact. If you make an effort, either by talking to the fetus, or feeling the fetus kick, or just listening to your partner talk about what is going on inside her body, there's a good chance that you'll feel more part of the process. Brant, like more and more fathers today, accompanied his wife on all the visits to the obstetrician. "I wanted to be part of it and see what was going on," he said. "I'm learning more about the baby all the time." A visit to the obstetrician is not only an opportunity to listen to your baby's heartbeat on the fetascope, but a chance to get to know the person who will be bringing this new life into the world. Reading up on fetal development also helps. Knowing the astonishing facts about what happens in those nine months can be more powerful than any fantasies or daydreams (see the list of recommended books in Appendix B).

The middle months of pregnancy are often an idyllic time for fathers-to-be. You can sense the baby growing just by looking at or holding your partner, you feel the kicks getting stronger, the baby seems more real all the time but not yet so real that he or she interrupts your pleasant dreams or fantasies by crying. Many couples begin their childbirth education classes at this time (see Chapter 6), and these can be a source of much good information for expectant fathers, information that may deepen one's feelings toward the fetus. Strangely, however, as the due date approaches, many men find themselves drawing back from the pregnancy, suppressing their fond fantasies about the fetus, or just feeling suddenly uninvolved. This denial can affect those who were the most enthusiastic about the pregnancy at the start and who will soon become the most enthusiastic fathers. Ron, who was so ecstatic at the first trimester sonogram, found himself withdrawing as the pregnancy neared term. "There are so many things going on now," he said when they were a few weeks from the due date. "I'll be starting a new job, I'm fixing up the apartment, I'm so preoccupied that I have felt more detached from the child and the pregnancy. Even feeling fetal movement doesn't mean as much as it used to. My wife, on the other hand, is becoming much more involved. My detachment more or less coincided with starting Lamaze."

Jim, a psychologist who lives near San Francisco, felt so detached from the pregnancy in the final weeks that he wondered whether he would love his baby. Like Ron, he felt himself drawing back as his wife became more and more preoccupied. The feeling was: It's so physically inescapable for her, but there doesn't seem to be any connection with the baby for me anymore. What does this say about the kind of father I'm going to be? (In both cases, nothing. Both men jumped into their roles as totally involved fathers without the slightest hesitation. Jim was boasting about what "a great little guy" his son was two days after he was born.) For other men, the whole pregnancy can seem more and more unreal the closer the due date gets. One expecting father with two weeks to go said, "When I start confronting the reality of the timetable, I pull back. I guess I'm just avoiding my anxiety over time." It's sort of like being drafted or receiving a notice from the IRS that your taxes are being audited: you can't believe this is happening to *you*.

Several fathers I interviewed who were expecting their second or third child said their involvement with the fetus was much smaller this time around. "The second pregnancy has been almost nonexistent for me," said one dad who was near-

Feeling About the Pregnancy

ing the birth of number two. "We've both been so busy the entire time. With the first there was a moment by moment discussion of what the baby is doing. Now we're not really focused on the baby except when it moves."

Late pregnancy denial can have a lot of causes: mounting anxiety about the birth, anxiety about how you will accept the baby, resentment over your partner's engrossment with it all, a desire to cling to your old, unburdened way of life. If you deny the reality of the pregnancy or detach yourself from it emotionally, you can live with the illusion that everything has returned to "normal"—an illusion that may seem more and more attractive on the eve of everything departing quite radically from normal. For some men, detachment from the fetus may arise out of fear for their wives during labor and delivery. New York-based childbirth educator Diana Simkin said that as the birth approaches, "Men are often more worried about their wives than about the baby and there can be guilt arising because of this. If something goes wrong, they want the wife to pull through." So, detaching oneself from the fetus is a way of protecting oneself from this guilt.

Worries about the baby can add to the expecting father's feeling of detachment. His pleasure in feeling the baby kick can turn to desperate concern late in pregnancy when the baby's kicks diminish (remember, there's less room for acrobatics now, so the baby simply *can't* be as active). The reveries about taking the baby to concerts or ballgames may be replaced by horrifying images of birth defects. Fear blots out whatever loving feelings had been developing inside the father-to-be. One fairly common way in which men cope with late pregnancy anxiety is to throw themselves into some project at home or in work. Ron finished renovating the kitchen just days before his daughter's arrival. Brant went into training for his first marathon. David started a rush job constructing a roof-deck over his apartment and was still working on it even as his wife's cervix began to efface. "I planned to finish in time for the baby," he said, "and now the complications with the pregnancy [his wife had developed high blood pressure] have made me crazy. I just have this feeling that once the baby is here, I won't have time for anything."

The point is: The final weeks of pregnancy are an extremely tense and intense time for everyone—expecting fathers, mothers, grandparents, and so on. Your feelings about everything are likely to go a little (or a lot) out of whack, and this may be especially true with your feelings toward your unborn baby. "The intensity level of *everything* has increased" is how one expecting father who was days away put it. "It's as if colors are brighter, events more vivid. Things have become heavier, there's no doubt about it. And yet I feel dazed from time to time."

You've been dreaming and fantasizing about this little being for months, and now you may find yourself almost dreading his or her arrival. Why, you wonder, is everyone else so much more worked up about it than you? You're *supposed* to be anticipating the "blessed event" with joyous excitement, and instead you find yourself working late every night, desperate to see all the new movies, and a bit sick of all the baby things piling up around the house. Knowing that all of this is perfectly normal may make your life a *little* easier, but you're still likely to be juggling a lot more conflicting emotions than you feel comfortable with.

Part of the difficulty might simply be that your nine-month relationship with the fetus—a decidedly one-way relationship based largely on fantasy, hope, and imagination, but a relationship nonetheless—is about to come to an end. Any day now you're going to find yourself in a totally new relationship—the very real, undeniable, and impossible-to-ignore relationship of a new father with a newborn baby. And this, as any father will instantly point out, is a whole different ballgame.

Common Worries and Symptoms of the Expecting Father

It is truly the rare, maybe even unique, man who has not worried about something during the course of his partner's pregnancy. In fact, according to a study conducted by D. R. Entwisle and S. G. Doering (*The First Birth*, Johns Hopkins University Press, 1981), men worry more during pregnancy than their wives, and worry more about their wives than the women do about themselves. So when a pregnant woman has a headache or feels a bit dizzy, her husband may very well be the one doing most of the fretting. This was certainly true for me, and it drove my wife crazy after a while. Charles, a doctor from Albuquerque and a father of three, said his worry level remained pretty much the same during each pregnancy. "Pregnancy is a neat and exciting time but also kind of a scary time. You don't know if something is really there, you don't know if it's 100 percent, you don't know about problems. I didn't really relax until I saw the babies born."

Much as they worry about their wives, pregnant fathers worry even more about "issues," mostly under the headings of economic, personal, and sexual. Money is the number one worry for expecting fathers, and it usually takes the form of "Can I make enough to support my family?" Other expecting father worries identified in a study conducted by Katharyn May, Doctor of Nursing Science and assistant professor of nursing at the University of California at San Francisco, include anxiety about whether their marriage is strong and stable enough to bear up under the stress of parenthood; doubts about whether they have done all the things they wanted to accomplish before the baby came (for example, get a graduate degree); insecurities about what kind of fathers they will be; anxiety about what impact pregnancy and parenthood will have on their sex life.

These major worry categories certainly came up in the interviews I conducted with expecting fathers. Money and practical problems—where to live, how to find and afford child care, how to juggle schedules—were at the top of everyone's pregnancy worry list. Said Brant, a banker from a small city in Colorado, "Most of what I worry about is how we will handle things after the birth. How we will swing it financially, about child care arrangements, and, looking into the future, about education." For some, the worries about money, their relationships, and their work were intimately bound up. Ron, a hard-working attorney married to a hard-working attorney, talked about the pressures that he and so many two-career couples are facing today. "I do feel anxious about the future of our relationship and the impact of a child on it. With me going back to a job with a heavy schedule and my wife's working until eight every night and one day each weekend, I worry about the time we'll have together. How will a child fit in unless we restructure the way we think about work? How will we have any time to see each other?"

Don expressed a slightly more abstract kind of worry by saying, "I worry about finding my own self so that the baby will have something to relate to. If I don't find a groove, will the baby respect and love me?" The flip side of this is the expecting father worrying about whether he will love his baby. As one father-to-be put it: "I sometimes wonder whether I'll like the child or be bored with it after a while. And the idea that the next eighteen years of your life are not your own, that you have to work a baby into your existence, is frightening."

Most of the men I spoke to were definitely worried about the responsibilities that would soon be closing in on them. Will I be up to the pressures of fatherhood? The relentlessness of it? The ceaseless demands of a young child? What if I find out that I don't like being a father? As Mike, a thirty-eight-year-old geneticist from New York, put it: "The responsibility is definitely my greatest fear: the money, the long-term commitment, the changes it will bring in my life. I have a brother I'm close to who has three kids and I was happy in the role of Uncle Mike. The great thing was: I could leave. Now I realize I won't be able to leave." (Without doubt, there will be aspects of fatherhood that all men will find unpleasant just as pregnancy also has its down side for men. But who said you had to like all of it? Expectations of this sort can get you into trouble.)

Lots of men worry about medical complications: difficult deliveries, stillbirths, birth defects, injuries to their wives. Some men skip ahead and start worrying about the stresses of adolescence—what if the kid gets into drugs, has emotional problems, drops out of school? Fathers who are expecting their second (or third) child often worry about the added stresses and strains. "Having one taxes you right to the limit," said one dad on the eve of his second child's birth. "Thinking about two is scary! Everyone says that two is more than twice the work of one. You really start to appreciate what your own parents went through." Lots of men worry about the air their

Feeling About the Pregnancy

wives breathe, the stress levels they're exposed to, the foods they eat. We've all read about deformities and low birthweights caused by pollution, radiation, chemicals in food, medication women take, alcohol, tobacco, and drugs. These are serious concerns, made worse by the fact that we have so little control over them.

Then there are the slightly less serious concerns. "My major anxiety now is getting my wife to the hospital on time," said one father-to-be nearing due date. "I'm just afraid of her giving birth in a taxi." A touch more eccentric was the expecting father who worried about his baby's first hour at home: "We get the baby home from the hospital—and then what do we do? Stare at the baby? I also worry about how to handle my large golden retriever and keep him off the baby. We've already begun talking to the dog about the baby to get him prepared." Yet another worry concerns grandparents: How are you going to keep the in-laws from fighting over visiting rights? How are you going to deal with your mother-in-law?

Then there is the whole area of superstitions. One father I spoke to selected a name for his baby girl right after his wife's amniocentesis, only to be told by nervous grandparents-to-be that it would bring bad luck. Some cultures say setting up the baby's room brings bad luck: you're supposed to have all the furniture and clothes delivered elsewhere or keep them at the store until the baby is born. (I bought into this one and it sure made life difficult when we brought the baby home and she didn't have a crib or a changing table and all her clothes were still packed in plastic bags!)

I'll stop before I get you worrying about things that haven't occurred to you yet. The universal advice from psychologists, counselors, and experienced parents is: If you've got these worries, admit it—first of all to yourself. Talk about them openly, especially with your partner. Men who think that the manly thing to do is keep their fears and worries to themselves (or deny them altogether) are doing no one a favor. These men are much more likely to end up angry, withdrawn from the pregnancy, and alienated from their babies. If you're worried about the pregnancy, don't worry about it. You're perfectly normal. And the perfectly normal response is to deal with it and get it off your chest.

* * *

Also perfectly normal for expecting fathers are physical symptoms similar to those their wives are experiencing. Yes. Weight gain, nausea, stomach problems, backache, insomnia, appetite loss, toothache—expecting fathers commonly experience all of these right alongside their expecting wives. Statistics vary widely, but one recent study conducted at the University of Wisconsin-Milwaukee School of Nursing found that 90 percent of men in a sample of 147 were having some of these symptoms (interestingly, very few of the men told their pregnant wives about it). This phenomenon even has a name—the couvade syndrome. The name (from the French *couver*—to brood or hatch) derives from a ritual practiced by men of certain primitive cultures, which British anthropologist Sir Edward Tylor dubbed "the couvade" in the late nineteenth century. Men performing the actual ritual will get into bed when their wives go into labor and act out the labor and birth of the baby, sometimes even dressing in their wives' clothes. One can see at least two functions of the ritual: to establish the real father's identity for everyone in the tribe or community and to trick evil spirits so that they will expend their wrath on the mock-mother and leave the actual mother and baby in peace.

The couvade ritual may seem utterly bizarre until you begin thinking about the reasons why you've gained nearly as much weight as your partner in the first half of the pregnancy. The couvade syndrome is the way fathers in modern Western societies act out their involvement and identification with their wives' pregnancies. It has less to do with evil spirits than with anxiety, which, come to think of it, might be our version of evil spirits. It's the male body's way of channeling pregnancy worry. One expecting father who was undergoing a mild version of the couvade syndrome analyzed it this way: "I do feel increased anxiety and the little aches and pains I have may be sympathy with what my wife is going through. I assume my every living moment is tied in with the pregnancy, and thus it seems safe to assume that the lower back aches I've been having are tied in with the pregnancy. It's been a stressful time."

If you do have some of these symptoms, you'll be pleased

Feeling About the Pregnancy

to know that they don't last. The couvade syndrome tends to peak in the third month, then tapers off until the last few weeks of pregnancy, when some of the symptoms may return. But as soon as the baby is born, the symptoms vanish.

Your Relationship

Somewhere deep in popular culture the idea was conceived that the first thing a man should do when his wife told him she was pregnant was to make her sit down. She wasn't to lift heavy burdens, to exert herself in sports or chores, to strain herself mentally or physically—and it was a man's duty to enforce her inertia. Being with child instantly elevated a woman's status from wife to sacred madonna—and instantly transformed a man's role from husband/partner to protector/provider/porter/guardian/handyman/crisis-handler. In a way, a wife's pregnancy instantly made a husband into a father—the father of his wife. Well, to lift a line from a long-running ad, we've all come a long way, baby.

Many men may still have the impulse to protect and coddle their wives upon finding out the big news, but for most of us, this impulse is just one in a range of feelings that keeps shifting throughout the pregnancy. For one thing, pregnancy is no longer considered or treated like a disability, and thus husbands no longer feel impelled to treat their wives as if they're suffering from some vague but beatific disease. A woman who is visibly pregnant and yet continues to work full-time, jog three miles a day, hang out with her friends, and stay on top of the chores clearly has no need to be told to "Rest, dear, and let me carry the groceries" (which is not to say she won't appreciate it now and then). On the other hand, a woman in her eighth week who is experiencing severe morning sickness and fatigue is unlikely to be enthusiastic about going out to restaurants, let alone sex, keeping the house clean, or playing tennis. This woman's husband will find himself confronting an entirely new marital situation almost as soon as he's heard the news—and the baffling part is that in four more weeks his partner may have recovered her former bounce and seem totally back to normal. Chances are that both you and your

Love and Stress

One of the best things about pregnancy is the way it can bring a couple closer together. When asked what impact the pregnancy had on their marriages, nearly all the men I interviewed first replied that it deepened their love. "I feel I love her more," one expecting father said simply. "And it's a much more intense love. We tell each other more. We're so excited to see each other when I get home from work. We've grown much closer, bonded even more. We do more together, we have more fun. I'm ecstatic with her." Don admitted that there were "inconvenient aspects" to the pregnancy, especially in its impact on their physical relationship, but "at the same time, I've experienced a new closeness to my wife. We always had an unusual closeness, and now we have become *emotionally* closer. I don't understand the reason. Something has been freed up in me. We've both become something more because of the pregnancy and we feel an even greater fulfillment at the prospect of becoming parents." And Michael said he felt proud of his wife, "but I've always felt this way. We have a very good relationship and the baby has drawn us a bit closer. I've been rather protective, keeping her from lifting heavy things and making sure she has no drinks when we go out to dinner. She is taking it really well. She even came out all summer to watch my softball games."

It's possible the sample I covered was unusually fortunate: all the men wanted to become fathers (with some minor ambivalence), and all welcomed the news of the pregnancy. So it would seem only natural for these men to feel closer to their wives and to feel proud of them for being pregnant. (By the way, a study has shown that the happier a man is about the pregnancy, the more likely that his wife will enjoy the first few weeks of the baby's life.) There is something indescribably moving about the knowledge that your wife is pregnant with your baby. "I felt proud of her—she was radiating" was the way one father put it. The two of you have succeeded

Feeling About the Pregnancy

together in making this miracle come to pass. Your wife, the person with whom you share a thousand mundane, day-to-day activities, seems somehow to be moving in a realm far removed from normal reality by the simple fact that she is carrying a growing life inside her. This all probably seems a little sappy until you've been through it, and then it may bring tears to your eyes. Even if there's no reason to take care of her, you're going to feel that deepening of love, that affirmation of your bond that the two expecting fathers described above. And having this feeling is an excellent way of starting out on the long journey of parenthood, a journey that inevitably leads you past emotions that are a good deal less pleasant.

Sometimes these less pleasant emotions arrive hard on the heels of pride and joy. No matter how close you feel to your wife, you may find yourself resenting the fact that everyone else feels so concerned about her, too. Once the word is out, no one ever asks how *you're* feeling, but it's always "How is Beth? Does she have morning sickness? Has she seen the doctor yet? What's the due date? Are you taking good care of her?" This can get a little tiresome quite quickly.

Of course, this kind of concern from others isn't *her* fault, but then again the fact that she's having a rocky first trimester isn't all her fault either. It may seem a little unfair of Mother Nature to saddle a woman with so many uncomfortable side effects so early in the pregnancy, but that's the way it is. Nausea, queasiness, and vomiting can set in almost as soon as a woman discovers she's pregnant and can stay with her until she has passed the three-month mark. Many women are blissfully free of these symptoms, but almost all women feel a degree of fatigue during the first trimester, and for some it may be overwhelming exhaustion. It's difficult to feel deeply intimate with a woman who spends all her spare time sleeping and/or sick to her stomach. Even the most saintly husband can become resentful. And the resentment may intensify precisely because your new feelings of closeness have been rebuffed. She's always telling me I'm so distant and preoccupied with work, you may be thinking, and now that I'm feeling so incredibly in love with her, all she can think of is sleeping. Before you get too carried away with being hurt and angry, remember that the second trimester is a wonderful break from discomfort in almost all pregnancies. Try saving all those loving words for week fifteen, when she's likely to be more receptive.

One favor you can do for yourself is to acknowledge that it's perfectly okay to have a number of feelings, even conflicting feelings, about your partner at the same time. Ron said that the pregnancy brought him very close to his wife, but it also introduced some new tensions into the relationship. "I'm more relaxed, she's more impatient, and the pregnancy has brought out this difference. For example, she worries about packing her bag, I'm just concerned with getting the kitchen finished. [Ron was renovating their apartment during the pregnancy.] She's having a problem fulfilling her nesting instinct because she's still working hard at her job, and there's tension over that. She takes out a lot of anger at her job." These were relatively minor problems for Ron, and they were the only ones I heard him complain about. But not all men are so lucky. A pregnancy, and especially a difficult pregnancy, can heighten basic personality differences between husband and wife and can leave a man feeling isolated, lonely, and increasingly bitter. You may come to see the growing fetus not as an expression of your love but as a symbol of your separateness. All her energy, all her care, all her thoughts go into *it*—but what about *me*? I'm still the same old guy with the same old needs. And if she's this tied up now, halfway through the pregnancy, what's it going to be like when the baby's here? I'm going to be the classic fifth wheel.

Coping with Marital Rough Spots: Jealousy, Fighting, Alienation

Jealousy becomes an issue for many men—jealousy of the woman's involvement with the baby, jealousy of how the baby is sapping the woman's energy and interest in him. There also may be jealousy of the woman for being the pregnant one. Some psychologists have identified an unconscious desire on the expecting father's part to carry the baby himself, a phenomenon sometimes known as "Zeus envy" (the name derives from the myth about the Greek god Zeus who swallowed

Feeling About the Pregnancy

Metis, a goddess he had made pregnant; their offspring—Athena, goddess of war and wisdom—sprang fully armed out of his head). A friend of mine joked late in his wife's fairly difficult pregnancy, "I wish I were the one carrying the baby. At least I wouldn't complain about it so damned much." Men whose outlooks are not so comic may become threatened by these feminine impulses and go overboard in proving how macho they really are. And jealousy of any sort can quickly degenerate into anger and fighting.

The odds are high that whatever rough spots you've had in your marriage will become rougher at some point during the pregnancy, or soon after the baby is born. If you bicker over chores, you're going to bicker even more when she's no longer able or willing to do her full share or when you insist on doing her chores and then resent her for it. (As one expecting father put it at the end of his wife's pregnancy: "In the last few months, almost *everything* has fallen on me, from painting the apartment to cooking and shopping. Work consumes everything in her and she's exhausted on weekends—so doing the chores is really up to me.") If working out the right balance of time with friends and time alone at home has been a problem, it's going to be even more of a problem when you feel the subtle (or not so subtle) tug of wife-and-baby dragging you away from your buddies. If budgeting time is difficult, it's going to be more difficult when she has so little energy at the start of the pregnancy and again at the end when you're trying to get everything in shape before the baby comes. And then there are work issues: she thinks you work too much and make too little—and you sense she thinks this even more now that there's a baby on the way and you're going to be on call for child care and under pressure to provide; you think she's obsessed by office politics and work pressure—and you really can't stand it when it seems that the office consumes her entire energy supply, except for a few bursts of griping about it that she saves for you. The list goes on and on: entertaining, budgets, in-laws, vacations, moving. One expecting father said he and his wife even fought about the baby's name! All these possible tension areas can become dangerous battlegrounds during the pregnant months and treacherous war zones after the baby arrives. And we haven't even mentioned sex (yet)!

It can all seem a little daunting when you're six months into a pregnancy that you both thought you wanted and you're fighting like cats and dogs. I'm not going to suggest that there are easy answers because it's simply not true. The stress that pregnancy puts on a marriage may be mild compared to the stress that parenthood involves, so it's no help either to assume that all the trouble will suddenly vanish when your beautiful baby arrives. Trite as it sounds, the best way of dealing with issues in a relationship is to get as much as you can out in the open. Start by being as honest as you can with yourself. Examine your motives. Are you doing all the chores only to place yourself in an unassailable position from which to resent your partner? Are you using the father-as-provider model as an excuse to retreat into your work because you feel excluded from the pregnancy? Do you feel angry that your partner works because it implies that you cannot support your family —or because you fear it may leave you "stuck" with more domestic duties? Try to separate out your own needs and desires from roles that have been imposed on you by society. Lots of men, for example, get into trouble by acting out the scenarios depicted at the opening of this section: they feel they *should* take care of the little woman, but they soon begin to feel that the little woman is taking advantage of them. Freeing yourself of these socially imposed norms can only be to your advantage.

Beyond this, it's a matter of working things out with your partner in the most constructive way possible. Couples get into ruts and remain in them contentedly until some stress forces them to reassess. Expecting a baby may be that stress. Many problems have practical solutions: change your schedules slightly and you'll have more time together; take more responsibility for certain domestic details and there will be less conflict. Jolting attitudes and expectations out of ruts can be more difficult than making scheduling adjustments. Talk openly about as many problems as you're aware of, and then give yourself a break. Sometimes just relaxing together can clear the air. One childbirth instructor advises expecting parents to set aside time together during which it is strictly forbidden to talk about the baby: couple time. Don't rule out

Feeling About the Pregnancy

counseling or family therapy, or just blowing off steam with friends.

Many men sentence themselves to a kind marital exile during a pregnancy. They may begin by feeling excluded and end by excluding themselves. The attitude is: There's nothing for me to do. She doesn't need me or she's too tired to offer me anything, so I'm just going to take myself off and do my own thing. For some this means extramarital affairs. For others a sulking pose of aloofness and pride. Others simply get lonely and miserable. The feelings that led to this kind of stance can feed on themselves. The more excluded you feel, the more you exclude yourself, the lonelier you feel, the less approachable you seem, the more your partner withdraws, the more excluded you feel, and so on. One good way out of this is to try to involve yourself in the pregnancy: feel the baby kick, go to doctor's appointments, see the sonogram, read. As noted in the previous section, you can and do have a relationship with the fetus, and acknowledging and participating in this can help end your isolation from your partner. The baby is something —some*one*—you share. Accepting this can open the way to sharing in all areas of your relationship.

How Your Partner Is Taking It

"She was great. She stayed active the entire time, never had any morning sickness or discomfort. The pregnancy really suited her: it added a new glow to her looks and made her feel great about the world."

"The pregnancy was one long ordeal for her. When she wasn't feeling physically rotten, she was mad at everything and everyone. She hated getting big and complained constantly about how unattractive she felt. She was convinced that any woman who claimed to enjoy being pregnant was lying."

These are the two extremes of how women handle being pregnant—and, of course, there are millions of variations in between. Most of us probably harbor a secret expectation that our partners will conform to the first attitude. After all, women are "supposed to" find pregnancy joyous and fulfilling just as men are "supposed to" welcome it with manly strength and pride. If your partner is having a miserable pregnancy, you may feel disappointed in her at first and then gradually grow more and more sick and tired of her complaints. Before the situation degenerates into blaming and fighting, it's worthwhile trying to put yourself in her place and understand what she's going through.

It's possible that in the future scientists will devise a method to implant a human fetus in a man's abdomen (not as farfetched as it sounds), but until they do, women are stuck with the job of conceiving and nurturing our babies to birth, and it's quite a demanding undertaking. Most of us are pretty good about sympathizing with our partners' most obvious physical stresses—the difficulties of carrying around the extra weight, the discomfort of a swollen abdomen, the increased need for sleep—but it's the invisible stresses that we too often overlook or come to resent.

Among these invisible stresses are hormonal changes. Pregnancy significantly alters the hormonal balance of a woman's body, and very often these hormonal changes trigger mood swings. Throughout most of the pregnancy your partner's body is producing great quantities of progesterone, a hormone that depresses the central nervous system. High progesterone levels hit many women with the same lousy mood that descends on them before their period arrives. Some women sink into an angry depression; others have fits of weeping or fly off the handle with the least provocation. Terry, a truckdriver and new father from Saint Paul, said his wife practically became a different person during the pregnancy. "I didn't know who she was. She just wasn't herself. She'd overreact and her moods were all twisted around." Knowing that your partner is the victim of high hormone levels may make it easier for you to weather the storms and to avoid blaming yourself (or her) for the turmoil.

Hormones don't explain everything about a pregnant woman's moods. Some of her moods are just plain moods: anxiety about the delivery and about raising a baby, joy at feeling the new life stirring within her, despair at all the things

Feeling About the Pregnancy

to do and buy, impatience with the endless months of waiting. Don't forget that the pregnancy is a major emotional transformation for her, just as it is for you. She's going through the same life-shift you are—the worries about money, about work, about what kind of parent she'll be—and on top of that she has the physical aspect of pregnancy to contend with. When you add up hormonal changes, the physical discomfort, and the emotional issues, you may find yourself marveling at how *well* she's handling it all. In any case, it can't hurt to put yourself in your partner's shoes now and then. If she's having a happy, problem-free pregnancy, let her know how pleased you are. If she's miserable, give her as much support as you can and remind her (and yourself) that the pregnancy *will* end and she *will* feel like her old self again.

Is *That* My Wife?

Late in the pregnancy you may experience a strange and unsettling moment when you find yourself gazing at your wife with almost total lack of recognition: Could that possibly be the woman I married, that enormously pregnant, waddling, moody, constantly exhausted person who can barely haul herself out of bed, who reads stacks of baby books when she isn't watching the most awful trash on TV, who never wants to go out or have anyone in, whose sole interest is the color scheme of the baby's room, who seems to be in constant communication with her mother? This may be the moment when it dawns on you in a tangible, immediate way that your wife is on the verge of becoming a mother, that she's never going to be "just" your wife anymore. It can make you feel all warm and protective and proud of her, or it can be a little chilling. Somehow it wasn't *quite* what you bargained for when you started on this baby business.

The new rapport with her (or your) mother (or both) also makes many men stop and wonder. More and more she may seem to be entering into this mothers' cabal—spending hours on the phone discussing "baby things" in agonizing detail, sharing developments in the pregnancy with the mothers that she hasn't even told *you* about, shopping with them, asking their advice in areas where she once insisted they mind their own business. Your wife's mother (or your mother) usually assumes she knows all about what a pregnant woman is going through, and not only does she know all, she and *only* she knows it. The weird part is the way pregnant women go along with this, identifying with their mothers, letting their mothers take over, welcoming daily calls when they once took the phone off the hook as a protection *against* her. Of course, the intensified mother-daughter bond leaves no place for you, which can get a little frustrating. And be prepared for mothers of the "old school" who feel that men have no business "meddling" in a pregnancy, which to them means wanting to be involved, accompanying your wife to the obstetrician, attending childbirth preparation classes, and—worst sin of all—being present at the birth when they, the all-knowing, all-caring mother of the mother, are excluded!

Inevitably, the thought arises: What if she turns out to be just like her mother? At some point late in the pregnancy you may remember that old saw about how if you really really want to know the woman you're marrying, look at her mother—a saying that struck you as utterly preposterous and irrelevant to your wife when you married her. But now you may be wondering. One father-to-be found himself staring at just this issue as the pregnancy neared term. "My wife's relationship with her mother is bad," he said, "and in fact her mother really has no motherly instincts and went back to work as soon as her kids were born. They seemed so distant. But now I've been thinking: What if she ends up being like her mother? What if she gets into the same nonnurturing relationship with our baby? After all, people do tend to recreate the familiar family situation. This is definitely a worry. Maybe part of my feeling of detachment from the pregnancy stems from this worry that my wife will be like her mother."

There's no easy answer here, because it really is bound to happen—*to some extent*—just as you're going to surprise yourself with how much you sound like your father when you're with the baby. But for most people, it's a matter of style, phrases recollected from their own childhoods, customs or rituals lodged in their unconscious, games. You might scold with the same words your father used, or your wife might go through the same bedtime routine her mother used, but this doesn't mean that the two of you have undergone a major personality shift. Previously unknown aspects of your personality will emerge: the parent buried within you. But you'll both still be you.

From Couple to Parents: Farewell to the Good Old Days?

As couples near the end of pregnancy, it's very common to feel nostalgic for the "good old days": late nights out on the town, late mornings in bed, spontaneous extravagances at restaurants, nightclubs, theaters, elaborate gourmet meals because you were in the mood, or just quiet evenings at home watching TV without interruptions. "Prior to the baby we had a fantastic relationship," said one Albuquerque father I interviewed. "I didn't want it to change and I worried how the addition of a baby would change it."

I remember looking at the calendar a few weeks before the due date and commenting to my wife that we had one last free weekend as "us." It was an unsettling notion. There was nothing we cherished more than these weekends when we could just be us. "Us" was an utterly known quantity. "Us" worked. And now "us" was about to turn forever into "we three." It was more than the sacrifice of freedom of movement, more than the shouldering of vast new responsibilities. What frightened us was the idea that having a baby would be like having a permanent house guest—and a house guest of the worst kind: fussy, demanding, immature, inconsiderate, expensive, constantly hungry, and in need of attention from us. What had we done to ourselves?

In a way this anxiety grew out of something basically positive: the value we put on our relationship, the supreme importance to us of being us, alone at home in our own way with no one to answer to. Having a baby, I can happily report, did not destroy this. The "us" part of our relationship is a little squeezed at times, but it has also expanded immeasurably. We discovered, as all couples quickly do, that having a baby is nothing like having a house guest; in fact, in no time at all, the baby became part of "us." As David, a graphics designer and self-described optimist, put it on the eve of his baby's birth: "My wife is worried that it will never be just the two of us again. 'It's going to be so different,' she said. I said, 'Yeah, it's going to be better.'"

Although this section dwells on the problems and tensions that a pregnancy can introduce into a marriage, I don't mean to leave out the joys that it brings to husband and wife. There is the closeness, which I've already touched on, a sharing that no other experience can rival. And for many, there is also the joy of discovering new sides to their partners during these nine long months. Don, on the verge of becoming a father, said it best: "My wife seems to be in better spirits as a result of the pregnancy. It has put her in touch with an aspect of herself that might otherwise have been denied her. We thought we might never have children—we never talked about it, but we sensed each was thinking privately that maybe it just wasn't necessary. But on the contrary, we've both become something more because of it. We're both feeling an even greater fulfillment at the prospect of becoming parents."

Sex

Your sex life with your partner, which got the whole thing started in the first place, is bound to undergo some major changes in the nine months of pregnancy and beyond. Not only major, but surprising changes. Pregnancy and parenthood raise a great sexual divide in many marriages, with heedless passion on one side and subdued, scheduled, "mature" lovemaking on the other. Men who have always been highly aroused by their wives may find themselves avoiding sex during the pregnancy. Couples who previously had a rather sober and dutiful attitude toward sex can experience a tremendous liberation in the pregnant months. Partners whose desires always seemed to be in sync may now find that they disagree about everything in bed from frequency to enthusiasm. One couple may go through all of these changes in the course of a pregnancy, with sexual appetites and compatibility shifting with the months. It affects everyone differently. The range is enormous.

There is, however, one constant that holds true for nearly all couples: Sex will be less frequent during the pregnancy than it was before. There are two general patterns that most couples fall into: decreased sex in the first trimester, followed by a sexual renaissance in the second, and then a return to infrequent sex in the final months; and a slow but steady decline in sexual activity throughout the pregnancy.

The reasons for diminished sex are many and obvious. In the first trimester when a woman is usually feeling exhausted and sick to her stomach or at least a bit queasy, sex is about as appealing to her as sitting by a roaring fire in July. From about six months on, sex becomes increasingly difficult from purely a physical/logistical point of view: with your partner's midsection protruding with your growing child, you simply are not going to be able to use the standard sexual positions. Also, as the baby grows, he or she seems so palpably present, what with the kicks and turns and little elbows and knees jabbing out, that it frightens many couples off sex. It's as if their privacy is being disturbed. And again, during the last few weeks of pregnancy, even if you've figured out comfortable positions, your partner will probably not be too much in the mood. She's exhausted from hauling the baby around inside her all day, she's preoccupied with the impending ordeal of labor and delivery, she's going to be rationing her very limited energy resources, and sexual energy may near the bottom of the list.

But in all likelihood, your partner is not the only one whose desire for sex tapers off during the pregnancy. Let's not get caught up in the myth that men are always hot for sex and women control the flow with headaches, fatigue, and other avoidance ploys. Studies have shown that a great many men experience a sharp drop in their sexual urge during their wives' pregnancies, and this has certainly been borne out by the conversations I've had with expectant fathers. "Sex started out fairly normally," one father told me, "but there has been a slow winding down. My interest has slackened. I just wasn't turned on by it." Another said flatly, "Some men are attracted to pregnant women, but I'm not. The changes in her shape have not especially pleased me. And she doesn't like it either. At the beginning she was less into sex, and now that the pregnancy is nearing term, I've been much less interested. I find the need for new positions more irritating than exciting. I guess there's nothing to do now but wait." Brant said that shared fatigue has slowed his sex life down. "She goes to bed pretty tired and I'm bushed, too, at night from training for the marathon." And M. Rossman, writing on pregnancy and sexuality in a collection of essays on fathers' experiences, called *The Father's Book*, went even further: "From the fourth month on, Karen might as well have been a pillow for all the sexual response I could summon up for her."

Once you get past male myths and expectations, it's not hard to see why many men experience this sexual slackening. Some of it is purely physical: your partner's body is undergoing some startling changes, some obvious and some much more intimate. Pregnancy affects much more than a woman's abdomen. Her breasts enlarge considerably, the nipples darken and become more prominent; the labia of her vagina, engorged with blood during pregnancy, will feel swollen to the touch and there will be a heavier flow of vaginal secretions with more intense odors; some women get bigger everywhere —their faces take on a new fullness, their feet grow, their ankles swell. If you are especially attracted to sylphs, you might find your partner's transformation into earth mother alarming. A lot of men worry that their wives might never get back to normal, and this can further dampen their sexual enthusiasm.

More difficult to identify but often more powerful is the psychological impact of pregnancy on a man's sex drive. If you've adopted a very protective attitude toward your pregnant partner, sex may begin to seem somehow inappropriate to you. You're playing a fatherly (or even motherly) role toward your partner, and sex would be a violation of this. Alternatively, as your partner becomes more and more obviously pregnant, she may begin to remind you unconsciously of your own mother. Sex thus becomes fraught with primal taboos and frightening conflicts. How could I be such an inconsiderate brute? may be the thought running through your head, when

Feeling About the Pregnancy

only a few short months ago you would have laughed at the very notion that sex with your partner could be brutal. For the narrator of Tolstoy's harrowing story "The Kreutzer Sonata," guilt over the "swinish" sexual demands that he has made on his wife during pregnancy becomes an obsession. He insists that sex at this time actually *destroys* a woman and is a perversion of nature.

Few contemporary men have such extreme fantasies, but many continue to be plagued by guilt and fears. Fear of hurting the fetus during sex is extremely common among men. Said Charles, a doctor from Albuquerque, "My wife had had two miscarriages prior to this pregnancy and both of us worried about the impact of sex on the baby. I was afraid to get rambunctious and thrust hard, but that didn't decrease the quality of our sex life."

Although I had read a slew of books that maintained that the fetus is wonderfully protected in the womb, that anything short of a kick or hard blow would not harm it, that it was impossible for the baby to be damaged during sex, I nonetheless worried about it. Not that I disbelieved modern medical science: I simply couldn't turn off this instinctive protective urge that keep warning me, *Don't squash the baby.* Crazy, maybe, but something that a great many men worry about.

If any complications arise in the course of the pregnancy, a couple is much more likely to give up sex, either from anxiety or because they think it may be detrimental to the pregnancy. Here, too, worries enforce a stricter standard than modern medical science. There are a few conditions for which doctors will advise against sexual intercourse during pregnancy— women who have had multiple miscarriages, for example, may be told not to have sex in the first trimester. But for the vast majority of pregnancies, sex is perfectly safe from conception until the moment labor begins. If you have any doubts, you and your partner should bring them to her obstetrician.

Of course, no matter what the doctor says, you, your partner, or both of you may not feel like having sex if you're living with the anxiety of even mild complications. One expecting father whose wife was experiencing high blood pressure and was worried about pre-eclampsia (see Chapter 5) said that the pregnancy had "nullified" their sex life. "We've had intercourse maybe three times in the last nine months. Yes, I'm frustrated, but I haven't let her know because I don't want to pressure her. I've been looking at women on the street like crazy, and getting sexual vibes from all sorts of women. But I'm very faithful. I assume that things will eventually go back to normal."

Frustration and sexual interest in other women are obvious fallouts from a sexual drought during pregnancy. Some respond to the pressure by looking for sexual fulfillment outside the marriage, but most men, like the father quoted above, deal with it by taking a philosophical attitude—they live with it and wait. More difficult to live with may be the *lack* of frustration and the absence of sexual fantasies. Men whose sex drive tapers off may begin to worry about their masculinity; they may try to compensate by proving themselves in other areas, such as sports; they may get angry at their wives and unborn babies; they may get depressed. Particularly hard on the male ego is the situation in which the wife is into sex and the husband isn't. Invariably, the husband feels threatened, inadequate, and "abnormal" in some way, and just as invariably the wife feels that the *real* reason is that he's turned off by her big belly, or worse, that he doesn't love her anymore. This is a setup for marital strife, and, again, the only way out is to talk about it openly. Your wife may actually be amused that it's you who is not in the mood, and she'll certainly be relieved to hear that you still love her and find her beautiful. Who knows, airing your concerns may actually restore your sexual energy. It happens all the time.

Sex may be less frequent during a pregnancy, but this doesn't mean it's less satisfying. For many, many couples pregnancy comes as a tremendous sexual liberation. For one thing, you finally don't have to worry about getting pregnant —either that she will or that she won't, because she is. If you've been trying for a while, you'll find the end of forced sex at set times each month frees you up to be sexually spontaneous again. And even if your wife got pregnant right away, it may be more relaxing not to be thinking that this time really *counts*. In any case, you'll be free of the tyranny of birth

Feeling About the Pregnancy

control devices and your wife will be free of the burden of menstrual periods. It's just such a relief to get in bed and do what comes naturally without worrying about the consequences.

Then, too, for lots of men pregnancy is a sexual turn-on. They like the new curves, the fuller breasts, the languor that comes over their wives; they love feeling her growing belly, which can become a new erogenous zone; they like the idea that their wife is pregnant, that the fruit of their sexual union is growing inside her, that by making love with their wives they are getting as close as possible to the growing baby. By the same token, pregnancy is a turn-on for many women: the engorgement of their labia with blood is like being in a state of continual sexual arousal, their orgasms are more numerous and more intense, they feel full and womanly and proud of their bodies.

There is a myth that the second trimester is one of huge, insatiable sexual appetites for a woman. Like most such myths, it's true to some degree in some cases—but for almost all women the fatigue and morning sickness abate, which means sex is much more welcome. And for those women who do experience a quickening of desire and who have husbands eager to enjoy this, the second trimester can be pure heaven.

The search for new positions, which becomes necessary around months five or six, can also spark new pleasures and, in some cases, great hilarity. With the standard missionary position (man on top and face to face with the woman) now out of the question, you're forced to be more inventive. Popular alternatives are woman on top, man and woman on their sides and facing each other, or rear entry with woman on knees and elbows or on her side. Some people start off one way and then shift around until they find something that works. It can be lots of fun if neither of you gets too self-conscious, and in any case, it will force your sex life out of any ruts into which it may have fallen. You may enjoy the new positions so much that you keep using them even after your wife's body returns to normal (don't worry, at least it will shrink most of the way back to normal).

Very late in pregnancy, the struggle to have intercourse may not seem worth it—but there are alternatives to intercourse that will sustain the intimacy that is so important to the marriage bond. Oral sex and mutual masturbation can be valuable sexual outlets; even massage, hugging, or any other kind of affectionate physical contact can mean a lot during the stressful periods of pregnancy. It's easier to resume your sex life after the baby is born if you and your partner have remained physically in touch throughout the pregnancy than if you've withdrawn into sullen isolation. It's not uncommon for men to ease some of their sexual frustration during pregnancy by masturbation; certainly not as satisfying as the real thing, but much less likely to complicate one's marriage than having an affair.

There is, by the way, a good book that covers the subject of marital sex and pregnancy with understanding and open-mindedness. It's called *Making Love During Pregnancy* by Elisabeth Bing and Libby Colman (Bantam Books, 1977), and although it doesn't have all the answers, it will probably make you realize that whatever is or isn't happening sexually in your marriage has been the experience of lots of other couples. This is perhaps the most important thing to remember during the pregnant months: You're not alone. You're not the only one who's having less sex or having trouble finding a comfortable position or who finds pregnant women unappealing or who never seems to be in the mood at the same time as your wife. (If your pregnant sex life has been fabulous, chances are you're not worried about it.) Lots of men get frantic about sex when *anything* goes wrong, and there are times during pregnancy when *everything* seems to be going wrong. There's no denying that pregnancy is a great sexual divide. But if you and your partner can cross it with understanding, patience, and a sense of humor, you're likely to find that not only does sex exist on the other side, but that in some deep and ineffable way it gets even better.

Becoming a Father

The day your baby is born will be a kind of birthday for you as well—the day you become someone's father. "Father," "fatherhood," "paternal"—the very words sound a rather

Feeling About the Pregnancy

somber toll in our culture. One thinks of God the father, the stern father, the all-knowing father, the care-worn, hard-working, ever-responsible *paterfamilias*. Less forbidding by far is dad—for dad is invariably a great guy, always willing to play one more game, to console his kids for any injury no matter how minor, to boost their egos with sympathetic heart-to-heart talks, and boost them on their way through life with college tuition, cars, and help on home mortgages. The stern father and the playful, supportive dad: these are the two poles of American fatherhood, and they form the image of fatherhood that most men begin to conceive of during the pregnant months.

For a lot of men, the idea that they are going to be someone's father has about the same level of reality as the fetus does during the pregnancy's early months: intellectually there is no denying it, but emotionally it seems about as plausible as their winning the next presidential election. How can I be someone's father when I'm still so very much someone's son? That is a question in some form running through many expecting fathers' minds. Somehow neither the stern father nor the great guy dad role seems to fit with one's own sense of self. Don, with two weeks to go, put it this way: "I still feel I'm on the move, that my life hasn't settled down yet. The idea of impending fatherhood has made me feel *more* restless."

Implicit in Don's concerns are certain assumptions about what being a father means: settled, stable, ultraresponsible, absolutely certain about one's identity—in fact, the very opposite of restless. Even the great guy dad is supposed to be on an even keel at all times: his role by definition excludes personal problems, doubts, job changes, unsatisfied longings. With all this to live up to, no wonder so many men experience something close to panic at the idea that they have to step into these shoes and run. And the worst part is that there's no preparation. Childbirth classes take you as far as delivery of the baby and then drop you off at the very moment your role as father (as opposed to husband/coach) begins. The old learning to swim by being thrown off a dock analogy fits this situation perfectly.

Actually, there is some preparation men provide for themselves in the months before the baby arrives just by imagining what they'll be like as fathers. Expecting fathers are great fantasizers and idealizers of fatherhood. "I see myself as very patient," one father told me, "very caring, very understanding. I see myself spending lots of time with the baby." Another imagined himself nurturing his child's artistic talents: "I hope to provide an environment where our son will be allowed to be as sensitive and as creative as he is capable of becoming." I went further than either of these and fantasized that I would be nothing less than the *perfect* dad: always loving, never angry or impatient, always ready to put my child's needs first, always happy to enter into my child's playing, learning, enjoying. (The question now occurs to me whether this indeed would not be more of a smothering father-monster than an ideal superdad, but at the time I found my daydreams very pleasant.)

We veteran fathers may feel tempted to snicker at some of the extravagant pipe dreams that expecting fathers indulge in, just as I now smile at my own fond wishes. Every expecting father I spoke to vowed that he was going to spend as much time as possible with his baby, that he was going to share the child care and be involved. Each time I heard this I found myself wondering, Will he feel the same when his baby is three weeks old, sleeping a maximum of four hours at a stretch and screaming a lot in between, and he has a big presentation scheduled at the office for the end of the week? I found the clash between my own fantasies and the realities of new fatherhood quite shocking. Not only did I fail to live up to my ideal of perfection, but I failed almost immediately: I became irritated by night feedings on the second night, I refused to enter into my baby's needs on long car trips when we were both exhausted, I shirked some of my paternal responsibilities in order to read, relax, or simply work. I soon realized that I was just the standard-brand father with the standard-brand limitations.

Although my fantasies did not come true, they at least introduced me to certain issues of fatherhood that I would soon confront. It's a way of trying on the role beforehand, and thus beginning to accept the reality. And unless you're seriously self-deluded, you'll keep in mind that your fantasies are just

Feeling About the Pregnancy

that and not be too hard on yourself (or your baby) when the actual experience doesn't quite measure up.

Expecting fathers also tend to spend a lot of time thinking about their own fathers. Memories of childhood experiences with their dads are very common at this time, and men often compare what they remember with what they hope to do themselves when they become fathers. Don told me that his associations to fatherhood are very positive "because of my relationship with my own father. I thought of my dad as basically a gentle man and he was this way largely because of his own children. I feel confident that if I can match up to my dad I'll be okay. I'm planning to take the gentle approach."

Michael also had very positive associations with fatherhood because of his own father: "I have very good relationships with my parents and I've always looked forward to having my own child. I know I'll be a good dad—there is no doubt in my mind about that. I just hope I'm as GREAT a dad as my dad has been to me."

David found himself thinking and dreaming a lot about his father as the baby's birth approached. "I'm close to my father and I picture myself being like him," he said, "but less serious and somber. My dad was from the Old World, very formal, and he resented too much familiarity. He was too serious and too tough on his children. I was always telling him to *lighten up*. I view myself as being a better father. I'm softer than he is. Yes, I'm a tough S.O.B. when I have to be, but I'm not as stoic as he is."

Most of the expecting fathers I talked to, even those who spoke most fondly of their own fathers, vowed that they would spend more time with their children than they remember their fathers spending with them. "He had incredible patience and, since he was a minister, he was home a lot," one said, "but I really don't recall doing a lot of things with him." "I would love for my child to have as enriching a childhood as my father gave me," another father-to-be began, but then he went on to describe how his dad worked the graveyard shift and "I never saw him much except on weekends. I don't want to do that with my child." Bob, a family therapist, said plainly, "I want to spend as much time as possible with my daughter because I didn't spend that much time with my own dad. He wasn't there emotionally." Michael, a clerical worker, had already planned certain changes in his work schedule so he could spend more time with the baby, especially after his wife returned to work and he would have responsibility for taking care of the baby by himself.

Again, as with the fantasies, it remains to be seen how these eager expecting fathers will act on their generous intentions. But what's encouraging is that they *have* these intentions, that a great many men now assume they will be involved in both the emotional and practical sides of parenting. A generation or two ago, you'd have to hunt far and wide to find an expecting father who said, "I want to be totally involved in the child care—at least 50 percent," but this attitude is increasingly common these days. And although many men fantasize wildly, a number of the fathers I talked to took a very realistic approach, already projecting ahead to how they would juggle schedules to share the child care equally with their wives. Ron described his own situation in which both parents are lawyers with long hours: "We're sort of planning to work out an alternating schedule so that primary responsibility will be on one person one night and one another night. But we are both workaholics, we buy into the six-day-a-week jobs. We're going to have to fight that."

Today's conception of fatherhood may have expanded to include shared responsibility for child care, but the "old-fashioned" notion of father as breadwinner remains very much in force. Fathers continue to assume it is their primary responsibility to provide economically for the family, and expecting fathers continue to take on extra jobs, work harder, or simply worry more about money. What this amounts to is that the role of father today is larger—more time-consuming, more stressful, more demanding—than it was in the past, just as the role of mother is more difficult for women who work. Conflicts are inevitable. As one father put it, "I want to be fully involved but I know that with the situation at work it will be impossible. I want to be included as much as I can, which will mean altering my schedule. But this is going to be difficult since I own my own business." Something is going to have to give.

Feeling About the Pregnancy

In later chapters we take a look at what *does* give and how fathers—and mothers—are dealing with the pressures caused by shifts in the roles of parents today.

It's always kind of funny to hear expecting fathers and veteran fathers talking together about children. You'd hardly guess they were on the same topic. One group seems alternately full of wonder and worry, whereas the other dwells almost exclusively on the concrete and practical—the exact numbers of hours slept, the precise progress baby has made with each body part, breast versus bottle feeding, bathing techniques. The two states of being are a world apart. It's the dream versus the reality, the anticipation versus the participation.

Expecting fathers are entitled to their extravagances, their impossible fantasies, their daydreams of undisturbed family peace and happiness. It's part of the pleasure, of the intensity of being in this state of neither here nor there. "Now that we have two weeks to go, it just gets better day by day," one father-to-be said. "Everything intensifies." That's it exactly. Expectant fatherhood, especially in its final weeks, is a heightened state of being. Anxious—undoubtedly; a bit unreal and rushed and confusing and, in a funny way, unconnected to the rest of your life. Your feelings, maybe even your *lack* of feelings, will come as a surprise to you. Those weeks surrounding the birth of your first child and the birth of yourself as a father form a little island in the life of a man. They're precious and vivid because they are like nothing else you'll ever experience.

5. Problems in Pregnancy

Most pregnancies in the United States today are normal and progress uneventfully to term without complication. But the word *most* becomes horribly meaningless if you are on the other side of it. That *most* is not going to matter much to you if your partner's pregnancy is one of the estimated 10 to 15 percent of pregnancies at risk of a problem or among the one in ten (a conservative estimate) pregnancies that end in miscarriage. And when you take a closer look at the statistics, *most* shrinks down a bit. According to *New Hope for Problem Pregnancies* by Dianne Hales and Robert K. Creasy, M.D. (Harper & Row, 1982), "in as many as 30 to 40 percent [of pregnancies], there is some exception to the usual course of development and delivery." So, yes, *most* pregnancies proceed normally, but a substantial minority do not.

What are the most common complications of pregnancy? What risks do these problems pose to the mother and the unborn child? How can the problems be detected? What can be done to treat or prevent them? What progress is science making in "solving" pregnancy problems? These are questions we find ourselves wondering about during the pregnant months. The lucky *most* of us wonder but have no pressing need to find out. But if your partner is experiencing any complications in her pregnancy, you'll want to get as many answers as you can. That's what this chapter is about.

Miscarriage

The medical term for miscarriage is "spontaneous abortion," and it means that the pregnancy ends before the fetus can survive outside the womb. In most cases, the fetus has already died. The woman's body goes through a kind of labor, with bleeding, cramps, and contractions until the fetus is expelled. A miscarriage has a good deal in common with the physical sensation of giving birth—but the labor brings tragedy instead of joy. At whatever stage in pregnancy it occurs, a miscarriage is frightening and more emotionally wrenching than anyone who has not been through it would imagine. In the vast majority of cases, once a spontaneous abortion begins, there is nothing medical science can do to stop it.

Miscarriage, as one book put it, is a "silent problem." Unless someone in your family or one of your close friends has suffered one, you don't hear much about it. But when you start asking around, you soon discover just how common—horribly common—a problem it is. Statistics vary a good deal, but the estimated range is that between 10 and 20 percent of pregnancies in this country end in miscarriage. On average, about 300,000 women miscarry each year. The risk of miscarriage increases the older the woman is; 12 percent of twenty-year-old women have spontaneous abortions; the figure jumps to 17 percent for thirty-year-olds, 22 percent for thirty-six-year-olds, and 31 percent for forty-year-olds.

These cold numbers are frightening. But there is some comfort to be had when you look past the numbers at other factors. A miscarriage—no matter how early it occurs—is a pregnancy: it means that you and your partner have conceived a baby and that you should be able to conceive again. Many believe that miscarriage carries off babies who never would have survived anyway or who would have been born with serious birth defects. It's better, say those who subscribe to this theory, to lose a twelve-week fetus than to have a newborn die days after birth. And perhaps they're right, although you're not likely to find this particularly cheering at the time you are suffering through a miscarriage.

Nearly all miscarriages—some 95 percent—occur before the fetus has reached sixteen weeks, with the largest number falling between weeks seven and fourteen. (This is why many couples choose to wait until after the third or fourth month of pregnancy to announce the news.) The much less common late miscarriages, occurring between weeks seventeen and twenty-eight, are believed to have different causes, often anatomical problems with the mother; and the woman suffering one will receive different medical treatment.

About a year and a half before the birth of our daughter, my wife had a miscarriage during the thirteenth week of the pregnancy. Because it was a classic "textbook" case, it's worth going through the details of what happened and when. The pregnancy seemed normal in the early weeks, though my wife had no morning sickness. Sometime around week eleven, her breasts ceased to feel tender and seemed to be getting a bit smaller. On Friday, at the end of her twelfth week, she had a terrific burst of energy—hosing down lawn furniture, raking leaves, taking the car into the shop and walking back home, cleaning windows, hanging pictures. Late on Saturday night she discovered she was "spotting," bleeding lightly from the vagina. She called the doctor, who advised her to rest in bed and keep her fingers crossed. The spotting continued on and off Sunday, and on Monday I drove her to the doctor's office. He said she *seemed* fine based on an internal exam, but that she should have a sonogram (discussed later) the next day to learn more about the condition of the fetus. Late Monday night she felt a low ache in her abdomen and by early Tuesday morning the ache had intensified to cramps and contractions and she was bleeding heavily—the sanitary napkins would be soaked almost as soon as she put them on. On the hour-long drive to the hospital, the pain became so intense that my wife was close to passing out. She couldn't walk unassisted from the car to the hospital admitting area. When the nurse undressed her in the hospital bed, the blood flow was unbelievable. How long, I wondered in terror, can she bleed that much? Before noon that day it was, in the words of the doctor, "all over": her cervix was open and thus the abortion was inevitable. She was given pitocin (a synthetic form of the hormone oxytocin used to induce labor or to intensify contractions in labor) intravenously so that her

Problems in Pregnancy

uterus would be forced to expel all the tissue. It was a kind of torture to have a chemical dripped into her veins that racked her body with even more pain. Early in the afternoon she had a dilation and curettage. (Known familiarly as a D and C, it is a procedure performed under anesthetic during which the doctor opens the cervix and removes whatever may have remained behind in the uterus. Without a D and C, there is some risk that the placenta or other tissue could remain in the uterus and cause severe bleeding or infection.) The D and C is a rapid operation, and she was back in her hospital room later in the afternoon. The gynecologist discharged her from the hospital on Wednesday morning, and we were told to avoid intercourse for several weeks and not to try for another pregnancy for three months.

Naturally, we wanted to know why this had happened, but we received no real explanation. I asked about the condition of the fetus, but the doctor said, rather crudely, that there was nothing to see—"it was just mush." He promised that an analysis of the tissue would be done, but he offered scant hope of any results because viruses invade rapidly as soon as the cervix opens, making it impossible to culture cells from the fetus in the lab. In any case, the fetus in all likelihood had been dead for several days or a week before my wife began spotting. The lab results, in fact, showed nothing, and we never learned why this pregnancy failed. In this regard, too, our miscarriage was "textbook," for seldom can doctors pinpoint the cause of a particular early miscarriage.

But even though the individual cause often remains a mystery, we do have some idea of the *general* causes of early miscarriages. We know that falls off a bike or down the stairs very rarely bring on miscarriage—so you can toss that myth and that fear out. Also toss out the idea that sex causes miscarriage: it doesn't. The cause of the majority of early miscarriages—an estimated one-half to two-thirds—is some genetic irregularity in a particular sperm or egg, often a missing chromosome or an extra chromosome. This doesn't mean your genes are messed up; it means you had bad luck in that particular conception. Although we don't yet know for sure, it is theorized that genetic "bad luck" is more common when the prospective parents are exposed to certain drugs, pollutants, and infections, including radiation, viruses such as rubella, herpes, and cytomegalovirus, infections including mycoplasma, toxoplasma, and brucella, and drugs including antineoplastics, diethylstilbestrol (DES), phenacetin, Dilantin, tetracyclines, lithium, large doses of vitamin D, alcohol, tobacco, and narcotics. It is believed that an "old egg"—one fertilized several days after its release from the ovaries—is more likely to miscarry. Fibroid tumors in the uterus have also been pointed to as a cause of miscarriage.

Another genetic irregularity linked to miscarriage is known as a balanced translocation. This means that an abnormality occurs in the arrangement of the chromosomes, although the total number of chromosomes remains the same. For reasons not yet fully understood, the genes have arranged themselves in an incorrect order along the chromosomes. Unlike the "bad luck" situation of a particular defective egg or sperm, a balanced translocation is an irregularity in the chromosomes themselves, and thus a permanent condition. If one or both of the prospective parents have such a translocation, it can cause serious defects in the developing embryo—serious enough to end the embryo's life in miscarriage. You and your partner can have yourselves tested for balanced translocations through an analysis of your chromosomes, performed by testing a sample of your blood. You should also see a genetic counselor, who will advise you about your odds in future pregnancies. A balanced translocation by no means rules out the possibility of having a successful pregnancy and normal children—far from it. Although research in this area remains scarce, some experts estimate that there is only a 5 percent chance that a given translocation will bring on repeated miscarriages. So the odds are excellent that your wife or partner can carry a baby to term. However, if either of you have this condition, she should have an amniocentesis (see below) performed during the next pregnancy to determine the well-being of the growing fetus.

Spontaneous abortion remains a subject about which science has more questions than answers. Defects in the egg or sperm and, much more infrequently, translocations are thought to account for the majority of miscarriages, but researchers can only speculate about the nongenetic causes. Fibroid tumors—benign growths in the uterus—and abnormalities in the shape of the uterus or uterine scar tissue have been linked with miscarriage. In some cases, surgery can correct these problems. Thyroid diseases and deficiencies in the hormone progesterone may also increase the likelihood of miscarriage, though many scientists would debate this. Also a subject of some debate is the role that viral and bacterial infection may play in causing early spontaneous abortions. Rubella, herpes simplex (see later in this chapter), and mycoplasmas, particularly T-mycoplasma (a microorganism that shares characteristics of viruses and bacteria and that invades the systems of both men and women without producing any noticeable symptoms), have all been implicated in miscarriage. Mycoplasma infections, which are quite common, can be wiped out with antibiotics (tetracycline is the most frequently prescribed, administered before the couple attempts to conceive again because it could cause staining of the teeth if a child is exposed to it in utero). It must be stressed that mystery still looms large in this area: tetracycline may take care of the infection and yet another abortion could *still* occur; or, alternatively, the next pregnancy might succeed without the tetracycline treatment. There are still no clear answers in miscarriage, but there is abundant hope. It is estimated that 70 to 85 percent of women who have experienced repeated miscarriages go on to have perfectly normal pregnancies and bear healthy children.

Second trimester miscarriages (weeks fourteen to twenty-eight) are quite rare compared to early miscarriages. In most cases the fetus is genetically normal, but the woman is unable to continue carrying it, usually because of some physical problem. If the spontaneous abortion is rapid, painless, and without bleeding or cramping, the cause is likely to be a condition known as an incompetent cervix. Either because of some congenital weakness or because of surgery, a roughly done D and C or even the vaginal birth of an extremely large baby, a woman's cervix is not strong enough to hold up under the weight of the growing fetus. When the growing fetus has become heavy enough to exert sufficient pressure on it, the cervix opens and the baby is born—too early to survive. This condition, which is relatively rare, has been treated surgically with good results. The doctor in effect stitches the cervix closed and leaves it that way until the thirty-eighth week of pregnancy.

A miscarriage is a medical emergency and your initial role will be to handle the crisis: to get your wife to the hospital, see that she receives good care, and just be with her throughout the ordeal. In the midst of my wife's miscarriage, I was advised to "be strong": the advice was well-intentioned but totally unnecessary. You have no alternative at the time but to be strong. Your chance to be something other than strong doesn't come until later. But one of the most horrible parts is that no matter how strong you are, there is still nothing you can do to prevent the loss of the baby: you are entirely helpless.

A miscarriage is a death—the death of someone you knew not at all but still loved, or hoped to love, very much. In all likelihood, you and your partner will mourn the way you would mourn a death in the family. The grief is all the more intense because it is so private: no one else quite understands your sense of loss, of dreams destroyed, your pain at never being able to know this child. People will try to soothe you by saying, "It's better than having a deformed child" or "Things will work out next time"—but this is quite beside the point. You're mourning *this* time, this baby who didn't make it.

There is a lot more to mourning than grief and the pain of loss. At first, you may not even believe that the pregnancy is over. I remember thinking that this couldn't be happening, and half believing that it wasn't happening. For days, when I woke up in the morning, I had to remind myself that the pregnancy was over. You may find yourself angry—at fate, at insensitive relatives, at yourself, at your wife, at doctors, even at the fetus for dying. Blame enters into many relationships: it was her fault for working too hard, my fault for insisting on that party, my genes, her uterus, and on and on. A common reaction is, "The pain was so intense—I don't want to put my wife through this ever again," a reaction that contains a hidden assumption of guilt.

For many men, the stress of being strong in the emergency catches up with them later. They handled the emergency, comforted their partners, supported them through their grief

Problems in Pregnancy

and depression—and finally, maybe even months later, these men fall apart themselves. Although a miscarriage happens to both of you as a couple, it is the woman who bears the awful physical pain and loss of it. And thus there is a tendency for the man to feel that it is *her* miscarriage and to shove his emotions underground. For some men the emotions sort of stay underground, and these men may feel bewildered and then resentful at the prolonged depression their wives are going through. Men who think they're doing their wives a favor by burying their own grief may have the whole thing blow up in their faces when their wives accuse them of not caring about the loss. It's a pop psychology cliché, but it's still worth repeating: you're better off letting these feelings show, acknowledging them and talking about them, even if it's not possible to do this until long after the actual event. You're serving no one by trying to "be strong" forever.

Even though the best "cure" for the depression of a miscarriage is another (and successful) pregnancy, you or your wife may feel extremely anxious about the possibility of repeating this ordeal. The first sixteen weeks of a succeeding pregnancy are going to pass very slowly.

Time is a great help in healing the pain caused by a miscarriage. And with time, you and your partner are more likely to be comforted by the encouraging statistics on those who succeed in bearing healthy children after repeated miscarriages.

Ectopic Pregnancy

Much less common than miscarriage, but more potentially life-threatening for the pregnant woman, is a condition known as ectopic pregnancy. Ectopic means "out of place," and what happens in ectopic pregnancy is that the fertilized egg implants in the wrong place, that is, somewhere outside the uterus. It can be the abdomen, one of the ovaries, the cervix —but 95 percent of the time, ectopic pregnancies occur in one of the Fallopian tubes leading from the ovary to the womb. It is theoretically possible for an ectopic pregnancy to succeed, and in fact there are cases of women giving birth to healthy babies that have implanted and grown in their abdomen. (According to *Omni* magazine, December 1985, about 9 percent of abdominal pregnancies succeed—a statistic cited as encouraging support for the notion of male pregnancy: that's right, an article in that issue explores the possibility of men having the embryo implanted into their abdomen and carrying it to term.) But for the 95 percent of women whose ectopic pregnancy occurs in the Fallopian tube, the fetus is not only doomed, but the condition can endanger the woman's life unless it is detected early enough. If the pregnancy is allowed to continue, the tube can burst and the woman can hemorrhage seriously. (In most cases this will occur between the eighth and twelfth weeks of pregnancy.) A woman with a tubal pregnancy will have to have an operation to remove the fetus and placenta, and in many cases the Fallopian tube in which the fetus lodged will also be lost. Half the women who have had a tubal pregnancy never become pregnant again and 10 percent have another ectopic pregnancy. Unlike with miscarriage, these are not very comforting odds.

A woman is unlikely to know she has an ectopic pregnancy until the situation has become an emergency. Her first sign of danger might be an intense tearing sensation low in her abdomen, a tenderness in the abdomen, or vaginal bleeding. When a Fallopian tube bursts, there is internal bleeding, the woman's pulse becomes rapid, and her blood pressure falls. With profuse bleeding, a woman could go into shock. A pregnant woman who experiences any of these symptoms should get to a doctor as soon as possible. It's better if the ectopic pregnancy can be detected, and ended, early on—before the tube bursts. In fact, the earlier a physician acts, the less damage will be done to the tube and the better chance the woman will have of bearing children in the future. This is one reason why a woman should see her gynecologist as soon as she suspects she's pregnant, and especially if there is any abdominal pain or bleeding or if she has had a previous ectopic pregnancy.

Rare though ectopic pregnancy is (it occurs in only about one out of one-hundred pregnancies), the condition is increasing in frequency. Women at greatest risk of a tubal pregnancy are those who have had pelvic infections, particularly pelvic inflammatory disease (PID), or salpingitis. An infection from an IUD can be the cause of PID. Also at risk are women who have had any type of surgery performed on their Fallopian tubes. There is still no medical technique to reverse the damage done to a Fallopian tube. And even if a doctor manages to save the tube of a woman who has had an ectopic pregnancy, she will have a difficult time getting pregnant again and still runs a considerable risk of having another ectopic pregnancy.

There is no getting around the severity of a tubal pregnancy. Added to the grief you and your partner will feel at losing the baby is the medical danger the woman is in and the high risk she runs of infertility or repeated ectopic pregnancies. If your partner has had a tubal pregnancy and suffered loss or considerable damage of a Fallopian tube, the two of you may want to discuss with a doctor the possibility of using one of the in vitro techniques in which the egg is fertilized outside the body and then inserted into the uterus (see Chapter 3).

High Blood Pressure Complications

It's obvious just by looking at a pregnant woman that her body is under increased stress: not only is she carrying a good deal more weight around, but she is creating and sustaining a new being entirely out of her tissue. The circulatory system is taxed especially hard during pregnancy—a woman's heart, enlarged by as much as half, will be pumping more than one-third as much blood (in volume)—and this is one reason why hypertension, otherwise known as high blood pressure, and problems that arise from it are so common in pregnant women. Even moderate hypertension can deprive the baby of enough nourishment to lower the birthweight considerably; and moderate to serious hypertension, if left untreated, can lead to the dangerous conditions known as preeclampsia and eclampsia, which threaten the lives of both mother and baby.

Some variation in a woman's blood pressure is normal during pregnancy: blood pressure generally falls in the first half of pregnancy and then climbs back to the regular prepregnancy levels in the second half. But when blood pressure climbs above this range, a woman has to be especially careful. Women at greatest risk of problems related to hypertension during pregnancy are those whose blood pressure is high to begin with or who have a history of hypertension in their families, who are over thirty-five, have diabetes or kidney disease, and who smoke. If hypertension is detected early on in the pregnancy, the doctor will prescribe lots of bed rest, good nutrition, and reduction of salt in the diet, and a decrease in physically taxing activities. The woman may be advised to lie for one or two hours each day on either side so that more blood flows to the baby.

Antihypertensive drugs and diuretics have been used successfully to treat hypertension, but these can cause complications during pregnancy. Diuretics, a type of drug that helps the body get rid of fluids more quickly, will lower blood pressure, but will also temporarily lower blood volume, which can endanger a fetus after week twenty-four. So diuretics will only be prescribed to a pregnant woman in the first half of her pregnancy. Certain antihypertensive drugs affect the flow of blood to the uterus, and these will obviously be avoided during pregnancy. Methyldopa and hydralazine, which don't have this side effect, are the antihypertensive drugs most doctors will choose.

Preeclampsia and Eclampsia

Although the causes of preeclampsia and eclampsia remain obscure, it is known that high blood pressure is one of the primary symptoms of these life-threatening pregnancy complications. Preeclampsia, the less severe form, complicates 5 to 7 percent of pregnancies, affecting for the most part young, otherwise healthy women in the last few months of their first pregnancy. Those at greater risk include women with diabetes, kidney disease, or who have high blood pressure to begin with or incidence of high blood pressure in their families, women under five-foot three, women carrying twins, and women who suffer from migraines. In addition to hypertension, symptoms of preeclampsia include edema (swelling of tissue and reten-

Problems in Pregnancy

tion of fluids), and/or protein in the urine. Preeclampsia used to be called "toxemia of pregnancy" because it was believed to be caused by a poison (toxin) in the mother's blood, but because researchers have been unable to identify such a toxin, the name "toxemia" is no longer used.

One danger of preeclampsia is that the woman will probably feel fine, and, unless she goes in for her regular checkups, the condition could go undetected. Preeclampsia left to progress untreated could develop into eclampsia: in addition to the symptoms of preeclampsia, the pregnant woman will have seizures or convulsions. The mortality rate for women with eclampsia is 3 to 5 percent, with a 20 percent increase in the likelihood that the baby will die.

One doctor has termed eclampsia "primarily a disease of neglect." Your wife or partner may get awfully tired of seeing her ob-gyn every month and then every two weeks in the last trimester of pregnancy, but these visits are necessary and are the best way of detecting eclampsia in its early stages. If the doctor finds that the mother is suffering from mild preeclampsia, he or she will insist on bed rest, with periods during which the woman lies on her side to increase the blood flow to the baby, and improved nutrition, particularly more protein in the diet. Your role is to see that your partner carries out this regimen and especially to make it possible for her to rest, relax, and not worry. The doctor may feel that it's advisable for the woman to come into the hospital for several days or until the condition shows some signs of improvement. If there is no improvement or the condition worsens, the doctor may choose to induce labor if the pregnancy is near term. And even if it is not near term, the baby may be better off outside the womb than inside, for preeclampsia seriously restricts the ability of the mother's body to nourish her baby.

Bed rest and good nutrition can control preeclampsia, but they will not cure it: the only real way to take care of the condition is to deliver the baby. Happily, in most cases this cure is both effective and enduring. Blood pressure drops soon after the baby is born and in most cases remains at normal levels. Mothers who have had this condition seldom have it again in subsequent pregnancies.

Herpes Simplex, Syphilis, and Gonorrhea

Three sexually transmitted diseases—herpes simplex, syphilis, and gonorrhea— can seriously complicate a pregnancy, damaging and in some cases killing the baby. It is crucial for a pregnant woman who has contracted one of these infections, either before or during the pregnancy, to get special care to prevent the disease from spreading to the baby.

Herpes simplex, a "newer" infection than syphilis or gonorrhea, has now probably overtaken them in number of cases. There are actually two herpes strains—herpes simplex virus type 1, the strain responsible for cold sores and fever blisters; and herpes 2, the sexually transmitted strain that, when infecting a woman, causes very painful blisters on the vulva, cervix, in the pubic region, buttocks, or thighs. Often the two strains will mix and a person will suffer from both. It is estimated that each year there are a half a million new cases of herpes 2. Herpes, which is caused by a virus, will not be cleared up by the antibiotics used to treat bacterial infections. Treatments such as sitz baths and topical anesthetics will reduce the pain of an active sore, but a cure for herpes has not yet been found.

The onset of herpes feels very much like the flu: fever, swollen lymph glands, and muscle aches. About a week after the flu symptoms, the person will feel a tingling or itching sensation in his or her genitals, and then painful blisters appear, which may break open and become encrusted. In most cases, about ten to twenty days later all symptoms disappear and the herpes sufferer is said to have a latent infection. A lucky 40 percent or so never get another outbreak of sores again, but for the unlucky victims, the sores will reappear at any time. Women are more likely to get them during their menstrual periods or during unusually stressful times.

The real risk a baby suffers from herpes 2 is at the time of birth. If there are active herpes sores in the birth canal, the baby could contract the infection, with the gravest consequences. As many as 60 percent of babies with active, visible herpes lesions die, and of the survivors, half suffer significant

Problems in Pregnancy 107

damage to their eyes and nervous systems. Fortunately, one can almost entirely eliminate the risk by delivering the baby by cesarean section (see Chapter 7), thus preventing the newborn from coming in contact with any active lesions. If the mother has had an episode of active herpes within a month of her due date, the obstetrician will in all likelihood perform a cesarean, just to be on the safe side. But if the infection has cleared up more than a month before the due date and if there is no sign of recurrence (active herpes in late pregnancy is relatively uncommon), then the woman can bear the baby vaginally.

Herpes poses a very real danger to a baby, but it is a danger that can be averted with proper care and precaution. As Dr. Paula Adams Hillard says in the book *As They Grow: Pregnancy and Childbirth* (Ballantine Books, 1985), "It is especially urgent that herpes infections be promptly diagnosed in women who are pregnant or who are considering having children, and it is imperative that any pregnant woman who knows she has had herpes inform her doctor. Given careful observation and proper medical supervision, women with genital herpes *can* have healthy babies."

Unlike herpes, syphilis and gonorrhea threaten a baby both inside and outside the womb. Gonorrhea impairs the growth of the fetus, raises the chances of premature birth, and is known to cause conjunctivitis so serious that it could lead to blindness. A woman with untreated gonorrhea may develop pelvic inflammatory disease (PID), which is known to raise the risk of ectopic pregnancies (see earlier). A mother with syphilis will infect her child in utero, raising the chances of fetal death and deformity. A fetus infected late in pregnancy might seem normal at birth and then, when the child is several months or even several years old, he or she could exhibit the symptoms of syphilis in its late stage, when the infection attacks the heart, spinal cord, or brain. A child born with syphilis has a 50 percent greater likelihood of dying in infancy than an uninfected child, and the survivors will bear the healed sores, inflamed eyes, jaundice, bowed legs, and disfigured teeth that are the marks of the disease.

Another key difference between herpes, gonorrhea, and

syphilis is that the latter two can be cured. Penicillin has been an effective treatment for these venereal diseases for years. And when the mother is cured, the unborn baby is cured as well. Thus, a woman can detect her own infection and prevent its spread to the fetus by seeking out competent medical care.

To put it harshly, there is no excuse for any informed woman to allow syphilis or gonorrhea to spread to her unborn children. And there is no excuse for any man with a venereal disease to keep this information from the woman with whom he is having sex; honesty becomes especially crucial if the couple is planning to have children. If you have any reason to suspect that you might have syphilis, gonorrhea, or herpes, have yourself checked by a doctor *before* you and your partner begin trying to conceive.

Diabetes

Diabetes is an impairment of the body's ability to metabolize sugar. One type, known as gestational diabetes, develops during pregnancy in fewer than 3 percent of women. Those women who have a family history of diabetes, who have borne very large children, who are significantly overweight themselves, or who have had previous pregnancy losses are more likely to get it. If detected by a doctor (the signs are sugar in the urine and elevated blood sugar levels), gestational diabetes can be treated by modifying the woman's diet. The doctor will prescribe different changes depending on the individual, but usually they include decreasing fat, sweets, and simple carbohydrates and cutting out alcohol. If these modifications return blood sugar levels to what is considered normal for pregnancy (blood sugar levels vary more widely during pregnancy), then the woman can pretty much stop worrying, so long as she continues on the modified diet and has the condition monitored regularly. If, however, glucose levels remain high, the pregnant woman may have to have insulin injections (insulin is the hormone that regulates the metabolism of glucose.)

Babies of women with gestational diabetes are likely to be

large because the fetus absorbs the glucose that accumulates, and there may be complications at birth. Doctors will not allow these pregnancies to go on longer than forty weeks, and since they are considered moderately high risk, the mothers will be monitored more strictly during labor and delivery. In most cases, the problem ends with delivery.

Women who have had diabetes since childhood and who require regular insulin injections face many more difficulties in pregnancy than women who develop diabetes during the pregnancy. An insulin-dependent diabetic is more likely to have preeclampsia (see earlier in this chapter) infection and to bear children with diabetes and congenital malformations. There is an increased risk that these babies will have respiratory distress syndrome (RDS—a condition of reduced lung development), although this danger passes about forty-eight hours after birth.

Before insulin shots were available, mortality rates for diabetic mothers and their babies were extremely high. The risk for mothers today has been substantially eliminated, but fetal death in the last two or three weeks of pregnancy remains a very real danger. As a result, babies of insulin-dependent diabetics are seldom allowed to go to term. Either labor is induced three to six weeks before the due date, or the baby is delivered prematurely by cesarean section. In order for the insulin-dependent mother to maintain fairly normal blood sugar levels, she may have to be hospitalized several times in the course of the pregnancy. Women with this condition are advised to seek the care of both an expert in diabetes *and* an obstetrician throughout the pregnancy.

Stillbirth

Each year approximately 20,000 babies die in the womb sometime after the twenty-eighth week of pregnancy. These babies were viable fetuses: they could have survived outside the womb if their lives had not ended inside it. These deaths are known as stillbirths.

In midcentury, syphilis was one of the major causes of

stillbirths, but it is no longer a significant factor. Today it is thought that most stillbirths occur because of problems with the placenta or the umbilical cord (including prolapse, meaning that the cord drops before the baby does, strangulation, knots), severe bleeding late in pregnancy, Rh incompatibility between mother and baby, and congenital malformations of the fetus. In problems with the cord or placenta, the baby dies because of lack of oxygen and nourishment.

Certain women are more at risk of stillbirth than others, including those with venereal disease, untreated preeclampsia, diabetes, kidney disease, heart disease, and women who are carrying twins. Although modern medical science has still not identified the causes of stillbirths with certainty, it has succeeded in greatly reducing the numbers. In 1935, the rate of perinatal death (stillbirth and death during or soon after birth) in the United States was 68.2 for every 1,000 live births; today the figure is about 16 deaths for every 1,000 live births.

A woman will know when her baby dies in utero: there will be no fetal movement for several days. Her body will eventually initiate labor, but this may not happen for several weeks. Many women have a strong urge to get the horror of this experience over with, in which case the doctor may induce labor, although sometimes the doctor may advise a woman to wait for her body to begin the labor. Either way, there is a labor and a birth of a dead baby.

Unlike a fetus who has died in a first trimester miscarriage, a stillborn baby is a fully formed recognizable person. Facing up to this person's death and saying good-bye to him or her is likely to be the most painful and difficult event a couple will ever endure. Many experience a sort of revulsion at the idea of holding or even looking at their dead baby. But months and years later couples may come to regret bitterly that they passed up their only opportunity to be with their child. Sensitive to these regrets and to the need most people have to focus their grief on some tangible object, psychologists often urge parents to spend time with their stillborn babies, to hold and touch the baby, and form an impression of what the baby looked like. Giving the baby a name and participating in the ritual of burial and mourning are symbolic acts that fulfill a real emotional need for many couples. The doctor may suggest that an autopsy be performed, and this can fill another need—the need to know *why* the baby died. Unfortunately, the question very often remains unanswered.

A sense of guilt, of blaming oneself, is very common for both men and women after a stillbirth. Both partners may punish themselves by feeling that "if only I hadn't done such-and-such (exhausted myself working, had so many affairs before marriage, consumed a bottle of wine), the baby would have lived." It can help tremendously to air these fears with a doctor; invariably he or she will put them to rest. A knot in the umbilical cord or a late pregnancy hemorrhage is no one's fault. Learning as many of the facts as possible about the baby's death will relieve the parents of some of their self-blame and destructive fantasies.

Men and women suffer through different kinds of crisis when a fetus dies, and sometimes these differences drive a couple apart. The man handles the medical arrangements while the woman suffers the physical pain of delivery. Unable to stop his wife's pain or to bring the baby back to life, the man stands by in the role of helpless onlooker to suffering. Even before he feels grief, a man in this position may feel anger—at the hospital staff, at the doctor, at fate, even at the fetus for causing everyone so much pain. His own time of mourning may not come until much later, perhaps because he is too numb to feel much of anything at first or perhaps because he is too busy handling practical matters and caring for his wife. A grieving woman may turn on him for not sharing her grief when all along he has been doing his best to hide his own feelings so her life would be easier. And it is not uncommon for a man to run away from the situation, to refuse to face up to his own emotions, to become angry at his wife for sinking into depression, to deny his dreams of knowing and loving the baby who died.

Sex is likely to be difficult for a long time after the stillbirth, even for couples who remained supportive of each other during the time of mourning. Both partners may find that sex calls up painful memories of the pregnancy and the baby's death. The strain of all these emotions may be too much for the relationship to bear. It can be a help to talk with someone outside the marriage, whether friends, family, or professional counselors. Occasionally those with the best intentions end up inflicting more pain. Family members or friends may think they're being kind by erasing all signs of this life unlived, stripping all baby furniture from the house before the woman returns from the hospital, never raising the subject, keeping their own children away. But most people who have lost a baby—or any loved one—need to talk about the loss with others. Those who carefully avoid the subject are in effect denying the reality of the child. Often those who have been through the experience themselves can offer the most comfort and understanding. A hospital social worker may be able to put a couple in touch with others; there are a number of national support groups for parents whose babies have died. Three are listed below.

>Amend
>4323 Berrywich Terrace
>Saint Louis, MO 63128

>SHARE
>St. John's Hospital
>800 E. Carpenter
>Springfield, IL 62702

>Compassionate Friends
>P.O. Box 1347
>Oak Brook, IL 60521

Some doctors urge a couple to conceive again as soon as possible after a stillbirth, on the assumption that a successful pregnancy is the only way of getting over the grief. But this is a matter a couple must decide for themselves. The grieving for a lost child never really ends, although with time the pain will soften.

Problem-Detection Tests:
Ultrasound and Amniocentesis

Until the latter half of the twentieth century, the womb of a pregnant woman was pretty much a private place, inaccessible to the probes of science. But now, with advances in medical technology, we have two windows on the womb that doctors routinely peer through to determine crucial information about the growing fetus.

Ultrasound is a technique for getting an early visual image of your baby on a screen. Here's how it works: high-frequency sound waves produced by a special ultrasound transducer are directed at the pregnant woman's abdomen. As the sound waves encounter the different densities of tissues inside, they are bounced back at different rates. The sound waves are converted into electrical signals and these create an image on a screen. To you, the image may look like a blur of dark and light shadows, but the obstetrician or radiologist will be able to "read" the image and point out your baby's features, heartbeat, limbs, and so on. An ultrasound examination, known as a *sonogram*, is used routinely to determine the age of the fetus (important if the woman must be delivered by cesarean section), to diagnose twins (before the days of ultrasound, as many as half the mothers carrying twins were surprised on delivery day), to detect certain birth defects and certain complications of pregnancy, including placenta previa, which means that the placenta is covering the cervix and cesarean delivery may be necessary. A sonogram is also performed before amniocentesis (see below) to locate the position of the fetus and the placenta. Sometimes the doctor can determine the sex of the fetus from a sonogram, but the test is by no means a foolproof way of discovering the sex and is not recommended for this purpose.

Studies have revealed no hard evidence that ultrasound endangers either the fetus or mother, and as a result many doctors perform sonograms routinely on all pregnancies for dating purposes and as a way of checking up on the fetus. Others take a more cautious approach and use the test only when there is a real need for the information it provides.

Although its dangers are minimal, a sonogram does involve some discomfort for the expecting mother because she must have a full bladder when the test is performed. The reason is that a full bladder elevates the fetus's head and the liquids provide a "clear window" for better viewing of the crucial organs.

In the *amniocentesis* test, a small amount of amniotic fluid is removed from the uterus and analyzed for the presence of certain diseases and birth defects. Amniotic fluid is the clear liquid in which your baby floats inside the womb. It contains weak solutions of sugar and minerals, skin cells, fetal hairs, and a good deal of baby urine. At around the sixteenth week of pregnancy, when this test is usually performed, most

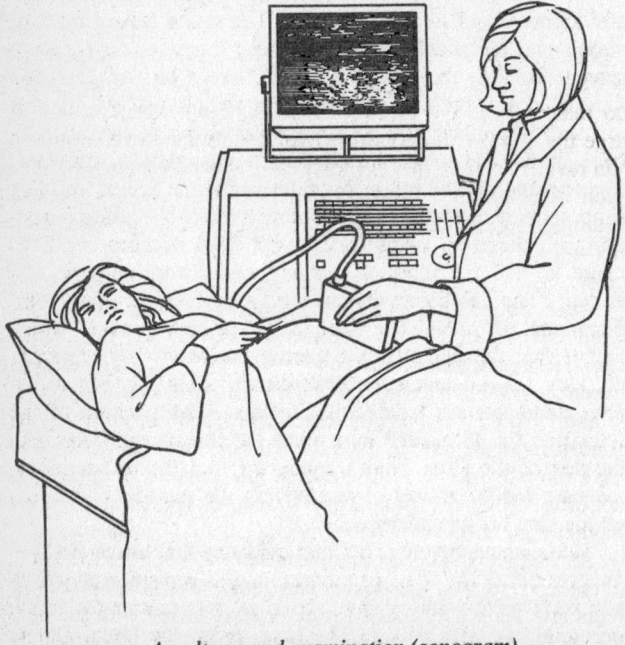

An ultrasound examination (sonogram)

women have about a cup of amniotic fluid, of which one ounce is removed for testing.

Amniocentesis analyzes both the chemical substances of the amniotic fluid and the fetal cells contained in it. The analysis of the cells, performed by culturing them in the lab, is especially important because this will show any abnormality in the chromosomes. The most common such genetic abnormality is known as Down's syndrome (the condition that often used to be called mongolism), which causes mental retardation and physical deformities, and often serious defects in the internal organs, including the heart. Down's syndrome, and genetic abnormalities in general, become much more common as a woman grows older. A recent study showed that thirty-four-year-old women have a 1 in 527 incidence of Down's syndrome, and that the incidence increases to 1 in 333 at age thirty-six, 1 in 183 at thirty-eight, and 1 in 83 by forty-one. This is why many doctors strongly suggest amniocentesis for women over age thirty-five. Also, if a couple's previous child had Down's syndrome, there is a 1 in 60 risk that it will recur no matter what age the woman is, so again, the doctor will urge the test. In addition to Down's syndrome, amniocentesis can reveal certain abnormalities of the central nervous system, such as spina bifida and anencephaly. And because the test examines the baby's genetic makeup, it also reveals the baby's sex—although some parents choose not to be told so as to preserve the surprise for delivery day.

An amniocentesis is a serious test and should not be entered into lightly for the purpose of ascertaining the child's sex. There is a slight, but nonetheless documented, risk (between 1 and 2 percent) that the test itself will cause the fetus to abort. And, if the results indicate the presence of a serious abnormality, the parents face the trial of deciding whether to have the baby aborted. Abortion at this stage of pregnancy is not only difficult emotionally, but it carries greater risks to the mother than an abortion performed in the first trimester.

As already noted, an amniocentesis is monitored through ultrasound so that the doctor can locate the position of the fetus and the placenta and avoid sticking either with the needle. A local anesthetic will be administered and a long hollow needle inserted into the woman's uterus. The needle extracts the small amount of amniotic fluid needed for the test.

Some doctors bar expecting fathers from the procedure because they have been known to faint at the sight of the needle. But for those who can handle it, the test is often a major turning point in their experience of the pregnancy. As one father put it: "For me, it was the realization that this was real stuff, that it was not a couple of cells but a real baby in there." And, of course, learning the baby's sex can make a difference in how you feel about him or her, in addition to making your baby shopping easier.

6. Preparing for the Birth

It may seem strange that something as basic and primordial as birth should be subject to the vagaries of fashion, but so it is and so it has been with increasing variation in the United States since the 1930s. The idea of choosing a childbirth method or attendant was alien to our mothers: in most cases, the woman went to a hospital when it was "her time" and she did what the obstetrician and obstetrical nurses told her to do. It was almost universally assumed that the father would be absent (consigned to pacing in the waiting room or sent home) and that the mother would receive some sort of medication—painkillers and either general or partial anesthesia. Our mothers were alone when they labored and in many cases not even aware when they gave birth. That was the fashion of the day, and even though the fashion was under attack by advocates of "natural" childbirth, such as Grantly Dick-Read, Fernand Lamaze, and Robert Bradley, few American parents in the 1940s, 1950s, and early 1960s were aware that a revolution in childbirth was underway.

Today that revolution continues, under a number of different banners, and alongside it other childbirth revolutions are transforming the way our children are born. From the point of view of fathers, the most important change in birth style is that we are now welcomed into the delivery room—indeed, almost expected to be present when our children are born. The rallying cry of our day is family-centered childbirth: childbirth that takes into account the *emotional* needs of parents to bear their babies in an atmosphere of human love, not technological control. And yet at the same time, more babies than ever are being delivered by cesarean section—a staggering 21.1 percent of the 3.7 million babies born in 1984.

The splintering of the childbirth revolution has engendered conflict and contradiction. In transforming the experience of childbirth, parents, doctors, midwives, and childbirth educators have also opened a fierce debate on the issues of how, where, and under whose control our children will come into the world. Today, we are no longer merely expecting parents; we are "consumers" with as many choices in childbirth as we have in VCR equipment or disposable diapers. We can have our babies at home, at alternative birthing centers, in hospital delivery rooms; we can learn breathing techniques, yoga, or meditation to cope with the pain; we can have our babies born under water, in soothingly lit, quiet rooms or under the white glare of hospital delivery room lights; an obstetrician, a certified nurse midwife, a lay midwife, or even you, the brand-new father, may be the one to deliver the baby.

You may be tempted, when faced with this array of options, to take the course of least resistance: to do as your friends and relatives have done or simply to follow the advice of the obstetrician. And this could be the right choice for you. But it could also be the cause of bitter regret after the baby's birth. "If only I'd *known* what it was going to be like" is a familiar refrain of disappointed new parents. Since the choices are out there, it makes sense to know what they are as you begin to prepare for the baby's birth. And since you, in all likelihood, will participate at the birth, it makes sense for you to participate in choosing the birth method as well. What is the range of options? What does each one typically involve? What are the costs? What are the risks? How and when do you make the arrangements? These are some of the questions this chapter answers.

The Basic Choices: Where and Who?

Where you want your baby to be born and whom you want to deliver your baby are the first decisions you and your partner will be making, and very often one decision decides the other. As for *where*, you have four possible choices: in a hospital delivery room, in a hospital "birthing room" (see below), at a birthing center, or at home. As for *who*, you have two basic alternatives—a doctor or a midwife.

Most of us—about 98 percent—still choose to have our babies in a hospital and with an obstetrician attending (statistics vary because it is thought that many home births go unreported). An obstetrician is, obviously, an M.D. with all that implies. He or she has received extensive theoretical and clinical training, is able to prescribe drugs, to perform surgery if necessary (cesarean section is the most likely), and, if he or she works at a large medical center, the obstetrician has all the latest medical technology and equipment at his or her disposal to use in the case of complications or emergency. The obstetrician is also bound by the ever-tightening net of malpractice regulations, a subject of enormous controversy at the moment. What it means for you and your partner and your baby is that the obstetrician will in all likelihood manage the labor and delivery in such a way as to avoid losing a malpractice suit. This, many opponents of medically managed birth would argue, is good for the doctor but not necessarily for the mother or baby.

Although all obstetricians are doctors, they are not all the same kinds of doctors—or the same kinds of people. There are rigid, remote, and businesslike obstetricians, and warm, flexible, people-oriented obstetricians. It's up to you and your partner to find one you like.

One factor that may influence your choice of a hospital is the birthing room. A relatively recent innovation, the birthing room is an attempt by hospitals to give you the best of both worlds—the comforts of home and the security of medical center backup. Most birthing rooms resemble pleasant motel rooms: there is "normal" furniture, a TV, curtains on the window, plants, phone, maybe even a radio. A mother labors and has her baby there. She is not rushed out to a delivery room at the last moment, unless there is some complication. The bed she rests on during labor will be the bed in which she gives birth. In most birthing room deliveries, only the mother, the father, a nurse, and obstetrician are present (no resident or anesthesiologist). It's not home, but neither is it as alienating as the harshly clinical delivery room. Not all hospitals have birthing rooms; even those that do have them usually don't have enough for everyone, and not all mothers may use them. To use the birthing room, the pregnancy and mother must be deemed "low risk" by the doctor, and the labor must be proceeding normally. If you are interested, take a look at the birthing room when you tour the hospital (see later in this chapter).

Bridging the abyss between hospital birth and home birth is an alternative known as the free-standing birth center or maternity center. A birth center is like a hospital birthing room *without the hospital*. This is a crucial distinction. The birth center offers not only family-centered childbirth, but does away with many hospital regulations. Only women with low-risk pregnancies may use a birth center, and a continuous screening process goes on to insure that women with problems transfer to hospital care.

At most birth centers, certified nurse midwives or teams of midwives and obstetricians attend the births, and the whole approach to birth is looser and less technologically oriented, with minimal interference in the process of labor and little or no medication offered. Not only fathers but other children may be present; the parents keep their baby after the birth and usually go home within twelve hours after the baby is born. One pattern for birth centers is to have nurse midwives handle the routine births, obstetricians on call for any problems, and a backup at medical centers in case of emergency.

The first free-standing birth center opened in New York in 1975 and now there are some 140 of them in thirty-five states. Their limited numbers make birth centers a possible alternative for only a relatively small number of parents, but more of them are opening up all the time. Another very attractive feature of the birth center is the cost: you'll pay about $1,600 for having a baby there as opposed to $3,200, the average cost of hospital delivery according to the Health Insurance Institute of America (which reports that cesarean delivery in a hospital now costs over $5,000).

More and more hospitals are opening up their own in-hospital birth centers as a separate part of the maternity units.

Preparing for the Birth

These facilities, known as alternative birth centers or ABCs, offer the birth center experience within the hospital, so that in case of emergency you're just down the hall from the latest technology. Although the ABCs have tried to incorporate many of the attitudes and practices of free-standing birth centers, critics insist that they are still basically hospital wards in pleasant disguise.

And then there is birth at home, at the furthest extreme from the hospital delivery room experience. For most of us the idea of home-birth seems truly radical, and the first question that comes to mind is, "But what if something goes wrong?" Most of us will never get past this question and so, despite the attractiveness of having total control over the birth environment, being surrounded by familiar things, and not having to drive off to the hospital or birth center, most of us will not make this choice. However, when you look at it from a purely statistical point of view, home-birth does not seem so radical a choice for normal, low-risk pregnancies—in fact, it seems rather conservative. Holland has the highest percentage of home-births of any developed country and among the lowest perinatal mortality rates. With a home-birth you greatly reduce the risk of infection that is ever-present in hospital maternity wards and nurseries.

Home-birth has become a battle cry for many in the so-called childbirth movement, and if you take the recent literature on childbirth as a sign, you will think that home-birth is a burning issue in the hearts and minds of most expecting parents. It isn't. For most of us, home-birth makes about as much sense as trading in our car for a horse and buggy. Yet, for a tiny but growing minority, home-birth offers the most wonderful way of bringing their children into the world. If you're thinking about it or simply intrigued by it, see below.

Obstetrician versus Midwife

Couples desiring family-centered childbirth have focused on the nurse midwife as a great new alternative to medical control, which is a bit ironic since midwives have been around a lot longer than obstetricians. But given our recent history of medically managed childbirth, the nurse midwife does offer something quite different and something very attractive to many parents. Jenny Whitman, a certified nurse midwife who practices at Kaunakaki, Hawaii, summed up the difference between the approach she takes and that of a medical doctor: "The main thing is the focus of the training. The nurse midwife is trained to promote normalcy. We look at pregnancy and birth as a normal healthy process and we're promoting that from conception to delivery. Whereas the training of an obstetrician is pathological and geared toward emergencies—they are trained to deal with the problems in pregnancy and childbirth. We expect the normal while they treat everyone as potentially abnormal. And it's amazing how that difference in philosophy and expectation can influence the outcome of the birth."

American midwives come in two varieties: certified nurse midwives and lay midwives. A certified nurse midwife is a registered nurse who does additional training in midwifery and receives her certification from the American College of Nurse-Midwives in Washington, DC. There are now some three thousand certified nurse midwives delivering babies in the United States. Forty-eight states license CNMs to perform deliveries. Lay midwifery is a less formally defined category: broadly speaking, lay midwives are women who have decided to attend home-births, often because their own home-births were so satisfying. Although there are schools where they can train, lay midwives are not certified, and many states outlaw them.

The difference in philosophy between midwives and obstetricians described by Jenny Whitman translates into some very basic differences in the birth experience for the parents. Because a midwife views labor and birth as natural, she allows it to progress at its own pace: let nature take its course is her guiding philosophy. She won't hurry it up with hormones or push painkillers on mothers who haven't asked for them, although she can offer pain-relieving medication to mothers who ask for it and can administer local anesthetic for episiotomy (see below). Midwives are not insensitive to the pain that nature inflicts on many women during childbirth. Whit-

Preparing for the Birth

man laughed at the image I had of the stern "all-natural" midwife telling the agonized mother to grit her teeth and bear it. She routinely dispenses Demerol, and in one case she had a laboring mother flown out to Honolulu when the pain became unbearable. Most CNMs work at hospitals or birthing centers and thus have full medical back-up.

Perhaps even more important, a midwife stays with a mother throughout her labor, unlike an obstetrician who darts in and out at long intervals and who may very well keep a mother waiting when she's ready to deliver. A midwife begins her relationship with a mother during the pregnancy, she is present and available to the mother from the onset of labor until the birth, and she follows through with postpartum care. And midwives encourage fathers to take an active, participative role. Some will actually let the fathers deliver the babies, but Whitman says she discourages this "because the main thing is what is happening between the men and their partners. If the father is concentrating on the technicality of delivery, the mother misses out on the emotional support. I do, however, let men cut the umbilical cord."

Midwives are supposed to deal only with normal, low-risk pregnancies, and when certain complications or emergency situations arise, an obstetrician will take over. Midwives do not do forceps deliveries (see Chapter 7) or perform cesarean sections and they cannot administer an epidural or spinal anesthesia.

If you and your partner opt for a birthing center or for home-birth, you will almost definitely have a nurse midwife attending (doctors *can* legally attend home-births, but very few will). And at some hospitals and hospital clinics, CNMs routinely attend births in labor rooms or birthing rooms. Check around at the hospitals in your area to see what they offer.

If you need help finding a CNM in your area, contact the American College of Nurse-Midwives, 1522 K Street, NW, Suite 1120, Washington, DC 20005; 202-347-5445.

Getting Prepared: Childbirth Classes

No matter who is going to deliver your baby or where, it makes good sense to take childbirth classes beforehand, especially if you are planning to attend the birth. The classes serve a number of purposes: they give you a rundown on the physical processes of labor and delivery; they teach you and your partner how to cope with the pain and stress of labor through breathing and relaxation techniques; they prepare you for most of the standard procedures used in hospital childbirth; they introduce you to other expecting parents; and for many they offer a much needed source of emotional support and easily accessible information. Taking a class is not going to make the pain of labor go away, but it is going to demystify the whole birth process and reduce (or eliminate) the panic that so many first-time parents experience when the big day arrives. Says Lois Fink, coordinator of childbirth education at the Long Island Jewish Medical Center in New York, "The classes provide basic knowledge so that the fear and anxiety level is lowered." Terry, a thirty-six-year-old truckdriver and new father from Saint Paul, Minnesota, wholeheartedly agrees: "I wanted to attend the birth but I was worried I'd be a bumbling idiot—more hindrance than help. In the classes I gained confidence that helped tremendously. I got security from knowing the tools."

Just as today we have many choices in childbirth, so we have a number of choices in childbirth classes. Most large teaching hospitals offer classes, and unless you live in a really remote area, you can usually find a private childbirth educator nearby who teaches one of the prepared childbirth methods (see below for Lamaze and Bradley methods). The Red Cross offers childbirth classes and good practical instruction in infant care at over 2,500 local chapters nationwide, and the YM/YWCA may also offer classes in your area. Whether they're at a hospital with a private instructor or with some community organization, classes generally meet for a couple hours once a week for about six to eight weeks. You and your partner will start attending sometime in the last trimester of

Preparing for the Birth

her pregnancy, timing things so that you finish the classes a couple of weeks before the due date. Costs vary—the range is from $30 to $200 for from six to twelve classes. Hospital and Red Cross classes are usually less expensive (they're free at some hospitals and sometimes the insurance company will pay for them), but they are also likely to be larger than private classes, with twelve or more couples in many hospital classes.

One advantage of hospital classes is that they really acquaint you with the procedures followed in the hospital: the instructor (usually a nurse) takes you through the admitting process, describes any routine preparation on the mother (see Standard Issue: The "Typical" Hospital Birth, later in this chapter), explains the roles of the various labor and delivery room nurses, and takes you through the first hours and days of your baby's life—when the baby is taken to the nursery, how long the baby and mother must stay in the hospital, fathers' visiting hours, and so on. The disadvantage of hospital classes, according to proponents of family-centered childbirth, is that in describing hospital procedure, the nurse also "sells" you on it. The message is: This is the way it's supposed to be so don't kick up a fuss. Private instructors are much more likely to encourage you to kick up a fuss at the hospital. "We were prepared to question everything the doctor did," one new father told me. This can be good or bad, depending on your personality and your own philosophy of childbirth. After reading a lot and taking classes with a private instructor (in addition to the hospital classes—yes, we overdid it!), my wife and I felt pressured to go in fighting. Somehow we both got the message that we were wimps if we abided by hospital procedures. Needless to say, this added pressure was the last thing we needed during labor. Then again, we were lucky: our hospital experience was positive, the nurses supportive, and the doctors humane. For those who aren't so lucky, private instructors will be useful in pointing out hospital shortcomings and in encouraging them to take control of the situation.

A lot of men gripe about the classes, whether they're private or at the hospital. As Diana Simkin, a private childbirth educator who works out of New York, put it: "Men tend not to like classes. They're busy, they don't like these organized group activities. They come in expecting some sort of indoctrination or sensitivity session, but when they realize it's not like that, that they won't have to spill their guts out, they relax a little more. Men's attitudes change as they learn more, too."

Another problem several men pointed out to me (and one that I had, too) was that the material covered in the class was repetitive and the substance rather slight. "I felt the six-week course could have been done in two weeks," said one dad. "In fact, it could have been taught in two hours. It became a bore." Other dads come away wondering what the point was: "There was lots of information, but I still have no idea of what to do when the time comes," an expecting father with three weeks to go told me. A common complaint from new fathers after the birth is that the classes did not really prepare them for their particular situation. "From the time her waters broke until delivery was three hours," said a dad in Minneapolis. "We just didn't have time to use the breathing or relaxation techniques." The classes tend to prepare you for textbook labor and delivery, but, of course, it seldom happens that way outside of the textbooks. Fathers in particular may come away feeling that the classes were a waste.

So why bother? First of all, there is the statistical evidence of the usefulness of classes. According to a poll conducted by *Parents* magazine of 64,000 women, 22.3 percent of those who took classes thought they were "indispensable" in controlling the pain of labor and delivery; 33 percent said they were "very helpful"; and 33 percent rated them as "helpful." Other studies have shown that men who have been through the classes feel a greater closeness with their wives during the experience of birth. Lois Fink pointed out that men who took the classes were more helpful, more open to communication, had a better idea of what to do and what was going on. For men who didn't take classes, "the anxiety tends to stay up there."

Lots of men go to classes because their partners want them to, and this really isn't such a bad reason. Women feel enormously grateful to their husbands for being prepared and being there. Says Simkin about the reaction of wives to the husbands after the birth: "I get glowing, glowing, glowing reports from women about their husbands' participation. According to one study, women commonly say 'I couldn't have done it without him' even if all he did was sit there and read the paper. The fact that he was there at all lends support." And, of course, if you've attended the classes, you're likely to do a lot more than read the paper. A slightly more abstract reason to attend classes is that it prepares you psychologically for the birth and the changes that having a baby will bring in your life. When you're sitting in a room full of pregnant women and you're learning how to recognize the onset of labor and how many centimeters your wife's cervix is supposed to dilate and what crowning means, somehow the birth becomes a whole lot more immediate, the idea of impending fatherhood more real. Quite aside from the information, the classes can help you make the emotional transition from pregnancy to fatherhood.

Prepared Childbirth Methods

The most popular prepared childbirth methods practiced in the United States today are the outgrowth of a few landmark books and the public's response to them. First came *Natural Childbirth* in 1933 by British obstetrician Grantly Dick-Read. Published as *Childbirth Without Fear* in America in 1944, it kicked off the "natural childbirth" movement, even though adherents and practitioners were few in the early days. (*Natural childbirth* is often confused with *prepared childbirth*, but the two are technically different: natural childbirth means that the woman bears her child without taking any painkillers or drugs and without intervention from a doctor; prepared childbirth means that the expecting parents have taken some sort of childbirth classes to help them get through labor and delivery with minimal medical intervention. Preparing for the birth through classes can lead to a natural childbirth, although it need not and in fact seldom does. Whereas totally natural childbirth remains relatively rare in the United States, prepared childbirth is increasingly common.) Next came *Painless Childbirth*, popularly known as the Lamaze method, published as *Qu'est-ce que l'accouchement sans douleur?* in France in 1956, and, around the same time, *Husband-Coached Childbirth* by Robert A. Bradley. Yet another method was developed by the British social anthropologist

Sheila Kitzinger in a number of books, including *The Experience of Childbirth* (first published in 1962 and revised several times).

There are very real differences between these various methods, but (although the doctors and writers would probably disagree), the distinctions may not matter all that much to most expecting couples. Many childbirth educators adopt an eclectic approach, selecting the aspects of each method that make the most sense to them. When the time really arrives, laboring mothers and their coaches tend to invent their own methods, using what works and discarding what doesn't.

However, despite the fact that the techniques you actually use may be a mix of the various methods, it's worth knowing the essential principles of each major school of thought and how they differ. Following is a rundown.

Dick-Read

The pioneer in natural and prepared childbirth, Grantly Dick-Read laid the foundation for the methods most widely practiced in this country today. Through his book *Childbirth Without Fear* and his own practice, he introduced the concepts of birth preparation classes, breathing and relaxation techniques, and having a "coach" along to support the laboring mother emotionally (in Dick-Read's practice the coach was more often a doctor than the baby's father). The essence of his childbirth philosophy, as his book title indicates, is that fear is the prime cause of pain in childbirth, and that without fear, a woman will not need to be drugged because it won't hurt as much. Dick-Read takes a rather high-minded, spiritual tone in his book, which may seem a bit quaint to modern readers. The book, however, has been updated and revised to include new information on nutrition, birth positions, family attendance, and the like. (The fifth edition was revised and edited by Helen Wessel and Harlan F. Ellis, M.D., and published by Harper & Row in 1984.)

There is no official certification for instructors who use the Dick-Read methods, but many private and hospital instructors trained in other methods incorporate his teachings into their approach. For further information, contact the Read Natural

Childbirth Foundation, P.O. Box 956, San Rafael, CA 94915; 415-456-8462.

Lamaze

Lamaze is currently the most popular prepared childbirth method in the United States (with some 10,000 Lamaze instructors here). The essence of the method, as French obstetrician Fernand Lamaze explains in his book *Painless Childbirth*, is a conditioned response whereby a woman learns to react to the pain of labor contractions by *relaxing* instead of tensing up. Most of us are familiar with the idea of conditioned response (or reflex) from the experiments of Russian physiologist Ivan Pavlov on dogs: by ringing a bell every time he fed the dogs, Pavlov conditioned them so that they would salivate whenever he rang the bell, even when no food was offered. In the Lamaze method, a woman practices relaxation and breathing exercises in the weeks before her due date in order to achieve the conditioned response of relaxing when the contractions of labor finally begin. The woman learns different breathing patterns for each stage of labor, and she distracts herself from the pain by focusing visually on some outside object—a picture, a crack in the wall, or a mental image.

As Lamaze is practiced in America, a coach (preferably the baby's father or a close friend or relative) is present to talk the laboring mother through contractions and to offer light massages (effleurage) to the mother's abdomen to relieve some of the pain and to further distract her. The Lamaze techniques were popularized in the United States by an American woman named Marjorie Karmel and her book *Thank You Doctor Lamaze*, and by Elisabeth Bing and her book entitled *Six Practical Lessons for an Easier Childbirth*. Bing, Karmel, and others founded the American Society for Psychoprophylaxis in Obstetrics (ASPO), which led the battle to get Lamaze methods accepted at hospitals and which certifies Lamaze instructors. For those interested in contacting the organization directly, the address of its national headquarters is ASPO, 1840 Wilson Blvd., Suite 204, Arlington, VA 22201; 800-368-4404; in Virginia, 703-524-7802.

Lamaze instructors, many of whom are nurses, must take

courses for a year or year and a half in order to meet the requirements set by the ASPO. Lamaze is the least "radical" of the prepared childbirth methods: although instructors prepare you and your partner to go through labor and delivery with minimal drugs, they do not forbid drugs and, in fact, a woman can use Lamaze in connection with various painkillers. Some critics point out that a woman using Lamaze techniques may be concentrating so hard on distracting herself from pain that she distracts herself from the emotional experience of pregnancy as well. Critics also say that the medical establishment has coopted Lamaze and uses it as way of retaining control over childbirth: the breathing and relaxation keeps a woman quieter while the doctor actually manages the labor. This may be true and childbirth purists may want to go a different route. But there is no doubt that the Lamaze method has done much to reduce the amount of anesthesia given in hospital deliveries, to help mothers remain conscious and in command of the situation during labor and delivery, and, as it is practiced here, to give fathers an important role during the labor and birth.

Bradley

The Bradley method, developed by Denver obstetrician Robert A. Bradley, is also known as husband-coached childbirth, and, as this name suggests, it emphasizes the role of the baby's father as an active participant and a source of emotional support during the labor and birth. Bradley stresses the need for quiet, comfort, and relaxation in labor, and part of the husband's role is to help his wife achieve these. A woman using the Bradley method assumes her natural sleep position during labor and relaxes through deep abdominal breathing. She does not try to distract herself from the pain by varying her breathing patterns, as a woman who prepared with the Lamaze method would, but rather she focuses *inward* on her uterine contractions, tuning in to her body and laboring with it. Bradley speaks of the pleasure and joy that a woman so prepared can experience. Another key difference between the Bradley and Lamaze methods is in their attitudes toward pain-

Preparing for the Birth

killing drugs. Where Lamaze attempts to minimize their use, Bradley encourages women to avoid them altogether during pregnancy, birth, and breastfeeding unless they are *absolutely* necessary. Bradley also puts strong emphasis on the importance of nutrition in pregnancy.

According to *The Whole Birth Catalog* (a very useful compendium of books, organizations, and information related to pregnancy, birth, and babyhood in America, edited by Janet Isaacs Ashford and published by Crossings Press in 1983): "The Bradley Method is particularly well suited for couples who are planning to give birth in a birth center or at home or who plan to labor without obstetrical intervention."

Classes in the Bradley method, usually taught by husband and wife teams, last several weeks longer than Lamaze classes. Bradley teachers receive accreditation from the American Academy of Husband-Coached Childbirth, the national Bradley method organization founded in California by Marjie and Jay Hathaway. Contact them for further information and for locating a Bradley method instructor near you: American Academy of Husband-Coached Childbirth, P.O. Box 5224, Sherman Oaks, CA 91413; 800-423-2397, in California 818-788-6662.

Kitzinger

Unlike the other originators of childbirth methods, Sheila Kitzinger is not an obstetrician—but she is a social anthropologist, teacher, writer, and, perhaps most importantly, a mother. The Kitzinger method, which has no national organization to codify it or accredit instructors, is based on what she calls a psychosexual approach. She takes into account the sexual aspect of birth and places the birth experience in both a psychological and social context. Her books, including *Education and Counseling for Childbirth*, *The Experience of Childbirth*, and *The Complete Book of Pregnancy and Childbirth*, contain detailed descriptions of how women can achieve deep relaxation during labor and encourage couples to use fantasy imagery. One technique she advises is known as "touch relaxation" in which a woman learns to relax various parts of her body in response to a partner's touch. She draws on a rich variety of sources, including the exercises devised by Russian "method acting" advocate Konstantin Stanislavsky to put people in touch with their bodies.

Many childbirth instructors incorporate Kitzinger's techniques and approaches into their classes. Those interested in finding out more about her methods should look into her highly readable and highly recommended books.

Other Childbirth Methods and Preparations

As childbirth styles, philosophies, and books proliferate, parents today have more and more choices in childbirth. Here is a brief sampling of some of the other methods and preparations available.

Leboyer Gentle Birth

A Leboyer birth is not so much a preparation for birth as a different way of bringing a child into the world. It is based on *Birth Without Violence* (first U.S. publication in 1975) by French obstetrician Frederick Leboyer, who considers birth from the baby's point of view—a simple but rather radical perspective. Birth is hard enough for a baby, Leboyer argues, without subjecting the newborn to the brutality of our hospital procedures—the glaring lights, the noise, the being turned upside down, the required crying. To reduce the stress of birth, Leboyer urges us to recreate the conditions of the womb as far as possible so that the baby comes into a familiar, warmly welcoming world. Thus, in a Leboyer gentle birth, the lights are dimmed, there is quiet and no rushing about, the umbilical cord in not severed until it stops pulsing, the baby rests for a short time on its mother's stomach with the mother gently caressing it, and then the father gives the baby a warm bath. Such a procedure, claims Leboyer, is not only good for the baby, but it helps the mother and father bond more readily with their newborn. Leboyer babies do in fact cry very little at birth and seem much more peaceful in their first moments of life than babies delivered by standard hospital methods. The downside, say the critics, is that the bath may lower the

Preparing for the Birth

baby's temperature, especially in a drafty hospital delivery room, and could cause infection.

If you're interested in a Leboyer gentle birth, read his book and also *The Gentle Birth Book: A Practical Guide to Leboyer Family-Centered Delivery* by Nancy Berezin (Simon & Schuster, 1980). Then discuss it with your doctor or midwife. A Leboyer birth is best suited to a birthing room or maternity center (many hospitals will not allow it). If you wish, you can eliminate the bath. There is no national Leboyer organization or Leboyer trained instructors, although most childbirth instructors are aware of his book and will discuss his ideas in class.

Underwater Birth

Advocates of the underwater birth method claim that a bath or hot tub is the most relaxing place for a woman to labor and that emerging from the watery environment of the womb into water is the most peaceful way for a baby to be born. The medical community feels otherwise, arguing that underwater birth prohibits a prompt examination of the baby and increases the risk of infection. Thus, you'll have a very hard time finding an American hospital that would permit an underwater birth. If you're interested in further information, contact Rima and Steve Star, 1000 Jousting Place, Austin, TX 78746; 512-327-7809.

Yoga

There are childbirth and exercise classes available that apply the techniques of yoga to labor and birth. The emphasis is on meditation, relaxation, and getting in touch with one's body through certain exercises and postures promoting limberness. A yoga birth would have the minimal medical intervention. Contact Positive Pregnancy Fitness, 4 Lauren Lane, Norwich, CT 06360; 203-887-4971.

Birth Works

In this holistic approach to childbirth, women explore their feelings toward birth and mothering, and during labor they are taught to release feelings by chanting, groaning, or making other noises. Labor coaches are mothers who have had positive birth experiences, not fathers, so there's little role for the man. The national organization of Birth Works is the Cesarean Prevention Movement, which also offers classes for women who have had one cesarean delivery and wish to avoid another. (The program is known as VBAC—vaginal birth after cesarean.) Contact them about either program at P.O. Box 152, Syracuse, NY 13210; 315-424-1942.

Biofeedback Relaxation Training

Biofeedback, a technique used to help hypertension, among other medical conditions, involves learning to relax through controlling certain bodily processes. One masters the techniques by using machines that record responses and then continuing to practice without the machines at home. The principles of biofeedback applied to labor help a woman to remain relaxed during painful contractions. It is expensive and time-consuming to learn, and a woman must practice a good deal on her own, but it does provide the most specific and scientifically grounded instruction on relaxation of any method. It is recommended that those interested in biofeedback use it in a combination with some other prepared childbirth method or course. Contact Association of Biofeedback Clinicians, 2424 Dempster, Des Plaines, IL 60016; 312-827-0440.

For further discussion of these and other alternative birth methods and preparations, see *The Maternity Source Book* by Wendy and Matthew Lesko (Warner Books, 1984).

Organizations to Help You Find Classes

The ASPO and the AAHCC (both listed above) will be able to help you locate instructors who specialize in Lamaze and Bradley techniques, respectively. Other organizations that will direct you to the kind of instruction you want include the following:

International Childbirth Education Association (ICEA)
P.O. Box 20048
Minneapolis, MN 55420
612-854-8660

National Association of Childbirth Education, Inc.
3940 Eleventh Street
Riverside, CA 92501
714-686-0422

NAPSAC, International (National Association of Parents
and Professionals for Safe Alternatives in Childbirth)
P.O. Box 267
Marble Hill, MO 63764
314-238-2010

La Leche League International
9616 Minneapolis Avenue
Franklin Park, IL 60131
312-455-7730

Hospital Tour

Even if you don't take any prepared childbirth classes, one bit of preparation that you and your partner should not miss is the hospital tour. It may sound trivial now, but when your partner is in active labor you'll be grateful that you don't have to wander around the endless hospital corridors searching for the admitting office. The tour is usually part of hospital childbirth classes; if you're using a private instructor, you can contact the hospital and find out when they're being offered.

The tour my wife and I went on was very complete. The obstetrical nurse told us where the hospital parking lot was and how much it cost for parking, she took the group to the admitting office and explained the procedure there, then we moved up to the "unit" as she called it (the labor, delivery, examination, birthing, and recovery rooms, the nursing station, and the newborn nurseries). We got to sit on the beds in the labor rooms, see the blackboard on which the nurses keep track of the laboring mothers' progress, look at a fetal monitor (see below), listen to the various sounds that the laboring women were making, peer through the window of the nursery at the incredibly tiny newborn babies, and meet some of the nurses. We even encountered a dazed and euphoric man still dressed in his scrub suit who had become a father minutes before. ("It was incredible," he assured us.)

The tour made the business of birth very real and it also relieved some of the anxiety we both felt about what kind of place our baby would be born in. When the time came, the "unit" already seemed familiar (it was to become a good deal more familiar in the course of an all-night labor). No one likes hospitals, but somehow familiarity with the setting and procedures makes them that much less forbidding. So if you're planning to have the baby in a large hospital, do yourselves a favor and take the tour ahead of time.

Standard Issue: The "Typical" Hospital Birth

Although midwives, birthing centers, and home-births are all on the rise in the United States, it nonetheless remains true that the overwhelming majority of American babies are still born in hospital delivery rooms with an obstetrician in attendance. So it makes sense to know beforehand what standard procedures, equipment, and operations to expect. If any of these bother you, you and your partner should talk it over with the obstetrician and find out how flexible he or she is. The scenario that follows is "typical" because it has become routine at a great many hospitals—but it's quite possible that your doctor and your hospital omit some of these procedures. The standard becomes less standard as more and more doctors and hospitals accept the principles of family-centered childbirth. In all cases, it's better to find out and discuss it ahead of time than when you're at the hospital having the baby.

Prep

When a woman in labor is admitted to the hospital, a doctor or nurse will examine her internally and then, very often,

Preparing for the Birth

the nurse will "prep" her. The prep consists of shaving or clipping the pubic hair and administering an enema to empty her bowels. The reason for these procedures is that they supposedly reduce infection in the case of episiotomy (see below), make more room for the baby's head in the pelvic area, and insure a "clean field" when the baby is born (if the mother's bowels are full, its contents will be expelled when the baby is born). Advocates of family-centered childbirth question this rationale. Studies have shown that far from reducing infection, a pubic shave may actually *cause* it. At best all the shave does is irritate the woman with painful scratches and abrasions. If any such prep is done, a clip of the hair between the vagina and the anus is all that is necessary. And in fact, this so-called mini-prep is increasingly replacing the pubic shave. An enema is unpleasant at the best of times and can be excruciating for a woman in labor. If a woman knows her bowels are empty, or if she has had mild diarrhea with the onset of labor, as some women do, there is no reason for her to be subjected to this procedure. Even with the enema, some women have a bowel movement on the delivery table, and it's no big deal. The nurse cleans it up, and given all the excitement of the moment, the mother doesn't much care.

Electronic Fetal Monitor

The electronic fetal monitor (EFM) is rapidly becoming the sine qua non of hospital labor. First introduced some thirty years ago and originally used only for high-risk pregnancies, the EFM is a device for checking on how the baby's heart rate is responding to labor contractions.

There are two types of monitors—internal and external. In the external monitor, two belts are strapped around the mother's abdomen: one contains a transducer that records the baby's heart rate and the other measures the frequency and duration of the uterine contractions. The internal monitor, which is more accurate, records the baby's heart rate through an electrode attached to the baby's scalp and measures the contractions through a catheter planted in the uterus. A small box spews out information from both types of monitor in the form of a continuous graph of the contractions, and every second an electronic display flashes the number of times per minute your baby's heart is beating. The machine also picks up and broadcasts the rapid thumping of your baby's heartbeat, although you can turn the sound off if you want to.

Arguments rage pro and con on the subject of EFM. Doctors tend to love them because they give immediate notice of any fetal distress, and the graph they draw is their permanent record of what happened in the labor. Many laboring mothers feel differently. They object to the external monitors because they severely restrict movement: once a woman is strapped in, she has to stay in bed, on her back, without shifting her position too much. If she sits up or rolls over, the transducers will no longer be positioned correctly. And many mothers also complain that once the monitor is hooked up, it becomes the center of attention. The doctor will check the machine before even looking at her, and the expecting father may find himself staring at the graph and the flashing heart rate as if it were a TV screen. Once this machine arrives, it becomes impossible to ignore.

There is even stronger objection to the internal monitors. For the internal monitor to be applied, the cervix must be dilated to a certain point and the amniotic sac (also called the bag of waters or the membranes) must be broken. If this hasn't already happened naturally in the labor, the membranes will be broken by the doctor. The internal monitor increases the risk of infection in the mother; the catheter may puncture her uterus; and the baby may develop abscesses or black and blue marks on his or her head where the electrodes had been implanted, not to mention the pain the baby feels. Critics also blame the EFM for the alarming rise in cesarean sections, arguing that the machine prompts all sorts of intervention that need not be taken and would not have been taken without it.

On the other hand, some parents find the machine quite comforting during labor. The graph that it draws can help the mother get ready for the next contraction and can help the coach talk her through the rise and fall. And the rapid thumping of the baby's heart can be a cheering rhythm indicating that all is going well. Almost all the fathers I interviewed gave the monitor rave reviews. As one dad put it: "Being an ama-

Preparing for the Birth

teur backyard mechanic, I found it intriguing to monitor the machine. Looking at the graph, listening to the sound of the heartbeat was neat. I used the machine to help my coaching." And another said, "The machine was wonderful! I was really impressed with how they work. It gave you something to do and really helped me anticipate the contractions."

There is no doubt that the EFM has its use, although maybe it's now being overused. In preparing for the birth, find out your obstetrician's views on the EFM. A good compromise is *occasional* monitoring, especially early in labor. This will permit your partner to be up and walk around as long as she feels like it. Toward the end of the labor, when she's more likely to want to be in bed, the monitor will be less of an intrusion for her and more of an aid in coaching for you.

INTRAVENOUS (IV)

Less common than EFMs but still standard practice for many obstetricians is to place an intravenous (IV) drip in a laboring mother's arm. The IV, through which fluids (usually sugar water) and any prescribed drugs pass, is necessitated in part by another standard hospital procedure—denying any food or drink to a laboring woman. This may sound like a piece of calculated cruelty, and is some cases it is, but again there's a medical rationale: in the event that anesthesia must be given, it's better for a woman to have an empty stomach so she won't vomit and choke by inhaling the vomitus. Few laboring women feel much like eating anyway, but most want and need more than the cupfuls of ice chips they're permitted. Opponents of medically managed birth have a very sound argument here. If the pregnancy is deemed low risk and the woman is planning to go through without anesthesia, why not let her have broth or tea when she wants it instead of giving her essentially the same nourishment through an IV that restricts her movements? Others point out that the sugar water dripping into the mother's veins will cross the placenta and can raise the baby's blood sugar level during labor; after birth, the baby's blood sugar level can plummet dangerously.

These objections are so sensible that many doctors have

discarded the practice and will permit the mother to take in fluids orally. Again, it's wise to find out what your doctor's policy is and whether he or she is willing to consider abiding by your wishes in the matter.

Labor in Bed, Give Birth on a Delivery Table

A woman who has an IV needle stuck in her arm and the two EFM straps secured around her middle has no choice but to lie on her back (or side) in bed. And so, during active labor, most American women are confined to hospital beds in labor rooms. There are two obvious disadvantages: the weight of the full uterus blocks the mother's blood circulation, possibly lowering her blood pressure, and the supine position prevents the force of gravity from assisting in the descent of the baby. Sitting, standing, walking, or squatting all make a lot more sense.

At most hospitals, women labor in labor rooms and give birth in delivery rooms. In the course of the labor, the obstetrician and obstetrical nurses will pop in and out of the labor room, check the EFM, check the mother, and occasionally the doctor will perform an internal exam to see how many centimeters the mother's cervix has dilated (for more on the process of labor and delivery, see Chapter 7). When the moment arrives in which the cervix is fully dilated, things move quickly. The mother is shifted from the labor room bed to a stretcher or wheelchair and wheeled into the delivery room, a brightly lit hospital "theater" (one father said he was "shocked by the overhardness of the delivery room; it looked like a food processing plant with a lot of seemingly gratuitous technology").

This switch to the delivery room is an exciting moment for the father-to-be but often a painful one for the soon-to-be mother. One father told me that although his wife had had a fast, easy labor, the pain was excruciating when she was moved to a wheelchair to be shifted to the delivery room. In some cases the disruption, the change in temperature and lighting, and the introduction of new faces and voices (the delivery room usually holds an obstetrician, obstetrical resi-

Preparing for the Birth 141

dent, anesthesiologist, nurse—and, of course, you, your partner, and soon your new baby) is enough to stop uterine contractions.

The delivery table looks a bit like an instrument of torture. There are stirrups to hold the mother's legs up and apart, and in some cases arm straps (so the mother won't touch the sterile field into which the baby is born). According to some historians, Louis XIV was responsible for the introduction of the modern delivery table: supposedly he enjoyed watching the births of his children and insisted on the high table so he could get a better view. The table also provides a better view for the doctor, nurse, and you. But it doesn't do much for the mother or baby. Because it forces the mother to push the baby out against, instead of with, the force of gravity, the birth becomes more difficult and episiotomies (see below) more common. For many women, more comfortable and sensible birth positions are squatting, sitting up, or being propped up (the birthing stool was common in Europe before Louis XIV changed the fashion), or resting on all fours. Obviously, your wife is not going to know what is most comfortable for her until the time comes. But it's still a good idea to find out your

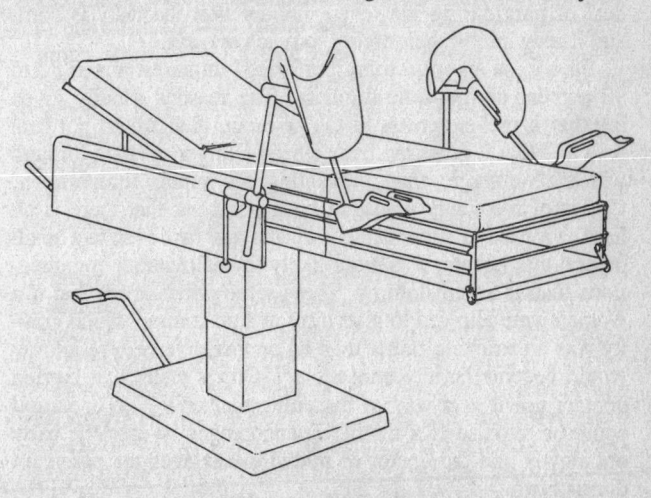

A standard hospital delivery table

doctor's views on the subject. At some hospitals, the mother is permitted to give birth in the labor room, and, of course, many hospitals have birthing rooms now (see earlier). If you're concerned about these issues, explore your options.

Episiotomy

A minor operation in which a small incision is made in the mother's perineum between the vagina and anus, an episiotomy is performed in order to enlarge the opening through which the baby emerges. It has become a standard feature of American hospital births, especially for first-time mothers. The doctor will administer a local anesthetic (known as a perineal block), open the incision with surgical scissors, and then, once the baby is born, stitch up the opening. The procedure is usually over quickly and doesn't hurt much compared to the pain of labor and birth. The new father, jubilant over the birth of his child, may not even notice what's going on (I didn't). But the pain of episiotomy often comes later. The healing period is uncomfortable for a lot of women and infection of the stitches does sometimes occur, requiring antibiotic treatment. For many women, an episiotomy causes a good deal of pain during sex, even months after the baby is born, and it may inhibit their ability to reach orgasm.

So why is an episiotomy performed on an estimated 80 to 90 percent of first-time mothers? The reasons usually given are that it prevents tears in the perineum that would not heal well and that it gives the baby's head a larger opening through which to emerge, thus preventing too much compression. Critics of medically managed birth point out that there is no hard evidence to support these claims and that even if a small natural tear occurs, it is more likely to heal without complications than is an episiotomy. These same critics argue that if a woman were allowed to give birth in a position in which gravity was an assisting rather than an opposing force, episiotomy would become largely unnecessary. Others claim that harried doctors use it as a way of hastening the birth. The operation could be avoided if a mother is encouraged to ease the baby out slowly and the doctor or midwife massages the perineum during birth.

Preparing for the Birth

Again, find time to talk over this procedure with your partner and her obstetrician. Ultimately, the decision about whether or not to perform an episiotomy rests with the doctor and it is made in the highly charged atmosphere that immediately precedes the birth. The time to discuss the pros and cons of the procedure is in the weeks before the birth. Some doctors are more willing than others to make the effort to avoid episiotomy. By making your views on the subject clear, you are more likely to have them respected.

Bonding Time

In most hospitals, bonding time is limited. Most likely the baby will be cleaned up and dressed immediately after the birth and then you may have some time (half an hour or so) together as a family in the recovery room before the baby is taken to the nursery to be weighed and measured. (At some hospitals, the dads are allowed to perform these tasks.) Although you can look at your new baby through the thick glass of the nursery window, you may not be able to hold him or her again until "father's hour" that evening. And even if the birth went wonderfully and mother and baby are fine, they will most likely remain in the hospital for a day or two or even three after the birth. Some men find this extra waiting period, coming on top of nine months of waiting, intolerable. And, of course, going home to an empty house after the birth of one's child can be depressing. At most hospitals there is not much place for the father between the time the baby is born and the time he takes his new family home. More liberal hospitals have rooming-in (baby spends most of the day in the mother's room with her) and the father is allowed to be present as long as he wants. Again, try to find out the policies of local hospitals and choose the one that best suits your needs.

If you'd like to find out more about standard hospital procedures and what's wrong with them, see the carefully researched *Birth-Rights: What Every Parent Should Know About Childbirth in Hospitals* by Sally Inch (Pantheon Books, 1982).

The Birthing Center: Departure from the Hospital Norm

"The childbearing center," says Kitty Ernst of the National Association of Childbearing Centers, "has taken birth and placed it in a homelike setting that is not controlled by acute-care administration." What this translates into for parents and their new babies is less technology, less intrusion, less rigidity, and more family togetherness. It must be stressed that these facilities, some 140 nationwide, are available only to mothers whose pregnancies have been deemed low-risk based on a detailed set of criteria, including the mother's age, medical history, obstetrical history, and the progress of the pregnancy. There is continuous evaluation for any risk during the course of the pregnancy and labor, and mothers who are "risked out" are transferred to hospital care.

"All childbearing centers operate as part of the overall health-care system," says Ernst, so that there is full backup at a nearby medical center in case problems arise at the birth. New York's Childbearing Center (operated by the Maternity Center Association) has an arrangement with an ambulance company that can get a mother to a hospital in four to six minutes. Emergency transfers are, however, extremely rare.

In terms of the actual birth experience, here is what birthing centers offer:

No routine prep (pubic shave, enema).
No routine electronic fetal heart monitor.
No routine IV hookup.
No confinement to bed until the laboring mother feels like getting in bed.
No hospital gowns—mothers and fathers wear what they want (many women choose to be naked when their children are born).
Laboring mothers may eat lightly and drink juice; families can bring food to prepare after the birth.
Siblings and other family members are allowed to be present.

Preparing for the Birth

Mothers choose whatever birth position is most comfortable for them.

Painkilling medication, although available, is not routinely dispensed unless women ask for it, which few do.

Episiotomy is performed sparingly.

Parents and baby remain together after the birth; the baby is never isolated in the nursery.

Parents go home with baby within twelve hours after birth.

Both obstetricians and certified midwives staff birthing centers, and the division of responsibility between the two varies. At New York's Childbearing Center, the obstetrician performs three prenatal examinations, including the first one, and the midwife does the rest. The midwife attends the actual birth and then a pediatrician checks out the baby before the parents go home. One guiding principle of birthing centers is, in Kitty Ernst's words, "that birth is a normal human event until proven otherwise." Parents using these facilities have much more freedom in determining the type of birth experience they desire than they have in hospitals. And fathers are encouraged to accompany their partners every step of the way, from prenatal visits, to classes, to the birth, and postpartum checkups. Said one father, whose son was born in a hospital and whose daughter in a birthing center, "I felt I was infinitely more involved at the birthing center—particularly during the birth itself. At the birthing center, my wife was in a normal, old-fashioned brass bed, with no stirrups, so I was holding up one of her legs while she pushed the baby out. Afterwards, I got to sleep over in the bed and we went home the following afternoon."

Although birthing centers permit older siblings to be present at the birth, this is a highly controversial topic. There is strong evidence that many children find it upsetting and some midwives actively discourage it. However, it has received good reviews from some parents (and children) who have done it. Brian, a twenty-seven-year-old contractor and father of three, described the experience of his family at the birth of their third child in New York's Childbearing Center: "The two kids [ages five and three] saw the birth and the looks on their faces were really wonderful. As soon as the head emerged, my second son said, 'Look, baby sister.' They knew exactly what was going on and where the baby came from. When kids don't see the birth and the mother comes home out of the blue with a new baby, they think you went out shopping and picked up this strange kid and now they have to share everything with him. Or they think maybe you got another kid because they were being a bad boy. But since my kids were there at birth, they didn't go through any of this. The kids have a lot more respect for each other and I think it started from seeing the birth. It definitely has a powerful and positive effect on them." Brian and his wife had arranged a "coach" for the boys to bring them to the birthing center and play with them there during most of the labor. They felt there was no reason for the boys to be subjected to the entire labor, so they came in only for periodic visits until the birth itself. For Brian's older son, this was the second birth he had witnessed.

The decision about whether to have your kids present at birth is one that you should weigh carefully. Do you really think they can handle a situation that many adults find quite wrenching? Do you and your partner really want the distraction of having the other kids around during this experience that requires supreme concentration? Is there someone reliable who can look after them and possibly take them home if the labor is prolonged or if there is any serious problem? In making this decision, you'll want to discuss the subject with each other, with the staff at the birthing center, and if possible, with other families who have had their older children present. Ultimately, the most important consideration is the children and what impact the experience might have on them. If you have deep-seated doubts, you may be better off involving them in the new baby's arrival in other ways; for example, by reading them books for children about childbirth or letting them help you arrange the baby's room.

Today, fewer than 1 percent of American babies are born at the 140 or so birthing centers around the country. But, as expecting parents continue to seek childbirth that is at once humane, noninterventional, and safe, it is likely that birthing centers will increase in numbers. If you want more information on the subject or would like to locate the birth center

Preparing for the Birth

nearest your home, contact the National Association of Childbirthing Centers, R.D. #1, Box 1, Perkiomenville, PA 18074; 215-234-8068.

Home-Birth

It's odd that home-birth now strikes so many people as a really daring choice because, until relatively recently, home-birth was the norm in America, and it remains the norm in most of the world today. According to Edward Shorter in *A History of Women's Bodies* (Basic Books, 1982), before 1900 only unwed mothers and poor women gave birth in American hospitals, and as late as 1935 only 37 percent of American births were taking place in hospitals. But hospital birth has become so prevalent over the past half century that we tend to picture home-birth as something remote and quaint, like a scene out of a Western with the mother groaning and tossing in a big four-poster bed and lots of hot water boiling away on the cast-iron stove and the harried doc galloping up just in time... as the nervous father, pacing in the parlor, pricks up his ears to catch the little critter's first wails.

But leap from the imagined past to the real present, and the associations of home-birth suddenly turn from romantic to risky. As noted earlier, the first question that pops into most of our minds when we contemplate home-birth is: Is it safe? We also wonder: Is it legal? What if something goes wrong? How do you keep everything sterile?

The question of safety, the most important in most people's minds, has not yet been answered satisfactorily. The American College of Obstetricians and Gynecologists flatly says no, and one of its executive directors has branded home-birth "child abuse." Home-birth advocates from NAPSAC (see above) and other organizations claim that it is as safe or *safer* than hospital birth for normal, low-risk mothers and babies. And certainly home-birth has advantages over the hospital in that the parents are free to manage the birth as they see fit, that all medical interventions (many of which are potentially damaging for normal births and yet routinely administered anyway) are eliminated, that the risk of infection—always present in hospital nurseries and maternity wards—is diminished, and that the disruption to family life is avoided. The last point can be especially significant if there are other children: it seems reasonable to assume that if the new sibling is born at home there will be less resentment and confusion than if the mother disappears for several days only to return with a new baby. The father's role is also magnified in home-birth since he, in effect, becomes the substitute for the hospital staff. There are no doctors and nurses telling him what to do, no hospital procedures for him to deal with: he's calling the shots in his own home, he's making the decisions and supporting his partner every step of the way. With home-birth there is no need to determine the precise moment labor sets in, no rushing back and forth between home and hospital, and no need to adjust to a foreign environment. You have all the comforts of home right there. And when your baby is born, there is no intrusive hospital staff around to inhibit the expression of your emotions. You can be yourself with your family from the instant your child is born.

On the legal question, yes, home-birth is legal in the United States, but the individual states regulate who may legally attend a home-birth. Generally, a nurse midwife cannot practice in this country unless she works in conjunction with a physician. Physicians can deliver babies at home, but for both philosophical and practical reasons there are very few who will. (Some doctors have been fired from their hospital jobs for attending home-births.) Thus, it may be difficult to find someone medically and legally qualified to attend a home-birth in your area. Many couples turn to lay midwives (who may be practicing outside the law), and as a result it is thought that American home-births are actually underreported. If you need help finding an attendant for a home-birth, if you want more information on the legal issues relevant to your state, or if you want to learn more about arranging for a safe home-birth, you can contact the following organizations:

Association for Childbirth at Home, International
P.O. Box 39498
Los Angeles, CA 90039
213-667-0839

Preparing for the Birth

American College of Home Obstetrics
664 North Michigan Avenue
Chicago, IL 60611
312-642-6414

La Leche League International
9616 Minneapolis Ave.
Franklin Park, IL 60131
312-455-7730

NAPSAC, International (National Association of Parents and Professionals for Safe Alternatives in Childbirth)
P.O. Box 267
Marble Hill, MO 63764
314-238-2010

If you're contemplating a home-birth, you should plan ahead of time what to do in case of emergency. This means getting to the closest hospital that will admit you. (Many hospitals will turn couples away who are having complications in home-birth.) The safest course is to have a relationship with a physician or obstetrician with admitting privileges at a hospital and to know your way around that hospital beforehand so you can get right to the emergency room (or wherever you're supposed to go). You should arrange to have a pediatrician check out the baby within twenty-four hours of birth. And it's also a good idea for mothers who bear their babies at home to breastfeed since this will reduce both the baby's chances of getting an infection and the mother's chances of hemorrhaging after the birth.

Maybe in the Western movies all they need for home-birth is boiling water and clean sheets, but for maximum safety and comfort you're going to have to lay in certain supplies and make certain preparations. You are going to have to educate yourselves about labor and delivery, which means taking childbirth classes for starters, and you are going to have to read and study so that you are aware of the special considerations for successful home-birth (see the list of books below). It's also an excellent idea to talk with people who have had their babies at home. They can share invaluable advice, both practical and emotional. You're going to have to get your home in order. It's best to have a good, hard mattress on your bed and to protect it with a plastic sheet or newspaper (which, though it seems unclean actually inhibits germ growth), and disposable bed pads. A big pot of boiling water is still essential for sterilizing instruments, and there should be plenty of rubbing alcohol and antiseptic solution or surgical soap for the birth attendant and mother to use to wash their hands. Some birth attendants like to have an infant ear syringe to suction mucus from the newborn baby's mouth and a pair of sterilized shoelaces with which to tie off the umbilical cord. Everyone who comes in contact with the mother at the time of the birth should wear freshly washed clothes and be aware of the importance of good hygiene. And, of course, you'll want receiving blankets and clothes for the baby.

This is only a partial list of the preparations necessary for safe home-birth. There are a number of books on the subject that will be of use in guiding your decision and helping you prepare. These include *Home Birth* by Alice Gilgoff (Coward, 1978), *Home Birth Book* by Charlotte and Fred Ward (Doubleday, 1977), *Childbirth at Home* by Marion Sousa (Prentice-Hall, 1977), *Birth at Home* by Sheila Kitzinger (Penguin, 1979), and various publications put out by the organizations listed above.

Home-birth is clearly not for everyone. Even if it harmonizes with your philosophical views on the "ideal birth experience," you and your partner may simply feel too nervous about the "what ifs." You may find you are stuck on the impossible question: How could we live with ourselves if something goes wrong that a doctor in a hospital might have prevented? If you can't get past this issue, perhaps it's best to conclude that home-birth is not for you. Peace of mind plays a tremendous part in how a couple deals with labor and delivery, and ultimately you and your partner are better off choosing the birth method and environment with which you feel safest, most comfortable, and most at home.

Preparing for the Birth 151

Easing the Pain

According to the Bible, the pain of childbirth is all Adam and Eve's fault. "In sorrow thou shalt bring forth children" was part of the punishment God meted out to Eve for eating the forbidden fruit ("thy husband shall rule over thee" was another burden that fell to her lot). Ever since then, pain has accompanied childbirth. For some fortunate women, the pain is of short duration and mild intensity; for others it is akin to the sensation of sex. But for many women, and particularly for first-time mothers, labor can be a prolonged agony too intense to handle with the breathing and relaxation techniques of prepared childbirth.

Today, many couples are reluctant to turn to medically administered painkillers during childbirth, and there are some very good reasons: all drugs cross the placenta and affect the baby; some anesthetics make it impossible for the mother to push; others have unpleasant side effects. But there are times when a painkiller of some sort will benefit the baby by speeding up the labor, and the proper anesthetic administered at the correct time can transform the experience of childbirth from a torment to a joy.

Because the drugs and anesthetics are available, and since many doctors still routinely offer some of them even when the parents have expressed the desire for a drug-free birth, it's a good idea to know what they are and what they do, both to mother and baby. The two main categories of childbirth medications are analgesia and anesthesia, the distinction being that analgesics deaden the sensation of pain, whereas anesthetics either remove all sensation in a specific part of the body (local) or render one unconscious (total). Following is a rundown of the most common drugs in each category.

Analgesia

Occasionally a doctor will prescribe mild tranquilizers to a women in early labor to reduce tension and calm jittery nerves. These relaxants include Valium, Miltown, and sparine. Valium has the odd side effect of causing amnesia during labor, with 12 percent of the women who have taken it initially unable to recall whether they have delivered a boy or a girl.

Demerol, a narcotic, is the painkiller most commonly given to ease the pain of labor. In most cases, it will be injected into the muscles of a woman in active labor. It will take effect in about fifteen minutes and its effects will last for around two hours. Some women say Demerol is great: it relaxes them, taking just enough of the edge off the pain to enable them to coast through labor. But for many, Demerol causes more discomfort than it relieves: dizziness, blurred vision, nausea to the point of vomiting, and a general feeling of unpleasant wooziness and emotional depression are very common reactions to the drug. Often Demerol makes a woman sleep between contractions, which can really throw off her concentration and her ability to prepare for the pain.

For you, the expectant father, the experience of seeing your partner all "doped up" on this narcotic can be quite upsetting. Even more upsetting is having a doped-up newborn, which will happen if the mother has been given an analgesic too soon before the baby's birth. Ideally, the last dosage of any drug should be given long enough in advance of the birth (about five hours) so that the baby can excrete it back into the mother's system. If given too soon before birth, the drug will still be in the baby's system and the newborn will have to metabolize the drug him- or herself. Tranquilizers may make a newborn floppy and sluggish, and Demerol could make it difficult for the baby to breathe.

Anesthesia

There was a time when American women were "knocked out" with general anesthesia for delivery and awakened when it was all over, but that time is past. Nowadays, the anesthetics used for labor and delivery are regional or local—the former blocks sensation in the entire lower half of the body

Preparing for the Birth

and the latter acts only on a specific area, such as the cervix or perineum.

Of the regional anesthetics, the two most common types used today are epidural and spinal. An anesthesiologist administers an epidural through a catheter inserted into the lower back near the spinal cord (epidural means at the dura, the outermost membrane covering the spinal cord). He or she will leave this catheter in place so that any additional doses of the anesthetic can be administered through it. A skilled anesthesiologist will localize the epidural just right so that the woman loses sensation in her lower half (she'll have a numbness similar to that of dental anesthetics) but remains fully awake. Epidural is very often the anesthetic used for cesarean sections. Lots of women report very positive experiences with this form of anesthetic. One mother I know said the epidural really transformed her labor: she was having agonizing back labor (see the next chapter) without making any progress until the anesthetic was administered and then she really enjoyed the whole thing and moved along quickly. But there are dangers and disadvantages. With the lower half of her body numb, a woman may have a very hard time pushing the baby out and thus a forceps delivery (Chapter 7) may become necessary. An epidural lowers a woman's blood pressure, and thus decreases the amount of oxygen going to the baby; it may slow the labor down and cause postdelivery backaches for some women. The full effects of epidural anesthetic on babies are still being studied.

Spinal anesthesia is injected directly into the spinal fluid in the lower back, numbing a woman's lower half. It will be given only during the last stage of labor, the pushing stage, which for many women is the best part. Like epidural, a spinal makes pushing quite difficult, lowers blood pressure, may slow down labor, and often means the baby must be extracted with forceps. After delivery, a woman who has received a spinal must lie flat on her back for eight hours or else she may suffer an excruciating "spinal headache."

The three most frequently administered local anesthetics are the paracervical, the pudendal, and the perineal blocks. A paracervical block, given in the first stage of labor as a series of anesthetic injections around the mother's cervix, numbs sensation in the region of the cervix. It is a highly controversial anesthetic because it slows the heartbeats of three babies out of ten, and some babies have died as a consequence. For this reason, the paracervical block is used less frequently than it once was. The perineal and pudendal blocks are often used for episiotomy (see earlier) because both numb the area between the vagina and the anus. In addition the pudendal block may be administered at the time of delivery to ease the pain in the vagina. Since these two forms of anesthesia will be given only at the time of the birth, neither helps with the pain of a prolonged labor.

Child-care Arrangements: Planning Ahead

As the pregnancy nears term, many of us have a tendency to think in terms of endings rather than beginnings. Those interminable nine months are over at last! But, of course, the end of the pregnancy is also the beginning of your baby's life as a person, and the beginning of your lives as parents. Caring for a baby, as you're about to discover, is a lot harder and a lot more time-consuming than caring for an unborn fetus. Caring for a baby presents you and your partner with major decisions, such as who is going to be the primary care-taker, or if the mother works, how soon must she return, or how much time is the father willing or able to take off from his work? Once both parents return to work (assuming this is the chosen or necessary arrangement), how will the day-care be managed: full-time baby-sitter, day-care center, family home situation? If the mother is planning to quit work to raise the baby herself, how does she feel about this? How *you* feel about it? What impact will it have on your finances or on your own involvement with the baby?

These are tough, practical, nuts-and-bolts questions, and there is no shirking them. In this day and age, few couples have the luxury of taking a "wait-and-see" attitude. Employers demand firm commitments from and impose strict timetables on their pregnant workers; most day-care centers, especially those for infants, have long waiting lists; and finding a reliable

Preparing for the Birth

baby-sitter takes time. Getting your child-care arrangements in place well before the baby is born not only makes good practical sense, it is often imperative.

Chapter 12 covers the subject of child care in depth, exploring each of the major options currently available to new parents. If you're wondering about how to make child-care arrangements, Chapter 12 will answer your questions. If you're *not* wondering about child-care arrangements, maybe you should be. All too often the whole burden—both logistical and emotional—of this decision falls on the new mother, and rare is the new mother who can shoulder this burden happily by herself. Choosing a childbirth method is crucial to your joint experience of your baby's birth day; but the repercussions of the decision about the baby's daily care may go on for years. It's up to both of you to think about and plan for the arrangement you feel is best. And the best time to begin is several months before the baby is born.

Thoughts on Attending the Birth

The one aspect of childbirth today that representatives of (almost) all the childbirth factions agree on is the desirability of having the father attend the birth. As social scientist Rob Palkovitz points out in the *Child Development* journal (April 1985), where the father in the delivery room was once viewed as "an unnecessary source of infection," he is now welcomed as "an essential source of affection for both the mother and newborn." In fact, not only are dads welcomed at the birth, they are really *expected* to attend, and, as Palkovitz says, many men perceive a subtle message that if they are not intimately involved in the pregnancy and delivery, they are somehow second-rate. Men who either can't or don't want to attend the birth worry that they won't bond with their children as quickly or as closely as men who watched their babies being born. There's this anxiety that missing the birth of your child is like missing the first ten minutes of a mystery movie: you never quite get what's going on.

People are beginning to question these assumptions. There is no doubt that men have found being present at the birth of their children to be one of the most moving experiences life has to offer—if they *want* to have this experience. Some men don't. They feel pressured into attending when inside they really feel that they have no business being there. Some men have no desire to see their partners in pain; others are put off by the "blood and mess" of childbirth. And many men who planned on attending are unable to because the hospital excludes them from cesarean birth, or because of business commitments, illness, or other circumstances. If you are one of these men, don't worry about it. According to Palkovitz's review of the literature on the subject in *Child Development*, there is no hard evidence that indicates that bonding with the baby results from attending the birth. Attending the birth "is neither necessary nor sufficient for the establishment of positive father-infant relationships," he concludes. Interestingly, the relationship that gains most from a father's birth attendance is that between the mother and father. Women appreciate having their men stand by them, and men feel closer to their women for supporting them through the transition to motherhood. The conclusion that more and more writers and educators in the field are drawing is that a man can play a wide range of roles during the pregnancy, birth, and parenthood, and still be a good father.

The message is: Do what you feel comfortable doing and don't blame yourself if your instincts lead you in a different direction from your friends and relatives. The superinvolved father has become something of a media hero in recent years, but superinvolvement may simply not be your style. Fine. You may be super at other things, things that could ultimately be just as important in establishing good relationships with your children.

A final word of advice on the subject of birth attendance: Keep an open mind. All the childbirth educators, midwives, nurses, and social workers I spoke with found that some of the most reluctant, uninterested, suspicious expecting fathers turned out to be the most helpful and enthusiastic at the time of the birth. "Even though they had real doubts about attending, they are transformed by the experience," one nurse-midwife said. "Just seeing what happens at the birth is plenty to

Preparing for the Birth

turn them around." So, if at all possible, keep your options open.

Although it may not be crucial to establishing a good bond, witnessing the birth of one's child *is* transforming. For men who attend, it is the focal point of their transformation into fathers. If you're planning to be there or wondering about it, read on. The next chapter examines the father's role in labor and birth.

7. Labor and Birth: The Father's Role

"As my daughter was being delivered, mostly I had this feeling of being totally helpless and scared. I was frightened by the changes in my wife's facial expressions and at seeing her in so much pain. I was dizzy. Though we had taken childbirth preparation classes, when it really happened I felt 'What is going on here?' But then, when the baby was out, there came this monster feeling of being IN AWE. It was like a great big slap across the face, a feeling of being shook so that I couldn't see straight. I wanted to jump up and grab her. It definitely made a big difference in how I felt toward the baby. I can't understand anyone who doesn't go in."—Pat, age thirty, on the birth of his daughter.

"I felt there was nothing I could do to change what was going on. My role really was to keep my wife calm. I did what I could to keep timing the contractions, stay on top of the details. I was not frightened but I was concerned. I was concerned that the doctor wasn't there yet, and worried that no one was paying attention to me. When my son was born, I felt relief more than anything else—relief that he was born and that my wife would feel normal again. The focus of my feelings during the birth was really with my wife's welfare."—Richard, age twenty-six, on the birth of his son.

"For my first son, my wife had progressed to six centimeters and then stopped. She had been in labor for eighteen hours and they decided to do a c-section. At that point it was

Labor and Birth: The Father's Role

really a relief to have it over with. The second child was also delivered by c-section. It was pretty relaxed this time. I could be there. It was fun. I cut the umbilical cord and then I carried the baby to the nursery. It really makes no difference to me now that the boys were delivered by cesarean. I believe the main goal is to get healthy kids. The only negative is that it took my wife longer to recover."—Philip, age thirty, on the birth of his two sons.

Awe. Fear. Relief. Helplessness. Concern. Fun. Love. Can you think of any other event in life that elicits all of these emotions—sometimes all at once? Witnessing the birth of one's child is one of those unforgettable, overwhelming "peak" experiences—maybe even *the* peak experience of a man's life. It leaves even the most eloquent men fumbling with words like "incredible," "awesome," "amazing." One friend of mine, a modest, sober book editor, described it as "the greatest natural high I've ever had." I wondered at his choice of phrase until I went through the experience myself a few months later. For weeks after our baby's birth, I went around like a new convert to some cult trying to describe the indescribable. I found it even more satisfying to play back in my mind each stage of the miracle like a movie I had memorized. I've talked to fathers who, years later, can recall the most minute details of what they said and thought and did during the labor and birth. They say women forget the pain of childbirth, but it seems men never forget the sheer wonder of their own births into fatherhood.

The "wonder," however, includes a lot that is not so wonderful. There's the helplessness and fear that Pat, the diemaker from Minneapolis quoted above, experienced. There's the ordeal that Jim, a clinical psychologist who lives outside San Francisco, went through as his wife failed to progress beyond six centimeters for the better part of a day. There's the physical exhaustion of staying up all night and the emotional exhaustion of seeing your partner in agony as yet another contraction grips her and the private, inner exhaustion of wondering what you're doing and whether you're doing any good. There's the worry about complications and sometimes the anger at the hospital staff. And there's the pressure of "keeping it together" when you might feel like falling apart. Attending a birth, as one book points out, is not a spectator sport. The term "coach" is apt for the role a participating father plays: you're not playing the game, but you're *involved* —vitally involved—every step of the way. "I couldn't have done it without him" is the line you'll hear more often than any other from new mothers who had their men beside them. Yes, you're on the sidelines, but your presence is crucial to the game. Mother and baby are undergoing a biological event, but the birth very much happens to you, too.

Like just about everything having to do with children, there is a practical and emotional side to birth. The practical side for the father includes helping to decide when it's time to go to the hospital (or call the midwife for a home-birth), arranging transportation, running interference with the hospital staff, providing the right kind of support, knowing what stage of labor the mother is in. The emotional side is largely a matter of reacting—to the onset of labor, to the hospital procedures, to the way the laboring mother is dealing with her pain, to the emergence of the head and face and body of one's child, to the first contact with this newly born person. Together these two aspects add up to a man's experience of the birth of his child. That's what this chapter is all about.

Labor: Is She or Isn't She?

How do we know when labor has begun? This question preoccupies many expecting couples in the last weeks before the due date. Luckily, medical science has a precise answer. There are three signs that labor has begun or will begin fairly soon.

The Bloody Show

The cervix is the narrow end of the uterus that opens out into the vagina. Shaped rather like a neck, it remains closed and hard throughout the pregnancy, blocking off the uterus with a plug of mucus. As the time for the baby's birth nears,

Labor and Birth: The Father's Role

the cervix begins to soften and stretch (it must become fully effaced—that is, completely flattened out—and fully dilated —that is, entirely open—before the baby is born). During the softening and stretching process, the mucous plug may be discharged through the vagina and appear as a pinkish blob known as the bloody show. For some women, this is a sign that labor is at hand, but for others the actual labor may not begin for two or three weeks. Other women discharge the mucous plug during active labor and never really notice it. So the bloody show does not necessarily signal that full-fledged contractions are going to start at once, but it is a sign that things are happening. It's your signal to be prepared, but not to drop everything and charge off to the hospital. Experts advise you and your partner to continue your normal activities, with the awareness that the baby could come any time now.

Breaking of the Water Bag

If your partner has a clear, odorless fluid leaking out of her—either in a gush or a slow trickle—this means that her bag of waters (or amniotic sac) has broken. The medical term for this is "ruptured membranes," which sounds rather dire but isn't. It just means that the baby's head is pressing down on the surrounding membranes with enough force to break them. The clear liquid leaking out is amniotic fluid, the element your baby has been living in for the past nine months. Breaking of the water bag usually means that true labor is about to start— and even if it doesn't start all by itself, most obstetricians today will induce labor (get it going artificially by giving the mother pitocin, a chemical that triggers contractions) soon after the membranes rupture. The reason for this is that there's an increased risk of infection once the amniotic sac is broken. In addition, there's a risk that, if the baby's head has not settled securely into the cervix, the waters will force the umbilical cord through the cervix and cut off the baby's oxygen. So, if her waters have broken, let the doctor know right away; he or she will probably want to check things out. Also, if the fluid leaking out is not clear but green and foul-smelling, you should have the situation checked out quickly. This means that the baby is passing meconium (the newborn's first stools) into the amniotic fluid, a sign of fetal distress. In this case, the doctor or midwife may want the mother to come into the hospital and stay there until the baby is born.

Breaking of the water bag is not something to worry about. It's a perfectly normal early signal of labor, although in the majority of cases the water bag doesn't break until contractions have begun (sometimes the doctor will break them during labor). There is no risk that all the amniotic fluid will leak out because a woman's body replaces it naturally. Stories about women causing floods when their waters break are exaggerated. Sanitary napkins and perhaps a towel are quite enough to soak up the fluid. There is no need for you to wear a raincoat to bed, as one joke has it, although a plastic sheet might not be a bad idea. Once the membranes have ruptured, you should not have intercourse, and your partner should not take a bath or use tampons.

Contractions Begin

The uterus is made of bundles of muscles and the contractions of true labor tighten these muscles in a regular, rhythmic pattern. The tightening of the uterine muscles pull up on the cervix and press the baby's head down on the cervix. This is the "work" of labor that effaces and dilates the cervix. Before your baby is born, the contractions must make the cervix paper-thin and open it ten centimeters (about four inches). When the first contractions start, your partner may not even know it. She may complain of vague aches in the lower back or she may feel as if she's getting her menstrual period. Or she may dismiss them as Braxton Hicks contractions—the "practice" contractions that the uterus goes through during pregnancy to get the muscles in shape. And, in fact, they may *be* practice contractions. At the end of pregnancy Braxton Hicks contractions can be so painful that a woman will be convinced she's in labor. The way to determine if the contractions are true labor contractions is to time them over a period of thirty to sixty minutes. If they're coming at regular intervals, she's in labor (early labor). If not, they are probably Braxton Hicks contractions. This is usually what people mean when they talk about "false" labor.

Labor and Birth: The Father's Role

If they are true labor contractions, they will begin to come at shorter intervals, to last longer, and to get stronger. This could be a gradual process or it might happen all of a sudden, with the interval decreasing from ten minutes to three minutes in half an hour. It's different for every woman and every labor. This is an important point to keep in mind throughout labor and delivery. Chances are in your childbirth preparation classes you learned about a classic "textbook" labor—and chances are that your partner's labor will seem like an entirely different ballgame. It might stop and start. The contractions might *begin* at three-minute intervals. She may not even be aware that her contractions have been working for hours and that the dilation is almost complete. Several of the men I spoke to were bitter because the classes did not prepare them for what really happened to them. This may be a fault in the classes, but it's also in the nature of the experience. Even if you've been through it before, you're not going to be fully prepared for the next time because the next time will be different. As one of the baby books wisely says: Expect the unexpected. Listen to your partner and encourage her to listen to her body.

Once your partner's labor has begun, it will pass through three stages: the first and longest stage goes from the start of labor to the full, ten-centimeter dilation of the cervix; the second stage, known as "expulsion," is the birth of the baby when the mother pushes the baby out through the birth canal; the third stage is the expulsion of the placenta. Most of the books divide stage one into three parts based on how dilated the cervix is: in the latent phase, the cervix goes to three centimeters; in active labor it progresses from four to seven; and in transition from eight to ten centimeters. Again, this is the textbook model and it's unlikely that any bells will go off announcing that active labor has commenced. Some labors are so short that the woman seems to skip stages entirely; others are so long that the stages blur together. But many people find the labels reassuring and feel a sense of progress if they can say: Now we're in the second part of stage one. There's only one rule I'll offer for labor: If it makes you and your partner feel better, do it.

Early Labor: Now What Do We Do?

When my wife was pregnant, we took two sets of childbirth preparation classes (one at the hospital, one with a private Lamaze instructor). I had read a fair amount on the subject of pregnancy, labor, and birth. I considered myself informed enough to be on top of the situation. Nonetheless, on the Friday evening two days before the baby's official due date, when my wife informed me that her water bag had broken, my rather stunned reply was: "Oh my GOD! Now what do we do?" It wasn't quite panic—but it was a long way from calm reassurance. Needless to say, I'm not recommending this as the ideal approach to the situation.

I wasn't the only one caught off guard. Despite the fact that her due date was upon us, my wife hadn't yet packed her bag, nor had we made any arrangement for our two large dogs in the event of a long in-hospital labor. In our childbirth classes, we had been taught that early labor should be a time for quiet relaxation. The teachers recommended taking a walk, if the mother-to-be felt up to it, or watching TV or listening to music, doing crossword puzzles or relaxation exercises. Instead, the two of us were flying through the house turning drawers upside down, making phone calls, and fussing about the dogs. Because, as it turned out, we didn't get any sleep that night, this last-minute frenzy was a waste of valuable energy. The moral of the story is: Be prepared. Make sure that arrangements for other children, pets, or whatever are in place, that your partner has her bags packed (see the list at the end of this section for what she should take), and, if possible, that you preregister with the hospital so you won't have to worry about that either. Being prepared means having all this together at least two weeks before the due date. Your first job as coach should be to take responsibility for getting all these things taken care of.

Once you are fairly certain that labor has begun, you face the question of when to call the doctor and/or go to the hospital. Often, this amounts to the same thing, because there's a good chance the doctor will want to check things out, which

Labor and Birth: The Father's Role

probably means doing an internal exam and hooking the laboring mother up to a fetal monitor (see Chapter 6) for a while to see how the baby is doing. If the baby is fine and the labor hasn't progressed much, you may very well be sent home and told to stay there until "something happens," that is, the contractions become more intense and closer together. This can be frustrating and, if you live far from the hospital, irritatingly inconvenient—another waste of energy. So if your partner feels comfortable and is still in early labor (that is, her contractions are coming five or more minutes apart and are lasting less than a minute), it's probably better to stay home and keep control of the situation yourselves. As Sheila Kitzinger sums up in *The Complete Book of Pregnancy and Childbirth* (Knopf, 1985), "Knowing that [the] contractions will be coming one every two minutes and will last about one minute or longer just before the baby is born may give you some perspective on [the] labor when it is just starting.... The baby cannot possibly be born when contractions are coming [every five minutes], so if you are happier at home, stay there."

An additional problem with going to the hospital too soon is that the contractions, which were coming regularly at home, may stop the instant your partner sets foot in the hospital. It may be psychological or it may have something to do with the physical environment of the hospital—the odor of disinfectant, the glaring fluorescent lights, the depressing atmosphere —that makes people tense up. In any case, an interruption in labor is demoralizing, and the doctor may insist on getting it going again artificially, that is, by giving your partner pitocin, to stimulate uterine contractions, intravenously. The so-called pit-drip wallops some women with sudden and intensely painful contractions, and for everyone it means the end of the freedom to be up and around.

Despite all the admonitions to stay home as long as possible, many couples, and especially first-time parents, jump the gun. Labor seems more advanced than it really is, or they're worried that something might go wrong, or they feel frightened and want to be near medical help. In our case I insisted on calling the obstetrician as soon as I got over my shock that the water bag had broken, and the doctor insisted we come into the hospital so he could check the baby on the fetal monitor. Everything was fine, he informed us that her cervix was "hard as a rock," and she had a long night of work ahead of her—so we should go home and stay there until something changed. We couldn't have been home more than an hour before my wife started vomiting repeatedly and trembling all over. The contractions were three minutes apart, although they were not lasting that long and were not that intense. Still, both of us got scared. Was this transition, we wondered, the stage immediately before birth? So off we sped to the hospital once more, only to be told that she was still in *very* early labor, she hadn't progressed beyond one centimeter in dilation, and that the best thing to do was walk. Which we did from midnight until 2:30 in the morning—up and down those same dreary hospital corridors. In short, we would have been better off at home, but there was no way of knowing that until afterward. There really is no right and wrong in the situation: it's a matter of personal comfort. But it's good to keep in mind that jumping the gun means you could be in for a long, boring, and exhausting haul in the hospital.

Whenever you decide it's time to go, it's going to be your job to get the two of you there. Be sure to call the doctor or midwife before you set out so they know you're coming. Labors have a way of starting at inconvenient times—during snowstorms, at rush hour, in the middle of the night, on national holidays, on the day the road crew has closed off the highway leading to the hospital—so be prepared for a longer or harder trip than usual. If you're driving, make sure your car is in good working condition, that you have enough gas, and that you know the way and any shortcuts that might speed up the trip during rush hour. If you're going by taxi, try to line up a cab company or car service ahead of time (ask around for reliable ones). If all else fails, you can always call the police and explain the situation.

When driving, don't speed, don't make sudden lurching stops, and don't panic. You *will* get to the hospital on time, your baby *won't* be born in the backseat (although if the baby is born on the way to the hospital, you can deal with this, too—see below). Concentrate on your driving: your partner needs your chauffeuring services now more than she needs

Labor and Birth: The Father's Role

your coaching. The less she has to worry about the trip, the more she will be able to focus on her labor.

What to Bring to the Hospital

For the father-to-be:

Insurance card
Checkbook and/or credit card
Childbirth education diploma or letter (some hospitals will not let dad into delivery room without proof that he has completed the course)
Watch with second hand for timing contractions
Pen and paper for writing down contraction times or journal of birth
Something to eat (sandwich, coffee, sweets)
Lightweight clothing (hospitals tend to be hot and you'll have to wear some kind of gown over your regular clothes)
Camera, flash, and film
Phone numbers of close family members

For the mother-to-be during labor:

Warm kneesocks
Sour sucking candies or lollipops to help ease dry mouth
Washcloths for dry mouth, cooling forehead
Extra pillows
Tennis ball (useful for easing pain of back labor)

For the mother-to-be during hospital stay:

Nightgowns, nursing bras, slippers, bathrobe
Toothpaste and brush, soap, makeup, and the like (let her do the packing, you carry the bag)
Books and magazines
Sanitary belt

Contact lens case, wetting solution, and glasses
Telephone and address book
Clothes for her and for baby to go home in (or you can bring these later)
Leave jewelry home

The Hospital: Admissions and Etiquette

Even though the overwhelming majority of hospitals now allow the father to be with the mother during labor and delivery, most hospitals still insist on separating the expecting parents during the admissions and prep (see previous chapter) procedures. The father is installed in some kind of waiting room, the laboring mother is seated in a wheelchair, and away she goes. For many couples this is the worst part of labor. The man is both nervous about his wife and anxious that the hospital staff has forgotten all about him (they sometimes do!), and the woman finds herself suddenly alone with her contractions, treated like a patient in a medical emergency, and subjected to procedures that are at best unpleasant (having needles poked in for blood samples) and at worst excruciating (some women's reaction to the enema).

Although this separation is part of standard procedure, many hospitals will waive it at the patient's request. And, I'd be willing to bet, the hospital staff will be much more likely to comply if the request is just that—a polite request rather than an arrogant demand. Many childbirth educators and baby books send parents into hospitals prepared to do battle. The attitude they instruct you to adopt is: *They're* going to take over our pregnancy and subject us to all these dehumanizing, dangerous high-tech procedures unless *we* stand up for ourselves and fight it out. There is some truth in this, and you do have to exercise a certain amount of vigilance if you want to have some control over the labor and birth, but my personal feeling is that courtesy and collaboration will get you what you want a lot more easily than combat. When the admissions clerk told me I'd have to wait in the lobby for my wife while she was being examined and prepped, I wanted to say: "No. She needs me and I refuse to leave her." But I thought about it

Labor and Birth: The Father's Role

for a second and instead I tried: "I'd like to stay with her. Is that possible?" The clerk called up to the maternity unit, explained my request and got the go-ahead. Battle won without the battle.

Of course, it's not always so easy, and there may be times in your partner's labor when your frustration or even anger gets the better of you. A shocking number of fathers told me stories about doctors who either failed to show up on time for the birth or who made it just in time—and in one case the mother, who was fully dilated and ready to give birth, was told to stop pushing and blow while they tried to page the hospital cafeteria. This is surely grounds for organizing a lynch mob. But until you confront a maddening situation, try not to get mad. At most hospitals, the nurses are really the ones who will be attending your partner during the labor and they can really make a huge difference in your experience. A nurse can be a valuable ally if treated with respect, humanity, and a spirit of cooperation. After all, your interests and hers coincide: you both want to get your partner through the labor and birth as quickly as possible and with the least amount of pain. And, as you may discover, many nurses view doctors and their high-handed ways with a certain amount of skepticism. By establishing solidarity with the nurses, you may get them to run interference with the doctor. It can really help you feel in control of the labor.

In dealing with the hospital, don't confuse courtesy with passivity. You have to make your wishes known. Be polite, but be assertive. If you don't know what they're putting in your partner's IV, ask, and if it's a medication she hasn't asked for and doesn't feel she needs, refuse it. If you have a request, make it clearly, positively, and immediately. Several fathers told me that their wives were given painkillers or "relaxants" (sometimes never even identified), although they had expressed a desire for a drug-free birth; few made any move to stop it. More serious was a story I heard about a woman ten days post-term whose doctor induced labor and then, when she failed to make speedy progress, insisted on a c-section so he could get home in time for dinner. The mother and father passively agreed to this possibly needless procedure.

Although my wife's labor showed no signs of slackening,

the obstetrician prescribed pitocin to "even out the contractions and speed things up." The contractions did become more regular, but they were also a lot more painful. If we had thought to object, he probably would have omitted the pit-drip. But we were passive. This brings up another point: you have to think pretty fast at times. The nurse will come bustling in with a tray of things and inject your partner with Demerol before you even know what's going on. Or they'll whip out the internal fetal monitor (see previous chapter) and attach electrodes to your baby's head in the blink of an eye. Don't just be prepared to question everything—do it, and do it before the procedures have been performed. Often the doctor or nurse has a very good reason, but often they don't—they're just doing the routine thing. Speaking up in time can stop it. And speaking up is part of *your* job as a coach.

Coaching: What It Is (... and What It Isn't)

Being a good labor coach involves a certain amount of knowledge, a certain amount of stamina, a certain amount of preparation—but mostly it involves good old common sense. Whatever reasons you might have for attending, you are fundamentally there for *her*: to be her support and her link to the "outside world" during the labor and birth. Knowledge—about the phases of labor, the changing shape of the cervix, the technical names of the various presentation positions, the pros and cons of medical technology—may help, but mostly it helps *you* understand what's going on and what the doctors and nurses are talking about. In terms of helping *her*, your best tools are attentiveness, concentration, confidence, cheerfulness, flexibility, a spirit of cooperation, and at times a thick skin so your feelings don't get bruised during some of the tenser moments. You don't have to be an expert in anything—you just have to be there mentally and physically.

What you'll actually do as a coach depends largely on the needs of your laboring partner. Jim told me his wife wanted back rubs for a while and then, at some point in labor, she didn't want him to touch her—so he didn't. Pat said his wife

Labor and Birth: The Father's Role

"put her full concentration on birthing, but when she was in pain she was grabbing out for me—and I was there largely to be a support to her." Rich felt that the "breathing helped minimally. There came a point where nothing did any good. It was her will that got her through. But my caring was the main thing I contributed. The comfort for her of knowing that family was there." Terry said he thought he was being a big help by calling out the numbers registering on the fetal monitor, giving a "play-by-play" account. "But it was too much information. It was getting her really wound up so I stopped." You can't know the right thing to do until the time comes. The methods you've used hundreds of times in the past to calm her down when she's upset—back rubs, kind words, jokes—may backfire during labor. This woman you know intimately may suddenly seem like a stranger utterly absorbed in her pain, or she may treat you like a stranger. The hours you spent practicing breathing and relaxing may seem like a total waste. The plan you made together to avoid medication may be tossed as soon as you get to the hospital. Your encouragement and excitement may be met by hostility. You may be surprised by her anger—or her strength. But, no matter how grim and strange and remote she seems, she needs you. The best thing you can do as a coach is let her call the shots and let her know that you're supporting her in the way she needs to be supported.

Although every labor and every woman's needs are different, there are a number of techniques that work at least part of the time for almost everyone. Timing contractions is one. First of all, it's a good way of determining what stage of labor she's in and, if she's in early labor, whether you should think about calling the doctor. Once active labor has started, timing the contractions can be a really helpful way of "talking her through." A number of the men I interviewed said that once they were in the hospital they used the fetal monitor to assist them in this aspect of coaching. They followed the progress of the contraction on the graph printout and could tell their partners when it was beginning, when it was peaking, and when it was coming down. Informing your partner of the progress of the contractions will give her a chance to rest—and maybe even sleep—between contractions. Remember that you time contractions from the start of one to the start of the following one: so if a contraction begins at 6:15, ends at 6:16 and 30 seconds, and the next one begins at 6:18, they are coming three minutes apart.

If you did prepared childbirth that uses breathing techniques, you will play a vital role in coaching her through the breathing, telling her when to take the deep cleansing breath, reminding her to breathe slowly, and to end the contraction with a deep breath. I remember developing a kind of patter that I would repeat each time a contraction came—something along the lines of "Take a deep one, okay, keep it slow, take another, okay it's peaking, deep, slow breaths, okay it's ending, one more, okay it's over, take a good deep breath and let it out with a sigh . . ." This worked pretty well for part of the labor, but at some point I noticed that the more I talked the more my wife would scowl. Finally, between contractions, she told me that the patter was distracting her and could I please just keep quiet. I felt a bit abashed, but from then on I spoke as little as possible, mostly to encourage her and to keep her from hyperventilating. This was not the first time she had corrected my coaching technique. Much earlier in the labor, before she had been hooked up to the fetal monitor, every time I noticed her face tensing up I'd ask "Are you having one?" and she would invariably nod. Finally she informed me rather sharply that each time I asked if she was having one, I ruined her concentration. That ended that annoying question! In general, most women prefer relative quiet from their coaches as the labor progresses: a hand squeeze and a single phrase work better than a stream of cheerful commands.

Concentration is really one of the key tools that a woman uses to deal with the pain of labor. You can't know just how important this is until you are with her at the time and you see the expression on her face. Anything you can do to help her maintain that concentration is great; any time you disrupt it, as I was doing with my questions, you're making it harder for her to handle the pain. One way of protecting that concentration is for you to run interference with the hospital staff, or, when possible, to take over some of the duties of the hospital staff yourself. Find out where the ice machine is, where the cups and washcloths are, where the extra pillows are stored so

Labor and Birth: The Father's Role

you don't have to run for the nurse every time she needs something. If two residents are having a lengthy conversation right outside her labor room and you can tell it's breaking her concentration, politely ask them to leave. If she tells you to shut up, to stop touching her, or to quit proffering wet washcloths, do so and let her know, by your positive attitude, that you're not sulking about it. The last thing she needs is to worry about your hurt feelings.

Encouragement and confidence are reliable tools of the trade for coaches, but again, there is often a right way and a wrong way. A woman who has been suffering excruciating pain for hours and is begging for an epidural does not want to hear that "she's doing great—keep it up!"; she wants you to get the doctor and see if the anesthetic can be arranged fast. On the other hand, a woman who is tired but hanging in there is going to feel better if you say, "You've dilated two centimeters in the past hour—it's really starting to move now" than if you join in her despair and agree that "this seems endless." Try to keep encouragement specific and brief, and always keep the brighter side before her, even if you're worried and exhausted yourself. Don't make promises you can't keep ("I promise the baby will come before noon," "I know you're in transition now"), but don't be brutally honest in a way that is going to upset her ("The doctor said you're stuck," "This is only the start of active labor"). Keep her focused on the present moment, the contraction that is happening now, and the relief that is coming as soon as it's over. If you get her looking down the road at the next hour of pain, she may crack.

Your physical presence is probably as or more important than what you say, and the way you touch her during labor can be enormously soothing. It can also, like the wrong kind of verbal encouragement, be annoying. Terry, the truckdriver from Saint Paul, said that when his wife had back labor he pushed the heel of his hand into her back and held on to one of her knees with the other hand so as not to push her off the bed. "That worked, but when my wrists and arms got sore and fatigued, I laid my head down on her hip. She didn't go for that at all and told me to get off." Michael, from Greeley, Colorado, coached his wife through a long and difficult labor that finally ended in cesarean section. He told me that "the breathing helped some, but just being there was the biggest help. She would reach out for me whenever a contraction was coming. I hated to see her in pain, but my being there for her to hold on to definitely gave her help." My wife and I had learned in one of the childbirth classes that "effleurage"—a light (but not ticklish) massage to the abdomen—can help the woman get through a contraction, but my wife wanted no part of that or any other kind of massage. Squeezing my hand was the only kind of touch that she could tolerate. As with everything else in labor, follow her directions in the kind of touch or massage you use.

One aspect of coaching that can be particularly hard on a man is the difference between the actual labor and what he has prepared for. You may have taken the classes, practiced your breathing and relaxing, remembered to bring her favorite picture as a focal point, and even planned out certain activities you were going to do in early labor—only to have your partner reject all of it when the time comes. Rich said that though they took the classes, the breathing and coaching techniques provided very little help: she got through mostly on willpower. Pat said that his wife's labor "did not really match up with what we learned in class: there was no chance to relax or do the breathing. The whole thing lasted three hours and it went like an instant. I was prepared to be waiting and keeping track of contractions but I never had the chance. I felt, What is going on here? I really had no control over the situation." Terry had been told in his class to wear shoes that wouldn't slip around on the hospital floor, but the shoes he choose made a squeaking sound that quickly got on his wife's nerves —so he had to remove them. We had failed to decide on a baby's name beforehand and we thought we'd bring the "Name Your Baby" book along to the hospital and go through it during the labor. But when the time came, the book lay forgotten at the bottom of the bag. Another surprise for us was the importance of the focal point. My wife said she found this aspect of the childbirth classes ridiculous and refused to use it. However, during her actual labor I noticed that every time she had a contraction she would stare fixedly at a Mary Cassatt poster of a mother bathing her child hanging directly opposite

Labor and Birth: The Father's Role

the bed. I asked her about it afterward and she said that the baby's belly button was her focal point: not only did she finally understand this technique, she found it indispensable for getting through contractions.

I'm not suggesting that you ignore all preparation, but rather that you should expect the unexpected. Even if you've already had a child, you can't predict what the next labor will be like. Use whatever works, and let go of everything that doesn't work, even if your childbirth instructor said it was important. When the time comes, you and your partner are going to invent your own childbirth methods based on her needs and your skill in coaching.

Don't try to force or control the situation. Be sensitive to your partner and be willing to change your approach as her needs change. Don't assume you know what's best for her just because you agreed on it beforehand. One childbirth educator told me about a comedy routine she had seen in which a nurse comes in to the labor room to find the mother jumping out of the bed with pain, and the husband tells the nurse, "We're fine, everything is under control and we don't want any medication." This kind of gung-ho, take-charge attitude seldom does the woman any good. In labor, mother knows best.

At the opposite extreme from the take-charge, know-it-all coaches are the worriers and wonderers. Will I do the right thing? Will I faint? Will I be able to handle seeing her in pain? Will I become disgusted? Will I know what to do? Will I get in the way? Actually, all of us have some of these concerns (including, I'd bet, the take-charge types, although they're less likely to acknowledge them). We all deal with them in different ways. One father told me that he'd had serious doubts about attending the birth because he thought he'd be squeamish, and he wondered whether he really wanted to see his wife in this situation. "But at the actual birth, there was no time to be squeamish," he said. "I felt I grew up a lot in that brief moment."

Often the things we worried about beforehand never come up, or we find we're dealing with them without even thinking about it. Childbirth educator Diana Simkin, drawing from her experience with hundreds of couples in the New York area, commented: "Men are afraid it will be bloody and disgusting, that there will be vomiting, but when they're there it just becomes part of the process. When she's nauseated, you simply hold the basin. Many men are fearful that they'll faint, and some actually do faint during the amnio [see the preceding chapter]. During labor, however, men are too busy to faint."

Simkin also found that men sometimes fear that they will be impotent to help their wives. And, in fact, a number of the fathers I spoke to felt they weren't really doing anything except squeezing their wives' hands and watching them suffer. The point to keep in mind, however, is that often this is enough. "You assume an importance beyond what you physically do," says Simkin. "You're more important than you know." And studies have borne this out: women who have coaches have easier labors and turn to drugs less often. One father worried he wasn't doing much to help until he thought about what the experience would have been like if she'd had to go through it alone. "All ladies need their husbands with them at a time like this," he concluded. Don't be discouraged if your partner ignores you or even turns on you at times during the labor. Very often the positive feedback doesn't come until it's all over—but when the mother is able to praise her coach, her praise is lavish.

The worries, for the most part, can be put to rest, but there are also real problems that coaches experience during labor and birth. There's the stress—both physical and psychological—of total concentration that must often be sustained for hours. No, it's nothing like the agony of labor itself, but still, it takes its toll. Men seldom faint, but some do get lightheaded or trembly. "There was all this fear and adrenaline and fatigue," one father told me, "and all the things happening to her so fast and having no control over the situation. I was dizzy. I had to get ice water and washcloths from the nurse to calm *me* down."

If you're feeling queasy, don't blame yourself—and don't try to be stoic and hide it. Sit down, take a break, get a bite to eat, or take a walk outside. It's the uninterrupted tension of labor that can be the hardest thing to bear, the endless hours of telling her to breathe slowly every four minutes and watching her face seize up with pain and worrying about how she's taking it and how the baby's taking it and whether the baby

Labor and Birth: The Father's Role

will *ever* arrive. Her break may be in the form of Demerol; your break could be a short stroll down the hospital corridor. Just tell her that you're going and how long you expect to be gone.

There are men who resent the position coaching puts them in—not just the helplessness but the sense they have of entering into a sort of conspiracy to deny their partners relief from the pain. They feel they're supposed to say "You can do it," while inside they're crying out "Why? Why am I standing here and watching you suffer and actually encouraging you to suffer more?" Some men, because of this experience, question whether they would attend another birth; others revise their opinion of the benefits of prepared childbirth. There is no easy answer to this problem because there is no easy way of "handling" the pain. The pressure very often comes from the outside: men and women feel they have to live up to some ideal set for them by their friends, by their childbirth instructors, by the hospital staff. It may be difficult to throw off these pressures and confront your own needs, but it's always worth trying. There is no such thing as *failing* as a coach, just as no laboring mothers fail. The goal is not to have a model, drug-free, supermellow labor and delivery; the goal is to have a healthy baby and mother and for both of you to feel good about the birth of that baby. Your presence is your commitment to that goal. Your success comes from giving her whatever kind of support she needs.

Coaching Through the Stages and Phases of Labor

There is no mistaking the three basic stages of labor: stage one, the dilation of the cervix; stage two, the birth of the baby; stage three, the expulsion of the placenta. It's the three phases of stage one (early labor, active labor, and transition) that give people trouble. Every mother passes through these phases, but not every mother (or father) is aware of what phase she is in or when. Women with short easy labors may sleep through early and most of active labor, arrive at the hospital in transition, and have the baby in a matter of minutes. Women with prolonged, difficult labors may say that the pain was relentless and monotonous from start to finish. But, although the textbook labor exists only in textbooks, chances are your partner's experience will correlate at least in part and at times to the model. As she progresses through labor, her needs and moods and attitude will change, and so will your role as coach.

Early (or warm-up or latent) labor is when the first contractions come, usually at intervals of about five minutes, and the cervix begins to dilate. For first babies, this can go on for eight or nine hours, but the pain is usually manageable. Encourage your partner to walk around during this stage of labor. It helps get the contractions going, is good for her circulation, and lessens the time she'll be confined to a bed.

The real work of labor kicks in with active labor, when the contractions start to come on strong and the cervix dilates from four to seven centimeters. Women who are fairly relaxed, communicative, and physically active in early labor often undergo a mood change when the contractions begin to intensify. Many retreat into themselves, devoting their full concentration to coping with the pain and then resting between contractions. Communication with you, the coach, may cease, so it can be pretty hard to know what she needs or what you should do. If you sense there may be something else you can do but don't know what, try asking her between contractions. Encourage her to shift positions occasionally, but not to thrash about restlessly. Textbook active labor lasts three to six hours for first babies and one to two hours for subsequent babies. Contractions last forty-five to sixty seconds.

Transition, the climax of labor, is the hardest phase on both mother and coach. The contractions are strong and so frequent they may almost seem continuous. The mother may start to vomit, tremble uncontrollably, and experience changes in body temperature. Just as drastic are the mood changes. A woman who was grim, silent, focused, and controlled during active labor may lose it during transition; she may start shouting for help; she may get bitchy and turn on her coach. After laboring all night with nothing but a dose or two of Demerol, my wife declared she couldn't take this anymore: she demanded an epidural and ordered me to get help. That was her

Labor and Birth: The Father's Role

transition. Another woman I heard about announced that she was going home, that she had decided to call the whole thing off and not have the baby after all. This is another classic response to transition. Men report their wives won't let them touch them, that they tell them to shut up or order them to stop saying, "You're doing great."

Transition sounds pretty dreadful, and it is, but it does have one terrific positive side: it is the shortest phase of labor (lasting anywhere from five minutes to two hours) and it means you're in the home stretch. Transition leads to the "pushing" stage of labor, which leads directly to the baby's birth. The pain is intense, but it's not going to get any worse. Transition is the light at the end of the tunnel, and just knowing this can be a tremendous relief, psychologically if not physically. You can help coach your partner through transition by reminding her that it means the baby is close to birth. For almost all women, this makes the pain more bearable. It also may make anesthetics unnecessary. In our case, when my wife asked for an epidural, I felt it was better to support her in this demand (even though I hoped she wouldn't have one). The doctor said okay, but he said he wanted to do an internal exam first. He found she was nine centimeters dilated—and we all instantly forgot about the anesthesia. The woman who insisted on going home only needed a single dose of Demerol to take her through to delivery.

Because a woman in transition cannot always feel when a contraction is subsiding, you can help by keeping her informed. That way she'll know when she can get a breather. It also helps some women in this very difficult stage to have their coaches breathing with them: they'll focus on your breathing patterns and use them as a guide. This can be quite exhausting, so pace yourself. And make sure neither of you hyperventilates. If you do hyperventilate, sit down and either lower your head between your knees for a minute or breathe into your cupped hands. It's probably a good idea not to talk about how it's all going to be over in an hour, but to take one contraction at a time. Even though transition may only last half an hour, this time-span can seem unendurable to a woman in agony. Somehow it's easier to face the sixty seconds on each individual contraction as it peaks and slackens off. Remember: each contraction is now bringing her closer to birth. A woman in transition who refuses to hear how well she's doing may respond more positively to a comment like "This is horrible! I can't believe how hard you're working." She'll let you know what she wants to hear. No matter how snappish and irrational she becomes, try to keep control of your own feelings. Don't take it personally and remember, both of you will be an awful lot more cheerful quite soon.

As a woman's cervix nears full dilation and the baby moves down toward the birth canal, she will probably feel an overwhelming urge to push. The baby is pressing against her anus and she feels that if she doesn't push, she'll explode. This is the point at which you instruct her to blow out and then run for the nurse. The blowing will keep her from pushing and the nurse will get someone to check her dilation. The danger of pushing too soon is that if the cervix is not fully dilated, the pushing may make it swell or cause it to tear. If she is fully dilated and gets the go-ahead, a nurse will instruct her on pushing technique and your role will shift from worried hand-holder to exuberant cheerleader as you encourage her to push the baby out. This is a magical moment. You've emerged from the long night of stage one labor into the wonder of stage two: birth.

Pushing, especially with a first baby or a very large baby, is not exactly a picnic. It's extremely hard work and requires immense physical energy at a time when most women are already drained. But the majority of women say it comes as a giant relief because at last they can fight back. Instead of lying there passively while contractions grip their bodies, they can work *with* the contractions. For both of you there comes a sense that something is FINALLY happening. In your excitement and cheering, don't forget that your partner still needs you for encouragement, support, and calming. Pushing can take as little as five minutes or as long as two hours. A new nurse (the "pushing nurse") may come in to teach (or remind) your wife how to push effectively and to show you what to do to help. One father I talked to said he counted to ten while his wife was pushing and she found this helpful. Another worried that his wife was pushing so hard she might pass out. The doctor assured him that this never happens.

Labor and Birth: The Father's Role

In long pushing sessions, despair and exhaustion may take over. Or it may go incredibly fast. Our bouncy enthusiastic "pushing nurse" kept saying how fantastically my wife was doing, until finally I decided this was the standard line she used on everyone. Then she pointed out the tiny strip of baby's scalp visible (it comes and goes at first with the contractions) and I realized she was being honest—my wife *was* doing a fabulous job.

At some point during the pushing stage, you will be instructed to change into a scrub suit (hospital gown, trousers, special booties for your shoes, cap, mask) that is required garb in most hospital delivery rooms. This can be a maddening moment. As Rich, the quality control inspector from Minneapolis, put it, "I was worried enough as it was and I was nervous about getting into the gown at that moment. I was really clumsy about it, especially the booties. It added an element of anxiety at the end." I worried that I wouldn't be able to find the changing room and, being a New Yorker, worried that someone would steal my wallet, which I had to leave behind. Then, as I was trying to get the five-inches-too-large pants to stay up, I decided the baby had been born and I rushed out. To avoid this last-minute frenzy, ask if you can change ahead of time, preferably before transition starts. After you've changed, wash your hands thoroughly so you'll be as germ-free as possible when you first hold your baby—which you'll be doing quite soon.

Although some hospitals allow women to give birth in the labor room, the standard practice is to move her into a delivery room when a section of the baby's head appears at the vagina (of course, in birthing rooms and birthing centers, the standard practice is for the woman to labor and give birth in the same room, as noted in Chapter 6). This is a moment of supreme excitement and also sometimes chaos and unexpected pain. Don't lose track of your partner's needs in the hubbub. The move from labor bed to stretcher to delivery table is usually hard on her. Stay with her and try to direct and help the hospital staff so she feels the least discomfort. One father I talked to said his wife was transferred to a wheelchair to go to the delivery room, a move that caused her severe pain. "I wondered why they had to do it this way," he said, but he didn't interfere. It's possible he could have spared her this pain if he'd said something. Before leaving the labor room, take along a pillow to prop her up on the delivery table, her glasses if she wears them, and if you're planning to photograph the birth, don't forget your camera.

The delivery room can come as quite a shock after the dimly lit, quiet, and private (or semiprivate) labor room. "The lights were so bright," said Terry. "They were really irritating to her, and she insisted on having them dimmed." It's more than the lights that can be irritating and alienating—it's the machinery, the delivery table, which looks like a medieval instrument of torture, and the sudden appearance of medical personnel—anesthesiologist, resident, other nurses, and, one hopes, the obstetrician. This is no joke: several fathers I interviewed said they worried whether the obstetrician would show up in time and one father said the resident had to do the delivery because the doctor was nowhere to be found; he arrived only in time to finish stitching a perineal tear.

The noise and action in the delivery room may distract your partner and thus make it harder for her to handle the contractions, which are still coming, although not as quickly as in transition, or the sudden change may alarm her so much that the contractions stop. Your presence and support are as important now as at any time during the labor.

You may feel that events have been taken out of your hands as your wife is settled onto the table, her legs put in stirrups, her body draped with sterile sheets that you're not supposed to touch; but, even with this crowd of medical personnel buzzing around and giving orders, you can still talk to her and help her make her wishes known. It sounds strange, but a woman giving birth often feels left out: everyone else is busy doing *something* and the coach may be totally wrapped up with watching the baby's head begin to emerge. Not only is everyone ignoring her, but, because of the size of her abdomen and her position, she cannot see herself give birth. She really may have little idea of what's going on unless you tell her. You can also help by making sure there's a mirror in the delivery room (many already have them or you can bring your own) so she can watch the baby appear. Don't forget to ask her if it's properly adjusted.

Experiencing the Birth

The moment has now arrived. As you watch, your baby is being transformed from an abstraction that you've been trying to imagine for the past nine months to first a small strip of head and then an entire top of head (the phase called crowning), then an entire head complete with face, and then, with incredible rapidity, to a complete little being with a pair of shoulders, a body, legs, feet: your newborn baby. In a matter of moments you leap from coach to father, and your partner, with this newly arrived person *on* instead of *in* her stomach, surfaces from the pain and remoteness of labor and becomes a mother.

It's over—and it's just begun. The birth instantly erases a good deal of the ordeal of labor and replaces it with an image and a feeling that you'll never forget and never tire of recalling. Birth is the most natural, normal thing in the world—and yet, when you're there experiencing it, birth is an utter mystery, a miracle past all comprehension. Don expressed well the feelings that so many fathers go through at this moment: "I felt I grew up a lot in that brief moment. I was overcome with joy and I was crying and so was my wife. It was the ultimate high—I'd never experienced anything like this before and, despite the classes, I wasn't prepared for what it would be like. I remember being moved by my wedding day, but that was *rational*, you knew what to anticipate. This was a totally different order of experience."

Part of what made the birth of his son so special for Don was his participation in some of the tasks of birth. Because the hospital was understaffed, he was asked to wheel his wife into the delivery room, to cut the umbilical cord, and to hold the baby right after birth ("I had him for the first fifteen minutes," he recalls. "It was wonderful.") Another father I talked to said he was a bit nervous when they asked him to cut the cord, but, as he explains now, "it was a no-miss situation." If you've chosen to have the baby at home or at a birthing center, you play an even greater role at the birth. Some midwives let the fathers deliver the babies themselves (with the midwife's supervision), although others discourage this because it shifts his focus from mother to baby at a time when she still needs him. Brian, the father of three, said that he wanted to deliver their third child himself (they had chosen a birthing center for the delivery), but "my wife wanted me to hold her and support her during the birth. She wanted to squat for the birth and she held her elbows on my knees while she was pushing the baby out."

As happy as they are to see their children being born, many men feel even more powerfully a sense of *relief* that the birth is finally over and their wives no longer in agony. "It was such a relief to have him out of the womb and in our arms," said Terry. "We had named him Grumpy before birth because of the way babies look all wrinkled up and squinting, and when he was born I said, 'Sarah, it's Grumpy. He's here.' It was a very close time. It was a climax. I had a tear in my eye. I didn't know how to hold him but he was ours—there was no giving him back." For other men, the combination of joy, relief, fatigue, adrenaline, and the sheer wonderment of witnessing a birth become overwhelming. There can be a strong physical reaction—dizziness, trembling—and a tremendous emotional release. Men who haven't cried in decades find themselves sobbing like babies.

One role many men play at the birth is family photographer. Try not to let your photography interfere with your coaching or with your own experience of the birth. If you sense your partner needs you right there with her, either put the camera aside until after the baby is born or try asking a nurse or resident to get some pictures for you.

Your baby is right there in the delivery room and you'll want to look at her (or him), touch her, talk to her, but your wife still needs your help, so it may be hard for you to decide how to divide your attention. "I was torn between being with the baby and being with my wife," Phil recalled. "I was standing in the middle of the delivery room kind of shifting my weight between the two of them."

The Afterbirth

As far as you're concerned, once your baby is born the birth is completed, but your partner still has one more stage of

Labor and Birth: The Father's Role

delivery to go through—the expulsion of the placenta, the water bag and the remainder of the umbilical cord known as the afterbirth. The new mother's uterus contracts to deliver the afterbirth, but the contractions are relatively painless compared to those she endures during labor. The afterbirth should take anywhere from five minutes to half an hour, but if it is slow, the obstetrician will *not* hasten it by tugging on the cord. This can cause the mother to hemorrhage. Once the afterbirth is completed, the doctor will stitch up the episiotomy if there was one (see Chapter 6). In a hospital, you are now ready to accompany your wife to the recovery room, and you'll have your baby with you now for a short time before the nurse brings him or her to the nursery. Although it may be only half an hour, it's really special because it's your first time alone as a family.

Now What Happens? You and Your Baby After the Birth

Even before your baby is fully born, the doctors and nurses go to work on him with certain standard procedures. As soon as the baby's head emerges, the doctor will suction the mucus out of his mouth and they may suction the baby again after birth. The holding upside down and spanking routine is now, thank God, mostly part of childbirth history, but if the baby is not yet breathing, the doctor may rub his feet or his back to get him started.

A lot of men (and women) are quite surprised at how their newborns look at birth. They may be alarmingly blue for the first few moments, their skin is often wrinkled and may be either bloody or covered with the cheesy protective coating known as vernix, and often the baby's head has been molded a bit in the birth canal so its shape is odd. Not to worry. Your baby's color will improve quickly, the blood and vernix will be cleaned off by a nurse, and the molding goes away in a few days. The part that doesn't go away quite so quickly is the smallness and apparent frailness. Before we have babies, most of us think newborns will look like those chubby smiling

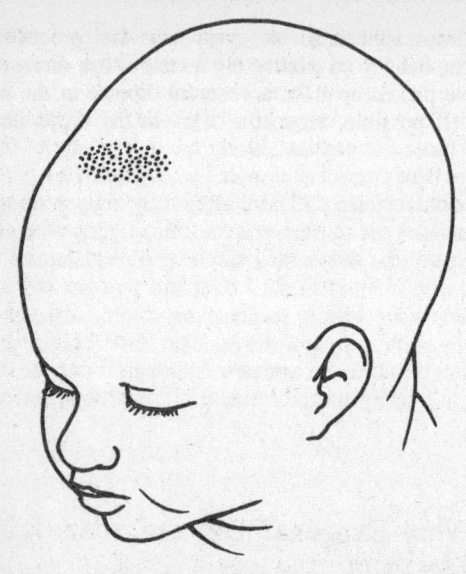

The front soft spot (fontanelle)

sturdy tykes in the Gerber ads, but many newborns seem so tiny and scrawny that their dads are scared they'll break them if they try to pick them up. (One dad said he held his baby at first "like she was a broken egg.") Babies do have their fragile spots—there are two soft spots on top of their heads you should be gentle with, and you should take care to support their heads when picking them up—but generally, newborns are a good deal sturdier than they look. One father told me a story about how the nurse hoisted up his one-day old baby and swung him around a bit. As the dad looked on nervously, the nurse informed him that "Babies are real *durable*. Don't be afraid of him. Just grab him and hold on. You won't break him."

Usually after the birth, the baby is placed on mom's stomach for a bit, and then the nurse will take the baby, clean and wrap him up, and put him in a warmer-crib. At some point in the first hour or so after birth your baby will be weighed, measured, footprinted, given a hospital tag, and have silver

Labor and Birth: The Father's Role

nitrate drops applied to his eyes. This last procedure is to protect the baby from contracting a serious eye disease that he may have picked up from a venereal disease in the mother's vagina. (If possible, request a delay in the drops until after your initial contact with the baby since they cause blurring of vision and thus distort his first impressions of his parents.) Your baby will also have his very first test! It's called the Apgar score and it measures the baby's appearance, vital signs, breathing and muscle tone on a ten-point scale. The test is performed one minute after birth and again at five minutes. Anything over a seven is fine, but don't worry about the score. The test is more for the medical staff than for you.

Some of the fathers I talked to were allowed to perform the weighing and measuring themselves and brought their newborns to the nursery. This is another aspect of standard hospital procedure: soon after the birth, your baby is taken away from you, placed in an isolette in the hospital nursery along with the other newborns, and left there, usually to have a good long sleep. (This separation does not occur in birthing centers, where the parents keep the baby after birth and then go home with the infant within twelve hours.)

There is a good deal of professional controversy over hospital nurseries, and even nonprofessionals wonder why new parents have to be separated from their babies, why the newborns, who have spent the last nine months in a dark and fairly quiet place, must be thrust under relentless fluorescent lights and subjected to the screams of their newborn neighbors. Many hospitals have responded to these criticisms by instituting "rooming in"—the baby may spend all or part of the day in the mother's hospital room and the father can be there, too. Policy varies from hospital to hospital, with the most conservative allowing new dads to be with their babies only during "father's hour" in the evening, and some really archaic hospital forbidding all contact between dads and their newborns. Try to find out ahead of time what the hospital policy is and talk over your desires in this regard with your partner. If you have strong feelings about spending a lot of time with your baby right away, makes these feelings known and see if you can choose a hospital with a liberal policy. I know from experience that an hour a day with my newborn seemed cruelly inadequate and that staring at her through the thick glass walls of the nursery was a miserable experience, especially when she started to cry and no one did anything.

Bonding, as already discussed, is one of the buzzwords of the baby business today. Everyone knows they should be doing it, but many are unsure exactly what it means or what it feels like. As one father put it, "After she was born, I kept thinking, 'Have I started to bond yet? Well . . . I don't know!' But in retrospect I can say that being there at the birth and afterwards really *did* help me bond." Father-infant bonding has become the subject of recent social science studies, and psychiatrist Martin Greenberg has come up with the term *engrossment* to describe this special relationship. Greenberg defines engrossment as "a father's sense of absorption, preoccupation, and interest in his baby. He feels gripped and held by this feeling. He has an intense desire to look at his baby, to touch and hold him. It is as if he is hooked, drawn to his newborn child by some involuntary force over which he has no control. He doesn't will it to happen, it just does" (*The Birth of a Father*, Continuum, 1985).

Greenberg feels engrossment is more likely to happen if the father attends the birth, but other researchers contest this, asserting that the bonding is just as strong and immediate for men who did not attend. One father I talked to stated this case very clearly when I asked whether he thought attending the birth was crucial to establishing a bond with his newborn son: "I feel very close to him, but I think this would have happened even if I hadn't attended the birth. I had lots of vacation time accumulated and I was able to take off two weeks when he was born and then every other week during the summer. I think spending this time with him was more responsible for my bonding than attending the birth." Others speak of the importance of close physical contact, including eye contact, holding, dressing, diapering, as ways that fathers can establish that bond with their infants (see Chapter 8). I think the major point about bonding is that it happens over time and that the bond grows stronger the more a man rolls up his sleeves and really *does* things with and for his baby. Men who attend the birth but are afraid to handle their newborns and unwilling to get involved in caring for them are less likely to bond than

Labor and Birth: The Father's Role

men who missed the birth but show a willingness to be "hands-on" fathers. Of course, men who were present *and* throw themselves into fathering have the advantage of getting in on the ground floor.

There is no denying that attending the birth of one's child is an enthralling experience, and part of the magic is getting to see and be with your baby from her very first moments of life. It's impossible to describe the thrill of seeing her open her eyes and stare into yours just seconds after she appears in the world. I had this amazing, amazed sensation that my daughter and I knew each other already and I imagined that she was fully aware of everything that was going on. It almost seemed as if she were thinking, 'Oh, so this is what it all looks like...' Of course, parents love to read in meaning and comprehension where there may be only undifferentiated sensation, but for me this sense that my daughter was aware of her surroundings and that we were communicating persisted from birth on. Now there seems to me to be a continuity between the one-minute-old newborn and the toddler—the same wide-eyed curiosity, the same alertness, the same refusal to take things on faith, the same eagerness to grow and know.

Don describes a similar reaction to his son. "I was very taken with his sweetness of disposition, which I sensed *immediately* after the birth. He opened his eyes right away—they are very large eyes—and I felt that he knew me. I had always talked to him in the womb and because we knew the sex after the amnio it gave him more personality. He didn't look babyish even at birth." And Pat describes his very first reaction to his daughter Emily: "My first words were, It's a girl and she's beautiful! She was when she was born and she still is."

Again, Pat would have thought Emily was beautiful, and Don would have thought his son was sweet, and I would have thought my daughter was alert even if we hadn't seen them arrive into the world. We would have bonded and loved our children just as much. But attending the birth has given us a kind of focus to our first feelings and our first impressions of our babies—as well as to our first memories. Not only have we had the satisfaction of supporting our wives through their labors, but we've had the pleasure of being included in our new family circle from the very start. Because our babies were never strangers to us, we never felt that we missed something or that we had to play catch-up in getting to know them. This is part of what men gain not only from attending the birth, but also from being with their partners and babies in the recovery room where they can finally get acquainted in peace and quiet.

For everyone's sake but most of all your own, try to extend this period as long as possible and try to be with your new baby as much as you can during the hospital stay. The more time you have with your baby initially and the more control you have over that time, the better you're likely to feel about your transition to fatherhood.

Early Arrival: Doing the Delivery Yourself

You're driving to the hospital along a deserted rural road in the middle of the night and suddenly you hear that stomach-clenching splut-splut-splut that can only mean flat tire. You're miles from a phone, no cars are passing, and you didn't bring a spare. You press your wife's hand and tell her to keep calm, but she squeezes your hand back fiercely. "I feel the baby coming," she tells you. "I think I'm going to have it . . . *now*!"

This is the ultimate nightmare scenario for many an expecting father (with variations depending on where they live: urban fathers feature horrendous traffic jams and grimy taxis). Men who dare to imagine to the end of the nightmare come up against the big question: What on earth do you do? Before the answer, here is a bit of reassurance: First of all, it *very seldom* happens and second of all, when it does, the babies who come popping out are almost always fine and the deliveries usually free of complications. In fact, one obstetrician jokes that you're actually better off with a taxi delivery because it's so fast and easy on the mother and baby.

Jokes aside, if you find yourself in this situation, there are certain things to do. First, keep calm yourself and reassure your partner that everything will be fine. Do whatever you can to minimize the anxiety level. Then, if there's a chance of getting to the hospital, tell your partner to blow so that she avoids pushing the baby out more quickly, but *do not* do any-

Labor and Birth: The Father's Role

thing else to stop the birth. *Do not* tell her to close her legs or push the baby back in: this can harm the baby. Try to get help. In a taxi, tell the driver to radio for an ambulance, flag down cars, call the police, or whatever seems most likely to get help soonest. If you're driving, pull over, put on the emergency flashers, and put up your hood. This way someone will stop to help you and you can send him or her for an ambulance. Don't go for help yourself if you can't be back in minutes: your partner needs you there, especially for the birth. Unless the weather is warm, don't turn off the car engine: you want to keep it warm for mother and baby.

A laboring mother knows when the birth is imminent. She'll feel a tremendous pressure and a powerful urge to push. Other signs are contractions coming less than two minutes apart and presentation of more than an inch of the baby's head at the vagina. Once any one of these occurs, you should prepare for the birth. Help prop your partner up in the position she feels most comfortable in, in the car or by the side of the road (weather permitting), and spread a clean sheet, towel newspapers, your coat (or whatever you have) under her. You're going to "catch" the baby, so be ready. Try to have your hands as clean and dry as possible and remember that newborns are slippery. Remind your partner to resist the urge to push by panting or blowing; you want the baby to come out as slowly as possible to minimize the risk of tearing.

As the baby's head emerges, guide it gently with your hands, but *do not* pull it out. Let the contractions do the work while you receive the baby. As soon as the head is out, run your fingers around the baby's neck to check if the umbilical cord has looped itself around the neck. If it has, gently unwind it and slip it over the baby's shoulders and then over the head. Once the head emerges, the rest of the baby is born fast. Keep a good grip on the newborn with one hand, supporting the head and the other under the body.

Your newborn may be a bit purple for the first few minutes: don't worry (unless this persists). As soon as your baby is born, you want to be sure his mouth and nose are clear of mucus (you can hold his head down so the mucus drains out or remove it with your fingers; best to cover the finger with a clean cloth before doing this). Help him start breathing by gently rubbing his tummy and back (no spanking necessary!), and keep him warm. Wipe him off with whatever clean absorbent material you have at hand, place him on his mother's stomach, and keep him warmly covered. Make sure his head is covered. Then, assuming he is breathing on his own and the mother is okay, proceed to the hospital or to get help. Do not cut the umbilical cord yourself and do not deliver the placenta. It will probably come out by itself, but if not, under no circumstances should you tug on the cord to get it out. Even if your partner is not planning to breastfeed, have her put the baby to her breast and try to get him to suck. This will stimulate the uterus to contract around the placenta and force it out.

If the baby does not start breathing by himself within two minutes, check again for mucus, and flick at the bottoms of his feet. If breathing does not begin, you should start mouth-to-mouth resuscitation. To do this you position the fingertips of one hand on the baby's chin, the other hand on his forehead and gently tilt his head back. Listen at his mouth and chest to see if he has begun breathing and, if not, cover both his mouth and nose with your mouth, give him four brief, shallow puffs, and listen again for breathing. *Do not* blow hard or deeply into his lungs. If he hasn't started, keep doing the mouth-to-mouth by giving him one gentle puff every three seconds and keep checking for the start of his own breathing.

If the cord breaks during the delivery, tie up the end nearest

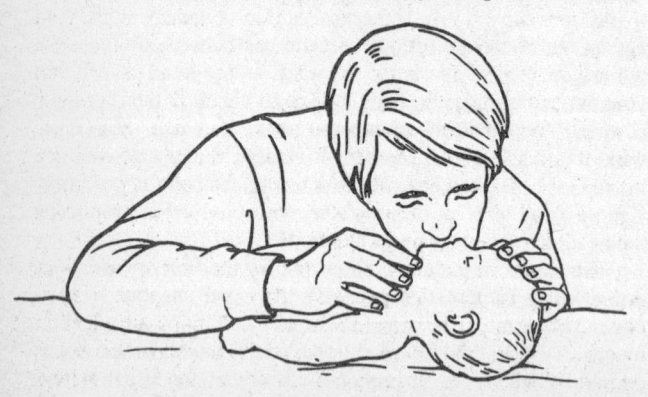

Mouth-to-mouth resuscitation on a newborn

the baby with a shoelace, string, or whatever you have handy. You can help your partner control heavy bleeding by massaging her uterus: feel along the lower part of her abdomen until you find it and then rub firmly but not too strenuously. Try to find her some clean towels or cloths of some kind to contain the flow of blood.

If you're still worried about emergency delivery, you'll probably want to prepare yourself even more thoroughly for the possibility—remote as it is. Discuss it with your childbirth educator, midwife, or obstetrician. And take a look at the *Emergency Childbirth Handbook* by Barbara Anderson and Pamela Shapiro (Van Nostrand Reinhold, 1982), or *Emergency Childbirth* by Gregory J. White, M.D. (Interstate Printers and Publishers, 1958). You can get this short and clear manual from the Police Training Foundation, 3412 Ruby St., Franklin Park, IL 60131.

Complications and How They Are Handled

Your partner may have something very similar to the textbook labor and delivery already described, but chances are that her experience will depart significantly at at least a couple of points. One stage will be longer or shorter, hurt more or less, or pass without anyone even noticing it. This is all fine and requires no intervention or special procedures. But when departures from the norm occur that are potentially dangerous to mother or baby, we have entered the realm of complications. Thanks to modern medical science, the danger remains *potential* in most complications. Doctors, hospitals, and their high-tech equipment can now keep amazingly tiny premature babies alive, detect drops in fetal heart rate quickly, and move fast to deliver emergency cases before any harm comes to mother or child. Chances are none of this will happen to you. The majority of births remain routine. But if something does happen, the more you know the less you'll panic. Following is a rundown on the most common complications in labor and birth and how they are handled at hospitals today.

Prematurity

Babies are considered premature if they are born before the thirty-eighth week of pregnancy or if their birthweight is under five pounds. Every year, about 250,000 premature babies (or "preemies") are born, and with each passing year they have a better chance of surviving and growing up as perfectly normal children. Progress in this field has been phenomenal. Nowadays, 85 percent of preemies weighing less than 3.3 pounds survive—the reverse of the late 1960s when only 15 percent made it. The frontier of fetal viability has been pushed back to twenty-five weeks after conception, and doctors are saving babies who weigh as little as a pound and a half at birth.

But with all the progress, serious problems persist. Preemies are much more vulnerable than full-term babies to physical and mental disabilities. A British study found that premature birth accounted for 85 percent of all infant mortality not related to birth defects. While they are fighting for their lives, preemies are kept in neonatal intensive care units and hooked up to an array of tubes and wires. For the new mother and father, this can be a terrifying way to embark on parenthood. And the cost of keeping a preemie alive may exceed $1,000 a day.

No one really knows what causes prematurity, but we do know that certain women are more at risk. These include women who have had two or more miscarriages or abortions (especially in the second trimester), who were exposed to DES (diethylstilbestrol—an artificial form of estrogen now known to increase the risk of miscarriage and cervical cancer in the daughters of women who took it while they were pregnant), who have had tissue samples taken that required dilation of the cervix, and who have suffered repeated kidney or urinary tract infections. Other women at risk of preterm labor are those who smoke heavily, experience excessive stress or tension, hold physically taxing jobs, or must make long commutes. Also, half of all twins are born preterm.

Although scientists have yet to pinpoint the causes of preterm labor, they are making some progress in preventing it. One of the keys to prevention is early detection. The warning

Labor and Birth: The Father's Role

signs may come in the form of a dull ache in the lower back, a feeling in the abdomen similar to menstrual cramps, and contractions. The contractions may not be painful to the mother, but she (or you) can feel them by pressing the fingertips on top of the uterus and feeling for a tensing and relaxing of the muscles. You should time the contractions: if they keep coming at intervals of ten minutes (or less) for an hour or more, call the doctor at once.

The doctor will tell you and your partner to come into the hospital and there, if the preterm labor is confirmed, he or she will take immediate steps to try to stop it—assuming the water bag hasn't broken and the labor hasn't already progressed too far. The usual treatment is for the woman to be put to bed with her feet higher than her head to keep the baby's head from pressing on the cervix. Then she will be given a contraction-inhibiting drug (probably Ritodrine) intravenously and both she and the baby will be watched closely. If the drug takes effect, the mother's contractions will stop and she will be switched to Ritodrine tablets and sent home. The doctor will most likely advise a strict regime of lots of rest, no sex, no physically taxing work, and regular office visits. And the Ritodrine will continue until the pregnancy is nearing term. Ritodrine is not without its side effects, however; it may cause racing of the heart in the mother and baby, affect the mother's blood pressure, and lower the fetal blood sugar level.

Many parents are quite understandably scared of handling their tiny, fragile-looking premature babies, and for some the scariest moment can be the day they finally take the baby home. More and more hospitals, responding to these fears, are involving parents right away in the care of their premature infants. The latest research, however, warns about the possibility of overstimulating a preemie. Dr. Peter A. Gorski of the University of San Francisco Medical Center found that preemies showed signs of stress after being stroked, hugged, or even being engaged in eye contact. Gorski believes that because their nervous systems are still poorly organized, preemies cannot block out stimuli the way full-term babies can, and thus even the gentlest interaction can overwhelm them (quoted in *Omni*, December 1985). Other researchers feel that preemies should not be deprived of handling, but that contact should be timed carefully and administered gently so as not to exhaust them.

If your baby is premature, you should also bear in mind that he or she will develop more slowly during the first year or so than full-term babies. But, in time, they do catch up and the only traces left of their prematurity will be the pictures you've saved.

Postmaturity

Couples have been known to fall into despair when their official due date comes and goes without a birth—or even a sign of labor. As one dad whose wife was two weeks late with their first child put it, "You have a certain date in your mind, and for nine months you're counting down the months, weeks, days—and it's really tough when that day passes and you have to wait some more." Another dad said the two weeks they had to wait after the due date felt like two months. It *is* really tough, not only psychologically but physically for a woman. But you should keep in mind that the official due date is only an *estimate* and two weeks plus or minus is normal. So your partner is not considered postterm or postmature until she has been pregnant for forty-two weeks.

Only about 10 percent of pregnancies fall within this category, and in the majority of these cases everything turns out fine. The risks involved for the baby in postmaturity are considerably smaller than the risks associated with prematurity. Some postmature babies grow so large in the uterus that they can only be delivered by cesarean section, but sometimes the placenta deteriorates and the baby begins to lose weight. Such babies are more likely to suffer distress at birth and may look long, thin, and stringy as newborns. One sign of distress of postmature babies is the passing of meconium, the infant's first stool. Normally, the baby excretes the dark, tarry substance soon after birth, but if the fetus's oxygen supply is interrupted for any reason, it may pass meconium into the amniotic fluid. When this happens, the doctor will probably want to observe the baby's heart rate on a fetal monitor to check for other signs of stress.

Labor and Birth: The Father's Role

Certain tests have become standard for women who have passed their forty-second week of pregnancy. One, known as the "nonstress" test, involves hooking a woman up to an external fetal monitor. Whenever she feels a fetal movement, she is supposed to push a button so the doctors can see if the baby's heart rate shows the normal increase during such exertions. If the heart rate fails to increase as it should, the doctor may advise a stress test, also known as the oytocin challenge test. Essentially, this is a simulation of labor, which indicates how well the baby responds to uterine contractions. The woman is given oxytocin, a synthetic hormone, to stimulate contractions and the baby's heart rate is measured on an external fetal monitor. If the baby is responding well to the test, the heart rate will show no significant change before, during, and after the contraction. However, if the heart rate slows down abnormally, it is considered a sign that the baby will not tolerate an actual labor and most doctors will then advise a c-section.

If the baby passes these tests, you will probably be told to relax and wait for labor to begin. Usually, the tests are repeated once or twice a week. If the pregnancy goes on and on with no signs of labor or if the baby shows some distress, the doctor may attempt to induce labor. This means the mother is given oxytocin (usually in the form of pitocin) intravenously in a high enough dosage to stimulate contractions and get the cervix to begin dilating. Induction doesn't always work: labor may start and then stop, or the contractions may not be strong enough to dilate the cervix. Phil, a New York writer, described the ordeal of seeing his wife (four weeks past her due date) through two inductions, the second of which went on for nearly twenty-four hours before their healthy and beautiful nine-pound girl finally emerged. Phil and his wife were fortunate in choosing an obstetrician who was willing to do almost anything to insure a vaginal delivery. Many doctors faced with this situation would insist on a c-section, and, of course, all doctors will perform a cesarean if the baby shows signs of severe distress during the induction.

Waiting for a postterm baby to be born is a real test of your patience and your frustration tolerance. Your partner may get angry at you, you may get angry at the baby ("What the hell are you waiting for?" is a common reaction), and both of you may get angry at all the people who call and ask how come you're not in the hospital yet. Also maddening are the couples in your childbirth education classes who have had their babies days—or weeks—ago. The best ways to cope are to detach yourselves as much as possible from the anticipation. Try to keep your partner busy with nontaxing activities, especially activities that are going to be difficult to perform once the baby comes (and, yes, the baby *will* come sooner or later). One father said his wife was actually "thrilled" to have the extra two weeks. She started her maternity leave from a high-stress job on her due date and used the waiting time to catch up on chores, rest, and fix up the baby's room. Go to the movies or out to eat. Get hold of some books you've always wanted to read. Get your camera equipment in order. Clean out that desk that's been buried in papers for years. Neither of you is likely to have much time or energy for these activities with a newborn to care for, and they can help the waiting time pass not only quickly but productively. And try to remember: Hard as it is to wait, you're soon going to be parents for a very long time.

Cesarean Delivery

A cesarean section is a surgical procedure in which the mother is anesthetized, an incision is made in her abdomen and uterus, the baby is removed, and the incision is then repaired with stitches. Babies have been delivered this way for thousands of years (the procedure, of course, is named for Julius Caesar, who was supposedly born via c-section around 100 B.C.), but in the West, our first recorded instance of both mother and baby surviving the operation dates to A.D. 1500. Nowadays, with improvements in anesthesia, antibiotic treatment for infection, and the greater availability of blood for transfusions, c-sections have become safer than ever. This may account, in part, for their astronomic rise. There is really no other way to describe the increase: from 1900 to 1909, 1 percent of American babies were born this way; from 1940 to 1949, 2.8 percent; 1960 to 1969, 6.8 percent); and by 1984,

Labor and Birth: The Father's Role

the figure had jumped to 21.1 percent, with numbers expected to keep rising by almost 1 percent a year. In other words, the odds are greater than one in five that your baby will be born through c-section.

The question one has to ask is: Why? First of all, why are c-sections performed, and second, why are they now being performed so much more often? Sometimes cesareans are performed because of a preexisting medical problem or condition, in which case the doctor will inform you ahead of time that this procedure is going to be necessary. The baby may be too large to fit through the mother's pelvis, or be positioned in such a way that vaginal birth would be impossible (for example, resting *across* the opening), or the mother may have active herpes lesions in the genital area or may have a condition such as high blood pressure, heart or kidney problems that would make labor too much of a strain, or her placenta may be positioned over the cervix (instead of up in the uterus, as it should be) in such a way that it would separate from the uterus as the cervix dilated in normal labor. This last condition is known as placenta previa. Also, if a woman has had a previous cesarean section, many obstetricians will perform cesareans for the succeeding children, although in many cases there is no medically sound reason for this (see below).

All of these are *planned* cesareans. You schedule an appointment at the hospital for the birth a week or two before the mother is likely to go into labor. You have plenty of time to read up on cesarean birth, to prepare yourselves for a longer hospital stay (six days on average), and a more difficult recovery.

Emergency cesareans are more difficult to cope with and likely to be more stressful. These occur when the labor fails to progress normally, becomes too difficult, or stops; when the baby shows signs of distress or, in many cases, when the baby is in the breech position (bottom or feet first, instead of the normal head-first position); or if the umbilical cord drops down below the baby's head in such a way that the head presses against it and cuts off the oxygen supply. This last case is an emergency situation known as prolapsed cord. The decision to perform an emergency cesarean is frequently made under rather pressured and hectic circumstances in the hospital. You may feel that the birth of your child has been entirely taken out of your hands—and to a large extent it has.

The answer to the question of why the enormous increase in c-sections since the early 1970s varies depending on whom you ask. Some obstetricians blame the current malpratice situation, in which doctors are being sued more often for more money. Advising a couple early on that a cesarean is necessary gives the doctors better protection if the case comes to court: they're practicing "defensive medicine." Critics of conventional medical practices insist this is merely an excuse. They say doctors are doing more cesareans because this operation is a lot quicker than waiting for a difficult labor to progress naturally, so it frees up their time and earns them more money. Others point the finger at the electronic fetal monitor as the culprit in increased c-sections: the machine gives early warning of any abnormality in the fetal heart rate and thus prompts nervous doctors to terminate the labor by an operation, perhaps unnecessarily. Still others say the increase has to do with the growing numbers of older women (over thirty-five) who are having babies. These women are considered higher risks than women in their twenties, and thus doctors will be more likely to intervene surgically in their deliveries.

Perhaps the major factor in the increase in c-sections is the tradition of "once a cesarean, always a cesarean." Repeat cesareans comprise over one-third of the c-sections being performed today, and critics of the rapid increase point out that a good many of these repeats can be avoided. The need for a repeat cesarean (assuming the mother and fetus are healthy) depends largely on the type of incision made in the uterus in the previous cesarean. The more common horizontal incision leaves the uterus quite strong when it heals, and experts feel that there is no danger in letting a woman who has had such an incision go into labor on a trial basis with the next baby. In fact, if you look at the statistics, she's better off having a vaginal delivery for her other children than repeated cesareans. This may not be true if the doctor made a vertical uterine incision, which is more likely than the horizontal incision to leave the uterus vulnerable to rupture during labor. (You should also keep in mind that there are two types of *abdominal* incisions: the horizontal bikini incision and the classic

Labor and Birth: The Father's Role

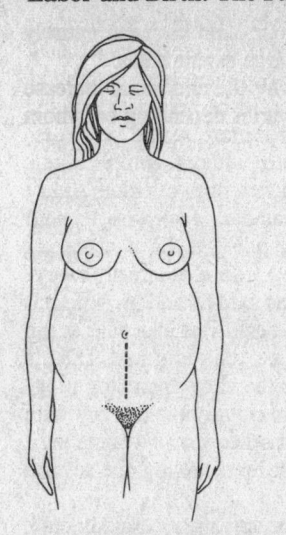

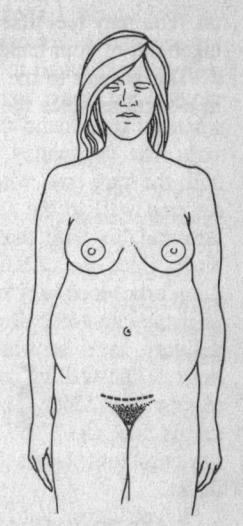

The vertical incision and horizontal bikini incision

vertical incision; but a vertical abdominal incision does not necessarily mean that the uterine incision is also vertical. When in doubt, consult the relevant medical records.)

The surgical procedure for a cesarean section lasts about an hour and a half; the birth itself happens quickly (usually in five to fifteen minutes), and the rest of the time is devoted to stitching up the incisions in the uterus and abdomen. Regional anesthesia, such as an epidural (see Chapter 6), is preferable to general anesthesia, which is usually reserved for extreme emergencies when there is no time to do an epidural.

At more and more hospitals, men are being given the opportunity to be present at the cesarean births of their children. Since your partner will be fully conscious if she has an epidural, she may find your presence tremendously reassuring, and, of course, being present at the birth of one's child is incredibly moving no matter whether the birth is vaginal or abdominal. If the idea makes you squeamish, you should know that you don't have to watch the incisions being made: the mother's abdomen is screened off from view during the surgery.

The fathers I spoke with were very positive about their experiences at cesarean deliveries. The consensus was that it really didn't matter to them how the baby was born so long as mother and baby were okay. Dan said he felt disappointed when he first found out that this procedure would be necessary. The pregnancy had progressed without complications until the very end, when the baby (a few days overdue) didn't respond well to the stress test. It came as a surprise to both him and his wife that they weren't going to have a normal birth. Once the decision was made to do a cesarean, everything proceeded very rapidly, and Dan said he and his wife felt as if they had lost all control of the birth. But Dan said at the delivery itself he was thinking: "Gee, this is great! There's none of the waiting, or the pain, or the slow agonizing progress through labor. They just lift him right out—and my wife seems fine, too." The pain, for the mother, doesn't come until the anesthetic wears off; and it can be disabling for several days.

If you know your partner will be having a cesarean, talk over the issue of your attending the birth with her and the obstetrician, and find out the hospital's policy. Check with your local chapter of the Childbirth Education Association for classes on preparing for cesarean delivery. You might want to take a look at *Cesarean Birth Experience* by Bonnie Donovan (Beacon Press, 1977) or get hold of the pamphlet *Father's Fact Sheet for the Unexpected Cesarean* (from C/Section Experience of Northern Illinois, 1220 Gentry Rd., Hoffman Estates, IL 60195).

Because of the mother's pain after the operation, and because on top of the pain she has a new baby to begin caring for, the recovery period is one of the hardest aspects of a cesarean section for the new parents to deal with. The hospital stay for mother and baby is likely to last three to four days longer than for a normal, vaginal delivery, and the new mother is going to need a lot of help during the first couple of weeks at home. If at all possible, she should be freed from housework, cooking, shopping, and strenuous chores. If you can manage it, try to take some time off from work or hire someone to help her out. Philip, father of two boys delivered by c-section, took one week off after the birth of his second son,

Labor and Birth: The Father's Role

his wife's mother came for one week, and his mother came for one—so, with the week she spent in the hospital, she had a full month of help before facing the demands of caring for two young children. Michael, who didn't have the luxury of vacation time or helpful in-laws, said that "the first week and a half was really tough after the c-section. I was doing everything in the way of chores *and* working, so the exhaustion was pretty severe." If the cesarean is planned, try to make as many arrangements beforehand to minimize the stress on yourself. And when the demands become overwhelming, don't be shy about asking family, friends, or neighbors to lend a helping hand.

Back Labor

Labor is bad enough when a woman feels most of the pain of the contractions in her abdomen, but when the pain is concentrated in her back it can become unbearable. Back labor, as this condition is called, occurs in most cases because the baby's head and back are pressed up against the mother's spine. One really rough part of back labor is that the mother feels the pressure during both her contractions and during the intervals between contractions (it's worse during contractions). As if all this weren't bad enough, back labors tend to drag on longer than normal labors because the baby's head doesn't work to dilate the cervix efficiently. Also, the contrac-

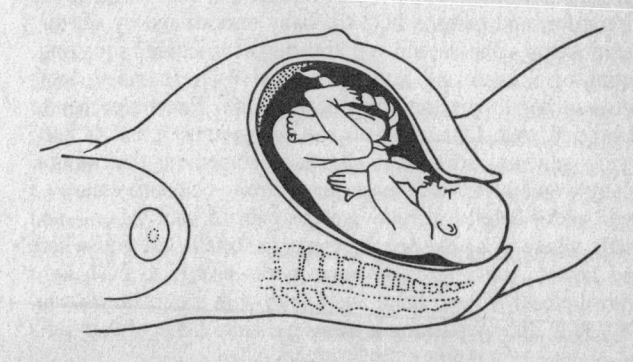

Position of baby in back labor

tions tend to be long and irregular, so the breathing and concentrating through them becomes much more difficult. About one in five women experience back labor.

Most babies will not be born in the posterior position (often called "sunny-side up": the baby's head and back are toward the back of the mother's body), so before they come out they will have to rotate to the standard anterior position (head toward the front of the body, with the baby born facing down

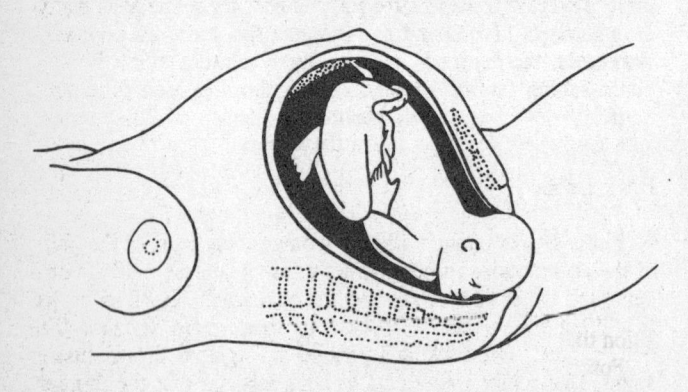

The standard anterior position

toward the floor). When this rotation happens naturally, the back labor ends and everything goes more smoothly. But if it doesn't happen, forceps may have to be used to assist in the delivery (see next section). The mother can ease some of her discomfort and perhaps help the baby turn around by shifting her position. She should try kneeling, crouching, squatting, sitting on a chair and leaning over with her abdomen down between her thighs, or lying on her side. Encourage her to stand and walk for as long as she can tolerate it and to keep trying new positions until she finds something that works. Many women find back massage or strong counterpressure on their backs helpful in relieving the pain of back labor—and that's where you, the coach, come in. She'll tell you where and how to press. Usually what works best is to push *hard* with the heel of your hand and to rub with a circular motion. Or you might try pushing a tennis ball into the spot that hurts

Labor and Birth: The Father's Role

her most. When your hands and arms become exhausted, try sitting back-to-back with your partner, pressing your lower back against hers. A hot water bottle can also relieve some of the pain of back labor.

Back labor is likely to push your coaching skills to the limit. But remember, most babies do turn around at some point, and all babies are eventually born. The labor won't last forever!

Forceps

If a woman has trouble pushing her baby out, the obstetrician may use forceps to aid in the delivery. Forceps are most often used for problems including an oversmall pelvis and large baby; anesthesia (such as an epidural) that makes it impossible for a woman to push; extreme fatigue for the mother; sudden drop in fetal heart rate requiring rapid delivery; a medical condition (such as heart problems or asthma) that limits the strain a woman should be subjected to; a presentation position that makes passage through the birth canal impossible.

Forceps look like two oversized spoons with holes in the bowls. They're shaped that way to conform to the shape of the baby's head. In a forceps delivery, the doctor will place one spoon (or "blade" as the official jargon has it) at a time around

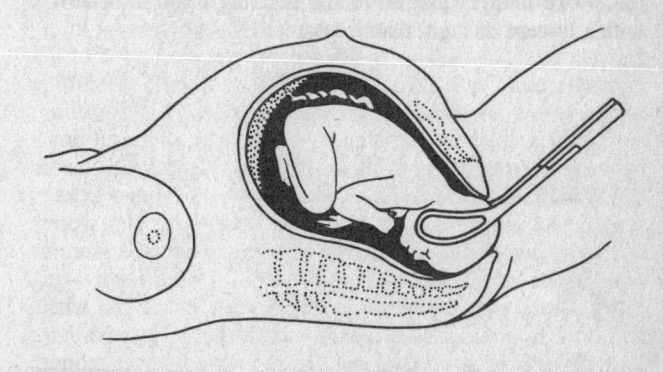

A forceps delivery

the baby's head during intervals between contractions. Once they're both in place, the blades are attached together so that they stay in place. Then, holding onto the handles, the doctor will use the forceps to pull on the baby's head during contractions, trying to replicate the mother's natural pushing force as closely as possible.

Forceps can be really painful for the woman and really difficult for you to watch (one father I talked to said it was the only time he had to look away during the delivery; and at some hospitals the coaches are sent out), but usually a good doctor won't have to use them for more than a minute, and when he or she is through, your baby is as good as born. Today, forceps are used only when the baby's head is engaged in the pelvis. Most common are the so-called low-forceps deliveries when the baby's head is just about to crown. When the baby is higher up in the pelvis with no progress being made, a cesarean is the usual course.

When handled skillfully, forceps can hasten a difficult birth without any harm to mother or baby, although it is not uncommon for babies to have *temporary* bruises on their foreheads. But when forceps are in the hands of an incompetent doctor, there is a risk of damage to a woman's cervix and injury to the baby's eyes, face, or even brain. In addition, forceps delivery usually necessitates a rather substantial episiotomy (see Chapter 6). Yet even with these risks (which are minimal if the doctor knows what he or she is doing), you're better off with a forceps delivery than a cesarean.

8. The First Weeks of Your Baby's Life

"There was nothing difficult about the labor and birth," said Don, a thirty-eight-year-old marketing manager from New York. "It all went so smoothly, everything was under control. The hardest part, really, was bringing the baby home from the hospital. Our major problems came from ignorance. I remember being up at two or three in the morning, frantically consulting baby books to find out what was wrong. Looking back, it's hard to believe we were so unschooled as parents. We had read so much for the birth, but somehow we neglected to read up on early childhood. The first couple of days were very hard."

Even if Don and his wife had read up on early childhood, it's likely they would have found the first few days at home with their new baby difficult. As Michael, the clerical worker from Colorado, put it, "You can't prepare yourself for the reality of the baby until it's there. You can't prepare yourself in any way for the fatigue and the demands. It just hits you." Jerry Sachs, who runs Father Focus, a New York–based organization that offers a number of programs for fathers, feels that most men don't even *try* to prepare themselves. He says: "Pregnant fathers seem only to be concerned with how they will do at the birth—they're wondering, What's going to happen? How can I help my wife? Only after the birth do they realize there is a child. At the beginning they worry about things like, Will I drop my baby? Will I hurt him when I pick him up? Few men have any experience in child care. For most of us, fatherhood is a leap into the unknown."

Once the unknown becomes a bit familiar, almost everyone says it's much more work and the work is much more relentless than they expected. And, when they're done wondering whether they can cope, almost everyone confides that it's also much more rewarding—and rewarding much more quickly—than they dreamed of.

Life with a new baby is a bit of an emotional rollercoaster. Exhilaration and exhaustion chase each other's tails. The sublime and ridiculous coexist in a single moment. While you're holding your new baby and marveling over the miracle of life, the bottle sterilizer will be quietly boiling over in the kitchen. Your precious infant son will pee in your face, burble on your suit, scream in your ear, scratch at your neck—and then fall asleep in your arms in the most unbelievably peaceful way. When you're up with him at four in the morning, you'll wonder how you're possibly going to function at work the next day, and at six the next evening you'll be dying to leave work and get home to him. The equipment—crib to assemble, snaps on baby clothes to fasten, formula to mix, car seat to install—will drive you nuts. But then, in no time at all, you'll be expert at all those chores and routines of bundling, changing, buckling, burping, rocking, soothing that once seemed so alien. Through all the fatigue, the hassles, the minor disasters, and the not so minor outlays of cash, there is this new person whose very existence still seems like the most marvelous gift imaginable.

Your new baby will give you a crash course in fatherhood with heavy emphasis on paternal responsibility. And on top of all the things you want to (or have to) do for the baby, you're more than likely to be errand boy, chauffeur, social director, chef, dishwasher, shopper, and house cleaner. No matter how well set up you thought you were before the baby arrived, you're going to discover things—lots and lots of little, tiny, expensive things you never even heard of—that are absolutely crucial to your baby's well-being and that *you* have to go to the drugstore, supermarket, toy store, whatever to pick up. We had bottles and nipples—but no nipple brush (a tiny cone-shaped brush for cleaning nipples). We had vaseline and baby powder, but no cornstarch or A&D ointment (doctor's recommended remedy for diaper rash). Josh's baby daughter ran through her entire wardrobe the first day. Alan had to run out and get formula at ten o'clock at night. Terry got his son home from the hospital, laid him on the carpet, and whipped off his diaper, only to discover that they had no wipes, no diapers handy, no washcloth, and no idea where to look for any of the necessary equipment. All of us quickly became masters of the baby-care sections of our local drugstores and supermarkets. (See the end of this chapter for more on necessary supplies.)

Dealing with "helpful" in-laws (or your own parents) can be one of the trials of this time. Pat recounted with a groan how "two hours after we got the baby home, my wife's parents showed up and stayed two weeks. We were stuck with them. Having no time alone was frustrating." And Don described the ten-day stay of his out-of-town in-laws as "more hardship than help. They're the types who feel as if they're interfering unless they're told to do something. So I was entertaining them on top of everything else." Yet another father, let's call him Lou, said bluntly: "I wanted my mother-in-law out of the house as soon as possible. It was stressful to have anyone around."

To be fair, there are probably as many helpful, organized, considerate in-laws as there are difficult nuisances. But the point is, as Lou put it, that for many men, it's stressful to have *anyone* around. Hard as the responsibilities of new fatherhood are, most of us want to jump in and figure them out for ourselves. We want to start on our lives as fathers, and the only way really to do this is to be with our families. Maybe there's an element of pride and control: *we* want to be calling the shots, not running errands at the behest of our mothers-in-law. But this is only natural. We've waited nine long months to become fathers, and now we want to do it, even if we don't really know how to yet. There will be plenty of time and plenty of caretaking left over for our in-laws later.

Defining Your Role

For most of us, the first weeks of fatherhood are a kind of heightened time in our lives, when everything seems at once vivid and unreal and nothing seems connected to our former existences. Colors look brighter, we notice our environment in a new way, we relate to our parents, friends, wives differently. Our emotional responses may be exaggerated, and we may feel physically odd, too. I remember being both full of nervous energy and utterly exhausted. Each morning, the birds seemed to be turned up to maximum volume. Every time I went outside I thought I heard a baby crying somewhere, as if each house on the block had a new arrival just like ours.

Part of it, of course, is sleep deprivation. But part of it is also the very real shock to our systems of having a new person move into our lives—a new person both so much a part of us and so alien, so lovable and so implacable, so fascinating and so ceaselessly needy. It's wonderful, but it's also bewildering—and as the bewilderment grows with sleepless nights and louder wails, many men begin asking themselves, "How do I deal with this? Just how do I fit in? What's in this for *me*?" The way you answer these questions will color your relationship with your baby—and your partner—for a long time to come, so it makes sense to face them squarely and openly and figure things out.

In an article entitled "Men's Entrance to Parenthood" (*Family Coordinator*, October 1976), Robert Fein reports his findings on how thirty different fathers adjusted to this transition in their lives. Fein concluded that one of the keys to men's adjustment to fatherhood was "developing some kind of coherent role (a pattern of behavior that met their needs and the needs of their wives and babies)." There were two broad categories of roles that Fein identified: breadwinners and nontraditional fathers. The breadwinners were the men who saw providing for their families economically as their primary parental responsibility. They tended to be proud of their babies, but not terribly involved in the day-to-day tasks of caretaking. Generally, their wives, who did not work, supported them in their choice of role. The nontraditional dads, on the other hand, considered the raising and caring for their new babies as much their responsibility as their wives', and most of them tried to arrange their schedules to spend more time with their babies in the first few weeks. The wives of nontraditional dads were much more likely to have jobs or careers of their own.

The men who adopted one of these two roles (of course, with their own individual variations) felt that they were functioning well as "family men" by the time their babies were six weeks old, and they felt much less anxiety about the wellbeing of their babies and about the "overall shape of their [own] lives." Fein's conclusion is, I think, reassuring. There is no single style of involvement or specific set of chores that will make a man feel comfortable in the role of father. The role a new father finds for himself depends on his own needs, his job, his relationship with his partner, the personality of his baby. The important thing is finding a role that one feels comfortable with. If you want to be directly involved in the child care, start right away, as soon as your baby comes home. Don't let yourself be squeezed out by the grandmothers or even by an overpossessive wife. And don't wait around for some magic moment when the baby is settled and less scary: *you* make that moment yourself. If you see yourself in the breadwinner role (and if your partner feels okay about doing most of the child care herself), try not to let yourself feel guilty or pressured by the superdad model. You don't necessarily have to change diapers and mix formula to be a good father.

Although breadwinners can indeed make good fathers, fewer men today feel satisfied in restricting their involvement to this role. It's not that we're dropping out of the breadwinning sphere in great numbers, but rather that we're adding active involvement with our babies to our breadwinning duties. Old cultural assumptions that fathers are less interested in their babies, less nurturant, and less competent in caregiving than mothers have been exploded. One study ("Father's Role in Infancy: A Reevaluation," by Ross D. Parke and Douglas B. Sawin, *Family Coordinator*, October 1976) found that dads are, in fact, more likely to hold and rock their newborns than are moms, and have just as much success in getting babies to drink their milk. And Fein, in his study, reports that the men who did more infant care had significantly less "infant-related anxiety" than did other men. None of the men in his study (and none of the men I interviewed) saw caring for a baby as a threat to their masculinity or felt that it was "unnatural" for a man to feed, change, hold, and soothe an infant. Fein concludes that "men's lives were enhanced ... by active involvement in infant caretaking." If anything, men have become even more involved and more comfortable with their involvement in the ten years that have passed since this study was published.

Involvement doesn't always come easy, even to men who looked forward during the pregnancy to becoming active, participating fathers. Few of us have spent much time around babies before our own arrives, and so we're usually in for some surprises. "My image of kids before we had them didn't match up with the reality at all," said Philip from Saint Paul and now the father of two sons. "I thought they were great— you know, cute and cuddly and you played with them and changed them and went to the park and played ball and that's all there was to it. I didn't realize the amount of time just taking care of their physical needs involves." Sometimes, by the time they leave the hospital, mothers have established a pattern of handling all the baby's physical needs and the fathers, a bit disappointed that playing ball in the park is still years away, kind of let things slide. If things slide long enough, the father might simply give up trying or he might try and fail and end up becoming frustrated and even kind of scared of handling the baby: What if I can't get her to stop crying? What if I put the diaper on backward? What if she spits up? Even though men *can be* as competent at infant care as women, they *won't be* if they don't start doing it.

A pattern can quickly develop in which the mother becomes the "expert" who, although proud and possessive of her expertise, nonetheless gets tired of doing all the caretaking. So she nags her husband to do more with the baby and then, when he does it "wrong" (that is, not her way), she criticizes whatever he does. The father may resent his wife's bossiness but may secretly agree that she's the better caretaker. When he

The First Weeks of Your Baby's Life

encounters the least frustration, he'll be only too glad to hand the baby back to his wife, and she'll be only too glad to prove how much better she is at feeding, soothing, whatever . . . until the next nagging bout begins. The father may begin to resent not only his wife for making him feel incompetent, but the baby for making him look like such a klutz. In short, there develops a vicious circle in which no one is getting what he or she wants: mother has no relief from child care, father is not getting to know his child, and baby is fussy because of all the tension in the air.

One way out of this trap is to stake out certain areas of caretaking as your own from the very start and become the resident expert in them. "I was Mr. Clean," said Terry, a Midwestern truckdriver. "I did all the bathing and a lot of changing. I'd get him as soon as I came back from work and this was sometimes the highlight of the day for me. He really likes having his diaper changed! So it was neat for me and a relief for my wife as well since she was tired of changing diapers all day." Other men I talked to said they made sure always to do one feeding a day or, if their wives were breastfeeding exclusively, they'd give the baby a bottle of water. For fathers with heavy weekday work schedules, weekends can be a time to get to know their infants. Saturday morning can be dad's time with baby (and mom's time to sleep in).

As all new fathers quickly learn, the only way really to get to know your baby is to take care of him or her. The playing ball in the park aspect comes later: for now, involvement means holding, rocking, feeding, changing, bathing, putting to sleep, making eye contact. And it's not a matter of ten minutes while your partner is in the shower. You've really got to put in some time. Jerry Sachs of Father Focus said that the only piece of advice he gives new dads is "to spend a day (or preferably a week, although this may not be feasible) *totally in charge* of the baby. Take total responsibility. You learn so much from this. Of course, part of it is a burden, but keeping track of a baby's bodily needs gives you an intimacy and a sense of confidence that you don't get any other way. There is a *connectedness* that develops—a sort of glue between father and child—that fathers who don't participate won't get."

Work Issues

We hear a lot these days about working mothers (there's even a magazine by that name), but have you ever heard the phrase "working father"? You don't hear it because there is no need for it. In our society, we take it for granted that fathers are working—and sometimes working harder and longer hours than ever to provide for their families. Paternity leaves exist, but still more in theory than in practice, and even at the few companies that have instituted such policies, many men are reluctant to take advantage of them. They worry how their superiors will view their putting family before job or they worry that they just can't take the time. It hardly seems wise to jeopardize one's job or one's chances of advancement at the very moment one has added the financial responsibilities of a new baby (and perhaps subtracted a spouse's salary).

The question naturally arises: Can you be a breadwinner and a nontraditional father at the same time? How do you juggle the demands of work with the desire to be involved in the upbringing of your child? For more and more of us, this is one of the crucial issues of our lives, and one for which there's no easy answer or solution.

The fortunate among the fathers I interviewed were able to take some time off when their children were born so they could get to know them and help their wives out. As noted earlier, Don, perhaps the most fortunate, had a lot of vacation time accumulated that he was not able to carry into the following year. He took off two weeks when his son was born in May and then every other week during the summer. "This was a rare opportunity for me," he says now. "If I'd carried out a regular job, I never would have this time. This time with my son was more responsible for my feeling close with him now than attending the birth. It was really crucial to giving him and me a good start." Phil, a writer, said he had more or less cleared two or three weeks in advance to be with his newborn. He really got off to a good start with his daughter and, because he was still able to get some work done during that time, he didn't feel that much dislocation in his work.

The First Weeks of Your Baby's Life

Few of the other men I talked to had this grace period. Michael, a clerical worker, said, "It would have been nice to have a couple weeks to stay home, especially since my wife had a cesarean and was really sore. But I had to work. In fact, I was working all week when my son was born. I took Friday off, that was the only day. I just couldn't afford to take the time without pay." Michael said he would definitely be in favor of paid paternity leave, but he didn't raise the issue with his employer (a major national corporation). Pat, who works at a tool and die company in the Midwest, had exactly the same story. "I'd love a paternity leave, and if I had my choice I would have stayed home at least a couple weeks," he said. "But there was no chance my company would allow this. I would have been laughed at for asking." Other men report taking a few "sick days" when their children were born.

It's possible that paternity leave will become more of a reality if Congress passes the bill sponsored by Representative Patricia Schroeder (Democrat from Colorado) guaranteeing both parents a leave of absence to care for a newborn, an adopted child, or a seriously ill child or parent. But legislation alone is not going to change everything. Even if Pat were entitled to a couple weeks off from the tool and die company, he'd still probably be laughed at (or at least worry about being laughed at) by coworkers for taking it. And, as a result, he might not take the time. In fact, a 1985 survey of 384 major American corporations, conducted by the New York–based research organization Catalyst, found that about one-third of the companies offered *unpaid* leave to new fathers, but in only 10 percent of them did the fathers actually take the time. This figure can be partly explained by simple economic necessity: few of us can afford an unpaid leave. But in Sweden, where fathers are able to take up to six months of *paid* leave to care for infants, only about 10 percent of dads took a day or more, and only 5 percent took a month or more (statistics from "Paternity Leave: Current and Future Prospects," by Joseph H. Pleck, Wellesley College Working Paper No. 157, 1985).

The reasons why fathers are not taking advantage of the paternity leaves to which they're legally entitled are complex. Part of the problem has to do with employers' attitudes toward men who take the time. Pleck cites two Swedish studies that found "a substantial proportion of both fathers and employers reported that employers do in fact view leave-taking fathers negatively and may penalize them in various ways... in spite of explicit legal prohibitions."

Another part of the problem has to do with us, the new fathers. The need to work—to define and fulfill and, of course, support ourselves through work—is something we learn before we're even out of diapers. (Isn't this part of the message of "what do you want to be when you grow up?") When we have children of our own, that need doesn't slacken —it just becomes tangled up in an unresolvable conflict. For a growing number of men today, the choice between work and children is really an impossible one: we lose no matter what we do.

Jerry Sachs said that work is a very big issue in the groups he runs for new fathers. "Most of the men I see want to work less, but they don't feel they can. They really have trouble with this. I've never met anybody yet who has cut back on his life-style to raise a child. It's seen as an *added* burden rather than something that's balanced by taking something else away." Rick Bell, a psychologist who runs a program for new fathers out of St. John's Hospital in Minneapolis, agrees that balancing work and family is a major problem for men today. He feels that part of pressure may be coming from outside, from norms that men feel that they have to live up to. "We may be doing to dads what was done to mothers a few years back—insisting on superdads," he says. "I think we may be creating a kind of superdad image—fast-track career and also nurturing to his children, balancing demands of job and family perfectly, sensitive to our wives, doing it all. These are worthwhile goals, but they're difficult to attain all at once, difficult to live up to. We childbirth educators and psychologists may be guilty of raising expectations or setting standards unrealistically high."

The ways we deal with these pressures and expectations will depend very much on our jobs, our personalities, our support from family and coworkers. Some men have stood up to employers and taken them to court for paternity leaves, but many more have knuckled under to work demands or positively thrown themselves into work with the arrival of a new baby. Sachs speculates that "many men compensate for their feelings of inadequacy in child care by becoming *more involved* in work. They say they want to be involved fathers, but then they get involved in new projects around the time of the birth, either as a distraction or as a compensation for feeling inadequate in dealing with the situation or because of a perceived financial need—the 'another mouth to feed' incentive. It's a very unfamiliar feeling for driven, high-powered executives who are used to success and results and getting things done. Dealing with a new baby is a whole different ballgame."

Yet another fairly common response to new fatherhood is for a man to put new pressure on himself to get ahead, to live up to success goals, to distinguish himself. For some it's a feeling of "now or never"; for others a desire to make something of themselves so their children will respect them. One new dad put it this way: "I worry about setting a good example. Will he be proud of me? Will I live up to his expectations? I know he will idolize me and I want to like the person he idolizes." Another father I talked to was pushing himself to act on his dreams of working in the movie business just around the time his son was born. It meant taking on a load of freelance work in addition to his nine-to-five job, but he felt he *had* to do it, and that this was the only time.

Balancing work and family is not a new issue for men, but it is an issue that has been thrown into relief by changes in our society over the past twenty years. It used to be okay for men to be breadwinners exclusively—in fact, there was a lot of social support, even pressure, for fathers to conform to this role. That pressure remains largely intact, but in a radically different society. Because our partners are likely to be in the work force, too, many of us now have to take time from our careers to help raise the children. But for many more of us, there is a real desire to be involved fathers, a desire that can be fulfilled only at a price to our work. Maybe we have to start being a little more imaginative and insistent about finding solutions. Long-term paternity leaves, even with full pay, may not yet be appealing, either to new fathers or employers, but there is a big, unexplored middle ground between six-month leaves and no leaves. To return to the example of the Western nation most advanced in this area, Sweden offers parents of both sexes the right to take twelve weeks of "special parental leave" at any time before the child reaches age eight. This last benefit is available in various forms, so, for example, the father can use it to lop off a few hours from his workday for a set period of time. Clearly, these kinds of flexible or spread-out paternity leaves would be less disruptive to one's career, less costly to employers, and less likely to make fathers vulnerable to penalties or stigmas on the job.

This work/family conflict is an issue that we surely will be reading a lot about through the rest of the 1980s and beyond. Although few of us feel that we've resolved it satisfactorily, at least more of us are aware of it and starting to talk about it. It's possible that the day is not too far off when parental leaves tailored to the needs of our families will become available in the United States. Right now, this area of social policy is still in its infancy. (For more on some of the ways men are finding to combine work and family, see Chapter 12.)

What Your Partner Is Going Through

During the first weeks of your baby's life, your wife has a lot to cope with. First there is the physical side. The ordeal of birth leaves many women exhausted for several days and sore for even longer; stitches from an episiotomy may begin to itch or hurt; breasts are often very painful when they begin to lactate and nipples frequently get extremely tender and sometimes infected when babies begin to nurse; mothers who have had cesarean sections are recovering from surgery, and just getting out of bed and walking around can be hard. Your partner is no longer so huge or weighted down around the middle, but many women see their postpartum shape as even less attractive. Loose, flabby folds of skin replace the firm, round abdomen of pregnancy; breasts may swell even larger if the woman is planning to breastfeed; and excess weight around the thighs and backside does not miraculously fall away with the birth. "Now I don't look pregnant—I just look fat" is how one woman put it.

Awful as some women feel about the lingering poundage of

The First Weeks of Your Baby's Life

pregnancy, many mourn the end of their intimate enveloping of the baby. They miss having the baby as a part of their bodies, they miss the special attention accorded obviously pregnant women, they miss feeling that they and they alone are nurturing this new life. The combination of this mourning over the end of pregnancy, fatigue, hormonal changes, the new and pressing responsibilities of motherhood, and the letdown that often follows a long-anticipated event can bring on a case of the postpartum blues. A good many women experience some version of this in the first week or two after the baby is born. One book compared it to the draggy, empty, disappointed mood so many of us sink into after Christmas.

For you, the new father, your partner's postpartum blues can be particularly baffling, even irritating. She wanted this baby for so long, you may be thinking, she insisted that nothing else would make her feel fulfilled—and now that the baby is here, all she can do is mope. You're right—but being right is no help in this case. If possible, try to sit on your own negative feelings for a while. Patience is probably the optimal response (although your reserves may be a bit depleted just at this time). Encourage her to talk about her mood and share your own feelings with her. Let her know that you're in this together. Both of you can take some comfort from the knowledge that postpartum blues are both normal and, in the overwhelming majority of cases, short-lived. In a week or two, the clouds will lift.

They don't, however, lift so quickly or easily for all women. Some women, even those who were not ambivalent about having a baby, find motherhood a trial. It can bring up difficult feelings from their own childhoods or confront them with painful feelings of inadequacy (not unlike the feelings many men experience). And not all mothers love their babies right away, a situation that is probably tougher for a woman than a man because of the cultural expectations placed on women. One father whose son had colic said, "It was a very tense time. My wife could not enjoy him. She thought she was unfit to be a mother because she didn't bond and she couldn't get him to stop crying. She started to resent me because I was so calm and more accepting than she was. Eventually, though, the colic ended and life got easier."

Mothers (and fathers) whose postpartum blues deepen into depression, whether because of some problem with the baby or because of psychological difficulties of their own, need help. Counseling for depressed parents is a good idea. Look to your physician, community organizations, church or synagogue, and friends and family members for ways of getting help. Try not to blame yourselves for being unnatural or unfit for parenthood. Take comfort in the knowledge that many new mothers and fathers find the transition much more difficult than they anticipated. New babies take a lot but seem to give very little in return: they don't smile yet, they don't seem to know you, they don't respond predictably, they don't play the way older babies play. Some parents find this first "sealed-off" phase of infancy impossible to deal with. It passes—and passes more quickly than you'd believe if you're suffering through it, but sometimes destructive patterns are so firmly in place that parents cannot enjoy their babies even after the babies "wake up" and begin to respond more recognizably. That's why getting help early on is so important.

Not all new mothers experience postpartum blues and those who do usually snap out of it—and into a real enjoyment of motherhood—quite soon. "My wife took to motherhood instantly," one father said. "It was as if she got in touch with some long-lost side of herself." The mother-infant bond, once established, is one of the elemental forces of nature, like gravity or magnetism. And particularly if the mother is breastfeeding (see below), this bond can seem all-encompassing and utterly sufficient unto itself. All the baby's physical and emotional needs are being met by the mother, the mother seems totally engrossed in the baby, and the father becomes the proverbial fifth wheel. Many mothers claim that they quickly develop special baby antennas that their partners utterly lack. Why is it, these mothers ask, that *I* always hear the baby crying in the middle of the night while *he* is sleeping soundly? How come only *I* know that you can't go visiting without three diapers and a change of clothes? Why does *he* so totally lack an intuitive sense of when the baby is hungry, when tired, when bored? We could point out that if she allowed us to get near the baby, we might develop antennas of our own, but this would probably only make matters worse. Couple all this with

The First Weeks of Your Baby's Life

the enforced abstinence from sexual intercourse (usually for at least a month after the delivery) and you have a potentially explosive situation in which the new father feels excluded from *everything* at home. No wonder so many men throw themselves into their work.

The best way out of this situation, as mentioned above, is to stake out areas of contact and baby care that are yours alone. Skin-to-skin contact is one key to bonding: breastfeeding mothers get this all the time; you can get it by taking baths with your baby (support the baby's back and head against your stomach and chest) and holding and changing your baby. Touch is as important to infants as food, and providing warm, loving contact can be a way of including yourself.

Some men blame breastfeeding, which is on the rise in the United States, for their alienation from wife and baby. But many of the men I talked to were totally supportive of it—for their wives, their babies, and themselves. Pat laughed at the idea of being jealous of his wife's breastfeeding: "I thought it was neat and fun to watch, though it was a partial pain for her." And Terry was grateful for the breastfeeding because it meant *he* didn't have to get up at night: "I almost felt guilty because I didn't miss any sleep after my son was born. My wife was the one who got up, breastfed him, and rocked him back to sleep." Other fathers felt pushed away by the physical closeness between mother and baby during breastfeeding and resentful that even after the birth, the mother was still providing all the baby's sustenance. And some used the breastfeeding as an excuse to avoid feeding the child later, when the baby needed more than breast milk.

Breastfeeding may raise issues not only for you, the father, but for your partner as well. Breastfeeding, like choosing a childbirth method, is a subject of some controversy today. Advocates, such as the La Leche League, insist there is no substitute for mother's milk and that, ideally, milk from the breast should be *all* the baby gets in the first months of life. There is no question that milk from the breast is the optimal way to feed baby. It provides the ideal nutrition, is easier for baby to digest, the sucking (more difficult from breast than from bottle) fulfills baby's need to suck and enhances jaw development and tooth formation later, the physical warmth and closeness is immensely satisfying to baby, and breast milk is cheaper than formula, more transportable, and ready to serve without sterilizing or heating. Yet even breastfeeding mothers who agree with all this in theory may feel overly pressured by the fanaticism of breastfeeding advocates. Breastfeeding definitely ties a mother down and makes it difficult to be away from her baby for any period of time. A working mother who breastfeeds will have to pump her breasts during the day to keep her milk supply going, and this is an irritating chore at best and an impossible one for many women. Your partner may want to breastfeed, but it may not work out for as long or as completely as the breastfeeding advocates insist is right. If a woman is highly stressed, overtired, or malnourished, her milk may not come in or it may dry up.

Breastfeeding advocates may make your partner feel guilty or inadequate every time she gives the baby a bottle, but opponents of breastfeeding can undermine her both emotionally and physically. These opponents may include all those who did not or cannot themselves breastfeed: grandmothers, friends, relatives, neighbors, baby-sitters, even old-fashioned family doctors. Although rarely as outspoken or organized as breastfeeding advocates (after all, the advocates have science on their side), these opponents can ruin a new mother's confidence and disrupt her milk supply. A number of women I know or have spoken with (including my wife) say they felt a definite if subtle pressure particularly from nonbreastfeeding women to switch to bottle-feeding or at least to supplement the breast with a daily bottle. The mother-in-law who asks, "Are you sure he's getting enough to eat?" may seem innocent enough to *you*, but what your breastfeeding partner hears is "Your milk is not plentiful enough to sustain my grandchild— give him a nice *full* bottle of formula and he'll stop crying." Unless baby-sitters are explicitly told that the mother is breastfeeding and that she wants to do *all* the feedings herself, they may find it more convenient to give the baby a bottle. Your partner (or you) may have to lay down the law not once but repeatedly until the message is clear.

The First Weeks of Your Baby's Life

A running battle with in-laws, mothers, and care-givers over how to feed the baby is the *last* thing a mother needs to face in the first weeks—or ever. Not only is it trying emotionally, but the emotional stress can have a physical effect on her milk supply. The more pressured and criticized a nursing mother feels, the tenser she becomes, and the tenser she becomes the less milk she produces. The hungry baby howls for more food, the insensitive grandmother suggests trying formula, the new mother grows angrier, and her milk supply diminishes even further. It's an explosive situation in which everyone is the loser. You can help by acting as your partner's buffer and support. Be sensitive to the criticism she may be getting, shield her from tense situations, let her know that you approve of her breastfeeding, and help her find quiet places and calm moments in which to feed the baby.

Not only do nursing mothers get caught in the crossfire between breastfeeding advocates and opponents, they may also experience their own physical and emotional difficulties. Breastfeeding, although "natural," is not as easy as it looks. Nipples can become sore, cracked, or infected; finding a comfortable position may be hard, breasts may hurt or leak. A nursing mother can have a harder time taking off the weight of pregnancy and the nursing may lower her self-esteem. "I feel like a cow," is the reaction some women have, and many feel embarrassed about the entire process, especially when they must nurse in a public or semipublic place. Even without a nagging mother-in-law, a nursing mother may wonder if her baby is getting enough to eat (at least with a bottle you can see how much formula goes into the baby); she may feel she is offering the breast as a kind of pacifier every time the baby cries and she may come to resent the baby's ceaseless demands. Even women who find breastfeeding more of a pain than a pleasure may still mourn when the baby is finally weaned. It can be difficult to surrender that last link between her body and her baby. Many mothers describe this as a mini replay of postpartum blues.

All of this can be extremely baffling to new fathers. The common male response—if you're having trouble with the breastfeeding, then switch to the bottle—although logical may be beside the point. We may have the best of intentions in our support for our partners' decision, only to find that she doesn't want us to interfere. Again, there is no easy answer because it's a complicated, many-sided issue. Probably the best advice is to back up your partner in whatever she feels and decides. Give her time to adjust, both to the demands of breastfeeding and the trials of weaning. Give her emotional space and remember that for many women breastfeeding is a highly charged emotional situation. Defuse as much of the negative emotion as you can by buffering her from stress and criticism, including your own. If the breastfeeding doesn't work out for some reason, comfort your partner as best you can and try to play up the positive side—that you'll be able to participate more in the bottle-feeding, that she'll get more rest, and so on. You may also find it helpful to take a look at books on the subject, such as *The Complete Book of Breastfeeding* by Marvin S. Eiger and Sally Wendkos Olds (Bantam Books, 1972), which contains a chapter for fathers, or *The Womanly Art of Breastfeeding* (La Leche League, 1963).

The first weeks of your baby's life are going to be a period of readjustment for you and your partner. You're both in very unfamiliar roles and you're both just learning to live with a very unfamiliar person. The transformation of your partner to mother may seem like the most beautiful thing in the world— or one of the most unsettling. You may feel as if you're living with *two* strangers who are utterly wrapped up in each other. Hang in there. Assert your need to be with and care for the baby, even if some of the tasks make you feel a bit uneasy at first. And when you've given her time to land on her feet, assert your need to be with your partner. While you're at it, don't forget to tell her you love her. (For more on the impact of children on one's relationship, see Chapter 10.)

Your Amazing Baby

Yes, you and your partner are going through a lot in these weeks, but let's not forget about your newborn and what he

The First Weeks of Your Baby's Life

(or she) is going through. After nine months in a warm, dark, wet, quiet, and increasingly snug-fitting cocoon, life in the open air is quite a shock! But even before he gets there, he's got to endure the contractions, squeezing, and pushing of birth, which child development expert Burton White speculates is "at least as tiring for the infant as it is for his mother" (*The First Three Years of Life*, Prentice-Hall, 1975). This is why, in White's view, babies tend to sleep so much in the period immediately following birth—maybe as much as twenty-four hours straight with only a few drowsy waking periods to suck.

The first, and most crucial, major adjustment your baby must make is getting his lungs to work. In the womb, the baby gets everything he needs from the mother, including oxygen. Now, in a matter of moments, he's got to start breathing on his own. Eating by himself is less of an immediate issue since infants are born with enough stored-up weight and energy to go for three or four days without much food. Babies are even expected to lose some weight (maybe half a pound) in the first five days after birth, and then gain it back in the next five. So don't worry if he doesn't seem to be eating well at first or if your partner's breast milk doesn't come in for a few days.

Newborns are a lot sturdier than they look to nervous new parents. Remember those just-born babies who survived for days buried under rubble after the earthquakes in Mexico City in 1985? Your baby is built to survive. By all means, don't be afraid to handle her: pick her up, cradle her in your arms, rock her, walk with her, explore her reflexes (see below). Just make sure you support the back of her head with your hand when you lift her and that you're gentle with the soft spots—or fontanelles—that you can see at the crown of the baby's head.

Not too many years back, people (or at least scientists) believed that human babies were rather like puppies or kittens: born insensate, with only the instinct to eat, sleep, and cry. Now scientists recognize what many parents have known all along: newborns can do a lot! Ten minutes after birth a baby can localize a sound, he can see something eight to twelve inches in front of him, and can track a slow-moving object. He prefers to look at patterns with colors than at solid blocks of color, and most of all he wants to look at a human face and listen to a human voice, especially one that is high-pitched. The best way to communicate with your new baby is to set your face fairly close to his and raise the pitch (not the volume) of your voice a bit. You may, in fact, find that you're doing this instinctively—a sign that parenting has its innate side, too.

Your new baby can hear and see you, he's incredibly sensitive and responsive to your touch, he's aware of certain changes in his environment and in his handling, he wants to look around and listen to the sound of human voices—but with all this burgeoning power of the brain and the senses, your baby still has very little control over his body. A range of protective reflexes guide the responses of just about every part of him: there is a gag reflex to prevent him from choking on mucus; a reflex to turn his head from side to side to keep from smothering and a reflex to raise his arms up over his face if an object seems to be coming toward him; when he's cold, he shrinks up into himself and shivers and cries to speed up circulation; when the lights are too bright he squeezes his eyes shut and when he's overstimulated, he tunes out the world by falling asleep. The so-called Moro reflex causes the baby to startle, arch his back, throw his arms out and bring them together rapidly in response to sudden shifts in position or loud noises. The tonic neck reflex makes the baby assume a kind of fencer's stance when he's on his back: if he turns his head to the right, for example, his right arm goes out to the side and his left arm draws into his body.

The newborn also has a swimming reflex that causes him to wriggle and paddle about like a little frog, and a walking reflex that you can activate by holding the baby upright on a bed or changing table: he'll actually take little steps, pushing the soles of his feet down and lifting one leg after another. These last-mentioned reflexes disappear quite quickly, and the Moro and tonic neck reflexes a bit more gradually over the first few months of life. Your baby's hands are also controlled by reflexes. You'll notice how tightly curled most babies keep their tiny fists, and if you stroke the palm of the hand or the sole of the foot, you can get your baby to grip your finger— and a fierce, clinging grip it is.

The First Weeks of Your Baby's Life

And on top of all these bodily reflexes there is, of course, the cry reflex—the baby's instinctive response to hunger, fatigue, distress, boredom, loneliness, transitions, and just about everything else. Babies cry: there is no getting around it and it's one of those things you have to live with. One thing that surprises a lot of new parents is how quickly a newborn can go from blissful peace to raging wails and back again. Such behavior in an adult would be a sign of serious mental disorder—but it's perfectly normal in a baby. Burton White says we should take the quick mood changes as "reminders that infants very probably experience life quite differently from adults at times." Newborns really do live for and in the moment. Each experience is fragmentary and isolated. The baby has no past experience to draw on, little memory, and no understanding of the future or the permanence of objects: once something falls out of her field of vision, it ceases to exist as far as the baby is concerned.

Even after your baby wakes up from her long snooze following birth, she's still going to spend a very large portion of her days with her eyes closed. In the first week or so, she may be awake and alert only three minutes out of every hour, and she'll probably drift from full wakefulness to a kind of dreamy trance to light sleep to deep sleep with no real pattern or schedule. "A newborn baby will sleep whenever he needs to and wherever he finds himself," says Penelope Leach, the author of well-known books on infant and child development. "There is nothing that you can do to make your baby sleep more than this amount and nothing that the baby can do to sleep less." (*Your Baby & Child: From Birth to Age Five*, Knopf, 1984).

What this means for new fathers is: Take advantage of the times your baby is awake. Three minutes an hour does not give you a lot of time to get acquainted, especially if you're out of the house working most of the week. Many newborns are happiest and most alert on the changing table, or in the moments right after eating (assuming all that happy sucking hasn't put them back to sleep). Try to be on hand to be with your baby when those moments occur. Look in her eyes and talk to her. You'll be delighted at how quickly you can get to know her and how much she responds to you. "I was surprised at how much she could do right from the start," one father told me. "It was amazing how fast the little creature became part of the world." (For a summary of baby's physical and mental progress from birth to age one, see the infant development chart in Appendix A.)

Are You Equipped?

In a consumer society catering to yuppies, it was inevitable that the baby products market would go upscale and out of control. If you've got the money and the desire, you can go truly wild setting up your baby's room, installing the latest in Italian high-fashion cribs with matching bumpers, blankets, curtains, stretchies—maybe even coordinated disposable diapers someday (don't laugh: disposable diaper fashion has become a very high-stakes, serious enterprise). If you want to go wild, you don't really need any advice or guidance here: just bring your plastic and let the baby supply store salespeople assist you in acquiring it all.

But if your budget is limited or if other parents have warned you how quickly baby clothes/toys/equipment become obsolete and thus given away, put away, or thrown away, you'll want to exercise a little restraint and rationality in your purchases (remember that other people are likely to give you presents, not to mention the presents you'll buy along the way yourselves). Following is a list of what you should have on hand to keep your baby happy, healthy, comfortable, and transportable in the first few weeks of life. In planning your purchases, keep in mind that you can usually find major items such as crib, changing table, or carriage second-hand and in very good condition, and you can also borrow a lot from family and friends who've been through it all before you.

For sleeping:

Crib with mattress and bumpers (or portable crib or sturdy old-fashioned baby carriage)
Waterproof sheet

The First Weeks of Your Baby's Life 229

Crib with mattress and bumpers

Regular fitted sheets
Blankets
Receiving blankets

For eating:

Bottles, nipples, bottle caps (You'll need fewer if mother is breastfeeding, but even so, have *some* bottles and formula

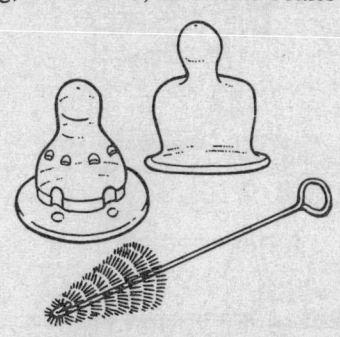

The natural nipple (left), orthodontic nipple (right), and nipple brush

on hand for times when her milk dries up, she's out, sick, and so on)
Bottle sterilizer (can be large pot and tongs)
Bottle and nipple brushes
Formula
High chair (a huge help in feeding the baby once baby can sit up alone at around 6 months)

Clothing:

4 stretchies
4 undershirts
2 nightgowns
2 sweaters
1 hat
(You might want to increase numbers here if you don't have ready access to a washing machine; otherwise you'll be spending a lot of your time at the laundromat.)

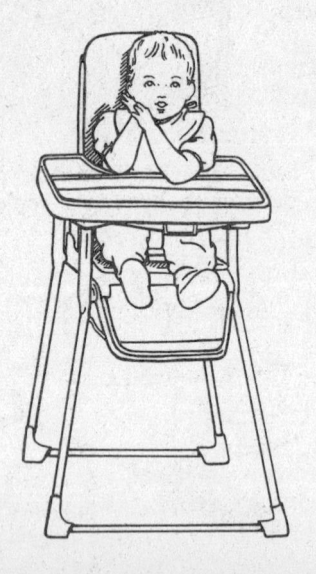

Infant high chair

The First Weeks of Your Baby's Life

For changing:

Padded changing mat
Changing table (This is not strictly necessary, but it's great to have because it will spare your back from bending awkwardly every time baby must be changed. See if you can get one second-hand.)
Several packs of disposable diapers, or
Two dozen terry diapers with pins and plastic pants
Disposable wipes and/or a good supply of washcloths
Baby powder or cornstarch
Vaseline
Baby oil or lotion

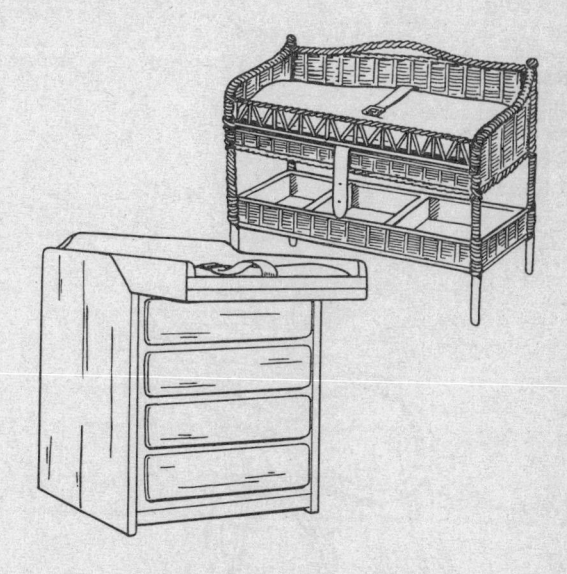

Two styles of changing tables

For bathing and hygiene:

Baby bathtub that supports baby's back (This is nice to have, although you *can* bathe baby in the kitchen sink.)

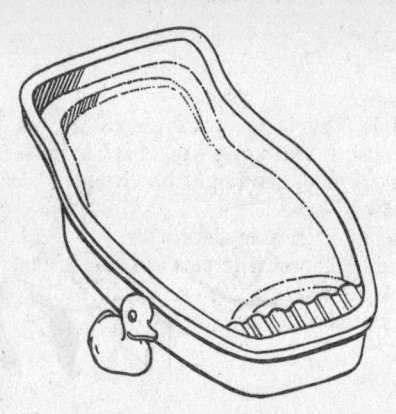

Baby bathtub

Cotton balls
Q-tips
Stork scissors
Soft brush
Soft towel and washcloth

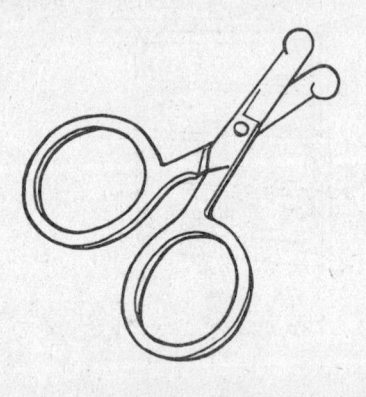

Stork scissors

The First Weeks of Your Baby's Life 233

The infant car seat (left) and toddler seat (right)

For transport:

Infant car seat (required by law in all states)
Baby sling or carrier (The best for newborns are the ones in which baby is nestled against your chest with good back and head support.)

Baby sling

A convertible baby carriage/stroller

Stroller or baby carriage (This nonessential item is highly recommended if you want to go on outings of any length.)

Furniture and toys:

Adjustable infant seat with strap (This is not essential, but it is useful for propping baby up and keeping entertained, and later when you start him or her on solid meals.)
First toys are brightly colored shapes for baby to look at (Make sure they are nontoxic and have no rough edges.)

These are the basic supplies. For how to use them in caring for and playing with your baby, see Chapter 9.

9. Now What Do We Do? Mastering the Practical Routines

Your mother-in-law has returned to Saint Louis. You are back on the job, with a backlog of work to catch up on. The UPS truck no longer pulls up at your door with boxes of tiny outfits and teddy bears. The phone calls from long-lost friends and checks from distant relatives have stopped. Your wife has recovered physically from the birth and is even starting to wear her prepregnancy clothes. In short, life is returning to "normal" with one very small (yet very large) addition: your infant son or daughter, now three weeks old.

For many couples, the real "work" of parenting begins when the wonder and magic of the first couple of weeks wears off and everything goes back to normal—except the baby, who, despite being a very normal baby, seems totally strange, unpredictable, and, in the words of one parent I know, eccentric. Now what do we do? new parents wonder when they're finally left all alone to care for their newborns. This can be a particularly pressing question for new fathers who—because of work, anxiety about handling the baby, fear of incompetence, or exclusion by possessive new mothers—haven't spent that much time with their newborns and thus really don't know what to do. The more time that passes in which new fathers remain in the dark, the more mysterious and difficult infant care will seem. Eventually, some fathers simply bow out, using their incompetence about practical matters as an excuse to retreat from their families.

When you break it down to its basic routines, caring for an infant is neither mysterious nor difficult, although it *is* demanding. It doesn't take special knowledge or skill so much as patience, love, confidence, stamina, and a willingness to do it day in and day out. For the most part, it's like starting a new job or taking up a new sport: you learn by doing it. But there are some tips from pediatricians, child development experts, and experienced parents that can get you started on the right foot, calm some common anxieties, answer some of your questions, and spare you from making a few mistakes. If you need help or advice or reassurance on mastering the practical routines of infant care, this is the chapter to read. (For a summary of baby's physical and mental progress from birth to age one, see the infant development chart in Appendix A.)

Holding

Babies not only love to be held, they *need* it. Studies have shown that babies in institutions who are fed, dressed, bathed, and medically cared for properly, but not picked up, held, cuddled, and loved, fail to develop at the same rate as babies raised in loving families. Their physical and emotional development is stunted and their vulnerability to disease is much higher than babies who receive loving touch. So by all means, pick up your baby! Hold her next to your skin, pat her back, kiss and hug her. It's good for both of you.

Don't listen to those self-appointed baby experts who tell you that picking up a baby too often will spoil her. They're wrong. It's impossible to spoil young babies because their mental capacities are not advanced enough yet. The spoiled toddler cries to get her way, and if she gets it, she cries all the more next time because she remembers how to manipulate you. But the infant does not—cannot—scheme for attention this way. In fact, she needs to figure out that she can get attention by asking for it. When her cries result in her being

Now What Do We Do? 237

picked up, held, fed, and comforted, she learns that her environment is responsive, that there is someone out there listening for her, that it's worth growing up and learning how to stop crying. So don't worry about loving and handling your baby too much. Especially if your partner is breastfeeding, it's your primary way of getting to know your baby. And don't worry if you become mildly aroused when holding your baby against your skin. This is a perfectly normal response to the sensual aspect of close contact with your baby.

In the first month or so of your baby's life, she won't be able to support her head by herself: if you just lifted her with your hands under her armpits, the way you see parents lift older babies and toddlers, her head would flop back, and she'd probably startle and cry. So, when you lift her you should be careful to slip one hand behind her neck and head to give it support. A favorite position for babies is having their

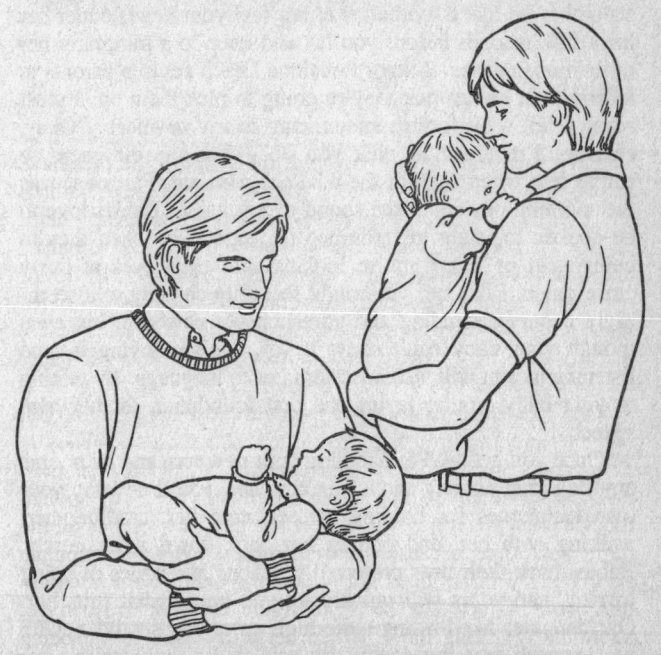

Two ways of holding baby with head supported

heads on or above your shoulder, with their bodies held securely against your chest. If your baby is on her back, you can get her into this position with one smooth motion by slipping one palm behind her head and the other behind her back and bottom and then, with all her crucial parts held securely, lifting her to your chest and shoulder. You may notice that it feels more natural to have her on your *left* side. Nature programmed us this way so that we'd hold our newborns next to our hearts: it soothes them to listen to the sounds and feel the vibrations that they lived with in their old familiar home in the womb. The next time you're in a museum, take a look at the paintings of the Madonna and Child. The Old Masters usually depict Mary holding her Child on her left side.

Since babies instinctively fear being dropped, they'll stay calmer if they feel safe and secure during the transition from crib to your shoulder. Don't swoop down on your baby and scoop her up like a football. Let her feel your hands under her for a few seconds before you lift and keep to a minimum her time in open space. Author Penelope Leach advises parents to inform their babies that they're going to pick them up. I must admit I felt a bit foolish announcing to my newborn, "Okay, sweetie, I'm about to pick you up"—but she did seem to startle less when she got the advance warning. Part of it was the soothing powers of the sound of my voice. Babies love to be spoken to, sung to, hummed to, especially when they're being held or when you're looking into their eyes at fairly close range. Like me, you might feel silly chatting to a seemingly uncomprehending and unresponsive newborn, but even though your baby can't show it yet, she's enjoying it, and listening to you will also accustom her to language. By talking to your baby, you're laying the first foundation for her own speech.

Once you get used to handling your newborn and overcome any lingering anxiety about breaking her, you'll develop your own techniques for holding her, calming her, cradling her, walking with her, and putting her back down again gently. Babies have their own preferred positions and styles of being carried, and yours will quickly let you know what suits her. Our daughter liked riding quite high up on my shoulder, with her stomach pressing against the top of the shoulder and her

Now What Do We Do?

arms dangling down my back. Some feel happy cradled in dad's arms, with head resting in the crook of the arm; others like to be held a bit away from the body and bounced or jiggled lightly.

Babies also have different preferences in how they're wrapped. Some like to be swaddled rather tightly in a light blanket: fold blanket into a triangle and place the baby on it with her feet pointing toward the apex; then fold up the apex over her middle and then fold in the two sides and tuck them in securely. Wrapping your baby up in this way may make her feel secure and it will keep her warm. It can also be a good substitute for holding her and may keep her happy for several hours when you need a break. On the other hand, your baby may hate it and thrash until the blanket comes loose. Some babies scream when they're undressed, making diapering a real trial. Others love to be naked and, if it's warm, you can

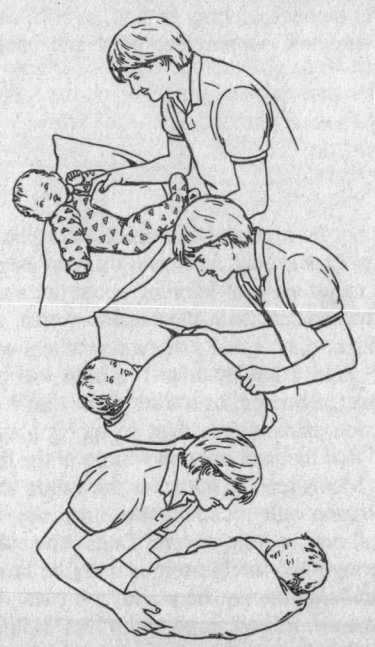

Wrapping baby in a blanket

spend long stretches (a long stretch for a newborn is ten minutes or so) letting them air out and playing with them on the changing table. If your baby can tolerate it, you might want to make this airing out time a regular part of your routine: exposing their bottoms to the air and letting them really dry out is the best way to clear up diaper rash.

Your baby will also let you know her preferred sleeping or resting position. Some pediatricians will advise you to place your baby on her stomach so that if she spits up it will run out of her mouth instead of down her throat. But babies do have a gag reflex (see the previous chapter) to protect them from choking, and if your baby will only settle on her back, then that's where you should put her. Until the scab from the umbilical cord falls off and heals, usually in about a week or two, you should put your baby on her side so that she won't irritate the spot. Prop her with a rolled-up blanket or two. Whether you're placing her on back, tummy or side, in crib, carriage or bassinet, make sure you support her head and back as you lower her in.

Playing

Playing may not be a crucial life function on the order of feeding, dressing, or sleeping, but from the very beginning it is one of baby's major ways of learning about the good things of life and making contact with the outside world. And in a great many families, play is dad's domain. Fathers who never change a diaper, hold a bottle, or give a bath still play with their babies. In fact, a number of studies show that dads spend a greater proportion of their time than do moms playing with their babies, and that they not only play more of the time, they play differently. Moms tend to go in for the gentle and verbal type of play: singing and rocking, showing baby toys and books, dangling things in front of him. Dads, however, prefer more physical, rough-and-tumble sort of activity: holding and tapping and stimulating the newborn and, a bit later on, tossing the baby in the air, rolling around with him, riding him on their shoulders. Dads are more active and inventive play-

Now What Do We Do?

mates, and they seem to take to it naturally. Of course, dads can nurture their babies, too, but if they don't or won't or can't get involved in the nurturing routines, they play.

Pediatrician and neonatologist T. Berry Brazelton comments that "most fathers seem to present a more playful, jazzing up approach... [he] is expecting a more heightened, playful response from the baby. And he gets it! Amazingly enough, an infant by two or three weeks displays an entirely different attitude (more wide-eyed, playful, and bright faced) toward his father than to his mother." Terry from Minneapolis confirmed Brazelton's laboratory observations with his own experiences with his three-month-old son in this way: "I try to stimulate him a lot while my wife is more comforting and handles the feedings. When he sees me he gets all goofy and crazy. We really have fun. In fact, it's good if I stay away from him at bed time, because having too much fun gets him worked up."

In terms of how or what to play, just about anything goes so long as the baby enjoys it. Play with a newborn is necessarily going to be gentler and calmer than play with a sturdy eight-month-old. At the start your playing might be an extension of your holding—jiggling the baby a bit, or moving him up and down against your body; or your "games" may relate to his urge to see, hold, and feel things. Explore him and explore with him to see what he likes. He'll certainly let you know which "game" is acceptable and which is not.

Other beginning playtime activities might be as elementary as sticking your tongue out at baby, dancing with him, propping him up on your knees and gently bouncing him up and down, tickling his tummy or his ear. Babies derive tremendous pleasure from making eye contact with their parents, and this can be the basis for all sorts of games (remember to place your face about twelve inches or so from your baby's face). Infant exercise is also a fine way for dad and baby to play: get him when he's warm and fed and alert and help him stretch his arms and legs (gently, of course; and do not lift a baby up by his hands or elbows—you could hurt his shoulders). You can also begin reading to your infant when he's still amazingly young. Way before they can understand the words, babies like the interaction of being propped on dad's lap while they listen to his voice and watch him flip the pages.

Although most of us dads are great at inventing our own games, occasionally we all run out of ideas. When that happens, you might want to consult a terrific series of books called *Your Child At Play*. The first volume, by Marilyn Segal, Ph.D., covers birth to one year, and the next two volumes, by Segal and Don Adcock, Ph.D., cover one to two and two to three (all published by Newmarket Press). They contain lots of tips for years of playing to come.

Feeding

Even if your partner is breastfeeding the baby, you should try to include yourself in some aspect of the feeding. Many couples like to supplement the breastfeeding with one bottle of expressed breast milk (or formula) a day, and this could be part of your routine. Or, if your partner feels strongly about giving the baby all his meals from the breast, you might give the baby a bottle of water now and then. It makes good sense to accustom even breastfed babies to taking a bottle because there will be times when mom wants to go out or cannot breastfeed. Babies who have never had bottles have been known to refuse to drink out of them later on, and this can be a real problem.

Night feedings can be a real battleground for couples, especially if the mother is nursing. Some men told me that their wives willingly got up twice or three times a night to breastfeed and soothe the baby back to sleep, but all of us are not so lucky. If your partner is suffering from serious sleep deprivation, you can help by taking over one of the night feedings with a bottle or else by getting up, changing the baby, bringing him into bed with your partner, where she can nurse without really getting up, and then putting the baby back to sleep. It's no fun for *anyone* to be roused at three A.M. to deal with a hungry baby, but it is part of the job description of new parenthood.

For the first several months of his life, your baby doesn't need anything but breastmilk or formula. There is absolutely

Now What Do We Do?

no question that breastmilk is better for the baby, which is one reason why more and more mothers are breastfeeding these days. As far as formula goes, ask your pediatrician which kind to use and then follow the directions on the can. If your baby is being fed formula exclusively, you'll want to buy it by the caseload and mix up a batch at a time. Baby supply stores carry bottle sterilizers or you can do it yourself with a big pot of boiling water and tongs. Don't forget to sterilize nipples and bottle caps, too.

Sterilizing the bottles, mixing up the formula, and getting everything all set is a bit of a pain, especially if your baby is screaming with hunger while you're doing it. If you know your baby is going to be formula-fed, you might want to practice the whole routine beforehand and have a fresh supply mixed up and waiting the day the baby comes home from the hospital. Making formula is one of those tiresome tasks of baby care—along with doing tons of laundry, buying diapers, stuffing little hands and feet into little outfits. Try to divide up the chores evenly so neither you nor your partner feels overburdened by the boredom and excluded from the fun.

Tips on bottle-feeding

The size of the hole in the nipple is important. It should be just big enough to allow you to shake out a few drops when you hold the bottle upside down. If the formula comes out in streams, the baby will choke and may spit it all up after gulping it down. If the hole is too small, the baby will exhaust himself sucking or may get frustrated and start raging. If the flow is too slow, heat up a needle on your stove burner and then slip it quickly through the nipple opening. Toss out nipples with overlarge holes. It makes sense to have lots of extra nipples on hand.

Find a quiet, comfortable, softly lit place to sit. A lot of noise or people bustling in and out may distract a baby, especially a slightly older baby, from his feeding. However, quiet music in the background may make the feeding more interesting and relaxing for you.

Many parents like to warm the formula up a bit (in a pan of

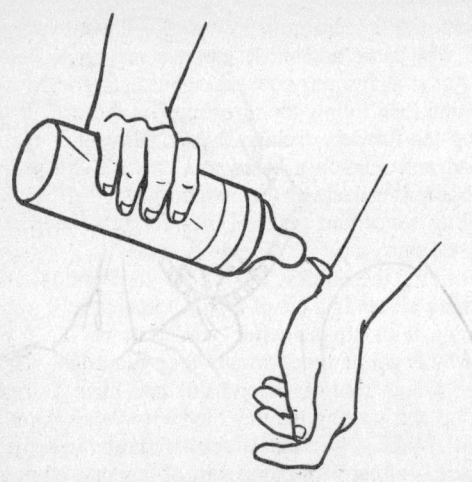

Testing formula on the wrist

water on the stove) before giving it to baby, although many books say this is not necessary and that the baby will drink whatever he's used to. If you have warmed the bottle, test it on your wrist before you give it to the baby to make sure it's not too hot (it should be lukewarm). Loosen the bottlecap a bit so the milk will flow freely without creating a vacuum inside.

Settle down with the baby's bottom in your lap and his head and neck supported in the crook of your arm. Make certain he's not lying flat, which would make it hard for him to swallow. If he seems reluctant to suck, try stroking the cheek nearest you with the back of a finger. This triggers the "rooting" reflex, causing the baby to turn and try to find the bottle.

Once he's got the nipple and is sucking happily, let him feed at his own pace. Make sure that you're holding the bottle in such a way that the nipple is always covered with milk; if you hold the bottle too much on the horizontal, your baby will be sucking in too much air.

Feedings are a great time to make contact with your baby. He's happy because he's satisfying one of his major urges, he's awake and alert (at least at the start of the feeding), and

Feeding baby his bottle

he may be interested in looking around. He's close enough to see your face clearly, so look in his eyes and give him a smile. The pleasure of contact can go a long way toward making up for the pain of getting up in the middle of the night. Partly because feedings offer such a wonderful opportunity for loving contact with your baby, it's not a good idea to prop him up on a pillow with the bottle in his mouth. This can also cause the baby to choke or swallow too much air.

Don't worry if the baby doesn't finish his bottle every time, and certainly don't try to force him to finish. You might want to give the baby a break in the middle of the feeding, let him rest and look around. And it might also be a good idea to burp him. To burp a baby you hold him on your shoulder, sit

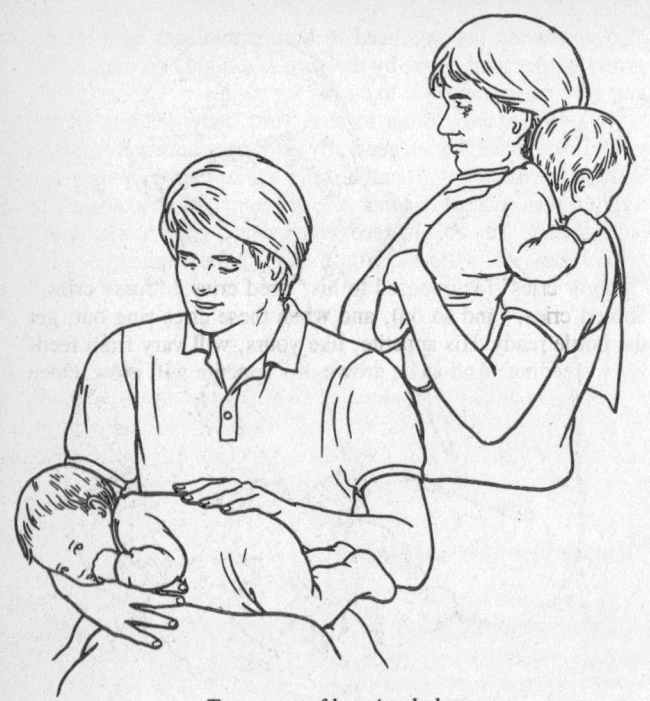

Two ways of burping baby

him up on your lap (supporting his chin with your hand), or lay him face down across your knees. Then you gently rub or pat his back until he brings up his burp, which is really just excess swallowed air. Authorities disagree on the need for burping—some say it's really more a chance for the parents to relax, slow the feeding down, cuddle the baby, and shift his position. Others say it really helps relieve stomach distress and helps babies keep their food down. Again, you should be guided by the needs of your baby and how he reacts to it. The best advice on the subject that I've seen comes in Miriam Stoppard's *Day-by-Day Baby Care* (Ballantine Books, 1983): "By all means do it ... but don't become fanatical about it.... Wait until your baby pauses naturally in the feeding, and take advantage of this pause to try burping her." Stoppard

Now What Do We Do?

also points out that the need to burp diminishes as the baby grows bigger. Her book, by the way, is a highly recommended and very complete guide to caring for babies.

In terms of how often to feed your baby, let him be the guide. Bottle-fed babies generally go longer between feedings than do breastfed babies and heavier babies can go longer than light babies, but *all babies are different* and it's absurd to suggest that you should feed yours every four hours, every three hours, or whatever. You'll soon come to recognize his "hungry cries" (as opposed to his "tired cries," "fussy cries," "bored cries," and so on), and when these cries ring out, get the bottle ready. His appetite, like yours, will vary from feeding to feeding. And as he grows, his appetite will grow. Once he hits ten pounds, he should be able to sleep for five or six hours at a stretch without needing to eat. Try to get him to take a bottle before you go to bed, and that way you might even get a full night's sleep (or almost) before too long.

Diapering and Dressing

Changing diapers has become a symbolic "great divide" between old-style and new-style fathers. My mother tells stories about my dad leaving us kids in diapers so wet and soiled they were hanging around our knees, and I've also heard of men of that generation who let their kids run around naked rather than put a diaper on them. Today's dads are champion diaperers! Of course, we don't all love every minute of it. Says Jim, father of a two-year-old boy and a newborn girl, "Doing ten diaper changes every day for two years gets to you after a while." But for several of the dads with whom I talked, changing diapers was the high point of their day with baby—a great opportunity to interact, play, and really get intimately acquainted.

Actually, Jim's estimate of ten diapers a day is a bit on the conservative side for newborns, who may need to be changed as often as once an hour! (There will be far fewer changes as your baby gets older.) A good rule of thumb is to change the baby's diaper after every meal, after every nap, at bathtime, and any time the diaper feels wet or soiled. Really young babies move their bowels quite frequently, and the stools of breastfed babies are loose and mustard-colored. So don't be alarmed when this is what you see. One compensation is that such stools are nearly odorless, which is not true of the stools that formula-fed babies pass.

Just about every dad has his early diaper change disaster story. It may be humorous to be peed or pooped on once or twice, but after that you'll want to be prepared. First of all, you should have a clean, dry, padded, and convenient place to change the baby (preferably a changing table, see Chapter 8) and second, you want all the necessary equipment handy, which includes the following:

Several diapers (either cloth or disposable, see below)
Washcloth, cotton, or disposable wipes
Tissues
Baby lotion or oil or petroleum jelly
Clean clothes
Diaper pail
Hamper
Something for baby to play with

Whatever kind of diaper you've chosen, the changing technique is basically the same. Take the old diaper off; if there's a bowel movement, use the front of the diaper to wipe away as much of it as you can. Fold up the diaper so nothing falls out of it and toss it in the diaper pail. Baby boys tend to pee the instant their diaper comes off, and it can squirt surprisingly high, so it's wise to cover them with a spare diaper while you're changing them. Wipe off and dry the baby's genital area: with a bowel movement, you'll probably want to use disposable wipes; urine can be wiped away with tissue, a damp washcloth, or cotton. Make sure you get the feces out of all the folds and creases in the baby's skin. Wipe girls from front to back so that you don't spread infection from rectum to vagina; never pull the labia apart to clean inside. With a boy, wipe from the inner thighs in toward the penis and then wipe his bottom off. If the boy has been circumcised, you'll want to keep the scab from sticking to the diaper until it heals. Most doctors recommend dabbing on a bit of petroleum jelly. Don't

Now What Do We Do?

pull back the foreskin of uncircumcised baby boys. When you're done, the baby should be completely clean and dry.

Now you must confront one of the burning issues of infant care today: powder or no powder? The prevailing wisdom of the times says no, unless you're really into it. The nurse at the hospital where our daughter was born recommended smearing a dab of petroleum jelly on the baby's bottom or into the disposable diaper as a guard against diaper rash, and this seemed to work pretty well. When rashes developed anyway, we dabbed A&D ointment on the rash area and sprinkled on a bit of baby cornstarch, and this helped clear it up quickly. Even better in curing diaper rash was to let the baby air out with nothing on her bottom at all; of course, this is easier in the warm months. These are my home remedies, and you and your partner will surely find your own. If you do decide to use baby powder or cornstarch, don't shake it out in thick clouds that the baby will inhale. Pour a little into your hands away from baby's face and then pat it on his bottom.

Even more fundamental than the powdering issue is the decision of whether to use disposable or cloth diapers. There is no doubt that disposables are easier: you just slip one (with the preattached tapes at the back) under your baby's bottom until it lines up with her waist, pull up the front of the diaper between her legs, and then secure the tapes to the front so the fit is good and snug. When the diaper is dirty, just take it off and throw it out. So easy... until you stop to think about the mounds of plastic piling up in garbage dumps all over the country and the energy and raw materials consumed in manufacturing this unrecyclable product. In addition to the environmental impact, there is the economic impact—on you. The *Wall Street Journal* reports that the average American family spends $535 on disposable diapers during the baby's first year. Cloth diapers are not free, of course, and they do have to be washed and dried, but ecologically and economically they have their advantages.

Cloth diapers come in a number of styles, materials, and methods of folding. And, in many areas you can arrange for a diaper service to pick up the dirty diapers and deliver fresh ones on a regular basis (still usually cheaper than buying disposables). As a rule of thumb in diaper folding, try to have the

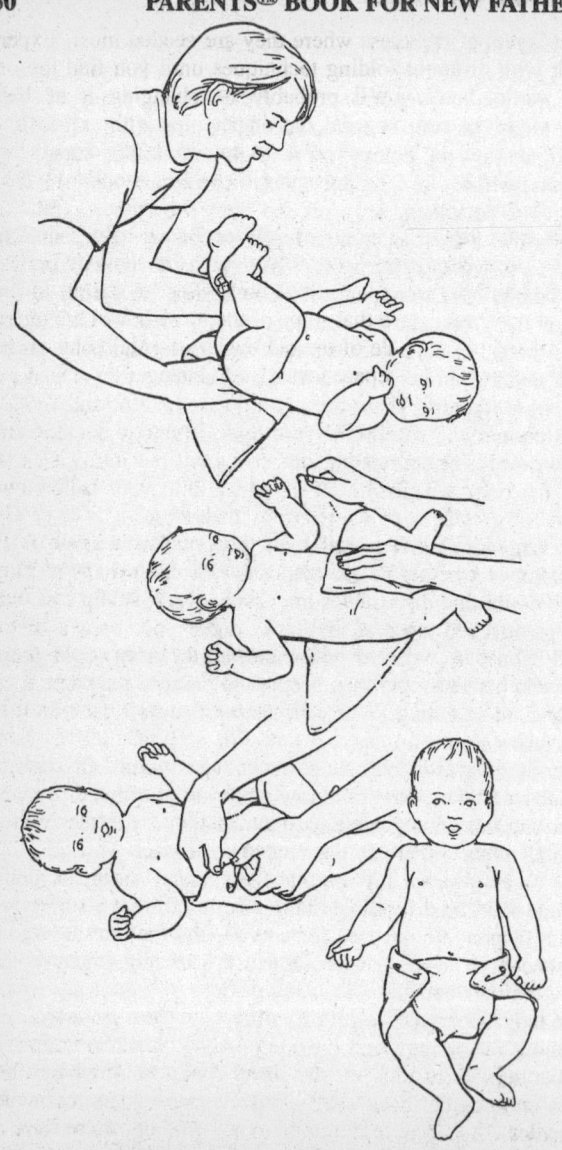

One folding technique for cloth diapers

Now What Do We Do? 251

most layers of thickness where they are needed most. Experiment with different folding techniques until you find the one that works best (you'll probably be changing it as baby grows). Make sure you get the diaper pins with self-locking heads. For an illustrated guide to folding cloth diapers and advice on washing and sterilizing them, see Stoppard's *Day-by-Day Baby Care*.

So now you've successfully cleaned your baby's bottom, had a nice chat with him as you got the new diaper on, showed him his favorite stuffed bird when he started to fuss —and now you notice that some of the loose bowel movement had leaked out the side of the old diaper and soiled his undershirt and stretchie. Prepare for an outfit change.

Since you've already unsnapped the stretchie in order to change the diaper, all you have to do is peel it off his little arms and legs (being careful not to soil the baby as you do this), unsnap the undershirt (assuming you have the easy wraparound kind that snaps in front), lift baby's head and back up a bit, and remove this, too. Of course, you remembered to have a change of clothes handy, so you don't have to go hunting through baby's room with a half-naked squirming baby balanced in your arms.

Now just reverse the undressing procedure: wrap the undershirt around the baby (the easiest way is to spread it out on the changing table and place the baby on top of it), pull his little arms through the little holes, and do up the snaps. Next, spread out the stretchie, insert the baby's feet into the stretchie feet, insert arms in armholes, and reach up through the sleeves until your hand finds baby's hand; then pull baby's hand through until all five fingers emerge through the cuff, and with all four limbs in the proper openings, do up the snaps. This is the really tricky part of the procedure. Stretchies, a single piece of cloth that covers everything without riding up, falling off, or binding baby's waist, are a really terrific invention, but they do have one small drawback—the snaps. Each stretchie comes equipped with a vast number of snaps, and each array of snaps has its own uniquely mysterious method of snapping together. There are front-snapping stretchies and back-snapping stretchies, ones that snap up the side of one leg and others that snap up the inseams of both legs; some have no

252 PARENTS™ BOOK FOR NEW FATHERS

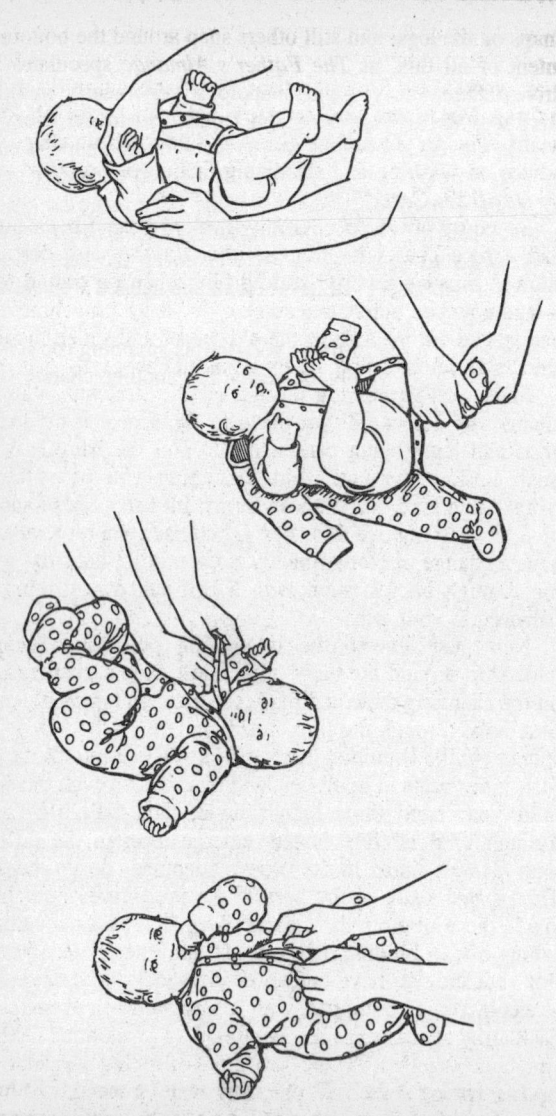

Dressing baby in an undershirt and stretchie

Now What Do We Do?

snaps on the legs, and still others snap around the bottom. The intent of all this, as *The Father's Almanac* speculates, is to drive fathers crazy—and snapology very nearly undid me. Rare was the change in which I managed to get every snap snapped; eventually I stopped trying and just snapped enough to keep baby covered. Occasionally I failed miserably and had to undo everything, get the baby out, turn the stretchie around, roll the baby (now screaming at maximum volume) over, and start snapping all over again up the back. Luckily, the hot weather soon came when all she needed was the diaper and undershirt.

The first couple of times you do this snapping routine solo, the baby will probably be ready for another change by the time you've finished stuffing hands into sleeves and snapping snaps. But you'll soon get the hang of it and even learn to live with snaps. And before you know it, your baby will be wearing overalls and sweatpants. (By the way, don't forget to wash your hands after changing the baby's diaper, especially if you're going to be feeding him later on.)

On the subject of how to tell if your baby is dressed warmly enough, Dr. Spock has an excellent piece of advice: don't try to judge by the feel of the baby's hands and feet, which are usually rather cool, but by her neck. If her neck is hot and sweaty, you've overdressed her. If it's cold and clammy, she needs another layer. You can also gauge how many layers to put on baby by what you're wearing: if you're in a t-shirt and shorts, it's crazy to wrap your baby up in a sweater and blanket—but you see this all the time. You do have to be careful, however, to protect a newborn baby from getting too much sun. A baby can get a serious sunburn in less than half an hour, so if you're at the beach, keep the baby in the shade.

Bathing

The fathers I interviewed were about equally divided between bathers and nonbathers. The bathers were all enthusiastic about their role as Mr. Clean. "It's part of our regular evening routine," said one new dad, "and it sure beats getting stuck with the dishes." Among the nonbathers there were several fathers who had a reluctance, even a fear of giving the bath. What if I drop him? what if he swallows water? what if he hollers when I wash his hair? were some of the standard anxieties. I was among these nonbathers with fear of water, and the first time I had to do the bath by myself (when my wife was out of town), I was pretty edgy. But the baby didn't drown or even scream, and the next time around we even had some fun. So ended my fear of the bath, and so yours will end. If you're really nervous about it, have your partner stand by the first couple of times. After that you'll be fine. For busy dads, and especially dads whose babies are being breastfed, the bath offers a really important opportunity for contact. As the baby grows, she'll start to enjoy her bath more and more, and this can be a wonderful daily ritual for father and child.

Before getting to the bathing techniques, let me repeat the standard bath warning: *Never leave your baby alone in the bath, even for a moment, even in a shallow bath.* You'd be amazed at how quickly your seemingly immobile newborn can slip, slide, or wriggle her way into trouble.

Newborn babies don't really need allover tub baths, and, in fact, until the navel and/or circumcision heals, you should keep the baby out of the water. "Topping and tailing" or a sponge bath is all that is called for. For "topping and tailing" in the first couple of weeks, you'll probably want to boil the water first and then pour it into a clean basin. Have lots of cotton balls handy, as well as cotton swabs, washcloth, towel, clean diaper, and change of clothes. Once the boiled water has cooled off to warm (test it on your wrist), dip in a cotton ball, wring it mostly dry, and clean the baby's eyes, wiping each eye gently from inside corner out. Then, with fresh cotton balls wipe behind baby's ears (but not inside them), and all around his face, especially around his mouth and chin and under the chin where dried milk could cause irritation. You can use a cotton swab to clean inside the nostrils, being careful not to push it into the nose. Once you finish with his face, get a washcloth, dampen it with warm water, and wipe his hands clean, then take off his diaper and get his bottom all

Now What Do We Do?

cleaned up. Pat him dry, get his diaper and clothes back on—and you're done.

The next step up is the sponge bath, which is easiest to do with baby on your lap (wear a bathing suit, a plastic apron, and a towel spread over your knees). You'll want the same equipment as described above, along with baby shampoo. Start at the top, soaping baby's front and back, under the arms and hands, then, with a damp squeezed-out washcloth, rinse off all the soap. To wash the hair, first wet it with a cloth, then shampoo (you won't even need a teaspoonful of shampoo), and then rinse out all the suds with a squeezed-out cloth (you'll probably get quite wet doing this). Dry baby's hair and top half, put his undershirt on, and then proceed to the lower half with the same soaping and sponging technique. You can do his face and ears as described above after he's all dried and dressed—or else do it before the sponge bath.

Now you can move up to a bath in a tub. Until your baby can sit up on his own, at around six months, he's going to need support in the bath—and it's a lot easier to give this support if you use a baby bathtub. There are a few different styles available: the ones for newborns look like little beds tipped up at an incline. The shape of the tub props the baby up and frees both of your hands for washing. When he outgrows this, you can use a flat-bottomed plastic tub, and then the regular bathtub, filled with a few inches of water. The baby will be less likely to slip if you line the bottom of the tub with a terrycloth towel. Always test the water temperature with your wrist or elbow before lowering baby in, and make sure you have everything you'll need—washcloth, towel, mild soap, nonsting shampoo, cottonballs, bath toys—at hand so you don't have to run around looking for things with a wriggling and wet baby in your arms.

For many babies and dads, the shampoo is the only part of bathtime when things get sticky. Most babies hate getting their faces and eyes wet, and the second they sense that shampoo time is upon them, some of them commence to howl. There are a couple of ways to minimize the stress. You can use a wet washcloth to wet down baby's hair and to remove the shampoo lather, carefully rubbing from front to back to keep water out of eyes. It's important to get baby to tilt his head back so

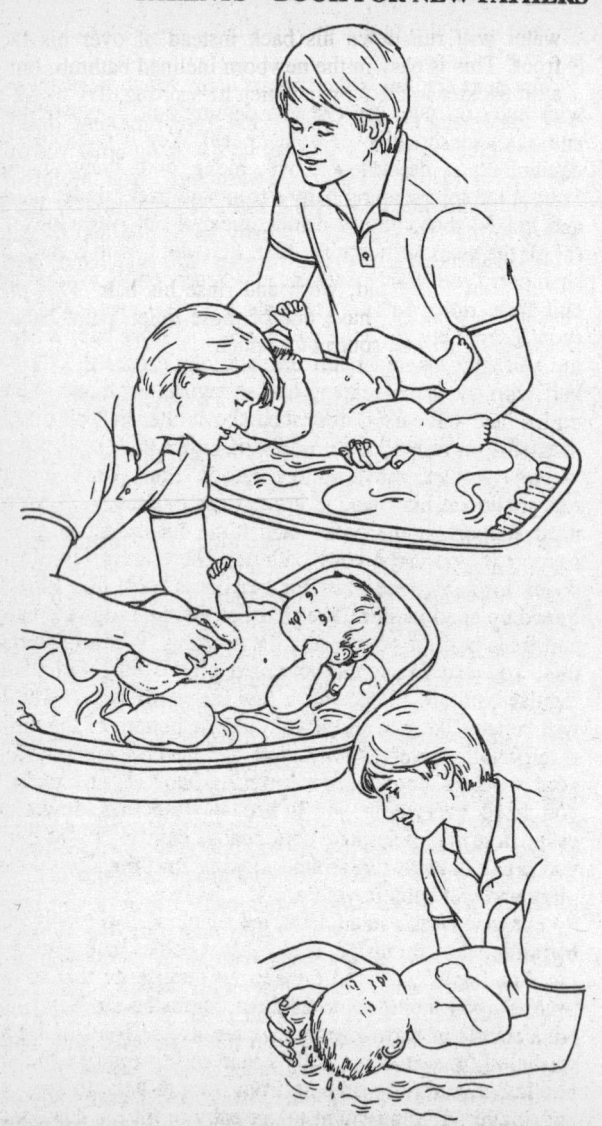

Bathing baby (make sure you test water temperature first)

Now What Do We Do?   257

water will run down his back instead of over his face and front. This is easy in the newborn inclined bathtub, but it gets a bit trickier in the tubs in which he's sitting. Try to get him to lie back against your hand and forearm, sing, talk, make funny faces, or whatever until he's looking up at you and then move in fast with the wet washcloth. You might also try washing his hair before the bath. Hold him over the tub or sink in the "football carry" (baby horizontal and face up with back and neck supported by your arm and hand) and then, with your free hand, wash and rinse his hair. This probably works best if you have one of those quiet, calm babies who won't wiggle and squirm too much.

If all fails and baby goes berserk every time you try a shampoo, lay off for a while. New babies don't really need to have a shampoo (or even a full-fledged tub bath) very often, especially if they don't have much hair. Keep the trouble spots—face, chin, eyes, ears, neck, and diaper area—clean and save the bath for weekends when you have lots of time and patience. Many babies hate their baths for the first couple of months and then develop a terrific fondness for them. Once they hit toddlerhood, they practically have to be pried out of the tub. So don't worry if your six-week-old is a reluctant bather, and don't turn it into a confrontation. Until the baths become fun, keep them to a minimum.

Once you've rinsed all the soap off of baby's body and hair, lift him out of the tub, and get him dried off and dressed again promptly. If your bathroom has a radiator near the tub, you can hang the baby's towel over it and warm it up ahead of time. Drying can be a great time for a hug and a cuddle, but while your baby is very young, don't let him spend too much time undressed. New babies tend to lose heat quickly.

One way to minimize your baby's fear of the bath (and your fear of bathing him) and to maximize the closeness for the two of you is to take a bath together. If you're really grubby, you might want to shower off first so your dirt doesn't flow onto baby. It's a lot easier to support a baby in the tub against your body than it is to hold his back with one hand while washing him with the other. It also makes the shampoo maneuvers more manageable. You'll feel secure knowing he's not going to slip and he'll feel secure having you right there with him. The only awkward part is getting out: there's no way to dry a baby and yourself simultaneously. If your wife is home, arrange for her to take the baby and dry him while you get dried and dressed; if not, have both your towels handy, wrap and dry baby first, then put him down for a moment on a soft bathmat while you get dried and cover up. It takes a bit of juggling, but it's worth it for the fun and extra security.

Sleeping

When it comes to sleeping, babies really assert their individuality. Newborns are "supposed to" sleep a tremendous amount—the *average* is sixteen out of twenty-four hours—but your baby will sleep as much (or as little) as she needs to sleep and will sleep different amounts on different days, so the average really doesn't mean that much for each individual baby. It's perfectly normal for a newborn to clock in as few as ten hours of sleep a day or as many as twenty. Your baby may fill her sleep needs through a series of catnaps—a half hour here, an hour there—or you may be one of those blessed dads whose newborn settles into five hours of nighttime sleep from birth and gradually ups it to twelve uninterrupted hours by eight months. There are night owl newborns who really start to rock 'n' roll after midnight and early birds who rise and shine several hours before dawn.

No matter what your baby's own sleep needs and style may be, your goal is to encourage her sleeping patterns to conform with your own so that everyone is asleep at the same time. This can either be a breeze or a prolonged exhausting struggle, depending on the baby. But again, there are techniques that parents have used successfully in getting babies to sleep longer stretches and at the preferred times of day.

One technique is to help new babies begin to distinguish between sleep time and waking time. When newborns are *really* asleep, practically nothing will wake them, and you can put them down in the middle of a party or with the TV or the vacuum on without disturbing them. (In fact, many babies find the regular whirring of household machines, even loud

Now What Do We Do?

ones, quite soothing.) But real sleep may be surrounded by long stretches of a kind of twilight zone between waking and sleeping. They'll doze in your arms, settle into a few minutes of sleep, then their eyes will flicker open, they'll wail for a bit, and doze off again. All of us, babies and grown-ups alike, have two basic sleep levels—light sleep and deep sleep—but for babies, light sleep accounts for about half of their total sleep time, whereas for adults it's more like 20 percent. Babies in that twilight zone are shifting back and forth between semiconsciousness and light sleep. It makes sense for you to try to "organize" their time into distinct periods of being awake and being asleep. When the baby gets drowsy, try putting her down in her crib for a nap. Even if she doesn't sleep much at first, you should think of it as nap time. Keep the lights dim and stimulation to a minimum. You might want to help soothe her by patting her, rocking her gently, or singing. When she surfaces again, treat it as a wake-up time. Interact with her, look in her eyes, talk and play and show her things. If you begin making a clear distinction between sleep time and awake time, your baby is likely to fall into this pattern, too. She'll have less twilight zone and more time both fully awake and deeply asleep.

You can also encourage her to sleep longer stretches by helping her learn to drop from light sleep into deep sleep by herself. A lot of new parents rush into their newborn's room at the first whimper, flip the lights on, pick her up, or discuss loudly what the problem might be. Sometimes there is a problem—the baby is hungry, cold, has gas pains, or is simply awake and ready to play—but sometimes she's merely stirring in her light sleep phase. The stimulation you provide is really jazzing her up at a moment when she might need either to be left alone or to be soothed into deeper sleep. I'm not suggesting that you let your baby "cry it out" because I really don't think this does anyone any good. But as you get to know your baby, you'll come to recognize what her cries mean and what her needs at a given time are—and when she needs to sleep, she should be allowed and encouraged to sleep. A baby's ability to put herself back to sleep and to make the transition from light sleep to deep sleep alone is crucial to getting her to sleep through the night.

In young babies, sleeping and eating are closely related. It's a pretty safe bet that if your baby is small, she'll wake up more often because her stomach cannot hold enough food to keep her content long. Most babies have to hit ten pounds before they can sleep five hours at a stretch, so unless your newborn is truly a giant, chances are one of you will be getting up a couple of times during the night to feed the baby. It will help your baby to distinguish between day and nighttime if night feedings are kept short and quiet. Save the wild games and stimulation for the day (or weekends if you work long hours). At night, try not to let the baby get totally awake: feed her quickly and soothe her quickly back to sleep. It's also a good idea to try to schedule feedings so that she's hungry for one right around your bedtime. If you can get a good meal into her then, she's more likely to leave you in peace for at least a few hours.

You can also help prolong nighttime sleep by making sure baby's room is warm (about seventy-five degrees; this is essential because babies will lose body heat quickly in a chilly room), that baby is well wrapped (see above on swaddling), and not lying in a cold puddle. Try to resist the urge to keep checking baby every twenty minutes. Almost everyone does this at first, but after the first couple of nights, you may be disturbing baby by going in all the time and poking around with her covers. Many new parents like to put the baby to sleep in their room, but experts discourage this, especially after the initial anxiety period has worn off. The baby's snorts and grunts may keep you up, and your rustling, snoring, or rolling over may wake the baby out of light sleep. If you live in a big place, you may have to rearrange things a bit so that baby's room is close to yours because you will want to listen for her cries (or you could invest in a nursery monitor, which picks up noises that the baby makes and broadcasts them through a portable transmitter). But it makes sense to move her out of your room and into her own permanent bedroom as soon as possible.

It's also a good idea to develop a nighttime routine early on and to make this a ritual. For a young infant this could be simply a last feeding followed by rocking and singing. A number of parents I talked to found a musical mobile a wonderful piece of crib equipment. The baby is mesmerized watching the little shapes go round and round, and the melody quickly becomes associated with sleep.

Even if you follow all this advice assiduously, you still might not be able to get your newborn to sleep easily or to sleep much at night. Some babies are more wakeful than others and some fall into a pattern of sleeping deeply during the day and fretfully at night. Until the baby settles, *someone* is going to be losing a lot of sleep tending to her. It makes sense to work out some sort of schedule so that you and your partner share the burden. If you let her do everything, you're going to have trouble on your hands. Severe sleep deprivation is a serious condition and can soon drag a person down into depression, anger, and physical sickness. If you're working long hours, try to do a late-night feeding before you turn in. Many women find they can't sleep even when their men are up and doing the feeding; but even if she's awake, try to get her to stay in bed. As she gains more confidence in your parenting, she'll probably relax more. And you'll have the dual satisfaction of making her life easier and spending time with your baby.

You can also take some comfort from the fact that your very wakeful baby is alert more hours of the day and thus learning more than those sleepyheads who give their parents such an easy time. Your payoff for lost sleep comes later when your baby bounds ahead in her developments.

Getting to Know Your Baby

Try to imagine how you'd feel if people judged your behavior and growth according to some Personal Development Chart set down in a book. For instance: Person, age 31, should be earning $22,000 a year, sleeping 7.4 hours a night, eating 3 balanced meals a day with a total of 3,213 calories, married with 1.33 children, having sex 2.25 times per week ... It's laughable, not to say insulting. Yet few of us think twice about judging our babies according to equally rigid, equally abstract norms. If she fails to sleep sixteen hours a day, we worry that she's hyperactive. If she doesn't roll over at three months, we worry that she's uncoordinated. And when we're not worrying and pressuring our kids, our friends and relatives are. "Isn't he walking *yet*?" everyone will be asking when your baby hits his first birthday. And then, "She's eighteen months and all she says is mama and dada? Maybe she has hearing problems...." And on and on through each hurdle of toddlerhood and kidhood. Watching the development clock is a consuming but ultimately futile pastime that all too many parents fall into.

It's certainly worth trying to avoid this trap and to start trying as soon as your baby is born. Although it may not be that obvious to you at the very beginning, your baby is born a thoroughly complex individual with his own style and temperament, his own needs, his own pace of development. Many of us go by a (perhaps unconscious) assumption that all newborns are basically alike—unformed little lumps of clay on which we parents imprint a personality. It certainly is true that as your child grows, he picks up a tremendous amount from you, and thus you do form his character in some very fundamental ways. But this doesn't contradict the point about your baby's innate individuality. Way before their parents can go to work building character, babies assert their own identities in how much they eat and sleep, how responsive they are, how aware, what sort of stimulus they prefer, and the pace at which they develop. Infant development charts are useful in giving a *ballpark range* of baby's progress month by month; it's fun to know what's on the horizon, as long as you keep in mind that the horizon may be a good deal closer or farther away for your own baby. If there are serious departures from the norm due to birth defects or disease, your pediatrician or a specialist will tell you about it.

Pediatrician and neonatologist T. Berry Brazelton takes a very useful approach to studying babies in his book *Infants and Mothers*, which traces the growth of three very different children during their first year. Brazelton, stressing the great range of developments and behaviors that are normal, classes the three babies in his book into three "styles": one is average, one he terms "quiet," and the third "active." He emphasizes the fact that all three are perfectly normal. The average baby

Now What Do We Do?

is the one who tracks the development charts most closely. The quiet baby is passive to the point of inertia. Physically she is limp, with very little muscle tone. She seldom cries, uses her limbs very little, demands almost nothing, and sleeps a great deal. Her only active feature is her eyes, which seem to take in even the smallest detail of her environment. The active baby is a bundle of explosive energy, wound up tight from his very first day. As soon as he wakes up he's kicking and screaming. He gets himself so wired he can't calm down enough to eat unless he's tightly swaddled. Rocking, patting, singing, and walking fail to settle him down, and in fact he sleeps far less than he "should." But his muscle tone is terrific and he sits, crawls, stands, and walks early. Interestingly, the parents in Brazelton's study who have the most trouble are the ones with the quiet baby: the mother finds it infuriating that her child does so little and makes so few demands.

Brazelton's book is both instructive and reassuring (even the average baby does his share of screaming). One of its underlying messages is that you'll enjoy your baby a good deal more if, instead of comparing her with the developmental norms, you really get to know her for herself. Take the time to notice what she can do and how she is changing. Find out what she is interested in looking at, what music she responds to, whether she finds a walk in a front-carrying baby sling relaxing. Experiment with different soothing techniques. Talk to her and see what tone of your voice she reacts to most. Is she one of those very passive "quiet" babies? Try to notice what she does with her hands, what she's looking at, how her facial expressions change. Is she calm and happy on the changing table? This might become your opportunity to slow down and just *be* with her for a while. Does she enjoy being propped up in an infant seat and looking around? One great thing about newborns is that you can prop up these seats almost anywhere—kitchen table, living room floor, even the bathroom—and let the baby watch the action.

When your baby is still quite new and spends most of his time either sleeping, eating, or crying, the idea of "getting to know him" may strike you as a touch absurd. You can't have a conversation (unless you enjoy monologues), you can't really *do* much with him, you can't be certain how he responds to much of what you do or say, you wonder whether anything (aside from milk) is getting through to him. Yes, you've read that he can see and hear and smell and feel, but it still seems pretty abstract on a minute-by-minute basis. But the one thing —so far the *only* thing—you can do for him is to take care of his physical needs. Hold him, feed him, change him, dress him, soothe him to sleep, pick him up when he fusses, and love him. It may not always be fun, but it's your opportunity to start to know your baby. That's why mastering the routines of child care is so important for new dads. Until you can talk with him, play ball, take him to museums, teach him to ride a bike, and all those other great father-child activities, caring for him is the name of the game. There may not be that much in it for you right away, but gradually at first and then with amazing swiftness, the routine business of caretaking blossoms into the complex pleasure of fathering. Sooner than you expect, your baby will wake up to the world and the people around him. Without quite knowing how it happened, you stop feeling like a "baby-sitter" and start feeling like somebody's dad. Those dirty diapers, those traumatic first baths, those bottles at three in the morning—they're worth it!

10. Coping with the Inevitable

"The low point was being up in the middle of the night and knowing you have to go to work the next morning."

"The chores were out of control. Being carless in Brooklyn is a terrible drag. You spend so much of your time doing silly little chores—the stress really gets to you."

"My son had colic for the first three months and there was nothing we could do to stop him from crying. It was very tough. He cried so much we worried what the neighbors thought. The most anger I felt was at not being able to help his pain."

"Our sex life changed *dramatically* after the baby was born. The fatigue was so extreme that all we wanted to do when we hit the sheets was sleep."

"In the first few weeks, both of us were always doing something for the baby. Everything revolves around him and his needs. Suddenly I realized that I can't just go out when I want to, I can't play golf, I can't do things for myself anymore."

Nobody said it would be easy—but nobody prepared you for how difficult it would be or exactly *how* it would be difficult. Maybe you were expecting crying—but not at three in the morning. Our maybe you were expecting crying at three in the morning, but not endless trips to the supermarket, endless loads of laundry, ten diapers a day to change. Or maybe you were expecting more chores, but not a cranky, demanding wife who seems on the edge of a breakdown after a day with the baby. Or maybe you were expecting to throw yourself into fatherhood, only to find yourself retreating as far and as fast as you can. Or maybe you desperately want to be involved but feel yourself shut out at every turn by mother and baby.

There is no getting around it: new fatherhood involves some major, maybe even wrenching adjustments. No matter how involved or uninvolved we are, no matter what style of baby we've been blessed with, we all have to face certain basic shifts and relocations. A new baby seems to change everything—our home life, our relationship with our partner, our sleep and meal schedules, the way we relax and entertain, even our work. For some of us, the first months of our babies' lives are a period of crisis. We find ourselves in a topsy-turvy world where the one constant is the sound of a baby wailing. Even if we've mastered all the practical routines discussed in the previous chapter, even if we've found our niche with the baby, we still feel at sea. At times we're strangers in our own homes and at other times we're trapped in an all-too-familiar world of night feedings, diaper changes, and Monday mornings back at work. It's not this grim for everyone, and it's rarely this grim for very long, but there are those times when it feels more like surviving (barely) than living. Everyone says it gets easier after three months—when the baby settles down, the colic goes away, the night feedings ease up—but three months is a year away when you're wondering how to make it through the next three *days*. (For a summary of baby's physical and mental progress from birth to age one, see the infant development chart in Appendix A.)

Being the father of a new baby involves a lot of just plain coping. And sometimes, when coping fails, you may have to back off, take a break, or simply step outside and blow off a little steam. It helps some of us to know that other men are going through the same thing. And it helps, too, to hear seasoned dads talk about the high points that follow hard on the low points. A couple of the dads I talked to said that being a new father was a breeze from day one: their babies slept five hours as soon as they brought them home, their wives always got up for the night feedings, there was practically no crying, no jealousy, no fighting, no difficult adjustments because life

Coping with the Inevitable

went on so smoothly. If you're one of these lucky dads, you can skip this chapter. But if you need a little advice on how to cope, this is the place. For every crisis, there are methods of crisis-handling. This is a chapter on crisis-handling.

Crying

Some babies seem to cry whenever they're awake. Some cry so little you hardly know they're there. Some work themselves up from little mewls to frantic screams. Some open up on their loudest note. Some settle down quickly when you comfort them. Some seem to need to cry it out. Some switch back and forth from wailing to smiling with amazing speed. Every baby has his or her very own, unique style of crying, but the plain, unavoidable truth of the matter is that *all* babies cry. At times, it may seem to you that *all* they do is cry, especially when you come home from work and when you're trying to get some sleep.

The first thing to keep in mind when the crying starts to get to you is that your baby is not crying to torture you, although that is exactly the effect it has. In fact, that's the effect a baby's crying is *supposed* to have. Nature designed crying to get on our nerves as a way to force us to *do* something to try to stop it. The crying makes it next to impossible for us to keep watching TV, talking on the phone, cooking dinner, or whatever. It makes us tense and edgy; our hearts beat faster and our blood pressure goes up a bit; it irritates us into action. Of course, when you stop to think about it, this makes perfect sense. Babies are born utterly defenseless and dependent, and crying is their sole way of making their needs known. The trouble is, it's not always that easy to know which need is fueling the cries. That's where parental experience, patience, and sometimes imagination come in.

The infant needs that most commonly provoke crying are hunger, fatigue, discomfort (being wet or cold or in an uncomfortable position), sickness, pain, boredom, loneliness, or any combination of these. So you're working with a finite list of possibilities, each of which has a fairly straightforward remedy. Because, especially in the early days, you can't be sure of the cause, you can work your way down the list. If you think she's hungry, feed her. If she seems tired, try rocking or patting her gently to sleep. Change her diaper. Maybe she has gas? Try changing her position, resting her tummy on your shoulder or holding her (securely) face down across your knees. The remedies for boredom and loneliness are obvious: pick her up, entertain her, talk to her, take her somewhere.

Often a baby will be comforted if she feels physically secure: try wrapping or swaddling her snugly (see the previous chapter) or holding her firmly against you. I had great success with a front baby carrier. We had the type that supported the baby's back and head, so both my hands were free while she was held securely against my chest and stomach. The warm contact, the security, and the movement calmed her down unfailingly while I went on walks or even did chores around the house. Or you can simply hold your baby and walk around the house with her, rock her in a cradle, or rock with her in a rocking chair.

Regular, rhythmic sounds will also soothe a baby. I heard of one baby who loved listening to the sound of the washing machine churning through its cycles; or you can play the radio or a record or get a recording of the human heart beating (sounds weird, but it really does settle them down!). Many parents use pacifiers to keep crying down, although this is a subject of some controversy. The prevailing wisdom of the day is that there is really nothing wrong with a pacifier so long as you don't use it too often or too long. It's usually better to try to handle the cause of the crying or pick the baby up first than to plug her up with a pacifier as soon as she emits her first wail. You might also try a swing. There are types available just for infants that come with seat straps and a wind-up mechanism that keeps the thing going for several minutes. A great way to buy peace while you're eating dinner. The only caution is that you must not leave baby unattended. Also keep in mind that there is no real substitute for human touch.

Every cry has a cause, right? And every cause has a remedy, right? But what about when you've tried everything and the baby is *still* crying? This happens a great deal with new-

Coping with the Inevitable

borns, so don't worry that you're doing something wrong or that you got a lemon. Sometimes babies *need* to cry. It's their way of releasing tension or letting off steam before they can settle down (it has nothing to do with that old wives' tale about exercising their lungs: lungs don't need exercise). Some babies who have been fed, changed, played with, cuddled, rocked, and walked will emit their loudest shrieks and then drop off to sleep for four hours. So add "need to cry" to the bottom of the list of causes, and once you've tried the other remedies, see if putting the baby down for a nap will take care of it.

If it does, fine. If it doesn't, you're stuck with a crying baby. And sometimes being stuck gets to be more than you can handle. Crying, as I said, is designed to be irritating. If you have to listen to it for hours after an especially irritating day at work, it can become infuriating. You might be furious at the baby for refusing to calm down or furious at yourself for failing to calm her or furious at the world in general for sticking you with this particular situation when you're least able to deal with it. Anger and babies do not mix. A friend of mine had an excellent piece of advice for exactly this situation: when you've reached the end of your rope, just put the baby down in her crib and get out of earshot until you calm down. The baby is not going to come to any harm in those ten or fifteen minutes (she may even fall asleep) and a break will put you in a lot better shape for dealing with her.

Timing has a lot to do with crying, and with time and greater knowledge of your baby, your timing will improve. The jouncing and funny faces that cheered her up on Saturday morning may send her into a tailspin Monday evening (you're overstimulating her when she's tired). Having her diaper changed when she's hungry may drive her wild. Your friends' baby may settle down to sleep after being left to cry it out for ten minutes, but you try the same technique on yours and the cries escalate to the level of high frenzy (every baby is different). You may also find that the longer and louder she cries, the longer it takes to calm her down. That's why trying to find the remedy fast is usually a good idea. Just as you gradually teach her to stop crying, she gradually teaches you how best to respond to her cries. The two of you grow together. That's part of the magic of parenthood.

Gradually you may learn to distinguish between the different cries your baby emits. There are the hungry cries, the cranky cries, the tired cries, the I-might-as-well-cry-because-I-can't-think-of-anything-else-to-do cries. And then there's colic. Colic remains something of a mystery to science: doctors aren't sure what colic is (they say it's not a disease but a "condition"), what causes it (the theories range from intestinal immaturity to oversensitivity to stimulation), or even what qualifies as colic. Some label any hard, uncontrollable crying as colic. Others insist that "true" colic is something known as evening colic—prolonged fits of screaming in the evening hours, which usually begin when the baby is about three weeks old, peak sometime around six weeks, and taper off around three months. Colicky crying is different from other sorts of crying: the baby will probably get red in the face and draw his legs up and the screams are really ear-piercing and nerve-shattering. The baby might respond momentarily to your attempts to calm him, but when he's in a real screaming jag, nothing works for long. When the baby finally stops crying, he may sob and pant for a while and then, just when you think he's about to settle down, he'll start it up all over again.

Here is how Rich, the quality control inspector from the Midwest, described his son's colic: "He was fine and normal for the first day or two and then he cried a lot to the point where he was only happy when he was being fed. He would fall asleep fine and then wake up crying. My wife didn't know what to do. You could hold him by his legs and he was stiff as a board. There was nothing we could do to stop him from crying. The only way to get him to sleep was driving. We started driving around with him at night. The doctors did tests, but he checked out physically normal. We tried different types of formula, but it only smelled bad. He finally settled down at around three months. It slowly faded. When he slept through for the first time, we kept checking him from surprise."

Dealing with a colicky baby is a tremendous strain on both parents. Rich described the atmosphere in his own household as "very tense" and said his wife resented him because he

Coping with the Inevitable

managed to stay calm and accept the situation. To preserve their sanity, Rich and his wife worked out a schedule: she had the baby during the day (she had taken a leave from work), Rich took him when he got home and cared for him during the early evening hours (the hardest part of the day for a colicky baby); then Rich went to bed from ten P.M. to two A.M., and whenever the baby got up after two A.M., Rich would take over again until he had to go to work. "I had a lot of tired days," Rich says. "But that's why we had him when we were young. Also, the shift schedule kept us from fighting."

The scheduling technique that Rich and his wife worked out for dealing with colic is probably the best one possible. Because colic is not a disease, there is no cure for it. You can try shifting the baby's position, giving him a different kind of formula, swaddling, unswaddling—but there's a good likelihood that nothing will be effective. (However, Rich's idea of going for a drive with the baby is a good one, even if your baby isn't colicky but just fussy: the drive may lull the baby to sleep and it might also be good for you to get out of the house for a while.) Penelope Leach advises parents to stop looking for a cause or a cure and try to adopt a mood of "constructive resignation." Remember that there is nothing really wrong with your baby, that colic does him no permanent harm, and that it *will* end.

Exhaustion

Parental exhaustion and infant crying seem to go hand in hand. Some of us have very large babies who enter the world able to sleep five or six hours at a stretch (and do it at night), and some very fortunate dads have partners who don't mind getting up for the night feedings. But the rest of us are going to lose some (maybe most) of our sleep during the first months of our babies' lives.

Our baby was small and restless. She went maybe three hours at a stretch during the first few weeks. And fairly often, when she got up at midnight, she wouldn't settle down again until one-thirty A.M. Then she was up and wailing again at four. I actually got to the point where I dreaded going to bed because I knew that as soon as I settled into deep sleep I'd be awakened by her cries. It almost seemed preferable not to sleep at all.

Mike, living in a small city in Colorado, found that his job schedule exacerbated the fatigue. "There were times," he said, "when I'd work the four P.M. to midnight shift and then I'd be up at six A.M. to feed him. Maybe I'd get a total of five hours of sleep. This was hard and the fatigue was getting real bad."

One way Mike found to cope with the fatigue was to sleep when the baby slept. "I went to bed at nine the other night, and I hardly *ever* did that before he was born." My wife and I, reduced to zombies, finally had to sit down and map out a sleep plan that took both of our sleep needs into consideration. We both hated having our first deep sleep interrupted, so we either traded off nights or else I would stay up as late as I could to feed the baby. My wife is more of a morning person, so she didn't mind doing the dawn feedings. Gradually, over the first few months, we pushed the midnight feeding up to eleven P.M. and the four A.M. feeding back to five-thirty or six A.M., and everyone was getting enough rest. (Long before her first birthday, our daughter was sleeping twelve hours at night and taking two substantial naps during the day—so there's hope on the horizon!)

"Nap when your baby naps" is advice often given to new moms, but it applies just as well to new fathers on weekends or evenings. It may also help the sleeping parent stay asleep if the parent who is up with the baby feeds and changes and soothes her out of earshot. If you've decided to switch off, try to make good use of your off-shifts and really sleep. This tends to be a more of a problem for new mothers who insist that they can't sleep once they know the baby is up. Even if she can't sleep, try to get your partner to stay in bed when it's your turn. There is no point in both of you being up all the time; also, you'll gain more confidence and control if you're handling the situation yourself.

Several fathers I talked to (and this was true for me as well) simply did not hear the baby crying at night, and so, even though they had agreed to take turns, their partners ended up doing all the night feedings. What often happens is that since the mother *expects* to be the one getting up, she develops more sensitive antennas than the father, and once she's up she decides for whatever reason to let her partner sleep. Interestingly, on the few nights that my wife was away on business, I seemed instantly to sprout my own fully functioning set of antennas that picked up the least little whimper. The point is that whoever *feels* responsible *becomes* responsible, a point that all too many of us fathers overlook when it's in our interest. If you really do intend to share the nighttime baby duties with your partner, the two of you may have to make an extra effort to break out of preestablished roles. You should try to understand the responsibilities that your partner has taken on herself as a matter of course and make her understand that you're going to assume some of these responsibilities; and she should try to understand that you mean it and that an occasional kick in the backside at three in the morning may be all it takes to get you into action.

It's not uncommon for new mothers who have quit work or taken time off to play the martyr: even though they're exhausted, they'll insist that since you're the one working and making money, you should be allowed to sleep while they're up half the night. Often this is a setup for a marital explosion (more on this subject follows). Even the most long-suffering martyr expects some ultimate payoff, and your partner's payoff may come in the form of excluding you from a relationship with the child or in a feeling of entitlement to anger and resentment. Sleep deprivation is a serious condition and can quickly lead to physical and emotional illness. The point is not to add your own sleep deprivation to your partner's, but to work out a system whereby you both lose the least amount of sleep possible. Once again, it helps to remember that this too shall pass. (For more on helping your baby to sleep longer, see Chapter 9.)

Stress on Your Relationship

One of the most difficult things to accept—or anticipate—about new parenthood is the pressure it puts on your relationship. The fantasy is: The baby will bring us closer together; it will cement our bond and turn us into a family. And the fantasy is very often true at a deep-down level, but at the level of daily life, a new baby may disrupt nearly every aspect of your relationship. Philip, a thirty-year-old accountant and the father of two boys, put it like this: "The kids have given me and my wife a good bond, and a really special bond, but they have also made it tougher to be close because we don't have the time. The bond is long-term, the toughness short-term."

"No time to be a couple" is a complaint that almost every father I interviewed had. "Because you have so much less time together, it changes your relationship enormously," said Jim, the father of a two-year-old son and a two-week-old daughter. "There's no talking anymore. We used to spend two to three hours over dinner, just talking, but that's gone. It's easy to see how people with kids grow apart in marriage. You really have to work on your relationship."

There's more than a time squeeze involved. A new baby shifts the entire center of gravity for a couple. With so much of your energy and your love going to the baby, you may fear that there's not much left for each other. If your partner is home all day with the baby and breastfeeding, you may soon feel that the mother-infant bond is a kind of field of gravity that you can't break into. "She fell head over heels in love with the baby," commented one father. "It really was like falling in love. She wasn't all there." It certainly is not unreasonable for a man in this position to feel jealous of the baby and to start making demands of his own. Jealousy is less likely to arise if both parents are wrapped up in the baby, but there's still some danger that the adult bond will get buried under the weight of the mother-infant and father-infant bonds.

With both of you so wrapped up in your own new experiences as parents, you may lose touch with what the other one is going through. Many of us work on the assumption that motherhood comes easier than fatherhood, that our partners somehow know instinctively what to do, that they're more tuned in to the baby and more rewarded and fulfilled by childcare routines than we are. Maybe. But that's not the case for every woman and certainly not all the time for any woman. When you really think about it, why should it necessarily be

Coping with the Inevitable

any easier for her than it is for us? New mothers can have just as much trouble coping with newborns as new fathers—in fact, more trouble because they're more likely to be primary caretakers. They may always have wanted a baby and still be shocked by how hard it is to care for one; they may be bored by the endlessly repeating routines; they may be overwhelmed by the chores, by the exhaustion, by the isolation; they may crave adult company and yet feel guilty whenever they succeed in escaping from the baby; they may resent both you and the baby and then feel terribly disappointed in themselves for feeling this way. Not all new mothers take to motherhood right away, or they may take to it so well that the idea of returning so quickly to work fills them with dread. They may feel trapped or liberated or both. They may feel desperate because they can't quite measure up to their image of the Supermom—infinitely competent, loving, organized, attractive, efficient, kind, energetic, and fulfilled. New conflicts may arise, new insecurities, new feelings of inadequacy. "How come I'm not enjoying this more?" is a question that more than one new mother has asked herself. "Is there something wrong with me?"

Your partner needs you to understand what she's going through, but she may feel that it's somehow wrong to tell you about it, either because she would be admitting failure or burdening you with problems at a time when you have enough of your own. You may be experiencing your own version of this same dilemma. The two of you may be keeping a tight lid on your feelings when you most need to express them. If you're finding the adjustment to parenthood stressful, keep in mind that you're probably not alone in this. Put yourself in your partner's shoes. Try to discuss what's going on without recriminating. Don't join the chorus of her critics and those who tell her what she *should* be doing and feeling. Remember, and remind her, that you're in this together.

Misunderstandings and tensions frequently arise over chores and child care, and if you're both exhausted from the night feedings, these tensions can easily explode into arguments. Finding the right balance of "who does what with the baby when" is harder for some couples than others. Pat said he and his wife used to get into childish arguments of the "I did this, I did that" variety. "We try to keep the chores as even as possible and back each other up. But lots of times she has to tell me what to do. And she does resent being the one in this role. Frequently she has to lay down the law and tell me to stop dinking around. I know she's right." Michael said, "There might be more tension between us if I wasn't able to help out so much. I've avoided arguments by doing so much of the child care."

In some ways, both Pat and Michael are lucky that their wives were able to surrender child-care responsibilities fairly easily. Many couples get into trouble because the woman demands more help with the baby, but then when the man takes over she criticizes what he does or snatches the baby back at the first cry. Her attitude is: If you can't do it right (that is, *my* way), don't do it at all. And all too often the man's attitude becomes: If you're such an expert, quit asking me for assistance. Sometimes what's going on here is a competition over who is a more competent adult. A woman whose sole "job" is child care may need to prove that she at least does *something* better than her partner. She'll resent her partner for spending so much time at work, but she'll also be jealous of the identity and status that his work gives him. The ultimate humiliation for her would be if he not only made all the money and had all the real-world adult status, but also was good with the baby. Obviously this situation not only undermines the father-infant bond, but spoils the couple's relationship as well. There are numerous variations on this theme depending on who feels more "stuck" with the baby: if the dad is home doing child care and the mother is pursuing her career, he's the one more likely to resent her job and to undercut her attempts at taking care of the baby.

Two-career couples may engage in a different kind of competition. Rick Bell, directing programs for fathers at John's Hospital in Saint Paul, says he hears about competition over "who does what in the evening: it's no fun to get stuck with the dishes if you'd like to be giving the baby a bath. There is also guilt over getting a baby-sitter. If you don't see the baby much during the week, it seems unfair to leave him with a baby-sitter on weekends." One father I know who works at home as a writer said that his wife, who works full-

Coping with the Inevitable

time in an office, is jealous of his time at home with the baby: "The most difficult thing for her is the feeling that I have so much more opportunity to be with the baby. She thinks she is being self-sacrificing for being at work; I feel self-sacrificing about getting a quart of milk at eleven in the morning."

The tension and competition over chores and child care may be exacerbated by what is going on—or rather, what *isn't* going on—in your sex life. Will we ever have sex again? is a question that preys on the minds of many new fathers. First, there's the ban on intercourse until the mother's uterus returns to normal, the bloody discharge stops, and the episiotomy heals. This may take from two to four weeks, or even longer. Most obstetrician-gynecologists advise abstinence until after they have checked the mother out during the first postpartum appointment. But it's more than the medical ban on sex. Neither your partner nor you may be much in the mood. For her there are the enormous changes her body has experienced, the lingering pain of childbirth, and the specific pain of the episiotomy, which may bother her during sex for months; for some women, there may be a subconscious dread of becoming pregnant again. For you, there may be some feeling that her body belongs to the baby, that it seems strange to make love to someone who is so wrapped up in the role of mother, or that you *want* to have sex but you never seem to feel aroused. For both of you there is the fatigue of new parenthood, never particularly conducive to passion, and the fear of being interrupted by the baby. You may begin to feel like strangers to each other's bodies. Weeks go by and you feel more and more like parents, and haggard parents at that, but less and less like lovers. And the longer you go without resuming your sex life, the harder it may be to find the "right moment."

Several couples said that they found it easier to get back into sex after reestablishing their intimacy and affection. They found a baby-sitter, often a grandmother at first, and went out to dinner. Sometimes it's almost as if you have to start all over again with dating, wining and dining, romancing and sweet talk. You have to make time to be a couple, and you have to learn to live with certain changes. "You change the way you show affection," one new dad told me. "You hug a lot. We knew what would happen for the first six weeks, so it wasn't a problem. And now sex is better than it was before the pregnancy. Having a baby makes you grow up."

Michael Hoyt, writing in *Working Mother* magazine (December 1985), humorously captures the sexual predicament of many new fathers: "A new father is learning the meaning of the word 'tired,' and if he does not come to a deep understanding of it on his own, the new mother explains it to him. Late-night passion and luxuriant mornings of love are something for those books on the racks in the grocery store. Bed is for sleeping. When I think of my sex life in the first year of my daughter's life, I think of a long trip across a desert, with occasional relief from a lukewarm canteen. Just enough to keep me alive." Funny—but also a little bit terrifying. Hoyt, however, goes on to say that "everything gets back to normal, more or less." So don't give up the faith!

The first few times you have sex after the baby are likely to be stressful and may be painful for your partner. It helps if you go slow and don't penetrate too deeply. Get your partner to show you where she's tender, and if intercourse becomes uncomfortable for her, hold off. Be open with each other about what you feel and need and try to keep a sense of humor. If your partner is breastfeeding, she may start to leak during sex—don't be alarmed at the sprinklings of milk. You may have a hard time feeling sexual about her breasts if she's breastfeeding, or you may be aroused by their increased size. You may feel that it's somehow wrong to include them in your lovemaking, or your may be curious about what her milk tastes like. Again, it helps to be open about your preferences in this regard so there is no misunderstanding or hurt feelings. Patience may be the biggest help of all. Give it time and your sex life will return to normal, or even better than normal. Even if neither of you is in the mood for sex, you can be affectionate with each other. Your shared love for the baby is a powerful bond between the two of you, and even if you don't feel like expressing this bond sexually now, you will in time.

Getting a baby-sitter and going out can be wonderful medicine for many bruised aspects of your relationship—not just your sex life. Brian, a twenty-seven-year-old contractor and the father of three (age five, three, and eight months), speaks from experience when he says, "You have to make time for yourselves because if you don't you grow bitter. When it's time to go out, we know it. We'll go out dancing, out to dinner. You have to do it." It may be difficult for you to leave your newborn on the first evening out, and you're likely to spend most of it talking about the baby. I remember on one of our first nights out calling home to see how everything was going (my mother was baby-sitting) and repeatedly getting a busy signal; finally, overcome with anxiety, I had the operator break into the line on an emergency basis, only to learn from my mother that the baby was sleeping peacefully and she'd been yakking with my aunt. But even with the initial stress, it's worth it, and the earlier you begin the easier it will be later on. Keep in mind also that your newborn is less aware of who is caring for him or her than a toddler, who may protest loudly whenever you get a nighttime baby-sitter.

Of course, having a baby may also change the kinds of things you enjoy doing as a couple. Rich summed this up eloquently in describing the changes he and his wife have gone through: "Having time together as a couple hasn't really been a problem for us because both our parents live nearby and help out a lot. But still, we used to go out dancing a lot and we haven't done that as much, and maybe we're not quite as romantic. Some things that we used to do are not as appealing. Maybe we're out of shape now. We could get out more, but we enjoy our time together at home. What we lost being intimate out, we gained with more time at home. I guess we were ready to have a child. We knew something was missing from our lives, and that's what it was. The closeness for us comes not so much from sharing tasks but from growing up with that extra person. We're working for him and working together for each other. It's the sharing not just with each other, but sharing with someone else."

There is no doubt that many couples feel pressured about what they *should* be feeling as new parents and that they punish themselves for not living up to the ideal. From somewhere we've imbibed the notion that having a baby is like returning to the Garden of Eden. It's not *supposed* to involve hard work and marital stress and frustration. If it does, we wonder what's wrong with us. "We're about as educated about babies as two people could possibly be," said one nurse-midwife (and new mother) whose husband is a community organizer who works a lot with families, "and yet new parenthood is a lot more than we expected. There is more work—and also more joy and love. And chaos. The order in our lives has gone out the window." The work is not just to make money and to take care of the baby and to run your home and to try to do all these things at the same time—the work is also to keep your relationship in good running condition.

It may sound strange that something like love could need something like work to sustain it. It's another one of those things that is not *supposed* to be. But it does take work—a kind of work in which the tools are sharing, and talking about things, and putting yourself in your partner's shoes, and making time for yourselves, and keeping a sense of humor. It also helps tremendously to remember that you're in this together and that you're very likely going through the same things: the same dislocations, the same fatigue, the same longing for the "good old days," the same craving for adult-time. Yes, in time a lot of the stress will ease, and the baby will bring you together. But you don't have to wait: with a little effort and a little sympathy, you can bring yourselves together now.

Shouldering New Responsibilities

New fatherhood means new responsibility, and for a great many men what it comes down to is financial responsibility. The word *providing* takes on a whole new dimension when it's linked with "family." And providing looms even larger when your partner has given up her job and income or taken a leave of absence in order to care for the baby. Like it or not, you're now *the* breadwinner—and that's responsibility with a vengeance.

On top of, and often conflicting with, the financial responsibility is the more immediate responsibility for taking care of the baby. Even if you want to participate in the upbringing of your child, your work may prevent you. Or, alternatively, you

Coping with the Inevitable

may be forced to sacrifice aspects of your career to child-care duties. Robert McCall, psychologist who contributes a column on fathers to *Parents* magazine, describes the complicated dilemma that many fathers face today: "Some guys say they would like to be involved, but that they have to hold two jobs to make ends meet and they don't have the time or energy when Friday rolls around. 'I want a little time in front of the TV, too' is the attitude. If your wife takes off a year or even six months, that means a real income loss, and the question is how to make up that loss *and* be involved. Flexibility of time is an upper-middle-class privilege, but most people don't have this flexibility. And if both parents are working, you have three full-time jobs and two workers. How do you handle it? It's just as threatening to men as to women to have to live with this situation."

The men I spoke with juggle their responsibilities in a variety of ways. Brian, the contractor and father of three, had to take on a second job. Between his two jobs he is out of the house from eight in the morning until eleven at night, every day except Wednesday. Wednesday, when his wife works in a restaurant, is his evening at home with the kids. "I try to spend as much time as possible with them, especially on weekends. There are some bitter feelings, but you have to put up with it and adapt and then some. My family life is lots of love, but it's hectic. And there is no denying that kids are expensive."

Pat, the Saint Paul diemaker, said he feels guilty for not taking care of his daughter more, and he described well the conflict he and so many men have between making money and spending time with the baby: "Should I be out hustling for money so I could get her anything she wanted? Finally I concluded that time is more important than things. Sure we could use more money, but it's not crucial. I've seen husbands out with two jobs who get into trouble at home."

Philip, accountant and father of two boys, agreed. "If I put in five to ten extra hours at work instead of taking care of the kids, it would help my career. But family is more important than a few extra thousand bucks. There are only so many hours in a day: what do you want to do with them? I don't tie financial problems to the kids. There is always a shortage of money and you feel the pressure of finances, but you work with the situation and live with it."

Phil, a free-lance writer who works at home—his wife works full-time in an office and they have a baby-sitter who comes from nine to five, five days a week—has accepted the added responsibility of being the parent at home: "I am definitely more tied down. It is hard to schedule out-of-town trips, and it has restricted what I can do somewhat. Lots of stories I'd never propose now because they would involve travel abroad. And it's frustrating not to be able to pursue something immediately. But it is relatively minor. What I gain is that I have a lot of opportunity to be with the baby, and I am grateful for that time."

Rich said he was definitely feeling the pinch of providing for the family, especially once his wife stopped working after the baby turned one. "I didn't throw myself into my work, but I did work smarter and keep the raises coming so I could get more money for the family—not to the point of greed, but to provide for my family. My wife had gone back to work when the baby was three months, but with the cost of child care so high, we really didn't feel like we were getting ahead. And she wanted to be home with him, so she left her job. We earn less money now, but everything else seems better."

Psychiatrist Martin Greenberg devotes a chapter of *The Birth of a Father* to "the perils of responsibility." He describes the double-bind many men get into when they work harder and longer to provide for their families and then catch it at home (or blame themselves) for not helping out with the baby more. With so much attention these days focused on nurturing fathers, men who stick to the traditional role of breadwinner may feel slighted or undervalued. But, as Greenberg points out, "There is a nobility in providing that is frequently ignored. . . . The act of providing, particularly for new fathers, is often experienced as an act of love. The father sees his work as directly connected to his wife and child, and this gives it a new meaning." And for many, the hard work springs from necessity or from a desire to give our children more than (or even just as much as) we had.

Greenberg advises men who are working harder out of love for their new families to discuss the situation with their

Coping with the Inevitable

partners. She may feel that you're running away and burying yourself in your work, when actually you're working very deliberately and consciously for her and the baby. Sometimes just the shared knowledge that you're both in this together and doing what you can in your own ways is enough to quell resentment and head off fights.

Of course, it's possible that you *are* burying yourself in your work as a way of avoiding child-care responsibilities, and maybe this is something worth thinking about. Some men develop a kind of fear of their infants, a fear that may be reinforced by new mothers who want to preserve their exclusive expertise. At least work is predictable and it's something they know they're good at, so they retreat. And once the process of retreat from the family begins, it can be difficult to break out of. As Rick Bell notes, "It becomes so painful to not have the relationship you want with your kids, that you opt out altogether instead of facing the pain." So rather than face the pain, you hide behind your work, an unassailable position since, of course, your work is necessary for the family to survive. (For more on issues of work and responsibility, see Chapters 8 and 12.)

The new responsibilities of fatherhood may put pressure not only on your work but on your leisure time as well. Michael had to give up golf. Jim said he hasn't played the piano or pursued his hobby of photography (except for baby pictures) since his son was born. Bob said he hardly has time to read anymore. Brian complained that he had to pass up a free trip to Mexico because of his three kids. Philip, the father of two, puts it this way: "You must plan every little thing in your free time. You can't do anything at the spur of the moment. You feel guilty if you want to go running because you know what you're doing to the other person who's at home with the kids." Going out to a movie becomes a major decision. Having people over for dinner becomes a major production. Sometimes just putting your feet up and reading the paper becomes fraught with the guilt of shirked responsibility. Every moment at home that we take off from child care is a moment that our partners must be on. If she's been with the baby for five long days in a row, the sight of you reading the paper on Saturday morning while the baby is hollering may push her over the edge. Of course, this cuts both ways: after five long days in a row at work, you feel entitled to a little time off and you'd rather take the baby when he's *not* hollering. When you're both feeing rested, relaxed, and refreshed, these problems evaporate and you're both *delighted* to take the baby. But how often are new parents (or even not so new parents) rested, relaxed, and refreshed? Who's going to pick up the slack? became a kind of battle cry in our household when the baby was a newborn, and responsibility issues tend to keep leaping out at us during times of stress.

There's another, more subtle level to this issue in terms of who *feels* responsible. As Robert McCall puts it, "It's not how people spend time but who is responsible. The traditional understanding is that the woman is responsible for child care, even though the man can help. And the man is responsible for the income, though the woman can help. It's the person who feels responsible who shoulders the psychological load." Unless your partner really feels herself freed of the psychological responsibility, your help with the child care may not be making that much difference. From your point of view, you're spending all day Saturday with the baby. But she can't really relax either because she's monitoring you or because she's still basically calling the shots, telling you when it's time to feed the baby, when to put him down, how to hold him, or she might feel compelled to use her time off to do child-care-related activities—shopping, cleaning, making formula. This is a fairly complicated problem and one that you can resolve only by first being aware of it and then by discussing it together. The ideal for many couples is *sharing*—not only the time but the feeling of responsibility. That way, when it's her turn for child care, you can play golf, or read, or garden, or whatever without guilt, and when it's your turn she can let you take full responsibility for the baby while she pursues her interests. That's the idea—but it may take a long time and a lot of work to get there.

One father, a highly educated clinical psychologist who was dealing with a formidable toddler and wondering what his life would be like in a month when the new baby arrived, said this of parenthood: "If you look at it as a rational person, you quickly realize that brains, education, logic don't take you far in preparing you for kids. So much raw emotion comes to the surface." This can be particularly true in the early weeks when everything is still so new, except for your sleep, which seems like a paradise lost long ago. A howling, squirming, wakeful, unresponsive, constantly hungry eight-pound bundle of chores hardly seems like a fair compensation for the loss of your sexual, emotional, cultural, and social lives, to say nothing of your civilized meals, your sleep, and a good part of your peace of mind. What have I done to myself? is a question that steals across many of our minds when we're feeling utterly bushed. There are moments, maybe even days, when we can honestly say that we do not love our babies—and certainly not the situation into which these babies have plunged us. Will my marriage survive? will my job survive? will I survive? are other questions that plague us. When stress levels get out of control, and you find yourself screaming back at your baby, fighting constantly with your partner, or miserably depressed and angry, it's time to seek help—either from a hotline telephone service (look in your phone book or the "personals" column of a local paper for Parents Anonymous, Parental Stress Hotline, COPE, CALM, the Warm Line, or similar organizations in your area) or from a doctor or psychologist.

By all means, do get help if you think you need it, but don't fall into despair or blame yourself if you feel angry now and then. Anger is as normal for parents as crying is for babies. In fact, many parents report not only anger in the first weeks but really gruesome fantasies about smothering their crying infants or throwing them out windows. As long as your fantasies are fleeting and as long as you don't cross the line and *act* on your violent fantasies or impulses, don't worry about it. Again, there is a good chance you'll feel better—less trapped and isolated—if you can share these feelings with your partner. You may discover that she's experiencing something quite similar.

Before you give up hope of ever really enjoying your home life again, remember: The verdict is not yet in on this new person in your lives. The early weeks may be tough, but they don't last forever. Babies change—and they change so rapidly that very soon you may actually wish you could slow it all down. It may seem unimaginable to you now, but many couples look back fondly on those first few weeks... once they're over. It's like a camping trip where it never stopped raining. When you look back, you can laugh about it together. And with parenthood, the best part is that when the trials of the newborn phase are over, you have your big, settled, smiling, playful baby to laugh with.

11. Feeling Like a Family

It hits all of us at different times and in different ways. Sometimes it doesn't "hit" so much as creep up on us. Sometimes it's so subtle and gradual that we're not even aware of it until we look back. We might be changing a diaper, taking the baby out for a walk, or sitting down to dinner. And we realize: None of this feels strange anymore. This child, these chores, these daily routines—they all seem like the most natural, accustomed things in the world. We don't have to pause and remind ourselves how to lift the baby. We don't have to go down a checklist of supplies before the bath. A walk around the block or a trip to the supermarket doesn't end in a hysterical screaming fit. The family dinner no longer has to be launched like a military campaign. We've emerged from the crisis atmosphere of the first weeks into the life of a family.

Part of it—perhaps most of it—is the baby's doing. He has, in the words of one father, "come out of the fog." At four or five months he seems so unbelievably grown up and accomplished. You now know what they mean by the term "settled baby." He sleeps six (or more) hours at a stretch at night. When he's awake, he's *really* awake—no more of that newborn space-out land—and he's really awake many more hours during the day. He holds his head up well, he pushes his chest up off the mattress, he wiggles and squirms and tries to roll over, he's *strong*. And maybe best of all from your point of view, he smiles—genuine, responsive social smiles that are undeniably the most wonderful things in the world. Getting

287

those first baby smiles is like a flood of sunshine after a month of rain.

Part of it, of course, is you. It's more than just getting used to the baby and the baby-care routines. It's getting to know and love and appreciate your baby. Newborns, let's face it, can be a little hard to relate to. "There was so little apparent development in the first few weeks," one father said. "For me it was mostly a matter of patience. I like her better now than when she was newborn. I appreciate more what she does now."

Even if you retreated during the first weeks, chances are you've come out of hiding now. Your baby has ceased to frighten you with his seeming fragility, his uncontrollable crying, his mysterious and ever-shifting needs. You can have fun with him! And, of course, you're awfully proud of him. One father told me in a prenatal interview that he worried he would get bored with his baby after a while. "I can't even believe I said that," he remarked at a second interview several months after the birth. "He's doing the most amazing things now. He looks so wise, as if he's a fully grown adult trapped in a baby's body. It makes one wonder about reincarnation. The glint in his eye is so full of wisdom, and he looks around with this sly expression as if he's fully aware of what's going on. I've always been struck by his intelligence." When this father talked about his son, there was a glint—of pure joy—in *his* eye.

Rich, whose son had colic for the first three months, said his life changed unbelievably once the colic faded away. Suddenly he began discovering some of the joys of fatherhood: "Seeing him do everyday things—playing with the cat, looking at a fire engine—fills your life moment to moment and makes you a happier person. For me, the joys are witnessing those everyday sparks of life." (For a summary of baby's physical and mental progress from birth to age one, see the infant development chart in Appendix A.)

Feeling Like a Family

Father-Baby Togetherness

Part of being comfortable with your baby comes from the confidence you've gained through success. Pat said he had a feeling of immense pride when he succeeded in putting his daughter to sleep. An even more special triumph for him as a father was the first time he took his baby to church alone. "My in-laws had their doubts, but I pulled it off. There were lots of people standing around looking at her, and I was full of pride. It really was fun."

I realized how far I'd come in my fathering abilities when my wife went away on a short business trip not long after our baby had turned three months and I was in charge of everything. I won't say there weren't a few tense moments, but overall, like Pat, I pulled it off. Not only was it a great boost to my confidence, but it made me see the enormous changes both the baby and I had been through. Just a few months back I'd been scared of taking care of her alone while my wife went to the supermarket! Being alone with your baby, being totally in charge of her care for a day or a weekend, is a terrific way to cement your bond. If you haven't done it already, try it: you'll be amazed at how much you learn. It also can open your eyes to just how much sheer work and attention baby care requires. Philip, the father of two, described a weekend when his wife went off for a trip with her brother: "I stayed home with the kids and that's *all* I did. It's a full-time job."

Perhaps even more important than the occasional triumphs of fathering are the regular day-to-day activities you perform with and for your family. Part of settling down into family life means finding your niche in child care and establishing the right balance between work and family. For fathers who work long hours during the week, weekend activities become particularly crucial. A couple of the dads I talked to said that Saturday mornings were their special times with the baby—for outings in the stroller, trips to the park, or just hanging out at home. Fathers whose jobs don't keep them too late have early evening hours for giving baths, reading, feeding the baby, and, of course, playing, holding, and cuddling. Charles, a thirty-eight-year-old doctor from Albuquerque, described his evening ritual with his four-month-old son: "I'm away all day and by the time I get home he might be a little fussy. I hold him on my lap and rock him. We talk and maintain eye contact and he starts to relax. It's funny, because he won't sit in this position for my wife, but it works great for me. He seems to enjoy it and I certainly enjoy it. This is our thing now."

For dads who work at home (as I do), there are also morning hours before the baby-sitter arrives or the day care begins. This can be an especially rewarding time because babies tend to be fresher, more receptive, and less cranky early in the day than in the late afternoon and evening periods. Once a routine gets going, babies come to rely on it, so if you're the one who bathes the baby, reads to her before bed, plays with her after breakfast, or whatever, she may insist that you keep it up. It's nice to be needed and it's also nice to have our own special province of activities and chores. There's no better way of overcoming jealousy of the mother-infant bond than to tighten the father-infant bond. Of course, for two-career couples there may be a tendency to play tug-of-war with the baby as each partner strives desperately to optimize his or her limited "quality time." But again, by three or four months, you'll have an easier time resolving this kind of competition than at three or four weeks.

As discussed in Chapter 9, play is very often the preeminent father-baby activity, and as the baby grows, the possibilities for play expand wonderfully. Each of the fathers I interviewed told of different father-baby games, but all the fathers said that roughhousing—rolling around with young babies, wrestling, and chasing around with older ones—was their department. One dad, who had two sons (one baby, one toddler) and a dog, said: "A couple times a week we all get on the floor with the dog and we chase each other around. My older son loves to help me with projects around the house while the second one watches or eats paper." Don said he has learned (and remembered) a lot about imaginative play by being with his son (age five months). "I'm more childish than my wife in many ways. I live with my imagination and so I find myself more on his level and he responds to that." Don

Feeling Like a Family

also told me that seeing his son can be the best antidote to a frustrating day at work. "He adds so much. In the past, when days went badly, I'd be ready to explode. Now I see Ben and his innocence is so infectious he makes you realize how far you've gotten away from that. I try to reach back for it. You realize how wonderful the innocence can be and how much of our adult cynicism is scar tissue."

Part of what makes babies in their third and fourth months such great playmates is the great mood they are so often in. As Burton White puts it in *The First Three Years of Life*: "The six-week-old baby... is a pretty sober individual. Not so the three-and-one-half-month-old—these babies seem to be happier than at any other time in life. Again, there will be exceptions to these general statements, and you need not be alarmed if your child is not regularly euphoric. By and large, however, this is a time when children seem to be chronically high."

Take advantage of this high! There is nothing more pleasing to a happy alert three-month-old than for you to get down on the floor with him and roll around together. Prop him up with pillows or put him in an infant chair and let him watch the action. Put him on his tummy on a blanket and encourage him to lift his head up and look around at you, at toys, at siblings, whatever. Babies this age are really discovering the world through their senses. Give baby new things to look at and touch; let him look at himself and at you in a mirror. Help your baby exercise by holding his feet and gently bicycling his legs or by holding his hands and showing him how to clap. Give him rattling toys and other noisemakers he can hold. He may enjoy looking at finger puppets, and it's not too early to start playing with a large, soft, brightly colored ball (he'll probably be into the color and texture and the feel of it on his mouth more than anything else). And by all means, talk to, sing to, and read to your baby. He'll enjoy your running commentary on his activities and will love the musical accompaniment to his exercise periods. Librarians in children's libraries are a great source of suggestions for baby books. You'll be surprised how early baby will sit and look at books with you. At first he will probably have more interest in devouring the book orally than intellectually, so buy a bunch of soft cloth and plastic books.

Your Relationship Revives

As the crisis of coping with a mysterious newborn passes, so does the crisis of readjustment in your relationship. There comes a moment when the two of you realize together that you can barely imagine life without this baby. She has become bound up with so many aspects of your lives together. The changes you have gone through no longer seem so radical or so hard to live with. Charles said that part of his reluctance about having more kids (he has a son and daughter from a previous marriage who live with his former wife) stemmed from worries about the impact of a baby on his new marriage. "Prior to the baby [a boy, now four months old], my second wife and I had a fantastic relationship and I didn't want it to change. I knew that becoming parents would change it, it had to. And yes, it has changed, but I think ultimately it has made it stronger."

Of course, even with a settled, cheerful baby, parenthood is hardly a romp through spring meadows. Charles pointed out that although having a baby strengthened the emotional side of his marriage, it wasn't quite so great for the practical aspects of day-to-day life: "Before the baby we could go to the movies or out to dinner at the spur of the moment, but those days are over. Now it's a major production just to go to the grocery store. But I can be patient and wait it out." Your couple time is still squeezed by the demands of work, child care, chores —but it's a lot easier to deal with the squeeze on six hours of uninterrupted sleep than it was on three.

Vincent, an engineer and father of two boys (with a third baby on the way), said the rough times in his marriage correlated directly to the fatigue of early infancy. "In the early days, when we were both getting up at night with the baby, I would be supportive and then I'd get tired and stop thinking about her and just think about myself. That causes stress. I remember a certain amount of complaining in the middle of the night—'It's *your* turn,' 'No, it's *your* turn.' But we were able to look past it, that's how we got through the problems.... We always tried to share as much of the child

Feeling Like a Family

care as possible. With our first boy, we had a tag-team approach: 'You take care of him and when you get tired, give me a holler and I'll take over.' Unfortunately, that doesn't work with two. We still try to split everything fifty-fifty until you see the other person is hitting bottom. If she's real tired, I'll take care of both the boys. When she's hitting the bottom of her biorhythm, I'll give her the car keys and tell her to go out and buy some clothes."

With the wisdom of a seasoned father, Vincent concluded: "The kids bring us lots and lots of joy and they're tremendous fun, but they are also a pain in the butt sometimes. That's why we make sure to get out of the house to get away." Philip, who also has two sons, said that he and his wife were able to "sneak in a few hours of time for ourselves now and then. Sometimes I call home from the office and that becomes our couple time."

With more sleep and less tension in the air, you've probably been able to resume your sex life—and maybe even improve it. Charles, whose wife had a cesarean section, said it took about three months for their sex life to go back to normal, but now, "it's as good if not better than before. Better because I feel so complete when we're joined together. It's having a family, a home, our work together [his wife works as the office manager of his medical practice]—all of it helps to bind us together." Other fathers spoke of the element of maturity that having a baby brought to the ways they showed affection. Again, it's not all roses. For some, sex became less frequent and the difficulties for the woman caused by the birth (pain during intercourse because of the episiotomy, inability to achieve orgasm) persisted for a long time. Others said that sex suffered from the same time squeeze that pressured all couple activities. One father said rather wistfully that it really wasn't until his son was a year old that the "old spark returned," and soon after that his wife became pregnant again and lost interest.

With a newborn, everything is so new and sometimes so impossible that life doesn't seem quite real. There's a sense of dislocation, a feeling that you'll wake up (after one of those agonizingly brief collapses into sleep) and it will all be a dream. Your present role (father) seems utterly unconnected with your past role (person), and the future seems unimaginable. But with a settled baby, it dawns on most of us that this is here to stay: this baby, this life-style, these changes in our relationship. So much is different, but gradually we perceive that a good deal has survived intact. Our relationship revives because with more sleep and more confidence about parenting and less conflict over the little things, love can breathe again. No more late Saturday mornings in bed (at least not together), but late Friday night dinners, out or at home, become possible again with a little planning. We also start to discover that many of the things we enjoyed doing as a couple—going to the beach or museums or long drives in the country or visiting friends during the day—we can now do as a family (again with a little—or sometimes a lot of—advance planning).

And, of course, for most of us, everything we've lost or sacrificed is more than made up for by what we've gained. As one father put it, "He has brought us closer together because my capacity for love has been expanded. The baby has opened my capacity for love with my wife." Another dad, a bit more reserved and private about his feelings, said he and his wife "sit there looking at the baby when she's asleep, mooning over her and recalling events of the day. This is definitely a good thing for us as a couple." And yet another dad, after discussing some of the minor problems that have arisen both for himself and his relationship, concluded: "The baby has definitely brought us closer. We were meant to be parents. More than our careers, more than making a lot of money, we were meant to be parents."

Time Alone

If you've been reluctant, afraid, or just too busy to spend time with your baby, now is a good time to jump in and do it. Really the best way of getting to know the baby and feeling comfortable with him is to spend time alone with him. A number of the fathers I talked to joined father-baby programs as a way of getting themselves to spend this time. These pro-

Feeling Like a Family

grams, which are springing up around the country, offer fathers and their babies the chance to get together with other fathers and babies and both talk and learn. Psychologist (and father) Rick Bell said his program for fathers focuses both on practical how-to matters and on emotional issues that fathers commonly face, including what to do about child care, the relationship with their partners, balancing work and family, dealing with their own role models. "For some dads," says Bell, "this is the first legitimate excuse to be alone with the child." One alumnus of Bell's program commented, "The benefit of the class is that I feel more comfortable with the baby. I knew my wife would be with the baby full-time, and I wanted to jump in and get involved. The baby may still cry, but now that I've taken the class I know how to calm him. Now I feel I could take care of most any kid."

To find one of these fathers groups, check with local community organizations, ask your childbirth educator, or consult *Fatherhood U.S.A.: The First National Guide to Programs, Services, and Resources for and about Fathers* by Debra G. Klinman and Rhiana Kohl (Garland Publishing, 1984).

Don't Miss the Magic

It may not happen during the first three months, but at some point in the baby's first year most of us come to realize how much this child needs us. The baby will be fussing when a friend or relative picks her up, but she'll relax the instant you take her. She'll cry when you turn your back on her and burst into a radiant smile when you come back. She'll rejoice when you return home from work. Charles recounted a moment of pure bliss with his three-month-old son: "I was holding the baby and rocking him and he was fighting to stay awake and then, all of a sudden, he closed his eyes and let out the biggest smile in the world. This was so great. I could hardly contain myself."

In some magical and yet utterly natural way, as this person comes to need you, your presence, your care, so you come to need *her*, her smiles, her little noises, her daily discoveries.

As one father put it when I asked him to describe the joys and trials of fatherhood, "The joys are easy. There is a feeling of almost constant elation when I'm in his presence. He has changed my life in ways I couldn't have imagined possible. Had anyone told me this I wouldn't have believed it. I've put my life in order in new ways, put a new timetable on things. It's going so fast. I don't want to miss out on this. It's such a magical time and I know it won't return." A father of two, with another one on the way, said simply, "It all runs by so quickly. That's why we spend as much time as we can with the kids."

One father I know, whenever I asked him how his baby boy was, used to comment, "This is a great age." This was before I had a baby of my own, and I wondered how can *every* age be so great? Now I know. Every age *is* so great; every age has its special joys. And every age seems to go so fast. It's funny, but even though time is speeding by, it somehow seems inconceivably long ago that you were just a person, not yet someone's father. Just as it feels completely right to have a baby in your arms, to roll around on the floor with him, to sing and dance and jiggle toys and make faces until you get that cherished smile, so it feels completely right to think of yourself as a father. So right that you may not bother to think about it at all. Without your knowing quite how it happened, feeling like a family has become the most natural thing in the world.

12. Caregiving: Who, How and When?

Before you have a child of your own, the question of child-care arrangements remains pretty abstract. The two of you have probably talked about it in a general sort of way. You might have looked into day care versus hiring a baby-sitter. You might even have begun to interview people. Your partner might have arranged to take off three months from her job and then return to work part-time. But it's not until you're actually in the situation with a baby who needs caring for and a demanding job (or jobs) that need to be done, that you begin to grapple with the real nitty-gritty issues—issues as trivial as how you're going to get the baby to day care and both of you to work on time when one car is in the shop, or as fundamental as whether your partner (or you) would prefer to stop working to raise the baby and, if so, how to swing it financially. This is just the tip of the issue iceberg. The question *Who Will Raise the Children?*, the title of James Levine's 1976 book, has if anything become more widely asked and more difficult to answer since the book was published. And clearly, it's not going to go away. Today nearly half of all married women with children under age one are working, and this figure is expected to rise. The U.S. Census Bureau estimates that by 1995 over 85 percent of women under age forty-five will be working.

How *are* we going to raise our children, and more specifically, our babies? Who is going to be there for them, and when? How do you find the right day care or the right baby-sitter? What are our priorities—work or family? What do our partners expect of us in terms of child care? What do we expect of *them* as mothers? How do we feel if *they* put work before family? Or if they put family before work and quit their jobs? And what about if we decide to quit *our* jobs (or get fired or don't get hired) and find ourselves full-time fathers? How do our partners handle it? How do *we* handle it? How do the babies handle it?

These are the issues this chapter explores, and they are just a few of the more pressing issues of this very pressing subject. The questions about child care seem especially difficult in part because for many of us they're so new. Our parents, for the most part, didn't have to worry about them. In the traditional family, the father worked, the mother raised the babies, and even if everybody wasn't always happy, that was the way it was. We've changed, but our social institutions—our jobs, our schedules, our workplace benefits, the child-care facilities available to us, the expectations put on us—have not caught up with us. Until they do, we're going to have figure things out on our own.

The Basic Issue: Where Do I Fit In?

No matter how much you planned for and organized and prearranged your baby's child care, there's a good chance that the arrangements will shift a bit (or a lot) when the baby is actually there needing to be cared for. For starters, you're dealing with three highly complex and unpredictable elements: you, your partner, your baby. Then there's the unpredictability of baby-sitters, day care, circumstances. And then there's time, which, as it unfolds, has a way of changing many things, perhaps most dramatically your baby. Your partner may start off an enthusiastic full-time mom and grow progressively more bored, irritable, and frustrated. You may feel that you're missing out on the best years of your baby's (and your own) life and decide to cut back on work and step up your child-care involvement. You may have made arrangements to

Caregiving: Who, How and When?

take the baby to work with you (several couples I talked to who had their own businesses did this) and it may work out fine until the baby learns to crawl and starts wrecking the office. You may be miserable about all the colds your baby is catching at day care and decide to keep him home with a sitter instead. You may find yourself with some intricate shifting schedule that includes mothers-in-law, play groups, baby-sitters, and the two of you juggling blocks of work time. The point is, child care is a process, often a makeshift one, not a fixed system; expect change and be ready to change yourself.

Where do you fit in all this? To a large extent, it's up to you. Of course, to start with there's the job situation in your household. If you're one of the 48 percent of married couples with two jobs and a baby under age one, you're going to have to figure out not only what to do with the baby when you're both at work, but who does what when you're both at home. If your partner stays at home with the baby, you may feel that there's *no* child-care role for you or that you're getting *all* of the care shoved at you the instant you walk in the door or that you're walking an impossibly thin line between her demands for more help and her criticisms of all your efforts. You may argue that every practical problem has a practical solution: I'll do this Tuesday, you do that Thursday, and so on. Sure, the practical side is important, but beneath nearly every practical issue there's an emotional issue—issues that, if left undiscussed, may disintegrate into power struggles. It's more than just changing diapers and giving baths; it's raw time, it's responsibility, it's being there day-in-day-out, it's who's going to take charge when one of you is sick, it's who's going to think and plan ahead. Yes, fatherhood has changed; yes, we're more involved (either from desire or necessity) than our dads were; but when you get right down to the basics of caretaking, responsibility, and decision making, all too often we fathers adopt a passive role. The father's attitude is: I've put in my five hours and now I'm off duty. And the mother's thinking: Yeah, five measly hours during which I was supposed to rush home from work, get my hair done, shop, and cook everyone's dinner—big deal! Our situations and life-styles may have changed, but both we and our partners are still basically working from traditional social norms that define work as dad's job, kids as mom's job. So when we work *and* do five hours of child care, we feel like heroes; unfortunately, it's rare that our partners feel like pinning any medals on us.

The point is not to beat our breasts with guilt, to blame ourselves, or to try to become instant superdads who do it all. Nor is the point to "reverse roles" and send our wives into the maw of corporate America while we rush around taking care of the babies, shopping, and getting our hair done. Practical, or impractical solutions, as most of us soon discover, only go so far. Part of the point, maybe, is to take a more active part not just in the *doing* but in the *thinking*—to develop an *active awareness* of our needs, our expectations, our desires, and our contributions, as well as those of our partners. Many men I talked to said their role in child care changed tremendously over the course of the first year—sometimes because of fights with their partners, sometimes because they began to wake up to how little they were really doing, sometimes because they gradually adjusted to the demands that raising a child involve. One father, a teacher whose partner did not work for the baby's first eighteen months, said that it took him some time to adjust to having his infant daughter "shoved" at him as soon as he came home from work: "It took a while, but over the course of time I accepted responsibility for the baby when my partner needed to get out. It was hard until I had assumed these added responsibilities into my life. Now we've reached an equilibrium state, an unwritten law. When I come home, I relieve her."

Another father, a clinical psychologist who lives outside San Francisco, described how it took a big fight to make him realize how passive a role he was playing in child-care responsibility: "My wife is naturally more interested in child care, so without intending it I was letting her do all of it. I didn't realize how burned out she got after five to six hours, how much stress she was under. She confronted me about how I hadn't been spending time with our son. I was totally angry and yelling for half a day because I knew she was right. I have been doing a lot more since then. She still does the lion's share, but I'm now doing a fair amount. We're trying to share more of the tasks. We move in when the other person becomes exasperated."

Aside from the private adjustments that each of us makes in his own home and with his family, there are changes we can push for in society and in the workplace to make family life more livable: flexible work schedules, decent part-time jobs (if we want them), and legislation that forces employers to take the special needs of parents into consideration.

The question of Where do I fit in? is one you may find yourself asking repeatedly as your baby grows. You'll ask yourself, your partner, and eventually you may start looking to your child for the answer. And really, it's a question that the three (or more!) of you will be figuring out together. If you leave it all to your partner, she'll assign you a role that you may grow to resent and she may resent the task of assigning. If you go off and ponder it all alone in the wilderness, you're likely to come back with a fairly wild answer. Again, it's a matter of awareness, openness, process, and change. Again, it's not easy—but no one has to tell you it's worth it.

Although the philosophical and emotional issues of child care may be the tough ones to work out, the practical issues are also crucial—and very often the two are bound together. Let's take a look at some of the child-care options available, how different couples are working with them, and how dads are fitting in to them.

When Both Parents Work: Two Workers and Three Jobs

"Two boys, two jobs, busy all the time: modern life." That's how one father summed up the life-style of the two-career family. When both of you work full-time and you have children, basically you have three full-time jobs to handle, and one of them includes no vacations, no weekends, overtime every night, and no pay (although the rewards are incalculable). Obviously, you're going to need some help. Before the children reach school age, you have three major options: find a baby-sitter who will come to your home, find a day-care center or a baby-sitter who will look after the baby in her own home (there are some male baby-sitters and professional caregivers, but the majority are female), or arrange for a relative or close friend to look after the baby. Or you can use some combination of the three.

Of the three options, the relative/friend arrangement is the least expensive, but it also the least likely to be available—how many of us have relatives or friends who live nearby and also have that kind of time? The in-home baby-sitter gives you the most control over the kind of care your child is receiving, but it is also the most expensive option in most parts of the country. The day care/out-of-home baby-sitter is the arrangement most commonly used by the fathers I talked to.

How do you go about finding a reliable baby-sitter or high-quality day care center? Most of us *don't* go about it: we leave it to our partners. No matter how egalitarian or liberated we are, most of us harbor the feeling that because *she* is the one going back to work, she better arrange the child care. At the most, we might get involved as the "boss" who has final say over her choice. As Daryl, a Philadelphia schoolteacher, put it, "I did not want to take part in the arrangements and she [his partner] did it all. I felt it would be a burden. Anyway, I wanted her to feel good about who the caregiver would be. She investigated all the child-care centers and came back and gave me the report."

Maybe we secretly don't want our partners to go back to work and "abandon" our children. Maybe at some deep, unconscious level (or with full consciousness and due deliberation) we really think mothers should stay home and raise their children. As one dad said, "Both my wife and I grew up with our mothers at home and there is some anxiety for both of us about not having that for our son." Or maybe we just kind of put it way at the back of our minds and assume it will take care of itself: the old passivity routine. This was certainly true in my situation. Even though I was the one who would be home with the baby-sitter (my wife is a teacher), I left the searching, most of the interviewing, and the real decision making to her. When she hired someone I really didn't like, I was stuck with her. When I complained, my wife got mad. "If you don't like her," she said, "why don't *you* find someone better!" Instant object lesson in taking responsibility.

Most fathers are spared this situation because most fathers

Caregiving: Who, How and When? 303

don't work at home; but that doesn't mean they don't care what kind of hired child care their babies are getting. They care a lot—they just don't do much about it. So here's what to do.

No matter what type of child-care arrangements you're going to use, the single most important thing is the personality of the caregiver. This person is going to have full responsibility for your precious baby—his or her physical *and* emotional needs. As you know from your own parenting experience, caring for a baby takes lots of love, patience, gentleness, energy, playfulness, good judgment, and common sense. You can't really ask a person in an interview whether they have these qualities: you have to go largely by your instincts and your gut sense. Above all, *you* have to be there to meet the baby-sitter or day-care provider. It's impossible to judge a person's abilities from a second-hand report. If you possibly can, take the time to be with your partner and meet the baby-sitter, to visit the day-care facility, and see the caregivers in action. Even if your partner does the initial screening, try to meet the "finalists." Two sets of instincts are always better than one in forming judgments. If you can't agree, it's probably a good sign that you should keep looking.

What Type of Care? Some Fundamental Considerations

Although the personality of the caregiver is the paramount factor in determining the quality of child care, there are some generalizations that can be drawn about the various types of child-care arrangements, and you may want to think about them before making the basic choice. We know that an infant requires loving stimulation in order to learn and develop and also that an infant thrives best when there is continuity in the way that stimulation is provided. Thus, the optimal situation is one in which the same creative, affectionate caregiver looks after your baby from the very start. This is least likely to occur in a large, institutional day-care center where many caregivers work in shifts, and most likely to occur with a loyal, loving, long-term baby-sitter who looks after your child alone. A recent book, *The Child Care Crisis* by Fredelle Maynard (Viking, 1985), reviews current studies on the effects of day care and concludes that "day care of average quality has no apparent ill effects on children's intellectual development." But Maynard cautions that caregivers rarely give children the kind of individual, sensitive responsiveness that parents hope for—that kind that is most nurturing of the child emotionally and intellectually. Sandra Scarr points out in *Mother Care/Other Care* (Basic Books, 1984) that day-care centers tend to employ caregivers trained in child development or early childhood education, and that these caregivers commonly offer educational programs and organized, scheduled group activities. Trained caregivers and organized programs, says Scarr, may well benefit a child over three, but an infant or early toddler is unlikely to get much out of them. For the child under two, individual attention, affection, unstructured play, and a schedule that takes his or her own needs into account are much more important. Thus, Scarr feels that the family home or baby-sitter is usually a better choice than institutional day care for children of this age.

Socially, children raised in day-care centers do very well: they show marked independence, they follow direction well, cooperate and interact with other children, and, according to some studies, show less timidity with strange adults (other studies have found that children put in day care before age two are *more* fearful). It should be noted that the studies found this increased social competence in children who have been in day-care centers but not in "family homes." On the downside socially, Maynard cites studies that indicate that day-care children feel more cut off from adults, less responsive to adult direction later on, and that they tend to be much more aggressive than other children (in one report day-care children committed fifteen times as many aggressive actions as children raised at home). There is concern that aggressive day-care children do not perform as well in school, that they're more impulsive and more easily distracted from their studies.

As noted above, day-care children lead much more regimented lives than children raised at home or in home environments: there is rest time, juice time, playtime, playground

Caregiving: Who, How and When?

time, and so on. Choices are necessarily limited and there is concern that these limits may suppress a child's creativity and moral sense. In the area of health, there is no doubt that an infant is better off at home. At even the most strictly run, sanitary day-care center, a child is far more likely to contract infections—ranging from colds to serious flus and viral hepatitis—for the simple reason that the child is coming into close contact with so many more children. As Scarr puts it, "In a day-care center there are countless new germs introduced every day." Maynard concludes that "the accumulated weight of evidence unquestionably points to day care as an increased health risk for young children."

On balance, the best place for your infant under age one is at home with a good baby-sitter, the second best is a family home with a top-quality caregiver who looks after a very small number of other children, and at the bottom of the pile is institutional day care (although for a mature, emotionally sturdy two-and-a-half or three-year-old, the day-care center makes a lot more sense). This is not to say that the day-care center in your area is *necessarily* going to be worse for your infant than a family home or a baby-sitter. There are terrific, small, cozy day-care centers staffed by superb caregivers, just as there are lazy, incompetent baby-sitters who will ignore your baby as he howls all day. Obviously, the individual situation is all that matters to you; but in contemplating the choices, you should be aware of the general picture painted by national studies. And the national studies indicate that day-care centers are prone to these shortcomings.

Unfortunately, many parents do not have all that much choice: they have to take what is available and what they can afford. But if you're on the borderline—if pinching a few extra pennies or driving a few extra miles or researching the local child-care situation just a little bit more fully could make the difference between more individualized care and large group institutional day care—you may well find that the sacrifice is worth it.

Finding and Hiring a Baby-Sitter

In hiring a baby-sitter, you either advertise by placing your own ad or you comb through local papers and look for ads placed by baby-sitters in need of work. In our community there is a particular local advertising circular in which the best baby-sitting ads appear. In New York City, parent word-of-mouth says that the *Irish Echo* is the place to look for ads. I suspect most cities and communities have their baby-sitting "underground" of preferred newspapers, bulletin boards, and the like. Ask around with other parents.

Placing an ad of your own may saddle you with a huge screening process. One New York City couple I talked to placed an ad in *The New York Times* and ended up with more than 200 people to interview. But there are ways to speed up the screening. As one mother pointed out, you can almost tell over the phone whether the person is someone you'd consider hiring or not. Try to be as specific as possible in your ad. Is it essential that the baby-sitter have her own transportation? Do you prefer (or insist on) a nonsmoker? What hours and days will you want her to work? Do you want a live-in baby-sitter? Is experience required? Is age a factor? English-speakers only (which can pose a real problem in some parts of the country)? You might want to specify "references required" in your ad, but in any case, before you hire someone it's a good idea to investigate her thoroughly. Follow up on all references she provides and ask probing, specific questions. Not just, Is she reliable? but Does she come on time? Does she do what you tell her? How did your baby like her? Why is she no longer working for you?

No doubt you've been on a number of job interviews yourself, so you have a good sense of what makes a good interviewer and what makes a poor one. Good interviewers ask intelligent, open-ended questions that require some thought and involve more than a yes or no answer; they put the job candidate at his or her ease at the start of the interview, but they also make the candidate work a little bit to prove him- or herself; they don't do all the talking; they don't seek to chal-

Caregiving: Who, How and When?

lenge, humiliate, or "catch out" the candidate. These are the qualities you should strive for in interviewing baby-sitters (or day-care providers). It's always a good idea to have the baby present, to let the prospective sitter hold the baby, and maybe even feed him or her. That's going to be her job, so you might as well find out how comfortable she is with handling a baby. A good icebreaker is to talk about her own children (if she has any), find out how old they are, and who takes care of them during the day. Why does she want this job? What is her previous work experience? You might want to set up hypothetical situations as little tests. What would you do if the baby got sick during the day? What are your techniques for putting an overtired baby to sleep? How would you handle it if both of us came home late? And, of course, cover all the practical considerations: hours the baby-sitter works, transportation, pay, how much housework you want the baby-sitter to do (this should be made as clear and specific as possible to avoid future disagreements), vacation time, pay raise schedule.

You can learn a lot about a person in an interview; you can learn even more by seeing them in action. Once you and your partner have narrowed down the candidates to three or four, have them come in and work a day or half a day. Again, try if possible to be present for at least part of the time. Let the person do the job just as you will expect her to do it if she's hired on a permanent basis and pay her what you would pay if she's hired. Don't hover over her, but work with her, be available for questions, and pop in and out to see how she's doing. My wife used this technique (again, I took a passive role even though I was home) and found out much more than the interview had revealed. One baby-sitter promised to do the housework *eventually*, but said she wanted to spend her trial period "just getting used to the baby." The "eventually" never came: she never got around to doing any housework and instead read magazines during the baby's naps. Another sitter had the opposite problem: she was so obsessed with the housework that she left the baby to scream in her crib while she took the refrigerator apart and cleaned it from top to toe, despite the fact that we said heavy cleaning was not part of the job. The baby-sitter we eventually hired found a good balance: for example, she put the baby on a blanket with some toys while she sat with her and folded the laundry and put it away. This seemed like the perfect way to combine housework and entertaining an infant. All three of these baby-sitters seemed responsible and caring in their interviews, but without a trial we never would have seen their very different approaches to handling the job. By the way, if you're planning to have a trial period, make sure you tell the baby-sitter about it so she doesn't assume she has the job.

In assessing baby-sitters, set your standards high but not unreasonably high. Obviously, you'd never hire someone you didn't trust or didn't like. But you're never going to replicate the care that you and your partner give. You can hire responsibility, competence, enthusiasm, fun, and even love—but you can't hire mother and father love. Once you find someone who works out, someone both you and the baby are happy with, hold on to that person. Continuity, especially in the second half of the first year, is crucial to the baby's happiness. Reward a baby-sitter you like with praise, with warm encouragement, with money, and with flexibility from you (for example, let her go home early on Christmas Eve or during a snowstorm or when her baby is sick). When you see something you don't like—the sitter is propping a young baby up on a cushion and giving him a bottle; too much television is being watched; the baby doesn't get outside enough; the nap schedule is not being adhered to—correct it quickly and with firm (polite) instruction. You may find (as I did) that the baby-sitter only listens to your partner on matters of child care, but if you're involved and have opinions, you may need to have a talk with her about the "new fatherhood." On the other hand, you may feel more comfortable leaving the baby-sitting management to your partner or you might simply never be around when the baby-sitter is on duty. As one father said of his situation, "I seldom see the baby-sitter and I don't interfere. I don't think it is fair for her to have two bosses."

Finding Good Day Care

Day care available in the United States ranges from informal, unlicensed arrangements known as family homes, where

Caregiving: Who, How and When?

a mother takes a few other young children into her home during the day, to slickly run and well-advertised centers that are part of national chains. In between are small day-care centers run out of church basements, licensed companies that consist of a single day-care center in a house or storefront, inner-city centers that have spots for children whose parents receive government subsidies to help pay the cost of day care. The current U.S. day-care scene has been described as a maze and finding your way through it to the right day-care setup for your baby can take some work, some time, and some luck.

Probably the most efficient way to begin looking is to hook up to some grapevine. Ask around—ask *anyone* with young children whether they know of decent day-care facilities in your area. Visit likely clearinghouses of parent information, such as children's libraries, YM/YWCAs, the Red Cross, community centers, churches active in community affairs. Check to see if your area is served by a child-care information and referral agency, an organization that provides lists of day-care facilities (licensed only) and that will arrange for families eligible for government subsidies to get slots in licensed day-care centers. If no such agency exists in your area, check with general social service administrations or local child development agencies to see whether they can provide you with lists of day-care facilities. Check the phone book under "social services." Another possible source of day care is through your local school district or through a university. Some large corporations provide day care to the children of their employees. And check your Yellow Pages under "day nurseries" and "child care."

The issue of licensing is part of the day-care maze. When the federal government was subsidizing day care more heavily in the 1970s, it established federal requirements for day-care centers. But when the Reagan administration cut back on such funding, it passed along the responsibility for regulating the centers to state and local governments. Therefore, licensing requirements now vary fairly widely from state to state, although most states maintain certain broad standards. The rules are usually stricter for those day-care centers that take in children under age three: in many states these centers must have one staff member for every four or five children, separate areas in which children eat, play, and sleep, and weekly visits by a nurse.

A state-licensed day-care center will thus deliver these minimum requirements, but that doesn't mean it will deliver the best day care for your child. First, there is not enough licensed day care to go around. Demand far outstrips supply in many areas, and waiting lists can be formidably long. Second, you may simply be turned off by an institutional day-care setting, no matter how carefully regulated by the state. Family home care remains the most popular and most widely available day-care option, and it is estimated that the overwhelming majority of such care is neither registered nor licensed. Very often it's "this terrific lady down the street who's great with kids." You hear about her from friends, you call her up (she doesn't advertise or list her services with any local agencies), she says she has a free spot, you visit her, like her, and that's that.

Ultimately, the quality of the caregiver matters more than whether the day-care facility is licensed. The most fundamental question you'll be asking yourselves is: Do we feel comfortable leaving our baby with this person (or people) and among these other babies? And the only way to answer that is to go to the center or family home with your baby and observe. The best way to start checking out a day-care facility is to meet and interview the director or, in a family home, the woman providing the care. Use this as an opportunity to find out as many practical details as you can: number of children, how long the center has been in operation, the physical setup of the center or home (such as where the children may play in- and outdoors, where they nap, where they eat), costs, background of the staff members, turnover of staff, costs, emergency arrangements.

If the center or home caregiver passes muster after the initial interview, you're ready to pay a visit to observe. In the case of a mother taking care of a few babies in her home, the situation is not that different from the trial period for a babysitter described earlier. She's doing her job and you want to see her in action. Bring your baby along and see how she treats him or her and how your child reacts to the situation. Keep your eye out for how she handles "crisis" situations

Caregiving: Who, How and When?

when a couple of the babies are fussing at once. Try to form an impression of how the other children relate to her, whether they like and trust her. Try to find out how regimented she is about feeding and nap schedules, what her policy is toward pacifiers, how often she changes the babies' diapers, how much television she watches with the children, how quickly she picks up babies when they cry, whether she has a gentle touch and a soothing tone of voice. How does she feel about her job? Does she see the babies as a series of irritating problems or as individuals? If she has her own children with her, does she give them special treatment?

Evaluating day care can be a bit more difficult because there are usually more caregivers and more children present. Bryna Siegel-Gorelick has some good advice in *The Working Parents' Guide to Child Care* (Little, Brown, 1983) on how to make the most of your observation time. She suggests picking out one child and following him for a few minutes to see what activities he engages in, how often he comes in contact with a caregiver, how happy he seems. Then pick one caregiver and follow that person for a while to see how much time she spends with the kids (as opposed to administering or preparing materials), what moods and emotions her face and "body language" reflect, how responsive she is to the needs of small children. Next, Siegel-Gorelick recommends an observation technique she calls "event-sampling": check out how the kids and caregivers act during stressful events such as fighting and crying. How long does the caregiver wait before intervening? How does she handle a fight between two kids?

It makes good sense when hunting for quality day care to visit a number of centers or family homes before making your decision. Even if there is one center that everyone in town insists is tops, check out some others before you follow the herd. Discuss and compare your impressions with your partner. If at all possible, get the names of parents who have used the center or family home and interview them about how pleased they and their children have been with the quality of the care. Putting together information and impressions from all these sources should give you sufficient guidance to make the right decision. Finding the right day care for an infant can be a very time-consuming and emotionally wrenching experience. Get a good head start on looking, and be prepared for some disappointments.

If your hunt does not turn up day care that satisfies you, perhaps you should consider some of the alternatives to hired child care discussed in the next section.

Other Child-Care Options for Working Parents

Help from relatives

Those of us who have relatives able and willing to look after our babies are lucky indeed. Nothing is more important in a caregiver than *caring* in the fullest sense of the word—and what caregiver could match the care of a grandparent, aunt, sister-in-law (or, more rarely, uncle, brother-in-law)? The other terrific advantage of care from a relative is that in most cases it is free. Free top-quality care: every working parent's dream! Too bad it's so rare. Of course, the dream is not entirely blissful. Grandmothers can be bossy know-it-alls who criticize the kind of care that you and your partner give. Since the relative is essentially doing the work as a favor, it's harder for you to make demands about schedules and activities than with a baby-sitter you're paying. You may find you resent being beholden to your mother-in-law (or whomever) and, if the relative in charge is elderly, she may have a harder and harder time dealing with your baby as he turns into a rambunctious toddler. Despite these drawbacks, if you have relative care available, give it a try.

Several of the fathers I interviewed were using relative care, each with a different setup. Daryl's partner, after checking out the day-care facilities in her city and finding them all lacking, approached her parents about baby-sitting. The grandparents agreed to do it together. At first they traveled across the city to Daryl's home, but soon they found the trip too burdensome so Daryl and his partner arranged to take the baby to their house. Terry from Saint Paul has a sister who loves babies so much that she was pressuring Terry and his wife to have one of their own. When Terry's wife went back to work part-time, Terry's sister jumped at the chance to look after her nephew two or three days a week. In my case, my wife and I had been using a baby-sitter who came to our home three days a week when the baby was very young and this worked out well; but when my wife took on a full-time job, we needed more child-care help—so on most Mondays, my wife's mother comes to baby-sit. Our arrangement remains informal—she comes when she can. But, of course, when she *can't* come, I do the child care because I'm the one at home. This has been great for my relationship with my daughter, but not so great for my work time. It's also been great for my daughter's relationship with her grandmother—an additional benefit of relative care.

Baby-sitting cooperative

A cooperative is an option only if one (or both) of you work part-time. Cooperatives function in many different ways, but the basic pattern is that a group of parents get together and divide the hours in the week among them. If there are only a couple of families involved, one parent could be in charge of all the kids. But once you have three or more babies, it's probably a good idea to have two parents on duty at a time. In any given week, you can probably get two or three days in the clear. The advantage is obvious: free baby-sitting from people who know about kids because they have kids of their own. The disadvantage is that it buys you only enough time for a flexibly scheduled part-time job. As with most child-care arrangements, the caregivers in baby-sitting cooperatives are usually women. It's possible that there would be some resistance to a father doing the sitting (assuming you have the time and that's the way your schedules work out). If you're committed to this idea and find a cooperative you like, why not ask them to give you a trial run?

Alternative work schedules

We Americans are an ingenious people and we're starting to come up with some ingenious solutions to juggling the demands of jobs and family. Flex-time is one way of altering work schedules to create more time for children. Flex-time means that you carry a full-time job, but not necessarily from nine to five. For example, Jim, a clinical psychologist on the West Coast, works ten-hour days on Monday through Thursday and takes care of his two kids on Friday. Jim's wife holds a part-time job as a social worker and puts in long days on Tuesday through Thursday; on those three days the kids (a boy age two and a girl three months) go to day care. In a poll of over 14,000 fathers published in *Parents* magazine in September 1985, 75 percent of the dads said they would take advantage of flex-time, even though 47 percent felt that it would count against them on their jobs.

Usually, flex-time only has a certain amount of flex: for most fields you must be on the job during a good portion of the regular workday. But by combining one flex-time job with either one part-time job or a job that has odd-hour shifts (evening or night), it would be possible for a couple to handle most of the child care themselves. Of course, your couple time would be squeezed to the vanishing point.

This squeeze on couple time is also a problem with job-sharing, another rather ingenious solution to the work-family problem. Job-sharing is just what it sounds like: a couple shares a single job, dividing responsibility and time between them. You might work mornings and your partner afternoons, or you might switch off days or even weeks. I've heard of one couple who share a newspaper reporter's job: one works a stint of five to six weeks while the other one stays home with the baby, and then they trade places. Since you're sharing a single job, one of you is always available for child care. (Of course, this means that you're also sharing a single salary, which might make job-sharing economically unfeasible.) Theoretically, almost any job from construction worker to bank president could be shared—the trick is getting your employer to agree to it. Couples tend to have better luck sharing jobs that are somewhat unstructured to begin with—university teaching or administrative positions, the reporter position already mentioned, jobs with small innovative companies not yet bogged down in bureaucratic procedures. And, of course, if you're both self-employed or run your own company, there is nothing to stop you from sharing the work in whatever manner suits you—and baby—best.

Although in the current employment environment, part-time work is an acceptable (if hard to find) option for working mothers, working fathers still have trouble with it, either from their employers or from themselves. Somehow a man is not considered sufficiently serious about his career if he only wants to work at it part-time. This, one hopes, will change; already we're hearing about lawyers working three-quarters time, doctors who are cutting back on their work schedules to be with their kids, and even corporate types who are dropping out of the seventy-hour-a-week rat race to spend time caring for their kids. In this way, professionals may be luckier than nonprofessional workers, who usually have less leeway in calling the shots on arranging alternative schedules. But with more and more mothers of young children entering the work force, the day-care supply increasing at a slower rate than day-care demand, and in-home baby-sitting prohibitively expensive in many areas, something is going to have to give. It certainly looks as if fathers, whether we or our employers like it or not, are going to be doing more and more child care in the future.

Special Issues for Fathers Whose Partners Are Full-time Mothers

Although the social trend is for more and more mothers of younger and younger children to work outside the home, over half of the married women with children under age one are *not* working in business. You might be thinking that these fathers have it made if you're in a two-job couple caught in the bind of juggling complex schedules and patching together child-care arrangements. And in some sense these dads do have it made: they can go off to work in the morning with the security of knowing that their babies are getting the best possible care —the most reliable, the most loving, the most stimulating, and the least expensive. But sometimes the return home from work—to a partner frazzled, exhausted, bored, and desperate for relief; a baby in a similar condition who hardly seems to know or respond to you; and a household barely afloat on your single paycheck—is not quite so blissful. True, nothing beats mother care (or father care) in terms of quality and dependability, but there is, very often, a price to pay—maybe not in cash, but in the more difficult currency of emotion.

Philip, the thirty-year-old controller with two sons (a toddler and an eight-month-old), gave a very vivid picture of what it's like to work full-time when your partner stays home with the kids. "My wife chose to stay home and raise the kids, but there are problems. First of all, she's really tired at the end of a day. There's lots of work just heading off disaster. She feels that it's a problem that she's not socializing, not working, and making a name for herself. She had been in nursing for four years, then she got her business degree and was ready to go back to work when she got pregnant. She feels cheated and envious of me. She has this desire to prove what she can do. All day she talks to two little boys, and she really misses adult companionship. At the end of a day she wants to get out and I want to stay home and be with the kids. We've discussed this issue a lot. We understand what we're talking about now and we make allowances. But the first year with our first boy was hard. It took me time to adjust to the fact that I couldn't go out with the guys and that my wife has to feel her freedom. At first we discussed these issues loudly. Now I understand a lot more what her life is like. When I take care of the boys, about three to four hours is my limit. I wonder how does she do it for ten hours a day? It helps for me to do some because it really puts me in her shoes."

The one issue Philip didn't bring up was money, but other fathers whose partners don't work discussed the financial pressure this has put on them. Said Daryl, who works as a schoolteacher in Philadelphia and whose partner did not go back to work until their baby was about a year and a half, "I am definitely under pressure to make more money. It's something I want to do, something I have to do, but not something I like." In the early months, Daryl's partner, like Philip's, desperately needed a relief from child care at the end of the day, so the pattern they worked out was for Daryl to take the baby and his partner to go out—to a movie, to be with

Caregiving: Who, How and When?

friends, whatever she wanted. In addition to his teaching job, Daryl started a home business selling subliminal tapes as a way to make more money, and as a result he feels tremendously squeezed. "I feel I'm working three jobs," he said. "I come home and take the baby and on top of that I have to earn more money. It's a triple whammy."

Rich, who works a seven-thirty A.M. to four P.M. day as a quality control inspector, offered a different perspective on the issue of finances. His wife went back to work in the accounting department of a big company when their baby was three months old, but after working for a while she decided to quit and become a full-time mother. "With the cost of day care so high, her working wasn't getting us ahead," Rich said. "She just decided she'd rather be home with him and enjoy him." Although his wife's situation changed dramatically, Rich said his role in child care has remained pretty much the same. "We still share. We both do all the chores and duties, from changing diapers to feeding. Now my wife and I have more time to do stuff together. It makes life easier and we're having more fun. I still get to spend a good deal of time with the baby and there is no longer the guilt of having him baby-sat at someone else's home. It's true that overall we earn less money, but everything else seems better. I don't really feel pressured by being the sole provider. In fact, I enjoy it. I don't feel that a woman's place is at home, but if she wants to be, that's great."

For Rich and his wife, having her stay home with the baby worked out well partly because they had a good pattern of sharing child-care responsibilities in place before she quit her job. Rich had been very involved with his son from the start and that involvement didn't stop when his wife quit her job. But for some fathers, this shuffling out of responsibilities can be a temptation, even if an unconscious one. I know it is for me. My wife, who works as a teacher, has long vacations at Christmas and during the summer. Every time one of these vacations rolls around, my child-care duties and involvement drop precipitously. It's not that I plan it that way—it just happens. My wife starts giving the baby dinner, something I would do when she was working; she takes the baby with her to the supermarket; puts her down for her nap. I continue doing all the fun things—playing wild games in the afternoon, reading, dancing—but all the chores begin mysteriously to gravitate to my wife. Invariably there's a quarrel, and then I have to be especially vigilant about doing my share.

If your partner stays home with the baby all of the time or some of the time, the two of you are going to have to work out a division of responsibility that you both feel happy with. Like me, a lot of men want to be involved and think it's right to share the child care and *do* share it when necessity dictates, but when necessity isn't there, we kind of sit back and let things ride. Sometimes our partners remind us—often heatedly—of our responsibilities, and sometimes they let things ride, too, and just keep doing everything with more or less resentment. Some women really *want* to be doing everything with the kids and some men really *don't* want to or *can't* do anything: dad makes the money, mom raises the kids is a formula that works for a lot of parents today, just as it worked for a lot of our parents. If it works, let it alone. But if it doesn't work—if dad feels excluded from the kids or mom feels burdened by them, or if dad agrees to share but weasels out or mom loves being with the kids but needs some time to herself come six o'clock—then it's time to make some changes. Sometimes all it takes is a talk—or a fight. Sometimes there are practical solutions: you change your schedule so you can be home earlier in the evening, when many babies are most difficult; you arrange for certain nights every week that your partner has off; you adjust the baby's bedtime so she's up when you get home from work. And sometimes it's a question of examining your basic assumptions about children, work, and the responsibilities of men and women. It takes work to get it right. But the payoff is a stronger relationship with your partner and your child and the satisfaction of living up to your own ideals as a father.

When Father Stays Home with the Baby

Full-time fathers. Nurturing fathers. Househusbands. Father primary caretakers. Mr. Moms. Our society hasn't yet settled on a name for them, but we all know what they are: fathers who take primary responsibility for raising their babies while their partners go out and work. A situation practically unthinkable a generation ago—and now the subject of press and television coverage, books, sociological studies, even a movie (albeit a comedy). Yet even in our enlightened age, full-time fathers (the term I prefer) provoke a certain uneasiness. Perhaps part of the reason for all the attention they're getting—out of all proportion to their tiny numbers—is that they challenge something basic about our culture, about the relations between and roles assumed by the sexes. Men really aren't supposed to do that—are they? we secretly (or openly) think. We wonder if there is something wrong with the man (can't find work, has a strange disease, isn't masculine) or the woman (is a workaholic, hates babies, insists on wearing the pants). As James Levine puts it so aptly in his book *Who Will Raise the Children?*: "A double standard applies to the man who cares for his own children. If he works and participates actively in the child care, he is a hero; if his work *is* to care for the children, he is a deviant." Perhaps the hardest part for us conventional types to accept is that some couples make this arrangement because they *want to*: the dad wants to be with the baby, the woman wants to work, and everybody's happy including baby. Or at least everybody's as happy as they are in "normal" households.

Choice is not the only factor that brings a couple to this situation. Circumstance also plays a role. The mother may have a better job (higher pay, more satisfaction) and not want to lose it. The father may have been fired or may have reached a point in his career when he yearns for something different. In his book *The Nurturing Father*, Yale psychiatry professor Kyle D. Pruett offers in-depth portraits of a number of families in which the father is the primary caretaker of a young child (or children). One nurturing father transformed his full-time job doing marketing data analysis for a utility company to a part-time job that he could do from his home. One young father kind of fell into full-time fathering when the family business he worked for had to suspend operations for a time. Another father was in a part-time sales job he wasn't too happy with; when the couple found out that the expecting mother could take a six-week maternity leave from her full-time job as a court reporter but with no pay, they decided together that the father-to-be should quit his job and raise the baby. Pruett focuses on these families as representative of the group of seventeen families he observed over a five-year period. As Pruett presents these fathers, they seem like perfectly normal, everyday guys. Part of his point is that "nurturing fathers" are not really special—they don't have overdeveloped nurturing instincts, they don't seem more feminine than masculine by any conventional scale. They're just men who, for their own personal and perfectly understandable reasons, happen to have taken over the primary care of their infants.

That doesn't mean that everything else in their lives stops. Just because they're primary caretakers doesn't mean they suddenly become parody 1950s housewives watching soap operas and waxing their linoleum when they're not changing diapers and giving bottles. Pruett's nurturing fathers continue to pursue some of their work and life interests, be it sports, hanging out with the guys, painting, home computers. His book effectively explodes the myth that when dad stays home the parents "reverse roles." The sharing of parental responsibilities, the blend of dad and mom caregiving and playing, the joint schedules, and the pursuit of individual interests is a great deal more complicated than that.

Pruett didn't just study the dads, but the babies as well. And he found that these father-raised infants "functioned above the expected norms on several of the standardized tests of development." (Other studies have found that children raised primarily by their fathers showed greater internal strength and were more advanced in verbal skills than children raised in traditional families, and that both girls and boys benefited from the arrangement: see N. Radin, "Childrearing Fathers in Intact Families," cited in *Fathers* by Ross D. Parke, 1981. The point of these studies is not that we should all quit work and become full-time nurturing fathers, but rather that if we have adopted this mode of caregiving, we don't have to worry that we're depriving our babies of some essential ingredient that only mother care can provide. Babies need *parent* care, and whether they get it in bigger doses from mother or father or in equal doses from both doesn't seem to matter.

Caregiving: Who, How and When?   321

Full-time fathers are in a very real sense pioneers, and like all pioneers they have to rely heavily on their own resourcefulness and self-assurance in dealing with new situations. How do you deal with the immense loss of prestige that any person, male or female, confronts the instant he or she leaves the working world to become a homemaker? (This issue, although difficult for both sexes, is particularly trying for men because our society has no conventional slot for the homemaker father as it does for the housewife. For men, fathers and nonfathers alike, paid work equals identity.) How do you deal with the almost inevitable disapproval of your own parents and in-laws? How do you handle the different kinds of stress this situation puts on your relationship with your partner? How do you retain your masculine self-image when you're spending your days doing "women's work"? How do you deal with the reactions of your friends? On a more mundane level, how do you handle the sandbox situation in which you are the only male in a group of mothers and babies at the park or playground? Do you become "one of the girls" or do you hold yourself in proud and lonely masculine isolation? Although I'm not a full-time father myself, I've had a taste of some of these conflicts on weekdays when my wife is working and I'm on duty. One problem I have, and a number of full-time fathers report, is a feeling of self-consciousness when I'm out with the baby, as if people are looking at me and thinking: Where is that baby's mother? Why isn't that man at work? And then there is the inner self-consciousness: If my college friends could see me now...

Full-time fathers also face many of the same problems as full-time mothers: how to find time for yourself when you're tied down by a demanding infant; how to avoid getting bored by the endless round of child-care chores; how to keep your mind sharp and alert in an environment dominated by demanding but fairly mindless activities; how to separate from the baby when the time comes for day care, nursery school, whatever; how to manage a partner who really doesn't seem to know what she's doing when it comes to baby care; how to cope at the end of a long day when you're dying to go out as a couple and do adult things and she's dying to spend some time with the baby; how to deal with being financially dependent on your partner. They also get the full-time mothers' payoff: the deep satisfaction of knowing one's child in the intimate, moment-by-moment, instinctive way that only comes from time and responsibility. It's not uncommon for full-time fathers to become feminists—or at least much more sympathetic to the role of women and mothers in our society.

There are no reliable statistics on how many men have adopted this role. We do know the numbers are small, but they appear to be growing. In the *Parents* magazine survey of over 14,000 dads cited above, 3 percent of the men reported that they were househusbands. But 42 percent of the responding fathers said they would *consider* adopting this role. *Considering* is still a long way from *doing*, but it's a step in that direction. And social trends indicate that the gap between considering and doing will continue to close for increasing numbers of men. *Newsweek* reports that working wives earn more than working husbands in nearly one-fifth of American marriages. Inevitably, for some of these couples, having the father take on the role of primary caretaker while the mother continues working full-time will make simple economic sense. And for many other couples, it will make complex emotional sense.

It may seem odd to think of today's families with full-time fathers as pioneers in the same sense as nineteenth-century families fighting to survive on the open prairies—but in many cases they share similar motives for breaking with the familiar: to stake out a life according to their own values, to find a way of earning a living that they could live with, to raise their children in a better environment than the one the conventional world offered. Although most of us will remain behind in the familiar world, we all have a lot to learn from pioneers.

In family life, as in so many areas of our society and culture, we seem to have entered an age of multiplicity. The ultra-traditional model—father as breadwinner, mother as child-rearer—coexists with the ultra-untraditional—mother as breadwinner, father as househusband—and in between there is the full spectrum of possible variations. For a great many of us, the question of who will care for the children, more than any of the social upheavals of the past twenty

Caregiving: Who, How and When?

years, has forced us to transform not only our values but our actions in work, in our relationships, in our leisure time. In answering this question, we have blurred distinctions between appropriate gender roles. In fact, for many couples, the question of "appropriateness" doesn't even come up. The issue is not who is *supposed* to do what, but who *can*: whose schedule or job or inclination permits him or her to take the baby to the doctor, to be home when the baby-sitter has to leave, to read the stories at night, or buy the milk in the morning. We're working out makeshift, crazy-quilts of child care—a grandmother on Monday, a baby-sitter on Tuesday, a father on Wednesday, a mother on Thursday—and hoping that they'll hold together long enough to see us and our children through. There are some who say that government has a responsibility to relieve parents of some of this burden through paid parental leaves, through job guarantees, through publicly funded child care, through promoting flex-time. That may well be. But in the meantime, we fathers have our work cut out for us—more work *fathering* than our fathers or their fathers had. Lucky for us—and lucky for our children—the "work" of child care is its own reward. Even if government does come through with parent-support legislation, for many fathers who have taken on a child-care role—either through desire or necessity—there is no going back. The rewards are too valuable.

13. Fathers in Special Situations: Adoptive and Single Fathers

Adoptive Fathers

Though he and his partner may have wanted a baby for many years, the adoptive father often becomes a father literally overnight. The adoption agency or lawyer calls with the long-anticipated message "we have a baby for you" and then in many cases tacks on the unanticipated proviso "if you want her, come and pick her up tomorrow." Said one father who used private channels to adopt a newborn: "For us, all the anxiety that expecting parents must feel over nine months was compressed into four weeks. We hardly slept. We were beside ourselves." Joy and stress are introduced simultaneously; the adjustment for the newly created parents—and for their baby—can be tremendously wrenching.

The way adoptive fathers adjust to fatherhood very often reflects the reasons they turned to adoption in the first place. For many, the reason is simple and clear: they and their partners want a baby but cannot have one biologically, either because of fertility problems or some medical condition. Others adopt out of altruism and idealism: they want to give a disadvantaged child a good home; they don't want to add an-

Fathers in Special Situations

other baby to an already overpopulated world; they have a special feeling for the plight of children in institutions. Often, though the reasons for adopting are fairly clear-cut, the actual decision to pursue it—and the long, drawn-out, and emotionally trying process of pursuit—becomes fraught with ambivalence. The woman may be more eager to pursue adoption than the man; the man may feel that adoption somehow draws attention to sexual failings (even if the couple's infertility has nothing to do with sex, as it usually doesn't); or the decision to adopt may arouse painful feelings of isolation and bitterness: why can't we be like everyone else? why do we have to subject ourselves to this public humiliation? For some, deciding to adopt means finally letting go of their dreams of having a biological child. In addition, fathers entering the adoption process have the same doubts and worries as pregnant fathers: how can I handle this financially? what will it do to my relationship with my wife? what about our careers? what if I don't like being a father? It all becomes more difficult because adopting an infant involves so much more effort and anxiety and sometimes money than trying to conceive. Is it worth it? is a question you may ask not once, but hundreds of times.

The process of adopting an infant in the United States today has been described as a "maze" of options, channels (some legal, some not), and foreign countries. If you are thinking about entering this maze, your best bet is to talk with other adoptive parents in your area about their experiences and to get hold of one of the better guides to adoption today and read it through before you begin. Recommended titles include these:

The Penguin Adoption Handbook: A Guide to Creating Your New Family by Edmund Blair Bolles (New York: The Viking Press, 1984).

The Adoption Resource Book by Lois Gilman (New York: Harper & Row, 1984).

Adoption and After by Louise Raymond (revised by Colette Taube Dywasuk) (New York: Harper & Row, 1974).

The Parent's Guide to Adoption by Robert S. Lasnik (New York: Sterling Publishing Co., 1979).

Successful Adoption by Jacqueline Horner Plumez (New York: Harmony Books, 1982).

You can obtain a copy of the pamphlet "Raising the Adopted Child" by sending $1 to the Public Affairs Committee, 381 Park Avenue South, New York, NY 10016.

Postadoptive Adjustments

One anxiety that comes up for many men during the adoption process is: Will I love my adopted baby? Or, more painfully unanswerable: Will I love my adopted baby as much as I would have loved a biological baby? The questions may become much more urgent and disturbing after you get your baby. For many biological parents, the birth of their children is a physically grueling ordeal that culminates in a moment of consuming joy; after the joy there frequently comes the letdown and adjustment period known as postpartum depression (see Chapter 8). Although adoptive parents are denied the joy (and pain) of experiencing the birth, they may share in their own version of postpartum depression. Adoptive parents may go from the logistical hassle of getting the baby to the practical burdens of caring for him or her without any time to celebrate, take stock, or rest. Paid parental leaves—rare enough when a couple has a biological baby—are almost unheard of for adoptive parents. It is becoming increasingly common for parents who cannot or will not wait to adopt an American infant to go abroad, usually to disadvantaged countries such as Korea, Peru, Chile, or other South or Central American nations. Traveling overseas with an infant is stressful enough, but when you're traveling for the first time with an infant you've never seen before, an infant who looks nothing like you, yet is irrevocably yours starting *now*, it can be overwhelming.

Even without these complications, you may feel let down by your adopted baby. You may feel you actually do not like him: the crying, the dirty diapers, the lack of response (or the frightened response) to you, the relentless routines of baby care. Very few fathers are prepared for the reality of life with a

Fathers in Special Situations

baby. Biological fathers at least have the nine months of expecting, the rite-of-passage of birth, and the buffer period of the hospital stay to begin adjusting and bonding. And, of course, they have the very powerful tie of knowing that their baby is their flesh and blood.

For adoptive fathers, the bonding process may take much longer and involve much more effort. Adoptive fathers will make their lives easier if they try to accept this and try not to worry about living up to unrealistic expectations. In the literature of adoption you read many accounts of parents who welcomed their adopted children as the answer to their prayers and began to love them instantly. This may well be true for some, but if it isn't true for you, don't punish or try to force yourself. One adoptive father said he felt fondly toward his adopted newborn at first, "but I did not feel the intense attachment that I feel now [at sixteen months]. That didn't happen until she started to smile." Many men (and women) find it difficult to love *any* new baby—be it their biological offspring or an adopted infant. It may take time. It's best to let the feelings come freely and to be as open as you can with your partner about what you're going through.

Of course, the postadoption period is not stressful for all couples. Said Irv, a thirty-six-year-old New York lawyer who privately adopted a baby just two days after her birth: "We just rode a high. I found out about the adoption and being made a partner in my firm the same week. Life was great! We had the world's most wonderful baby. I really thought I could be objective about this since I wasn't related to her and I hadn't given her any upbringing yet. She was happy and open and easygoing right from the start." Irv also pointed out that adoptive fathers feel less excluded than some biological fathers in the newborn period because in almost all cases the adoptive mother is not breastfeeding: that opens up a big area of child care to the father.

Part of what made Irv's life so carefree in the early days was that he and his wife had a few weeks notice before the birth to prepare for the baby. It was difficult enough for them to set up the baby's nursery and acquire all the necessary equipment in less than a month—but many adopting couples don't even have this much notice. (See Chapter 8 for a checklist of essential baby supplies.) If at all possible, try to minimize the stress of practical arrangements by getting help from others. If you have to travel to pick up the baby, see if you can arrange for a relative or friend to stock your house with diapers, formula, bottles, and such. Don't worry about getting everything exactly right (curtains, wallpaper, toys) immediately: focus on the essentials of food, clothing, and sleep. Borrow as much as you can from friends or relatives. And don't forget that you'll be caring for the baby from the instant that he or she is given to you. If you're traveling to pick up the baby, you'll need an infant car seat, formula (buy the prebottled kind for the trip so you won't have to worry about sterilizing bottles or refrigeration), some diapers, and changes of outfit to bring with you. (For a summary of baby's physical and mental progress from birth to age one, see the infant development chart in Appendix A.)

The Impact of Adoption on Your Infant

We've all heard stories about the depression, withdrawal, and anger that older adopted children often experience when they first move in with their adoptive families. Many adoptive parents assume they won't have to worry about this with an infant: they assume a baby under six months can't have formed a meaningful bond with his mother (or father) and thus switching parents won't matter to him. We now know this assumption is wrong. Adoptive parents have seen infants as young as three and four months old mourn for their biological mothers. The babies become listless and depressed; they won't smile or respond; their sleeping and feeding are erratic. Attachment begins at birth, and an infant who has formed an attachment will suffer when that attachment is broken. As Lois Gilman says in her useful *The Adoption Resource Book* (Harper & Row, 1984): "Adopted infants can be expected to grieve. They have suffered a major dislocation in their lives. They cannot verbalize their feelings, but they can vocalize them. Their feelings are there. They may cry; they may withdraw; they may refuse to smile. They are reacting normally to the changes going on in their lives."

Patience and love are the best ways of helping the baby to recover from his loss and to begin forming an attachment to you. Some adoptive parents find that the baby initially forms an attachment only to one parent (often the one who came to get him from the agency or foreign country). If you're excluded from the relationship, you may feel hurt and resentful. But if the baby clings exclusively to you, you may find yourself exhausted by child-care chores and mightily resented by your wife. The process of adjustment may be long and painful. Life with any infant involves crises and dislocations; with an adopted infant the crises may be more severe, the dislocations more baffling. It will take time—to bond with the baby, to adjust, to feel like a parent, to regain the balance in your relationship with your partner, to relax into the love of family life. Give it time. Don't expect too much too fast from yourself or your baby.

Getting Help with Problems: Parents Groups and Resources

All parents need help in the early months, but getting help can be particularly difficult for adoptive parents. If you grouse that your biological baby is keeping you up half the night wailing, chances are your colleagues and friends will feel sorry for you or maybe tease you in a sympathetic sort of way. If you voice the same complaints about an adopted infant, friends and relatives may call into question your fitness to be a parent or they may worry that you're thinking of taking the baby back. Their worries and criticisms of you are the last thing you need, particularly if you are in fact thinking about returning the baby (permissible at agencies until the adoption is finalized in court). This is one reason why adoptive parents very often do better seeking help from other adoptive parents or from trained counselors.

If you adopted your baby from an agency, this might be the best place to call when you need help. The agency might have some sort of postadoption program, or the staff may be able to help you find one or put you in touch with other parents in your situation. There are several national organizations that may help you find a parents-support group:

North American Council on Adoptable Children
(NACAC)
2001 S Street N.W.
Washington, DC 20009
202-466-7570
(They have lists of parent groups and will put you in touch with state representatives.)

OURS, Inc.
3307 Highway 100 North, Suite 203
Minneapolis, MN 55422
612-535-4829
(Has affiliations with about one hundred parent support groups around the country.)

Dealing with Family, Friends, and the "Outside World"

Long after you have settled into family life with your adopted baby, you may encounter subtle (or overt) resistance to the adoption, and insensitive questions and comments from members of your family, your friends, or perfect strangers. One father I interviewed told of a terrific fight he had with his own parents when he announced that he and his wife were thinking about adopting, a fight that intensified when they actually adopted a baby. Others tell of being given the third-degree by friends or colleagues about their motives, their philosophy, how they would feel about getting a "genetically inferior" child. Though our society is more accepting of adoption than it used to be, we still have a long way to go. Even well-intentioned people may come out with comments like, "You're really helping her overcome her origins" or "You're so good with her, you really seem just like her father." Strangers may comment on how little (or how much) the baby looks like you or ask your partner how the birth went. Or you may be quizzed about the baby's "real" parents: did you meet them? what were they like? why did they put this baby up for adoption? are you sure they can't claim her back? Even fellow parents may try to assert that their parenting abilities and bond with their baby must be superior to yours since theirs is based on biology.

Fathers in Special Situations

All of these questions, comments, and unconscious assumptions, no matter how well-meaning or innocent, may hurt you and make you angry. There's no way to shield yourself from this situation entirely, just as your child cannot be completely protected from similar comments once he enters the world of school and friendship with other kids; but you can prepare yourself—and later your child—to handle it. Most adoptive parents soon develop a strategy of response to defuse the situation or end it. With close friends and family members you can be open and precise about what offends you and why. Usually one talk is enough. The father whose parents put up such a fight about the adoption said that after one final confrontation the situation is now calm, if not totally amicable. "I told them I don't want to discuss these issues with them ever again, and they are now reconciled to the adoption. I knew they would eventually start to love the baby. How can you resist your grandchild—especially the first?"

With the "outside world" you'll probably have to decide how open or private you want to be about the adoption. If you've adopted a child of a different race, you have no choice in this matter, and you're going to be dealing with a much more difficult situation. Again, groups of parents in the same circumstances can be the best way of getting support and talking through strategies for handling practical problems (for example, how to deal with racist parents, how to prepare your baby for life in a society where racism is a fact of daily life).

All adoptive parents face the issue of how—and when—to tell their children that they are adopted. The issue is likely to arise much sooner when the child is of a different race due to pressures from the outside world. But even with a child of the same race, it's an issue that demands delicate and sensitive handling. One adoptive father described the approach he was planning to take: "I want my daughter to find out about her adoption from *me*, not from someone on the street or some child teasing her. A good time would be when she starts to ask where babies come from. Also, we're planning to adopt another baby, and that might be the time to start talking about it." Several adoptive parents have said that when they tell their young children about the adoption they are careful to provide lots of reassurance. The message they want to convey is "Yes you are adopted and, yes, you are my child and I am your father."

"Being adopted is a fact about my child's life," one adoptive father said. "I don't forget it nor would I want to. I'm always aware that she is someone else's baby in one sense and yet in another sense she is entirely mine. A woman gave birth to her—but that is not her mother. And her biological father's contribution was physically much smaller than her biological mother's. His physical contribution seems like nothing at all compared with actually being her father and raising her." After the stress and turmoil of getting settled with your adoptive child, after the adjustments of the first few months, after the difficulties with insensitive friends or family members, come the rewards of actually being a child's father and raising that child. And this ultimately has nothing to do with blood ties. What it comes down to, for biological and adoptive fathers alike, is loving and caring for the children. That's fathering.

Single Fathers

One thing we can say with absolute certainty about single fathers is that their numbers are growing rapidly. According to the Census Bureau, Marriage and Family Statistics Branch, in 1985 there were 136,000 male householders living alone with their own children ages three and under. This represents 11.2 percent of all single parent families with children under age three. The comparable figures for 1980 were 83,000 single fathers (8 percent of all single-parent families with children under three), and in 1970, 31,000 single fathers (5 percent of all single-parent families with children under three). The number of white single fathers who raise their children (under age eighteen) increased 22 percent from 1975 to 1980 and 56 percent from 1980 to 1985. It's not just single fathers who are on the rise. The total number of single-parent families doubled from 1970 to 1985. By all estimates, these increases will continue. According to *U.S. News & World Report*, three out of

Fathers in Special Situations

five children born today will live with a single parent by age eighteen.

Being part of an ever-growing national phenomenon doesn't make single fathering any easier. Just about every aspect of life for the single father is a challenge. There's work: how are you going to earn enough money to support your family alone when you have full responsibility for a young child? There are chores: how do you shop, cook, clean, buy clothes, and so on, when you're the sole parent? There's your social life: how do you go out with friends, entertain, and maybe even date and become involved with women when you have a young child to care for? There's your personal life: how do you maintain your interests (or just your sanity) without neglecting your child? The list goes on and on. If you're a single father you have your work cut out for you—and a lot of the work is juggling conflicting demands on you and your time. There is not enough of you to go around for everything, and yet none of the demands go away. Life is tough: there is no getting around it.

About half of America's single fathers are divorced. Not many years ago, it was almost unheard of for a father to be awarded custody of his young children, but today this is becoming increasingly common. Joint custody (also called coparenting) is an alternative that more and more divorced couples are turning to. If you're a father with full or joint custody of a young child, you're going to have to be entirely prepared to care for this child either all the time or, in the case of joint custody, part of the time. That means your house or apartment is going to need all the equipment necessary to feed, clothe, change, transport, and put to sleep a baby (see Chapter 8). Many single fathers find that getting control of the chores becomes the most frustrating and burdensome aspect of parenting. A trap that some men fall into is to try to compete with their ex-wives: they feel they must replicate (or improve on) the household standards and life-style that she provided. If she ironed the baby's clothes, they'll iron the baby's clothes; if she cooked a hot meal every night, they'll cook a hot meal every night, and so on. This can be okay if you love housework and find it a pleasant way to hang out with your child. But if you don't, it can become a consuming form of torture.

One piece of advice that many single fathers offer is: cut corners on the chores. Hire as much help as you can afford and what you can't afford, don't be too proud to accept from relatives and friends. Make a list of priorities and only do what you must. Send out the laundry. Serve frozen meals. Shop efficiently and infrequently. Stock your freezer and cupboards with back-up emergency meals. Maybe your ex-wife would never dream of letting the baby wear the same outfit two days in a row, serving take-out for dinner, or buying those expensive premixed bottles of formula. But if it makes your life easier, and gives you more time to relax and be with your child (or relax away from your child), do it.

Don't expect miracles of yourself, especially in the early days. Almost inevitably there will be a "crazy time" when you first take on the role of single father. If you've just gone through a divorce and custody battle, you're going to be emotionally (and probably financially) drained at the very moment when you have to shoulder massive new responsibilities. If your wife has died, you'll be in shock and so will your baby. You're going to need lots of help just to get yourself on your feet. The situation may seem impossible at first—and sometimes it *is* impossible. Widowed fathers with young children may turn to their parents (or other close relatives) for assistance or they may need to put the children in a relative's home until they get their lives in order. The beginning may be the most stressful because everything is so new, or the stress may accumulate as the pressures of day-to-day life mount without ever letting up. It's worth taking as much time as you can at the start to arrange for the best possible child care, to get your home in order, to figure out the logistics of daily life.

Many parents of young children complain that their lives are overscheduled and overfrantic: one parent has to appear at the day-care center before it closes, one parent has to shop while the baby naps and while the other parent catches up on weekend work, one parent has to fix dinner while the other deals with the evening fussy hour, gives a bath, or reads. If they're lucky, maybe they can find a minute to relax, either alone or together. What the two-parent family calls frenzy, the single parent considers luxury. When there is a couple, at least one parent *can* shop while the baby naps, or cook while the

Fathers in Special Situations

other parent reads. If you're single, you have to manage all of it all of the time by yourself. Unless you're incredibly organized and efficient, it might make sense to sit down and actually map out your week. Set aside certain days for certain chores. See if you can find some time without chores that you can use to be with your child. How flexible is your work schedule? Would your employer consider flex-time? How flexible is your child-care arrangement? If you have to work late (or shop late) one night, is there someone who could watch the baby? You may always have scoffed at people who live by lists, but making lists and schedules and planning ahead even for something so routine as a doctor's appointment might be a key to surviving the early days as a single father.

In your scheduling and planning, don't forget to make time for yourself. This should be one of your priorities, something you build in to your schedule. At first it may seem selfish or unfair when your child seems to need you so much, but you won't be doing the child any favors if you don't refresh yourself with time away. Henry Biller and Dennis Meredith point out in their book *Father Power* that single fathers may develop a "chronic intolerance" of their children if they feel compelled to spend every spare moment with them. Some men, say Biller and Meredith, feel they must try to compensate for the loss of the mother by being there for the baby whenever she would have been. This simply isn't possible. You'll be a better parent (and a better person) if you refresh yourself with "grown-up time" than if you try to be two parents at once. Time for yourself may mean hiring a baby-sitter one or two nights a week and seeing friends; it may mean an occasional weekend away or finding time to pursue romantic relationships; or it could be time you set aside for exercise, reading, or a sport or hobby. Much as we love our children, much as we need our work, if these are the only tings we do, our lives quickly grow stale and flat. Without time for yourself, depression, which is a common problem for single parents, may become your constant state.

Loneliness is also a common problem for single fathers. Though you're seldom alone, you may find you have less and less adult contact outside of your work situation. You may feel uncomfortable with former friends who are in couples or in two-parent families; you may not have time for other people (particularly if your time for yourself involves some solitary activity); or you may feel that you can't be away from your child. As time goes by, your circle of acquaintances narrows (some people stop calling you; you stop calling others) and you begin to feel that the whole world consists of you and your child. When this happens, it's time to get help. There are a number of national organizations that single fathers can contact for assistance and information (see the end of this chapter for a listing). Joining such an organization or a parents group can be the best way of meeting other single fathers, and sharing your experiences and problems with men in the same situation can be an excellent way of overcoming isolation. Some single fathers make changes in their living situations or their child-care arrangements. Sharing an apartment or house with another single father and his children can be a terrific way of solving a number of practical problems and gaining some adult companionship.

For some single fathers, the very thing that makes the whole situation worthwhile—their love for their children—can become a problem. If you have no partner to share with, your bond with your child can become all-consuming and all-encompassing. Your child becomes your sole reason for being and you become as dependent on the child's love as he is on yours. This is a damaging situation for both parent and child. You need more in your life than a child, and your child needs more than just you. Too much love and dependence will stifle a child. When this starts to become a problem, it's time to reach out to others and maybe to get help.

Single fathering is not all stress and crisis-handling. Like most challenging undertakings, it has rewards that are all the richer for being hard-earned. The first reward is your relationship with your child, and this is a reward you get every single day (though on the bad days it may not come until he's asleep). The second reward is the knowledge that you did it alone, that you have the courage and stamina and patience to raise your child by yourself. Most parents are proud of their children, but single parents can also be proud of themselves for making the most difficult parenting situation work.

Fathers in Special Situations

Though you may lose some friends along the way, you will also gain others. Some single fathers report that their special situation can make their relationships with women easier: many women are rightfully impressed by a man who raises his children alone and they feel attracted to men who are sympathetic to the situation of mothers (something that happens to most single and full-time fathers). The challenge of single fathering can be an opportunity for tremendous personal growth. Single fathers and their children may benefit from the contact with a larger community of other single-parent families. It's a way of breaking out of the insularity that the nuclear family imposes. Single fathers who give their children responsibility at an early age may be encouraging self-reliance and inner strength.

Few men become single fathers out of preference. For the growing numbers of fathers who are in this situation, single fathering is something they *have to do*—not only for their children, but for themselves. It's the challenge of a lifetime; but for those who rise to the challenge, it can also be the accomplishment for which they feel the greatest pride.

Resources for Single Parents

The largest single-parent organization in the United States is:
Parents Without Partners, Inc.
8807 Colesville Road
Silver Spring, MD 20910
301-588-9354
Contact the national headquarters to find a local chapter and for further information about books, magazines, and parents groups.

A national organization that deals with the legal problems of fathers after divorce is:
National Congress for Men
210 7th Street SE
Washington, DC 20003

202-FATHERS

For a copy of their directory (updated monthly) of local groups for divorced fathers, send a check for $7 to: NCM Directory, 68 Deering Street, Portland, ME 04101.

A network of 300 family counseling services nationwide, some with programs geared to the needs of single parents, is offered by:
Family Service America
11700 West Lake Park Drive
Milwaukee, WI 53224
800-221-2681
Write to them for the name of member agencies in your area. Fees for counseling are usually adjusted according to your ability to pay.

For the names of support groups for gay fathers who are raising their kids by themselves, who have joint custody, or who want to maintain closer ties with their children, contact:
Gay Fathers Coalition
P.O. Box 28317
Washington, DC 20005
703-548-3238

A hotline for parents (including single parents) who are having trouble coping with the frustrations of child care is:
National Child Help Child Abuse Hotline
800-421-0353

Also see *Fatherhood U.S.A.* by Debra G. Klinman and Rhiana Kohl (Garland Publishing, 1984) for local organizations, books, and magazines, and *The Official Parents Without Partners Sourcebook* by Stephen L. Atlas (Running Press, 1984).

14. The Growth of a Relationship

Change. Does any life experience change us as much and as quickly as fatherhood? When we stand at the threshold of this transformation and wonder about the new life we're about to step into, change seems both a promise and threat. We realize—and perhaps fear—that our lives will change: our relationships, our priorities, our responsibilities, how we work and play. But it's not until we become fathers, until we pass through the crises of adjustment and settle into family life, that we begin to perceive how much *we ourselves* have changed. The external changes in our time and energy seem trivial in comparison with the changes going on inside of us, really startling changes we didn't even dream of. Changes in our emotional center of gravity. Changes in our values. Changes in what gives us joy. Changes in how we think about the world and its future.

Our own changes are profound and radical enough—but what about the changes our babies are experiencing? A child's development from birth to one year seems nothing short of miraculous. How did that tiny, helpless, unreachable, wailing creature turn so quickly into this dynamo of motion, curiosity, laughter, and will? The infant who didn't know us or cried when we reached for him now practically jumps for joy when we walk through the door. The ten-month-old spends as much time smiling as the ten-week-old did crying. He's getting strong! He watches you in a new way. He seems to add a new skill every week. He's starting to talk. (For a summary of baby's physical and mental progress from birth to age one, see the infant development chart in Appendix A.)

Changes. You watch him playing in the sandbox shoulder to shoulder with the neighborhood children and you suddenly see the "kid" emerging from the baby. Before you know it he'll be in nursery school. *It goes so fast!* That cliché of parenthood that seemed so cruelly false when you were up half the night, when you were fumbling with the formula, or failing to control the piercing cries—all of a sudden it rings true. Your child's babyhood is precious. And you remind yourself to enjoy every moment of it.

The best changes of all are those you have created together —you and your baby, you and your partner, you and your partner and your baby. The father who held his newborn "like a broken egg" now swings his year-old daughter around the living room. The parents who fought over chores and night feedings now have a schedule that takes everyone's needs into account and they fight much less about *everything* now that their son sleeps ten hours at night. The father who had trouble expressing affection tells his son he loves him every night and, because of that, feels freed to tell his wife the same. The father who seldom cracks a smile in the office can't wait to get home and start rolling around on the floor with his kids. The father whose wife went away for four days discovered that he *could* do it all and enjoy it (though he was sure glad to see her when she returned).

New accomplishments. New games. New activities. New words. New discoveries. The changes seem to mount as the first year draws to a close. For busy fathers in the thick of these changes, baby's first birthday is a natural time for taking stock. We can still remember the birth as if it were yesterday. And then we look around us—at our babies, our lives, our relationships—and we realize in a terrific rush of emotion how far we've all come together.

Special Activities for Dad and Baby

By the second half of our babies' first year, most of us have staked out our own turf in child care, play, chores, and routines. Almost all the fathers I talked to said that they and their partners had worked out an arrangement based on sharing: if mom was home with the baby, dad would take over when he returned from work; if both partners worked out of the home, they would divide the "fun" activities in the mornings and evenings. Many father activities that began in baby's first days home from the hospital continue throughout the first year (and beyond): diaper changes, baths, giving the baby bottles, putting her to sleep, keeping an eye on her. But, although the routines themselves remain the same, the way we perform them and the way baby responds to them have changed dramatically. Bathing a newborn is a delicate, and occasionally nerve-wracking, operation as you struggle to prop the baby up, keep the soap out of her eyes, finish the bath before she begins to holler, get her dry before she loses all her body heat. Bathing a one-year-old is more like an aquatic circus with toys and bubbles flying through the air, baby attempting to "swim," and dad sitting back to enjoy the show. Meals, which used to be a matter of sitting quietly, holding a bottle, and burping the baby, are now frequently a different kind of circus. If you've got the patience and good humor to put up with baby's antics, the two of you can really have a blast as she makes her way through cottage cheese, overcooked carrots, mashed potatoes, or whatever baby delicacy you've dished up. You may not enjoy the mess, but you can have a good time just supervising baby as she sits in her high chair and immerses herself in her food.

Along with the accustomed routines of baby care are lots of new purely fun activities that become possible as your baby matures. Perhaps the most enjoyable is simply hanging out. Gradually it becomes possible just to *be* with your child without having to *do* anything for him. As he crawls or toddles or cruises around the house, you can keep him company or just

Precious time—just playing and relaxing

sit back and watch him. You can set him down in a playground and let him follow his whims (the whims of our baby at this age were to experience each piece of playground equipment methodically: she had to ride on *every* swing, play in all the sandboxes, look through every tunnel, and so on). Or you can follow his lead in selecting toys, books, furniture to climb on, pots to bang on, or whatever.

The Growth of a Relationship

One good piece of advice that the *Father's Almanac* offers is that when you're hanging out with baby, let this be your activity. If you try to accomplish something else at the same time—be it painting a chair, making a phone call, or reading the newspaper—you're going to disappoint your child and most likely fail to finish your own project. Whenever possible, undivided (even if passive) attention is best. Of course, you may not always have the luxury of just plain hanging out, but sometimes you can find activities that meet your needs and baby's needs at the same time. Part of my routine in the early evening is to play music and exercise: sometimes my daughter joins in with her own baby exercises, sometimes she dances to the music, and sometimes she insists that I stop exercising and read her books, play with her blocks, or whatever. I try to be available to her and make a point of including her in the exercise regime. I probably spend as much time playing with her as exercising, but it makes the whole activity a lot more fun for both of us (although occasionally we differ over the choice of music).

The possibilities of play become limitless in the second half of the first year. Once your baby can crawl, he'll want you to chase him around the house, and this game will gradually grow more elaborate as he becomes more mobile. Forty minutes of hide-and-seek per evening is de rigueur for one father and daughter I know. Babies who can sit up by themselves have a lot more fun because they can use both hands to play with. You can start to play ball games of all sorts. As your baby sits amid his toys, your role will range from active participant to silent observer to header-off of frustration when the rings won't stack or the wooden spoon falls out of reach. And as baby becomes sturdier, roughhousing becomes ever rougher and wilder.

Outings in the stroller or baby backpack to the park, to the yard, to the children's library, to friends' or relatives' houses, or to shops become a lot more enjoyable for both of you as the baby can do more and develops a longer cheerful attention span. Babies in the six- to twelve-month range are loads of fun to take along on trips of all sorts. They're old enough to enjoy the change of scene and to take advantage of playground facilities, but they haven't yet reached the age of opposition when the phrase "time to go home" invariably provokes a storm of protest.

The fathers I interviewed lit up when I asked them about the special activities they had with their babies. Don said that because he lived in his imagination more than his wife did, he found himself more on his son's level, to which the baby really responded. Don had wanted to be a cartoonist, and that side of him influences the way he plays with his son. Rich said that his special time with his son comes on Saturday morning when his wife sleeps late. They hang out and watch cartoons on TV. Often on weekends his son "helps" Rich work on the car: the baby fiddles in the toolbox while Rich keeps one eye on him. Brian loves playing in the water with his three kids (the youngest is eight months) and taking them out fishing on his boat. Vincent, the father of two with a third on the way, said, "I give more baths and I do all the wrestling, running around the house, and roughhousing. As for the diapers and reading, we split those fifty-fifty." Daryl said he takes his daughter on outings around Philadelphia and is very involved in selecting her food and clothing since he strongly believes that she shouldn't eat meat or wear synthetic fibers. Pat said that one of the high points in his daughter's first year was when he took her to a modeling agency and she was chosen for an ad. "I swelled with pride," he told me proudly.

As babies emerge from the "fog" of early infancy, as they gain control of their bodies and become mobile, as they focus their attention and respond to our attentions with smiles and laughter, as they show more and more curiosity for their surroundings and more and more enjoyment of their activities, as they return the love we give them, as they seek us out when they need us, cry when we leave, and rejoice when we return, as they do all of these things with the special wonder and innocence of babyhood, they become irresistible. Even reluctant fathers, even aloof fathers who formerly restricted their involvement to picture-taking, feel themselves drawn to their babies in their second six months. "One of the neat things about kids is that they enable you to be a child again," said Charles, a thirty-eight-year-old doctor and father of three. This happens even to the least childish, least playful of fathers. Sides of yourself you never knew you had will bloom when you're with your child.

Some of us jump into full-fledged fatherhood the moment our babies are born. Vincent, a thirty-four-year-old engineer from Albuquerque and the father of two, is one of these dads, and he says about himself: "I never had any reluctance to get involved. I always had lots of confidence in my fathering abilities. It wasn't because I had experience with babies before my own were born—it just came from extreme wanting to help and to share in bringing the kids up." But for lots of dads, there *is* a reluctance to enter into relationships: they find their babies scary, needy, demanding, unreachable, or just kind of boring. As Jim, a clinical psychologist who lives outside San Francisco, said of his own experience: "My son was hard to be with when he was a baby. I had less interest when he was very young. But with the development of language, he's more fun to be with and there's more in it for me."

For Jim, it was his son's first words that opened up the relationship. For other dads it's the child's first steps or the ability to play active games or even to sit in their laps and look at books together. What sparks the change is the full awareness of the baby as a *person* you can be with, talk to, play with, share with. Whether the awareness comes at birth, with the first smile or on the day your baby looks at you and says, "Dada"—it's marvelous when it happens. It's the bridge that joins you with your child. And as soon as it's up, the bridge carries traffic two ways. As you raise your child, he raises you as a father; as you love him and teach him about your world, he loves you back and teaches you about his world. It sounds very serious—and some of it *is* very serious, and some of it is hard and stressful and irritating and exhausting. But luckily, a lot of it is just plain fun.

Joys and Trials of Fatherhood

What are some of the joys of fatherhood for you? What are the tough parts? What are your best memories of the first year? What are your worst? I asked all the fathers I interviewed these questions, and the answers I got reveal a lot about what we expect as fathers, our attitudes toward our children, the roles we play in our families, our values and priorities. Here is a roundup of the most representative responses.

Irv, age thirty-six, a lawyer from New York and father of a daughter, age sixteen months:

> *Joys:* Having the opportunity to give of myself in a way that is unique. Watching my daughter learn to talk is the most exciting thing in the world. Watching her develop and giving what I can to that. The best reward is the opportunity to see a person become.
>
> *Trials:* The hardest part is the tension between my career and my desire to be with my daughter. I love my child, but it's a very demanding job, which I also love. Since I don't get home until after she's asleep, the only time I'm with her during the week is in the morning and I'm getting ready for work then so I can't give her my full attention. It's frustrating. I try to have maximum time on weekends to devote to being together as a family. The balance is hard. My wife needs attention on her own, too. She can't just be loved as a mother. So there is tension and compromise in my roles as a father, a husband, and with my career.

Philip, age thirty, a controller from Saint Paul and the father of two boys, ages eight months and two and a half:

> *Joys:* Watching the boys do something and be proud of it. We got the older boy a pool for his first birthday. That was the first time he stood by himself. Then when we all clapped, he clapped for himself. When you come home from work, they hug you. That's nice. If they cry when you leave you feel good, because you know they care about you. The special time of reading and when they fall asleep in your arms.
>
> *Trials:* I get home at five-thirty; we're feeding the kids until six-thirty; then we clean up, give them baths, and

don't get them both into bed until nine and that is the evening. I'm just coming to the realization that that's how it will be. There is constant work keeping everyone fed, clean, dry, and happy. The first isn't too bad—you can handle that easily. But adding a second more than doubles the work. Meals are hard. You're making three meals a day—one for each child and one for the grownups—for every meal. Disciplining is hard for me. It tears your heart out when you're washing their hair and they're screaming so loud it sounds like they're dying and you think they'll hate you forever.

Michael, age twenty-nine, a clerical worker from Greeley, Colorado, father of a five-month-old son:

Joys: His smile when you play with him. Just watching him grow is a joy. I look forward to him getting older and more mature so we can do more together.

Trials: There has been the lost sleep and also worries. The other night I asked my wife if she had checked the baby. She said no and I jumped up and ran in just to make sure he was breathing. I also worry about him getting sick.

Donald, age thirty-eight, a marketing manager from New York, father of a seven-month-old son:

Joys: The joys are easy to describe. There is a feeling of almost constant elation when I'm in his presence. He has changed my life in a way I couldn't have imagined possible. Had anyone told me this I wouldn't have believed it. There is an actual change and reordering of priorities. It's going so fast and it's such a magical time. It's such a gift and I don't want to miss out on this. I know it sounds corny, but I feel blessed at having this.

Trials: Seem so minimal. The lack of sleep. The feeling of losing control, but I know that changes. I'm working sixty hours a week, trying to squeeze in everything. I get up at five A.M. and work until the baby gets up.

Between the constant work and care, I can't find time for myself. I haven't read a book in months. It's the best of times and the worst of times.

Charles, age thirty-eight, a doctor from Albuquerque, father of a nine-year-old son and a five-year-old daughter from a previous marriage and a four-month-old son from his present marriage:

> *Joys:* The kids from my previous marriage love the baby. My son really wanted the baby, and especially wanted to have a little brother. When the baby was born and it was a boy, he said, "My dreams have come true." Each day my five-year-old girl says she loves her little brother. She's a great helper. It's a great joy for me and my wife to see the reflection of both of us in the baby's smile. His health, his disposition—these bring lots of warmth.
>
> *Trials:* He had the flu. He was fussy and not sleeping well. It places stress on time. Basically, the time my wife and I enjoy together has been put on hold. We're not the types to leave the baby with a sitter.

Daryl, age thirty-one, a schoolteacher from Philadelphia, father of a daughter, age twenty months:

> *Joys:* Changing her diaper. Being with her. Taking her out for walks, being with her among people, watching her interact with people, having her sleep right alongside me, watching her, playing with her, dancing with her, taking her to work with me, and having her meet my students, having fun, loving and kissing her, giving her baths. I am always proud when I'm with her and people are enjoying her. Proud that this is my daughter and I am her father.
>
> *Trials:* At times I've been short-tempered, not patient with her eating and making a mess when I know I would have to clean it up. It's difficult when we both throw a tantrum at the same time. My time is squeezed

The Growth of a Relationship

because I feel I'm working three jobs: I come home and there is the baby and on top of that we have to earn more money [he has started a business in addition to his teaching job]. It's a triple whammy. But it's also tremendously empowering being the one who is doing it all. I've never been as responsible, mature, and productive and awake in all my life.

Vincent, age thirty-four, an engineer from Albuquerque, father of two sons, ages five and two and a half, with a third baby on the way:

Joys: Playing with them and physical contact. Hugs. Having them close. Laughter. I get more energy back from wrestling with them than I do from a nap. Seeing them laugh is great.

Trials: I worry about giving them an example that is good for the future, worry about teaching them right and wrong, and teaching them to respect each other. I always want them to feel free to come and talk to me. I'm hoping it will work now so it will stay in place when they're fifteen. I am quicker to anger and more demanding. Sometimes it worries me. I have to stop to remind myself, "Hey, they're only kids." I worry I am being too heavy-handed.

Me, age thirty-three, a writer from New York and father of a daughter, twenty-two months old:

Joys: Seeing her discover the world and discover nature, watching her smell flowers, listen to birds, look at the ocean; seeing her create imaginary worlds with her toys and stuffed animals; being physically affectionate (when she lets me) and verbally affectionate the rest of the time. Watching her incredible determination to master new skills, be it crawling, walking, or putting puzzles together. Dancing with her. Traveling with her. The development of language is a continuing joy and also a source of great hilarity. Her taste in books and music never ceases to astonish me (she has progressed from Pete Seeger to the Beach Boys and James Brown in a matter of weeks).

Trials: Every day at around five-fifteen our otherwise fairly content, inventive, easily amused, and charming child turns into a nonstop need-and-whine machine. Dinners when I'm doing it alone can be stressful. One night there was something burning on the stove, the baby smashed a glass on the floor and started hollering, the dogs nearly slashed their paws on the wreckage— and I was ready to call the 911 help line. Setting limits and disciplining, though necessary, are no fun and often make me feel guilty. I worry: is she spoiled because, as the first and so far only child, she gets too much attention? are we pushing her too hard to achieve? will she be as difficult to live with at age fifteen as I was? I never dreamed that I would spend so much of my adult life washing dishes, bibs, high chairs, bottles, little hands, little chins, and so on.

Who Does What? Playing and Modeling Roles

Chances are that from the instant your baby came into the world, you and your partner have taken on very different child-care roles. Although many of us have come a long way from the dad as breadwinner, mom as child-rearer model, some vestige of this traditional pattern remains in place in most households. Dads are doing more child care; moms are doing more out-of-the-home paid work; but when push comes to shove, mom is usually still the primary caretaker and dad the primary breadwinner (even if mom actually wins more bread). But even though most dads play a secondary role in child-rearing, that role expands as the babies progress from early infancy toward toddlerhood. As babies become more complex beings, our responsibilities as fathers also take on a new complexity. Caring for a twelve-month-old on an hour-by-hour basis is certainly easier (and a lot more fun) than caring for a twelve-week-old; but the big, long-term issues—

issues of setting a good example, issues of discipline and setting limits, issues of sex roles, issues of stimulating our children without pressuring them—loom larger. In many families, dealing with and resolving these issues is more the province of fathers than of mothers.

The question of role modeling occurs to most of us the first time we notice our children copying our behavior exactly. It can be a great revelation about the power we have to influence their actions and the responsibility we have in setting a good example. With a one-year-old we're more likely to notice a physical action—the attempt to throw a ball in the same way we do or to imitate some facial expression or gesture of ours. Less obvious but ultimately more important is the example we set in social and ethical contexts. What ideas about love between adults do our children form by observing our relationships with our spouses? What ideas about sharing, handling aggression, being friendly, helping or ignoring others do they gather from the way we act in the world? What attitudes toward work do we convey? What attitudes toward fun? These are all areas in which children look to their parents—and perhaps especially to their fathers—for guidance. And very often what we *do* exerts a more powerful influence than what we *say*. If we preach peace, love, and understanding but confront the world with our fists raised, we're more likely to make our young children into fighters, and confused fighters at that, than into lovers of their neighbors.

With the spreading influence of feminism, more parents are becoming aware of how they are presenting sex roles to their children and how the sex of the child influences their relationship with him or her. We know from a number of research studies that fathers very often treat their sons in a different way from their daughters. As one might expect, with boys there is more rough and tumble, with girls more reading and cuddling. Fathers talk more to their sons than to their daughters and presumably expect more from them. These differences in interaction often begin right at birth. In one study, parents, asked to comment on a newborn baby dressed as a boy, described "him" as big, strong, and independent and jostled "him" about more; the same baby dressed as a girl was described as soft and little, held more gently, and played with more tenderly. (Jeffrey Rubin, Frank Provenzano, and Zella Luria, "The Eye of the Beholder: Parents' Views on Sex of Newborns," *American Journal of Orthopsychiatry*, 44, 1974, pp. 512–519, as cited in *The Nurturing Father* by Kyle D. Pruett.)

Interestingly, Kyle Pruett finds in *The Nurturing Father* that dads who are the primary caretakers of their children are less likely to make these distinctions between their sons and daughters than dads who are not as involved in their upbringing. But even dads in a secondary caretaking role are making an effort to raise their children in a nonsexist way. Says Pat, the father of a one-year-old daughter, "My wife and I are trying not to take on roles. Neither of us likes to play roles. I try to roughhouse with the baby. I try to treat her as a *baby*, not as a little girl. I think of her as a little baby first. I want her to be a feminist and think for herself." A young child learns about sex roles not only from the way you treat the child, but from the way he or she sees you and your partner behaving toward each other and toward the child. If your partner does all the traditional female chores and child-care routines and you confine yourself to breadwinning and play, even if it's rough-and-tumble play with a girl, you're sending a pretty clear message about which activities are appropriate for which sex.

Very few of us can, or want to, raise our children in an *entirely* sex-neutral way. For many of us, traditional sex roles "feel" right: we're content to set traditional examples and content to see our children adopt traditional feminine or masculine behavior. As one dad said, a bit sheepishly, "To me, it seems more natural for women to do more of the child care. Maybe I sound like a chauvinist, but that's how I feel. But I also think it's good for sanity's sake to share. I know a woman who does all the work for three kids—she must be going crazy! I think it's nice to share and I like giving my wife relief. That is the best setup." Another dad said that even though he took a very active role in raising his daughter, his partner was still the primary nurturer. "She gives her complete, undivided attention, something I could never do. She never seems to have the worries about work, money, bills that I have. I could never be that free for that length of time and I admire that." But even

The Growth of a Relationship

being involved with our children's care to a limited extent does them—and us—a lot of good. It's worth noting that if you want to reinforce traditional masculine behavior in your sons, your best bet, according to several studies, is to be warm and nurturing, not remote and macho.

For dads who are more concerned about breaking out of traditional sex roles, there is going to be more work, both in terms of awareness and involvement. With very young children who are not yet exposed to a lot of outside cultural influences, often the best way of countering sexism is simply for the father to jump in and do a lot of child care. I had a very clear example of this in my own family without even trying to convey a message about sex roles. During a month-long period when my wife was working late most nights, I was spending a lot more time caring for and just being with our daughter than she was. One morning I was reading my daughter a favorite book of hers about a duck that goes searching for a lost duckling. Without thinking about it, I had always referred to the duck as the mommy; but on this particular morning, my daughter corrected me. "That daddy," she said, pointing to the duck that cared for the ducklings and went hunting through the marsh for the missing one. I took it as a very great compliment.

Discipline

For better or worse, discipline is one aspect of child-rearing that fathers have traditionally handled, and if the fathers I interviewed are a representative sample, it remains primarily a paternal responsibility. Of course, the issue of discipline does not come up very often during the child's first year, since he or she is still for the most part too young to be disciplined. You can't correct a one-year-old's behavior through punishment because he quite literally doesn't know any better. But you can, and will, begin to set limits on unacceptable behavior: although your one-year-old is not *deliberately* misbehaving, he does very often do things that are bad—either for him or for you. There are times when you feel that every other word you address to your child is no (in a few months the tables will be turned and he'll be telling you no with every breath). This can be exasperating, to say the least. Experienced parents offer some good advice for easing the strain on both of you:

Draw your battle lines sensibly

The curious baby who has just learned to crawl or walk will want to get into everything. She'll pull all the books off your shelves, unload drawers, knock over garbage cans, and so on. If you forbid every household exploration, you'll turn your child into a zombie and drive yourself crazy into the bargain. Decide what you can live with and try to cordon off or remove the things you can't live with (obviously you'll have to baby-proof the house and get everything that is dangerous or unsanitary out of baby's reach). Let your baby get into the things that don't matter to you that much (for example, your socks and t-shirt drawer) and limit your no-no's to a few items (the stereo, pulling the cat's tail, and the like).

Try to be consistent

Your baby will never learn the rules if you keep changing them. Optimally, you and your partner should agree on what rules to enforce—but this is less important than each of you being consistent in the limits you set individually. Your baby will soon learn that dad doesn't tolerate gymnastics on the changing table, but mom puts up with it. But if both mom and dad keep changing their minds about what they allow, baby will become confused.

Try to distract before you confront

Your one-year-old has gotten hold of your wristwatch and is headed down the hall with it. You don't want it to be lost or thrown into the bathtub. Your impulse is to say, "No. That is not a toy" and grab it away. And this is likely to provoke a crying fit or tantrum. But with a one-year-old it's still fairly easy to avoid the tantrum by distracting him. Offer to trade him for another object or turn the flight down the hall into a game by pursuing him or suggest that the two of you sit down and listen to the watch go "tick-tock" together. You'll be surprised how quickly he forgets all about it. Of course, it's easier to invent a distraction when you're in a good mood. And when you're not in a good mood, you may actually seek out confrontation as an outlet for your anger. Provoking a toddler is just about the easiest thing in the world. Cheering him up again is another matter entirely. We all lose our tempers. But if you're actually picking fights with your child, it's time to find a way out of it.

Find the right balance of discipline and leniency

Your child depends on you to set limits for him. You're not doing him any favors by always giving in and never saying no. In fact, you will ultimately undermine his confidence in you and in himself and you will be sowing the seeds for irreconcilable conflicts. Part of parenting is teaching our children what is right and wrong, good and bad, acceptable and unacceptable, and to hold them to standards of behavior that we find appropriate. Appropriate takes both our needs and the child's abilities into account. You can't expect a one-year-old to eat neatly in a restaurant when he has never eaten neatly at home, but you can begin to teach him to respect other people's property. The child who always gets his way without being punished or corrected will keep pushing until he hurts himself. On the other hand, the child who *never* gets his way will be sitting on a volcano of repression. Let your child win some of the battles. Show him you respect his feelings.

The question of physical punishment should not arise with a one-year-old, but it may arise later. Again, spanking has traditionally been dad's province, but maybe it's a tradition that we fathers (and mothers) will want to abandon. I'll offer the reflections of one father on the subject: "My wife and I had a debate over physical punishment [their child was pushing two at the time]. She said never, I said sometimes. We fought about that. Since then I have made the decision that it wasn't accomplishing what I wanted. Now I see hitting as a lazy way out of child-rearing. It's easier to lash out, but it doesn't work long-term."

Because we as parents are questioning many traditional roles and assumptions, we might want to stop and question not only the usefulness of spanking, but the traditional role of father as disciplinarian. If you find yourself assuming this role and you're comfortable with it, fine. But all too often men get the role thrust upon them because that's the way things are "supposed to" be. "Wait till your father gets home" is a threat that lots of children grow up hearing, and then when father gets home, he's supposed to mete out the punishment. Thus, father becomes bad guy and mother preserves her own passive accord with the kids. This really isn't fair. If you resent doing your partner's disciplining for her, let her know. You might, as one father put it, have to "coach" her on discipline. Since we fathers are rolling up our sleeves and doing a lot more child care, it seems only right that our partners roll up *their* sleeves and lay down the law themselves.

Love

Irv, the New York lawyer, expressed eloquently and movingly the impact of having a child on his relationship with his wife: "If you both want kids and are ready, being parents together is a wonderful sharing experience. Loving the child becomes a way of sharing love with family. When my wife does something loving for our daughter, I feel good. There is a whole multiplication of love. Adults can take care of themselves, and so there are not that many opportunities to express love. With a child, it's a lot easier to express love for the child and thus for each other. It's also important to us to show our child about love between adults. I really believe there is no difference in kind in the love of an adult for another adult and the love of an adult for a child. The most important thing is respecting the separateness and individuality of the person you love."

The Growth of a Relationship

What Irv has put his finger on is the way that having a child both changes and sustains the love we share with our partners. The old saw about how a child will bring you together is really true when, as Irv points out, both of you want a child and are ready for one. It's not that a child solves or resolves problems in our relationships—far from it. Nor, as we all discover rapidly, does a child give us much time to relax together, to go out and enjoy ourselves, or simply to sit and converse as one adult to another. We sacrifice something free and unhurried and spontaneous in our romances; there is no question of that. But it's a sacrifice that yields up growth. When we have a child, some elusive element of romantic love settles and grows into family love. There's the same love that we started with, only it seems to be rooted now. It has shed some of its selfishness and heedlessness. There's less wild fun and more deep joy. All parents who have exchanged a look and a smile when they witness their child perform some antic or new accomplishment know exactly what I mean.

Of course, there are moments—or even stretches of time—when we long for the "good old days" of life before baby or maybe even life before marriage. But sometimes when circumstances return us temporarily to these good old days, we may discover to our surprise how very much family-centered we've become. Brian, twenty-seven, and father of three, described his own reactions to a temporary return to bachelorhood: "I sent my whole family to Oregon for six weeks, and I thought I'd have a super-blast, back to my bachelor days. But by the second night, I was just about in tears. I was family-sick. It was weird. It just shows the impact of what I'd go through if something happened to one of them. The lesson is to spend as much time as you can with your family, because you never know." Another lesson is that having a family changes us in ways we don't even realize. Though we don't always enjoy the stability, the maturity, the routines, the chores, and organization that come with family life, family love has become central to our lives. It's part of us and without it we'd feel lost—"family-sick" as Brian put it.

Family love certainly engenders the "multiplication of love" that Irv describes, binding parents to their children and through these bonds binding parents closer to each other. But family love alone is not enough. Without some romance and passion, our relationships with our partners will gradually starve. Finding or making time for passion can be one of the greatest challenges of parenthood. As Charles mentioned earlier in the "trials" of fatherhood, "Basically, the time my wife and I enjoy together has been put on hold." When it stays on hold there can be trouble. Sometimes parents unconsciously *prefer* their relationship to be on hold. They blame the child for an alienation that would probably have arisen anyway or they use the baby as an excuse to avoid intimacy. And sometimes there's an imbalance when one parent is totally wrapped up in the baby and the other feels excluded and ignored. But more often it's just the simple fact of both partners being too consumed by work, child care, chores, and modern life to have time or energy for passion. We know we love each other, we know we both love our child, and we figure the other stuff—the intimacy, the sex, the private sharing, the mutual interests, the laughter, the escapes that make up passion—will still be there when we get around to it again. Sometimes it is—but maybe it's better not to risk it. Once there are children around, passion takes work. Work to find the time, work to convince each other that escapes from the children are okay, work to put passionate feelings into words and into action.

One father of two told me he and his wife had just returned from their first long weekend off by themselves since their honeymoon. He raved about how great it was and he also mentioned how much advance planning and work it took. In his case, it was certainly worth it. Even one long weekend away a year and a handful of dinners out can be enough to keep that spark alive.

Just as we have changed as fathers (and as people) over the course of our child's first year, so we have changed as partners in a love relationship, and that relationship has changed, too. Some of our old interests have fallen away or been squeezed out by new interests and new demands. Some of our friends without children might find us dreadfully boring—and we might find some of them a bit irrelevant (or alternatively, we might crave their company as a *relief* from parental concerns). Some of our greatest pleasures as a couple—be it travel abroad, dancing half the night, staying in bed till noon on weekends, whipping up gourmet extravaganzas, jogging, or playing tennis together—may now seem inconceivable. "I can't believe what parents we've become" we may say to each other rather wistfully, or even bitterly. It's true. All the trappings of parenthood—the ceaseless responsibilities, the sensible life-style, the meticulous attention to practical details, the harried rushing through endless chores—now adhere to almost every aspect of our relationships. We certainly don't love every minute of it—but we do in some fierce and unfathomable way love the sum total of it. If we're careful to guard and feed the flame, love and passion in all their old guises endure. The many, many new guises of love are the blessing of being parents.

Firsts

The second six months bring a thrilling parade of firsts— firsts for baby, firsts for dad, firsts for dad and baby together. Our babies are forging ahead at breakneck speed. There's the first time she gets up on her hands and knees, the first time she sits by herself, the first time she crawls (often backwards at first), the first time she pulls herself to a stand, stands by herself, and just maybe by her first birthday takes her first step. Once she's up, there's no stopping her. There are language firsts: the use of vowels and then consonants, new babble that sounds so much like language, the first words (very often it's "dada," addressed to us, to mom, to her bottle, to the ceiling). There are all those thousands of daily discoveries: that water splashes and pours, that she can make a terrific racket by banging pot covers on the floor, that she has one nose, two eyes, and two ears—just like dada, that sand is irresistible to eat even though it tastes awful, that climbing stairs is something to be attempted the instant dad has his back turned, that dad is quite a comic fellow, particularly when he stubs his toe on your toy truck and hops around yowling on one foot. It was during this period that I found myself commenting about my daughter, at least once a month, "She seems to be in a new phase." I didn't have any precise, measurable scientific definition of *phase* in mind. I just meant it "felt" different to be with her. She did new things with her hands and feet and legs; she looked at me differently; she responded differently; she played differently. It really is an exhilarating time to be a father.

Baby's firsts have a way of prompting dad's firsts. A baby who can sit up, crawl, or walk is a lot more fun to take places and do things with. Dads who were reluctant to go out (or stay home) alone with their new babies—what if he cries? how do I snap him into the car seat? what if he needs to nurse?—find new confidence to venture forth with their very mature eight-month-olds. If you haven't already taken your baby to the park by yourself, or downtown to shop, or just out for a stroller or backpack ride, now is the time to do it. This can also be a great time to hang out with other dads and their babies, either informally or through organized father-baby groups. Take your baby to the zoo, to work with you (on a half day or during holiday season), to a museum, to grandma's house, to the swings in your neighbor's backyard, or simply give mom the day off and hang out with baby for the day. One father described his first weekend alone with his one-year-old daughter as a "breakthrough" in his fathering: "I found out I could do it and that it was okay." Finding out we can do it does wonders for our confidence as parents. The knowledge that we can be competent on our own frees us from dependence on our partners and frees them from the burden of feeling that they can never get away. It's also nice for baby to find out that dad can do it.

And then there are family firsts. Travel becomes possible —even fun—with a baby this age. Pat and his wife took their eleven-month-old daughter on a camping trip. Rich and his fourteen-month-old son and the grandparents got a cabin in the woods and went fishing for a few days. Jim and his wife took off for Europe for a month with their eleven-month-old son. Jim reported that the baby did really well: he napped through museums in his stroller or front baby carrier; he adjusted to the time change in a couple days; he slept well in a variety of makeshift cribs; and he only "lost it" once or twice when he was totally exhausted. Before her first birthday, our daughter had traveled with us to Maine, South Carolina, and Georgia.

The Growth of a Relationship

She did wonderfully in motels and relished the full spectrum of American fast food.

Family meals out in restaurants also become possible, provided you've chosen a place where the messy eating and noise of a baby will be tolerated. Most parents report that they have better success with lunch (or breakfast) than with dinners out.

Other firsts may include trips to the beach or pool, trips to the supermarket (usually a lot more fun for baby than for you), visits to the houses of your friends (or her friends). One impediment to socializing and traveling that occurs for many babies in this age range is separation anxiety. All of a sudden your gregarious, outgoing, smiling nine-month-old starts to cling to you, cries when a stranger (or even grandparent) talks to her, seems frightened in new surroundings, panics when she loses sight of you for an instant, and won't crack a smile unless she's safely alone with you and your partner in her own home. Separation anxiety is a perfectly normal phase of development. It's a sign of your child's growing attachment to you and growing awareness that that attachment can be interrupted. Separation anxiety may strike suddenly and depart suddenly; it may build and slacken gradually; or it may come in waves. It's inconvenient, but not permanent. The best way to help the child over it is to provide lots of reassurance and curtail some of the exciting "firsts" that involve strange people and places. There's lots of time to resume your family visits, travels, outings, and explorations later.

In your child's first year, everything is happening for the first time and everything becomes more special and more memorable because of this. The first smile. The first night slept through. The first Christmas. The first dunk in the ocean. The first step. The first clap. The first time he meets you joyously at the door when you come home from work. And, at the end of this magical, ever-changing, and incredibly fleeting year, another first: your child's first birthday. It's your first birthday, too: the anniversary of your "birth" into fatherhood. When you look back, you can hardly believe how much you and your baby have changed in the course of a single year. When you look ahead, you can hardly wait for all those other amazing developments and events to come—language, increased physical prowess, school, sports, riding a bike, taking walks together, talking things over father-to-son or father-to-daughter. Can this child who sits up at the table, eats birthday cake, laughs, claps for himself, and crawls (or toddles) off to play with his new presents be the same baby you saw come into the world naked, helpless, wailing, and tiny? Can this man who casually tosses his child in the air, whips diapers on and off without thinking about it, expertly consoles him for bumped knees and hurt feelings, reads him hundreds of books, and knows instinctively when and how to get him to sleep be the same person who trembled at the idea of lifting the newborn from crib to changing table? Yes and no to both questions: you're the same two people, only transformed by your experiences together.

You'll never have another year quite like the first. On your first birthdays, you both have a lot to celebrate.

Appendix A
Infant Development Chart

Your Developing Child

During the first few weeks of your baby's life, you will, of course, be noticing how he or she is developing. Is my child "normal"? Is he okay? Is she reacting as she should? To help ease your mind, the following is an infant development chart to serve as a guide to the *average* progress of babies through their first year. Remember, however, that your baby will invariably be ahead in some development areas and behind in others. Each baby is unique and develops at his or her own rate.

INFANT DEVELOPMENT CHART: BIRTH TO SIX WEEKS	
Physical:	Reflexes control most physical movements: will startle at sudden noise or position change, gag to avoid choking, grip your finger tightly, open eyes when pulled to sit.
	Limb motion jerky, hands curled into tight balls, may move head from side to side but can't support it.
Sensory:	*Vision.* Can see 8–12 inches ahead at birth; range increases during first weeks. Prefers colors and patterns over blocks of solid color. Favorite visual object is human face; will stare at it for increas-

Sensory, *continued*	ingly longer periods. Begins to "discover" own hands visually, spending time dangling them in front of own face.

Hearing. Well developed at birth. Evidence suggests baby of 5 weeks may recognize mother's voice. Loves sound of human, especially high-pitched, voice.

Smell and taste. Well developed. Newborns show taste preferences. Recognizes mother by smell early on. |
| **Language:** | Mostly limited to crying; grows louder and lustier. By 6 weeks may be making first "aahs" and "gaahs," which may begin in response to human talking. |
| **Social:** | Becoming increasingly alert to parents' presence. May begin to smile. Shows excitement by waving arms and legs. Shows unhappiness by crying, quiets when picked up, held, rocked, sung to, soothed.

Fun and games: Can begin to play games involving looking at things, making faces, singing, touching in different ways, shifting positions. Enjoys "conversations," especially close eye contact. May show interest in new sights and sounds. |
| **Care:** | Feeding. Food limited to breast milk or formula. Breastfed babies eat "on demand" (when they ask for it); bottle-fed babies usually eat less frequently—about every 3 to 4 hours (each has different needs). Probably won't adhere to strict, regular feeding schedule, but you may be able to begin settling night feedings into a pattern.

Sleeping. Great variation from baby to baby, some sleeping 18 hours out of 24, others as little as 8 or 10. Will probably sleep in naps no longer than 4 or 5 hours; if you're lucky you may get 5 hours sleep a night.

Dressing and changing. Keep baby warm and protected from the sun, but avoid overdressing and overbundling. Many babies like to be swad- |

Care, *continued*

dled in blanket for the first 2 weeks. Diapers may have to be changed as often as once an hour, but this tapers off as baby matures.

Bathing. Unnecessary to do every day unless you and baby really like it. In between tub baths, keep diaper area, face, chin, and neck sponged off and dry.

SIX WEEKS TO THREE MONTHS

Physical:

As reflexes lose their grip, baby has more control over own movements; movements (including grasping and swallowing) become voluntary. Bodily control progresses from head down and from center outward: baby will begin to hold head up first and then begin to hold back steady; will control movement of arms before movement of fingers.

Lots of "bicycling" movement of legs and waving of arms; limb movement is less jerky, more smooth, and deliberate.

On tummy, may begin to push head and chest up and look around.

Sitting, with support of pillows or in infant chair, becomes favorite posture; will enjoy long stretches of observation.

When pulled to a stand, may push feet to floor and stiffen legs for a few seconds.

Will start to roll from side to back and from back to side.

Hands have uncurled; baby begins to use them to swipe at things, although without much accuracy. May begin to grasp and hold objects. Will use fingers to explore textures.

Sensory:

Vision. By 3 months, visual range from 3 to 20 inches; baby has keen visual appetite. Will focus on an object dangled before him; can follow it as you move it around; will look from one object to another. Still loves to look at the human face, and now recognizes yours. Prefers three-dimensional

Sensory, *continued*

objects to two-dimensional. Spends long periods studying own hands and feet. Will stare at an object in his hand, then bring it to his mouth.

Hearing. A 3-month-old baby hears just about as well as an adult. When she hears your voice, baby will turn to look for you. The sound of your voice will quiet her when she cries. Hearing you speak will prompt her to vocalize back. Shows enjoyment of music, musical toys, and singing.

Language: Makes one-syllable cooing sounds using vowels. May repeat the same sound over and over; many babies "talk" the most when they are by themselves; others will vocalize, smile, and squeal with delight when you talk to them. The uncontrollable crying of early infancy is much diminished. Beginnings of laughter emerge in chortles.

Social: Baby is a delightfully social, gregarious individual; smiles joyously when he sees you and may even "greet" you by smiling and arching toward you, kicking vigorously. Also smiles readily at smiling strangers, but the most enthusiastic smiles go to you.

You can begin to have "conversations" with baby: when you smile and look at him and talk, he will smile and vocalize back.

You can reliably "get through" to baby now, soothing him when he cries, calming him down by talking to him, telling him you're going to feed him when he's hungry. You usually know what his cries are about and can usually stop them quickly.

Fun and games: Enjoys playing with crib gym, loves outings in stroller or front carrier, may enjoy watching cars or planes go by. Enjoys more and more physical games involving rolling, swinging, being pulled to sit, or held to stand. Has fun with rattles, bells, balls, new textures. Changing diapers can be a fine time for singing, tickling, massage, or showing him new toys.

Care:

Feeding. By 3 months, baby will have about 5 or 6 feedings every 24 hours from breast or bottle. You may start to introduce easily digestible strained solids—mashed banana, baby cereals (ask pediatrician about when and what to start with).

Sleeping. Most babies settle into sleeping patterns (if not yet fixed schedules) by this age. May sleep around 16 hours out of the 24, with as much as 10 straight hours at night and two naps during day (there is great individual variation). More truly awake when awake and more often deeply asleep when asleep.

Dressing and changing. Can begin to wear real clothes (overalls, stretch pants, sweatshirts) instead of nightgowns and stretchies all the time. Make sure baby is comfortable and that clothes allow her free movement of arms and legs. As baby settles down, the number of bowel movements decreases and diaper changes become a bit less frequent.

Bathing. Most parents like to start giving baby daily tub baths during this period; usually it's best to make them part of routine and always give bath at same time of day. Bath time can be a great opportunity for singing, splashing, exploration—even more fun if you bathe together. But if baby hates bath, it's not necessary to do so every day. Try to keep water and soap out of her eyes when washing hair.

THREE MONTHS TO SIX MONTHS

Physical:

Great leaps forward in major physical developments. At 4 months lifts tummy off floor on extended arms and holds head up for a minute or more. Next comes rolling over, usually from stomach to back first and then from back to stomach. On stomach baby will arch back and rock back and forth.

By 6 months many babies get themselves into a crawl position on hands and knees, and a few babies will actually begin to crawl, often back-

Physical, *continued*

wards first. Before learning to crawl, babies use all sorts of "creeping" and wriggling techniques to propel themselves around rooms (and off beds and changing tables if you're not careful).

Sits up with less and less support during this period until by 6 months most babies can sit for a few seconds with no support at all or will support themselves with their hands.

Baby is sturdy, well padded, and shows muscle development and increasing physical coordination. No longer "floppy" when you pick him up.

The urge to stand (with your support) grows as baby gets stronger, and by 6 months baby will try to be vertical as often as he can. Can begin to pull self to stand using your hands as guides. May insist on standing every time you put him in your lap: uses your lap as springboard, bouncing up and down as he tightens and relaxes knees.

Has perfected ability to reach for object, take it in his hands, and hold onto it, invariably bringing it to mouth. Uses entire hand to grasp object. May transfer object from hand to hand.

Sensory: Vision. Approaches adult standards at around 4 months. Sees the world in living color, perceives depth, and can adjust between near and far viewing rapidly. Shows great proficiency in following moving objects through space. Increasingly alert visually and perceptive about changes in objects or in environment: will begin to recognize favorite objects when they are partially hidden. Likes bright colors and visual variety.

Hearing. Continues to love listening to human voice as well as music, humming motors, and all sorts of new sounds such as dogs barking, paper crinkling, rattles shaking. Turns toward source of sound. More sensitive to differences in your vocal intonations.

Language: Undergoes a burst during this period. Babies add consonants to their early vowel sounds; they giggle, laugh, chortle, squeal, and babble (often

Language, *continued*

most intensely when they're alone). May use babble to comment on discoveries and to converse with you (or interrupt you). May "study" your jaw and mouth as you talk and begin to try to imitate your facial movements. They love it when you imitate their vocalizing, and the two of you can spend long stretches conversing in baby talk.

Social: Becomes very much bound up with primary caretaker during this period. This intense bond is crucial for baby's development and the source of a great deal of her joy. May protest when parent leaves, anticipate parent's return, initiate social interaction by vocalizing or smiling. More active participation in "conversations" and will keep them up longer.

Enjoys company and may show a strong preference for the company of other (usually older) children.

Shows very clear moods of contentment, hilarity, anger, frustration, and fear.

Enjoys looking in mirrors, will smile at her reflection, and look from your reflection to your face.

Fun and games: With increasing strength and mobility, can play more and more games and you can have more and more fun with her. Baby will enjoy exploring your face, pulling at your nose, and grabbing your glasses or mustache. Peek-a-boo becomes a favorite at this age. May enjoy "Johnny Jump-Up" door swing. Babies like all sorts of roughhousing: being tossed in air, sat across your stomach as you bounce them up and down, getting rolled in a blanket, or held on your shoulders. Dancing, singing, and clapping also become the sources of loads of baby games. Once baby can sit, you can begin to play ball: roll a soft cloth ball to baby and encourage her to roll it back to you. Baths become more and more fun with much splashing, delighting in bubbles, and throwing things.

Care:

Feeding. By 6 months, baby will be sitting up in high chair (or infant seat) and having 3 meals a day, plus a few extra feedings consisting of breast milk or formula. You can feed your baby almost anything so long as you mash, puree, strain, or chop it into a form that he can gum. Don't introduce a lot of new foods all at once. Give baby one new food at a time and see how he reacts to it. You can start to give baby zwiebacks. Baby will probably try to grasp spoon, and it might be a good idea to have two spoons handy—one for baby, one for you. Meals are likely to be extremely messy, but if you have the patience, let baby make a mess and explore (within reasonable limits). Don't worry if baby doesn't eat much in the way of solids or if his eating is erratic. He is still getting a lot of his nourishment from milk. Baby may start taking milk from a cup.

Sleeping. Average is 12 hours or so at night with two naps during the day—but range is very wide. Will probably sleep on fairly regular schedule. Most babies are up at the crack of dawn.

Clothing. Avoid clothes that hamper baby's urge to creep, crawl, roll, and wriggle. Best are comfortable loose-fitting outfits that do not bind baby around the middle or at the knees.

SIX MONTHS TO ONE YEAR

Physical:

Explosive physical development in the second half of baby's first year. Becomes mobile and keeps in motion nearly all the time. Most babies will crawl quickly and efficiently; will pull themselves to a stand using furniture for support; "cruise" around a room holding on to furniture with one hand. Some babies can stand alone for a few seconds; a few will be taking their first steps or even walking quite well by their first birthdays.

Baby's hands are nearly always busy and nearly always holding, manipulating, pulling, dropping, or poking something. Sometime between 6 and 9 months, babies perfect the "pincer" movement of thumb and forefinger, giving them even greater

Physical, *continued*	manual dexterity. As they get more and more manually adept, babies will pick up smaller and smaller objects. You should have a fairly good idea whether your 12-month-old is left- or right-handed. Baby will enjoy banging things together and will explore his or her body, including genitals, with hands.

Climbing becomes another favorite activity; will climb furniture, stairs, bookshelves. Baby-proofing becomes a must. One good way of finding out what to baby-proof is to crawl through the house after your baby and see what he gets into. Increased mobility, manual dexterity, and relentless curiosity will motivate baby to get into just about everything—kitchen cupboards, drawers, laundry, stereos and record collections, plants, newspapers. |
| **Sensory and intellectual:** | Recognizes familiar objects and shows understanding of the placement of objects in space. Enjoys shifts in visual perspective, for example, looking at things upside-down. Shows understanding of inside, outside, filling up, and emptying out. Visually focuses on minute details of objects and compares things. Looks at books with increasing interest and comprehension.

Rapid development in memory and intellectual capacities. Develops "object permanence," the understanding that an object continues to exist when it is no longer in visual field. Will look for things that drop off high chair, search for things that he sees you hide, is much more sensitive to your comings and goings.

Has sense of own identity as baby; strongly identifies with pictures of other babies in books.

Focuses attention much longer and tries to solve problems. Grows bored more easily with same old routines.

With improved memory comes much broader range of associations. Remembers from day to day which toys do what, what happens at particu- |

Sensory and intellectual, *continued*	lar times, how things work. Is familiar with basics of cause and effect; may begin using trial and error to accomplish goals.

Intense curiosity leads baby to explore all aspects of world through senses and body. |
| **Language:** | Understands a good many simple sentences you say; demonstrates understanding by carrying out simple commands. Her own language may consist largely of highly complex and inflected form of babble known as "jargoning": will talk baby-talk that *sounds* almost like English, with exclamations, questions, sentences, great variation of syllables and tones.

Some babies say 3 or 4 real words (commonly "mama," "dada," "baba"); often same word may mean many different things. Some have far larger vocabularies by this age; some will really not start to talk until age 2—variation in rate of language acquisition is great. Nearly all 1-year-olds are fully aware of expressive function of language: they're not just babbling to hear sound of their voices; they're trying to convey some meaning. |
| **Social:** | Very attached to parents, highly interactive, and incessantly imitative; 9-month-old will try to copy you in clapping, yawning, smiling, talking; 1-year-old may try to "help" you cook, clean, work. Sexual identities emerge: boys act like boys and model themselves on their dads; girls act like girls and imitate their mothers more. Girls exhibit more social attentiveness and talk earlier; boys are rougher in their play and more determined in their explorations.

More and more sensitive to moods of others, particularly parents. By age 1, have begun to test limits: they know when you "really mean it" and determinedly push to and past this point. Much more aware of consequences of own actions. Know when they've done something naughty and can predict your response.

Emergence of much greater range of emotions and facility in expressing them. Rage at frustra- |

Social, *continued*

tion coexists with keen sense of humor. Laughs at incongruity. Loves to perform and be laughed at.

Separation anxiety. Fear of being separated from parents and distrust or outright horror of strangers often begins at around 8 months and may continue past age 1 (or may subside and start up again). New fears of objects and situations may arise: fear of the vacuum, sudden fear of the bath or other children. Babies who were once sunny and cheerful may go through period of being clingy and whiny.

Will show strong interest in other children, but probably not interact much with babies his own age. May imitate their actions.

Strong urge to please parents. Will frequently seek your approval and demand your attention.

Many babies become attached to some sort of security object—blanket, pillow, stuffed animal, cloth diaper. Considered a healthy sign that they've separated enough from parents to form "outside" relationships.

Fun and games: Toys take on new importance as baby can do more with them; many excellent toys for this age can be found among standard household equipment: wooden spoons, plastic stacking containers, aluminum pie plates, anything that floats in the bath, and lots of room to play. Empty cereal and oatmeal cartons, wooden clothespins, straws, hats, paper (watch out for eating!), and telephones are other favorite "toys." Baby will get into all sorts of hiding games—hide and seek, peek-a-boo, hiding their toys. Boxes and cans in which to deposit and from which to remove objects provide hours of amusement and help teach baby about concepts of inside/outside. Stacking toys, cars and trucks, musical toys, and anything with which to pour water are favorites. Will also enjoy looking at books for longer periods and with greater concentration; many dads make reading a part of the bedtime ritual. Babies begin imaginative play: "feeding" their stuffed animals, putting them to bed, pounding on them, and throwing them around. Favorite pastime of many

Fun and Games, *continued*

is to try to point to the body part or facial feature that you name; later enjoy shouting out the names of the part you point to. Blocks and puzzles may soon be fun. Encourage baby to begin playing alone by leaving her in her room when she's fresh and in a good mood. When learning to walk, many babies like walking aid such as toy plastic shopping cart they can hold onto for extra balance. Once walking, she'll enjoy toys with strings to pull after her. You and baby can play ball games of all sorts, and the possibilities of roughhousing are limited only by your imagination and endurance.

Care:

Feeding. Most babies have 2 front upper and lower teeth by age 1; many are cutting molars, so they can chew much wider range of foods. Can eat anything you eat (no alcohol or caffeine, obviously) as long as you mince it up, remove pits and bones and anything else they could choke on. Pattern of 3 meals a day with supplementary snacks and bottles (or cups) of milk is fixed. Enjoy self-feeding; provide them with variety of finger foods—cooked beans, crackers, pieces of cheese. Let baby experiment with different foods; will have definite (and probably shifting) likes and dislikes. Will probably want to taste whatever you're eating; may show surprisingly sophisticated palate. Try to avoid meal-time contests or forcing baby to finish everything on plate. Most babies are irregular eaters and may specialize in one food group at a time while rejecting all others. One good meal a day is about all you can expect at this age.

Sleeping. Pattern of 12 or so hours at night continues; many babies drop their second nap by age 1; may still be persuaded to go into their cribs for quiet play alone.

Baby-proofing. As soon as baby can move around the house, baby-proofing is a must. Lock or reorganize cabinets so all potentially harmful household products are out of reach; block off stairs; remove precious breakables; block off electrical sockets; keep toilet lids closed; keep garbage cans

Social, *continued*

out of reach; scour house regularly for small objects (coins, paperclips, buttons) that baby might put in mouth. Though you won't be able to rely on your child's judgment for several years, it's not too soon to begin teaching about safety.

Appendix B
Resources for Fathers

Books

Expecting Fathers

Bittman, Sam, and Rosenberg-Zalk, Sue. *Expectant Fathers* (New York: Hawthorn Books, 1978). The groundbreaking popular study of the experiences and changes that men go through during their partners' pregnancies. Useful, informative, and highly recommended.

Colman, Arthur, and Colman, Libby. *Pregnancy: The Psychological Experience* (New York: Seabury Press, 1971). Considers the psychological impact of pregnancy on both expecting mothers and fathers.

Grad, Rae; Bash, Deborah; Guyer, Ruth, et al. *The Father Book: Pregnancy and Beyond* (Washington, DC: Acropolis Books, 1981). Covers fathers' issues from pregnancy to life with baby. Written by women but based on interviews and research about men.

Gresh, Sean. *Becoming a Father* (New York: Bantam Books, 1981). Issues, both emotional and medical, faced by the expecting father.

Heinowitz, Jack. *Pregnant Fathers: How Fathers Can Enjoy and Share the Experiences of Pregnancy and Childbirth* (Englewood Cliffs, NJ: Prentice-Hall, 1982). Discusses the feelings and changes that men go through in the pregnant months. Includes suggestions and exercises for how men can get in touch with their feelings.

Trimmer, Eric. *Father-To-Be: Questions and Answers About Pregnancy, Birth and the New Baby* (Tucson, AZ: HP Books, 1983). A popularly written book answering questions fathers commonly ask about pregnancy and childbirth.

Fertility Problems

Andrews, L. B. *New Conceptions: A Consumer's Guide to the Newest Infertility Treatments* (New York: St. Martins, 1984). A guide to the traditional and new high-tech methods of achieving conception. Contains a good section on resources.

Barker, G. H. *Your Search for Fertility* (New York: William Morrow, 1982). Focuses on treatments for infertility.

Glass, Robert H., and Ericsson, Ronald J. *Getting Pregnant in the 1980s* (Berkeley: University of California Press, 1982). Up-to-date information on infertility causes and developments in human reproduction.

Menning, Barbara Eck. *Infertility* (Englewood Cliffs, NJ: Prentice-Hall, 1977). Discusses the psychological and social impact of infertility on a couple.

Silber, Sherman J. *How to Get Pregnant* (New York: Scribner's, 1980). Discusses infertility as a shared problem and offers good information on how husband and wife can treat the problem together.

Stangel, J. J. *Fertility and Conception* (New York: Paddington Press, 1979). A useful discussion of male and female fertility problems and what can be done to treat them.

Fetal Development

Annis, L. F. *The Child Before Birth* (Ithaca, NY: Cornell University Press, 1978). Scientifically detailed but still accessible description of the fetus's development from conception to birth.

Montagu, Ashley. *Life Before Birth* (New York: New American Library, 1964). One of the classic books for a general audience about the conception and growth of the fetus.

Rugh, Roberts, and Shettles, Landrum. *From Conception to Birth: The Drama of Life's Beginnings* (New York: Harper & Row, 1971). A popularly written account of the development of the human fetus.

Pregnancy and Childbirth

Ashford, Janet Isaacs, ed. *The Whole Birth Catalog: A Sourcebook for Choices in Childbirth* (Trumansburg, NY: Crossing Press, 1983). A useful compendium of information on everything from pregnancy to child-rearing. Contains very extensive lists of books, organizations, resources, articles.

Berezin, Nancy. *The Gentle Birth Book: A Practical Guide to Leboyer Family-Centered Delivery* (New York: Simon & Schuster, 1980). Applies the Leboyer method to the American birth situation.

Bing, Elisabeth, and Colman, Libby. *Making Love During Pregnancy* (New York: Bantam Books, 1977). A reassuring guide to sex during the pregnant months. Discusses common anxieties and questions of expecting parents.

Bradley, Dr. Robert. *Husband-Coached Childbirth* (New York: Harper & Row, 1980). Sets forth the principles and practice of the "Bradley method" of childbirth.

Dick-Read, Grantly, M.D. *Childbirth Without Fear: The Original Approach to Natural Childbirth*, 5th ed., rev. and ed. by Helen Wessel and Harlan F. Ellis, M.D. (New York: Harper & Row, 1984). The classic "natural childbirth" text, updated for the 1980s.

Feldman, Dr. Silvia. *Choices in Childbirth* (New York: Grosset & Dunlap, 1978). A good source of practical information on various childbirth methods commonly practiced in the United States.

Hannon, Sharron. *Childbirth: A Source Book for Conception, Pregnancy, Birth and the First Weeks of Life* (New York: Evans and Co., 1980). Lots of good common-sense advice for the pregnant months and for choosing childbirth method. Addresses issues, answers common questions, and contains suggestions for further reading.

Hillard, Paula Adams, M.D., and Panter, Gideon G., M.D. *As They Grow: Pregnancy and Childbirth* (New York: Ballantine Books, 1985). Selections from the popular column appearing in *Parents* magazine. Deals usefully with common issues and problems.

Hotchner, Tracy. *Pregnancy and Childbirth: The Complete Guide for a New Life* (New York: Avon Books, 1979). One of the better and more thorough books on the subject. Covers choosing a childbirth method, sex during pregnancy, labor, the postpartum period, and the basics of baby care.

Inch, Sally. *Birth-Rights: What Every Parent Should Know About Childbirth in Hospitals* (New York: Pantheon Books, 1984). A detailed and scathingly critical study of high-tech hospital birth as it is practiced in the West today. Contains a chapter on alternatives and improvements.

Kitzinger, Sheila. *The Complete Book of Pregnancy and Childbirth* (New York: Knopf, 1985). Social anthropologist and mother, Kitzinger has written a number of excellent books on pregnancy, birth, and parenting. This one is highly practical, reassuring, and complete. Good illustrations. Also see her *The Experience of Childbirth* (New York: Penguin Books, 1981).

Lamaze, Fernand. *Painless Childbirth* (Chicago: Henry Regnery, 1970). The renowned French obstetrician sets forth the theory behind the childbirth method now practiced most widely in America.

Leboyer, Frederick. *Birth Without Violence* (New York: Knopf, 1975). The impassioned and poetically written text in which the French obstetrician explains his philosophy of gentle birth. With photos.

Lesko, Wendy, and Lesko, Matthew. *The Maternity Source Book* (New York: Warner Books, 1984). Addresses all the major decisions today's couples face in pregnancy, childbirth, and early parenting. Format geared to practical decision making, readily accessible information.

Savage, Beverly, and Simkin, Diana. *Preparation for Birth: The Complete Guide to the Lamaze Method* (New York: Ballantine Books, 1987). Superbly written and extremely thorough guide to the Lamaze method; takes you from choosing a doctor, through preparing for the birth, to the birth itself, and postpartum period. Contains a chapter for coaches. Highly recommended.

Worth, Cecilia. *Labor and Birth: A Coaching Guide for Fathers and Friends* (New York: McGraw-Hill, 1983). A good, thorough, and accessibly written "guidebook" to everything a coach needs to know, do, bring, etc. Useful checklists, tips.

Yarrow, Leah. *Parents Book of Pregnancy and Birth* (New York: Ballantine Books, 1984). Useful, practical, and readable information covering pregnancy, birth, and postpartum.

Problems in Pregnancy

Borg, Susan, and Lasker, Judith. *When Pregnancy Fails: Families Coping With Miscarriage, Stillbirth and Infant Death* (Boston: Beacon Press, 1981). A book for parents dealing with the medical and emotional trauma of failed pregnancy written by two mothers who have lived through deaths of their babies.

Hales, Dianne, and Creasy, Dr. Robert K. *New Hope for Problem Pregnancies: Helping Babies Before They're Born* (New York: Harper & Row, 1982). Covers the major complications of pregnancy including genetic factors, drugs and chemicals, miscarriage, fetal growth problems, postmaturity. Includes a reading list.

Pizer, Hank, and Palinski, Christine O'Brien. *Coping With a Miscarriage* (New York: New American Library, 1980). Author Palinski relates her personal experience of miscarriage, and the book also presents information on the causes of miscarriage and the emotional impact on both men and women.

Fathering: Issues, Experiences, and Activities

Biller, Henry, and Meredith, Dennis. *Father Power* (New York: David McKay, 1974). Though dated, this still has some useful information on the role that fathers play in their children's development. Includes chapters on divorced fathers, stepfathers, single fathers, fathers with problem children, and fathers with special problems.

The Family Coordinator, October 1976, Vol. 25 #4 (Minneapolis: National Council on Family Relations). A collection of professional articles on the changing roles of fathers today. Includes studies of father-infant bonding, single fathers, older fathers, and stepfathers. Though written by and for academics, the articles are accessible to nonprofessional readers.

Greenberg, Martin, M.D. *The Birth of a Father* (New York: Continuum Publishing Co., 1985). A psychiatrist and researcher on father-infant bonding tells of his own transformation to fatherhood and offers good advice to all fathers about issues that arise during the births and early months of their babies' lives.

Kort, Carol, and Friedland, Ronnie, eds. *The Father's Book: Shared Experiences* (Boston: G.K. Hall, 1986). A collection of essays, poems, personal narratives from a number of fathers on a wide range of issues, including work, marriage, fathers and sons, caretaking, gay fathers, etc.

Lamb, Michael, ed. *The Role of the Father in Child Development* (New York: John Wiley, 1981). An excellent collection of academic essays about how fathers affect the development of their children. Includes a detailed bibliography.

Parke, Ross D. *Fathers* (Cambridge: Harvard University Press, 1981). A good review of the literature on fatherhood.

Includes chapters on expectant father, fathers and infants, socialization, divorce and custody, and new developments in fatherhood.

Pogrebin, Letty Cottin. *Growing up Free: Raising Your Child in the 80's* (New York: McGraw-Hill, 1980). Guide for nonsexist child-rearing. Good coverage of the nurturing role played by more and more fathers.

Pruett, Kyle D., M.D. *The Nurturing Father* (New York: Warner Books, 1987). A valuable study of fathers who act as primary caretakers of their children. Includes in-depth case studies and profiles as well as an overview of the changing roles of fathers today.

Reynolds, William. *The American Father: A New Approach to Understanding Himself, His Woman, His Child* (New York: Paddington Press, 1978). A psychology professor and father of seven offers his thoughts on marriage, sex, fatherhood, and society.

Russell, Graeme. *A Practical Guide for Fathers* (Melbourne, Australia: Sphere Books, 1983). A highly recommended guide for fathers who want to take a more active role in raising and caring for their children.

Sullivan, S. Adams. *The Father's Almanac* (New York: Doubleday, 1980). An entertaining book chock full of good advice and helpful tips on being with, playing with, raising, and dealing with children. Covers pregnancy and childbirth, early infancy, and good games for older kids.

Child Development and Care

Bernath, Maja. *Parents Book for Your Baby's First Year* (New York: Ballantine Books, 1983). Accessible and practical, this book takes you through the first year of your child's life, describing developments and all aspects of infant care.

Brazelton, T. Berry, M.D. *Infants and Mothers: Differences in Development* (New York: Delacorte Press/Seymour Lawrence, 1969). Traces the month-by-month development of three typical babies in their first year: the average baby, the quiet baby, and the active baby. Offers a good picture of the range of infant styles and paces of growth.

Caplan, Frank. *The First Twelve Months of Life: Your Baby's Growth Month by Month* (New York: Bantam Books, 1971). Warmly and accessibly written description of how your baby develops each month from birth to age one. Contains development charts for each month.

Jones, Sandy. *Crying Baby, Sleepless Nights* (New York: Warner Books, 1983). Good practical help for getting babies to be happier, sleep better, and cry less.

Leach, Penelope. *Your Baby & Child: From Birth to Age Five* (New York: Knopf, 1977). Excellent guide to daily care, physical and mental development. Practical and informative. Useful illustrations. For more in-depth treatment of child development, see her *Babyhood* (Knopf, 1983).

Segal, Marilyn, Ph.D. *Your Child at Play: Birth to One Year* (New York: Newmarket Press, 1983). A very useful book that describes a baby's development month by month in the first year and suggests numerous games and activities appropriate for each month. Includes suggestions for meal time, bath time, daily routines, and quiet time. Other volumes in the series cover ages one to two, and ages two to three.

Spock, Benjamin, M.D., and Rothenberg, Michael B., M.D. *Baby and Child Care*, revised and updated edition (New York: Pocket Books, 1985). The baby care bible, updated to reflect the changing role of fathers. Covers necessary equipment, feeding, care, illness, and behavior problems.

Stoppard, Miriam, M.D. *Day-by-Day Baby Care* (New York: Ballantine Books, 1983). Extremely useful and practical guide to taking care of your baby from birth to age three. Excellent drawings and illustrations, many checklists on equipment, feeding, growth charts, home safety, first aid. Really takes you by the hand and leads you through all the basics.

White, Burton L. *The First Three Years of Life* (New York: Avon Books, 1975). Describes the child's physical, mental, social, and emotional development. Contains good recommendations on age-appropriate toys and advice on dealing with problems of all sorts.

Child-Care Options and Arrangements

Dreskin, William, and Dreskin, Wendy. *The Day Care Decision: What's Best for You and Your Child* (New York: Evans and Co., 1983). Examines the current day-care situation and its impact on children and on parents.

Fallows, Deborah. *A Mother's Work* (Boston: Houghton Mifflin, 1985). A critical, searching study of child-care alternatives in America today by a highly educated mother who decided to stay home and raise her children.

Filstrup, Jane Merrill, with Gross, Dorothy W. *Monday Through Friday: Day Care Alternatives* (New York: Teachers College Press, 1982). Runs through the day-care alternatives from househusband to day-care center by presenting in-depth interviews and case studies of parents who use them.

Levine, James A. *Who Will Raise the Children? New Options for Fathers (and Mothers)* (Philadelphia: J.B. Lippincott, 1976). Through interviews and profiles, presents cases for fathers who want to take a more active role in caring for their children. With chapters on custody, part-time work, job-sharing, single adoptive fathers, and househusbands.

Maynard, Fredelle. *The Child Care Crisis* (New York: Viking, 1985). Examines the issues that working parents face, the options they have in child care, the effects of day care on a child's emotional and intellectual development, and explains how to choose and evaluate day care.

Scarr, Sandra. *Mother Care Other Care* (New York: Basic Books, 1984). Takes a look at the dilemmas that modern mothers face in deciding whether or not to work and compares "mother care" with "other care," i.e., day care, sitters, family homes. Includes a section on "what children need," exploring the nature of babies and preschoolers.

Siegel-Gorelick, Bryna, Ph.D. *The Working Parents' Guide to Child Care: How to Find the Best Care for Your Child* (Boston: Little, Brown, 1983). Just what the title promises: practical how-to advice on finding, evaluating, choosing, and preparing yourself and child for day care.

Adoption

Arms, Suzanne. *To Love and Let Go* (New York: Knopf, 1983). Intimate portraits of American parents who have adopted, of the children they have adopted, of women who have given up their children. Includes listings of adoption resource organizations.

Bolles, Edmund Blair. *The Penguin Adoption Handbook* (New York: Viking, 1984). Practical advice for adopting and a good guide to the "adoption maze" of agencies, international adoption, independent adoptions, legal questions, foster homes. Includes directory of parent organizations.

Gilman, Lois. *The Adoption Resource Book* (New York: Harper & Row, 1984). A recommended guide to adoption today, including how to go about it and adjusting to the special problems it may involve. Includes a state-by-state adoption directory and intercountry adoption directory.

Lasnik, Robert S. *A Parent's Guide to Adoption*. (New York: Sterling Publishing Co., 1979). Addresses both legal and psychological issues of adoption, looks at American adoption agencies as well as the black and "gray" markets in adoption.

Plumez, Jacqueline Horner. *Successful Adoption* (New York: Harmony Books, 1982). Covers the various methods of adoption open to American parents today and includes good advice on raising the adopted child. Excellent resources and references section.

Raymond, Louise (rev. by Colette Taube Dywasuk). *Adoption and After* (New York: Harper & Row, 1974). Talks to parents who are thinking of adopting and takes them through the process of adoption, adjustment, and change. Includes chapters on telling the child about adoption, adopting an older child, dealing with problems.

Single Fathers

Atlas, Stephen L. *Single Parenting: A Practical Resource Guide*. (Englewood Cliffs, NJ: Prentice-Hall, 1981). Practical guidance, resources, advice, and reassurance for single parents.

Gatley, Richard, Ph.D., and Koulack, David, Ph.D. *Single Father's Handbook: A Guide for Separated and Divorced Fathers* (New York: Anchor Press/Doubleday, 1979). Advice for the separated or divorced father about dealing with his children, his former wife, setting up a household, work, etc. Contains a chapter on "father as 'mother'" about single fathers caring for children of all ages.

McCoy, Kathleen. *Solo Parenting: Your Essential Guide* (New York: New American Library, 1987). Upbeat advice for single parents about getting control of their lives, their feelings and raising their children. Good listings of other books for parents and children, organizations, and resources.

Rosenthal, Kristine, and Keshet, Harry. *Fathers Without Partners: A Study of Fathers and the Family* (Totowa, NJ: Rowman and Littlefield, 1981). Using research about divorced fathers' relationships with their children, analyzes a number of issues that come up for fathers after divorce. Includes discussions of fathers with full custody, joint custody, and without custody.

ORGANIZATIONS

For a very comprehensive listing of programs and services for fathers all over the United States, see *Fatherhood U.S.A. The First National Guide to Programs, Services, and Resources for and about Fathers* by Debra G. Kinman, Ph.D. and Rhiana Kohl, The Fatherhood Project at Bank Street Col-

Appendix B

lege of Education (New York: Garland Publishing Co., 1984). Includes statewide listings of programs for expectant and new fathers, fathers of special needs children, support groups for fathers in general, for single fathers, for stepfathers, services for teen fathers and gay fathers. Includes extensive bibliographies organized by subject. Obtain a copy directly from the publisher or send to The Fatherhood Project, Bank Street College of Education, 610 West 112 St., New York, NY 11025.

Fertility Problems

American Fertility Society
1608 Thirteenth Avenue South
Birmingham, AL 35205

Planned Parenthood of New York City, Inc.
Family Planning and Information Service
810 Seventh Avenue
New York, NY 10019

Resolve, Inc.
P.O. Box 474
Belmont, MA 02178

The Barren Foundation
6 East Monroe Street
Chicago, IL 60603

United Infertility Organization
P.O. Box 23
Scarsdale, NY 10583

National Support Groups for Parents Whose Babies Have Died

Amend
4323 Berrywich Terrace
St. Louis, MO 63128

Compassionate Friends
P.O. Box 1347
Oak Brook, IL 60521

National Sudden Infant Death Syndrome Foundation
2 Metro Plaza, Suite 205
8240 Professional Place
Landover, MD 20785

SHARE
St. John's Hospital
800 E. Carpenter
Springfield, IL 62702

Childbirth

American Academy of Husband-Coached Childbirth
P.O. Box 5224
Sherman Oaks, CA 91413

American College of Nurse-Midwives
1522 K Street, NW, Suite 1120
Washington, DC 20005

American Society for Psychoprophylaxis in Obstetrics (ASPO)
1840 Wilson Blvd., Suite 204
Arlington, VA 22201

Read Natural Childbirth Foundation
P.O. Box 956
San Rafael, CA 94915

Vaginal Birth After Cesarean
P.O. Box 152
Syracuse, NY 13210

Organizations to Help You Find Classes

The ASPO and the AAHCC (both listed above) will be able to help you locate instructors who specialize in Lamaze and Bradley techniques, respectively. Other organizations listed below will direct you to the kind of childbirth instruction you want.

Appendix B 389

International Childbirth Education Association (ICEA)
P.O. Box 20048
Minneapolis, MN 55420

La Leche League International
9616 Minneapolis Avenue
Franklin Park, IL 60131

National Association of Childbirth Education, Inc.
3940 Eleventh Street
Riverside, CA 92501

NAPSAC, International (National Association of Parents and Professionals for Safe Alternatives in Childbirth)
P.O. Box 267
Marble Hill, MO 63764

Maternity Centers

National Association of Childbearing Centers
R.D. #1, Box 1
Perkiomenville, PA 18074

Home-Birth

American College of Home Obstetrics
664 North Michigan Avenue
Chicago, IL 60611

Association for Childbirth at Home, International
P.O. Box 39498
Los Angeles, CA 90039

La Leche League International
9616 Minneapolis Ave.
Franklin Park, IL 60131

NAPSAC, International (National Association of Parents and Professionals for Safe Alternatives in Childbirth)
P.O. Box 267
Marble Hill, MO 63764

National Men's Organizations

Free Men, Inc.
P.O. Box 15489
Washington, DC 20003

National Organization for Men
814 Blackhawk Drive
Park Forest South, IL 60466

Parents in Crisis

Family Service America
11700 West Lake Park Drive
Milwaukee, WI 53224

National Child Help Child Abuse Hotline
800-421-0353

Adoption

North American Council on Adoptable Children (NACAC)
2001 S Street N.W.
Washington, DC 20009

OURS, Inc.
3307 Highway 100 North, Suite 203
Minneapolis, MN 55422

Resources for Single Parents

Family Service America
11700 West Lake Park Drive
Milwaukee, WI 53224

Gay Fathers Coalition
P.O. Box 28317
Washington, DC 20005

National Congress for Men
210 7th Street SE
Washington, DC 20003

Appendix B

Parents Without Partners, Inc.
8807 Colesville Road
Silver Spring, MD 20910

United Fathers of America, Inc.
415 North Sycamore, Suite 207
Santa Ana, CA 92701

National Organizations Dealing With Fathers' Custody Issues

Child Custody Evaluation Service
P.O. Box 202
Glenside, PA 19038

Fathers United for Equal Rights
P.O. Box 1323
Arlington, VA 22210

Joint Custody Association
10606 Wilkins Avenue
Los Angeles, CA 90024

Parents® MAGAZINE READ ALOUD BOOK CLUB

READING ALOUD—the loving, personal gift for you and your child to share.

Children's reading experts agree... reading aloud offers the easiest, most effective way to turn your child into a lifelong reader. And, it's as much fun for you as it is for your child.

Easy access to a variety of such important "first" books (read-aloud books) has presented a major problem for busy parents. And a challenge that *Parents* Magazine was well suited to undertake.

The result—a book club that can be your child's *first club*. A club for sharing and reading aloud. An early reading habit to last a lifetime, with books designed, created and published solely for this purpose. *Parents* Magazine Read Aloud Book Club.

If you're a concerned parent, and would like more information about our club and your free gift, just fill in the coupon below, and mail it in.

Parents® MAGAZINE READ ALOUD BOOK CLUB

1 PARENTS CIRCLE
P.O. BOX 10264
DES MOINES, IA 50380-0264

Yes, I would like to receive free information on *Parents* Magazine Read Aloud Book Club.

To find out how to receive free gifts along with membership, simply fill out this coupon and mail it today. There's no risk or obligation.

YOUR NAME	(PLEASE PRINT)	
ADDRESS		APT. NO.
CITY	STATE	ZIP

Index

Adcock, Don, 242
Adoptive fathers, 324–332
  adoption
    effect on infant, 328–329
    feelings related to, 325
    reactions of others, 330–331
    reasons for, 234–235
    source books for, 325–326, 328
    telling child about, 331–332
  groups/resources for, 329–330
  postadoption period, 326–328
    bonding, 327
    stresses, 326–327
  preparation for baby, 328
Afterbirth, 184–185
Alienation of father
  and breastfeeding, 221
  from mother-to-be, 77
Alternative birth centers, 121
American Society for Psychoprophylaxis in Obstetrics (ASPO), 129–130, 134
Amniocentesis, 114–116
Amniotic sac, breaking of, 161–162
Anderson, Barbara, 193
Anesthesia, 152–154
  epidural, 153
  local anesthesia, 153–154
    paracervical block, 153–154
    perineal block, 154
    pudendal block, 154
  spinal, 153
Apgar score, 187
Arguments, during pregnancy, 75–76
Artificial embryonation, 42–43
Artificial insemination, 40–41
  by donor (AID), 40–41, 43
  by husband (AIH), 40
Ashford, Janet Isaacs, 131
Aspermia, and infertility, 34
As They Grow: Pregnancy and Childbirth (Hillard), 107

Baby boomers, delaying parenthood, 16–17
Baby's firsts, 359–362
  baby's discoveries, 359–360
  first trips/excursions, 360–361
  language, 359
Baby-sitters, 305, 306–308
  ad for finding sitter, 306
  instructing sitter, 308
  interviewing sitter, 307
  trial period, 307–308

Index

Baby-sitting cooperative, 313
Back labor, 203–205
  relief for, 204–205
  and rotation of baby, 204
Bathing newborn, 253–258
  baby's fear, minimizing, 257–258
  caution about, 254
  and fathers, 254
  shampoo, 255, 257
  sponge bath, 255
  "topping and tailing," 254
  tub bath, 255
Bell, Rick, 216, 276, 283, 295
Biller, Henry, 335
Bing, Elisabeth, 88
Biofeedback, use in childbirth, 134
Biological factors, 20–53
  choosing child's sex, 27–28
  conception, 25
  embryonic development, 29–32
  fertilization, 23–25
  fetal development, 44–53
  male infertility, 32–40
    alternative conception methods, 40–44
  ovulation, 26–27
  sperm production, 21–22
  See also specific topics.
Birth at Home (Kitzinger), 150
Birth experience, 183–190
  bonding, father-infant, 188
  father's feelings, 184, 188–189
  newborn at birth, physical aspects, 185–186
  post-birth procedures, 186–188
    Apgar score, 187
    silver nitrate in eyes, 187
Birth of a Father, The (Greenberg), 188, 282
Birthing center, 120
  typical birth, 144–147
    children at birth, 145–146
    differences from hospital, 144–145
Birthing room in hospital, 119–120
Birth-Rights: What Every Parent Should Know About Childbirth in Hospitals (Inch), 143
Birth Without Violence (Leboyer), 132
Birth works, 133–134
Bittman, Sam, 56, 62
Bonding
  adoptive fathers, 327
  and breastfeeding, 221
  father-infant, 188
    engrossment, 188
  and hospital birth, 143
  and touch, 221
Bottle-feeding tips, 243–247
  holding baby, 244–245
  nipple opening, 243
  preparing formula, 243
  sterilizing equipment, 243
  warming bottle, 243–244
Bradley, Robert A., 130
Bradley method, 130–131
Brazelton T. Berry, 241, 262–263
Breadwinners, father's role, 210, 214, 217
Breastfeeding, 221–224
  advocates of, 221–222
  and alienation of father, 221
  and bonding, 221
  difficulties of, 223
  expressing milk, 242
  father's support and, 224
  opponents of, 222–223
  and sex, 278

Caregiving
  basic issues for fathers, 298–301
  and dual-career couples, 301–303
  See also Child-care arrangements.
Caregiving routines, 236–264

Index

bathing newborn, 253–258
diapering newborn, 247–251
dressing newborn, 251–253
feeding newborn, 242–247
holding newborn, 236–240
playing with newborn, 240–242
See also individual routines.
Cervix, 23
change at ovulation, 26–27
incompetent, 99
Cesarean delivery, 198–203
father's attendance, 201–202
increases in, 198–199, 200
planned cesareans, 199
post-birth, mother during, 202–203
reasons for, 199
surgical procedure in, 201
Cesarean Prevention Movement, 134
Childbirth at Home (Sousa), 150
Childbirth preparation
childbirth classes, 124–127
criticisms of, 126
hospital classes, 125
options available, 124–125
usefulness of, 126–127
child-care arrangements, 154–155
father attending birth, 155–157
hospital tour, 135–136
midwives, use of, 121–123
place of birth, 118–121
alternative birth centers, 121
birthing centers, 120
birthing room in hospital, 119–120
home birth, 121
hospital delivery, 119
See also Birthing center; Home birth; Hospital delivery; Prepared childbirth methods.
Childbirth Without Fear (Dick-Read), 127, 128

Child-care arrangements, 154–155
age factors, 305
baby-sitters, 305, 306–308
baby-sitting cooperative, 313
day-care, 304, 308–312
full-time fathers, 318–322
full-time mothers, 315–318
relatives and child-care, 312–313
See also specific topics.
Child Care Crisis, The (Maynard), 304
Children, older, present at birth, 145–146
Chromosomes
and conception, 25
in sperm, 21
Circumcision, and diapering, 248–249
Classes in prepared childbirth. *See* Childbirth preparation; Prepared childbirth methods
Cloth diapers, 249, 251
Coaching, 170–182
birth, experience of, 183–190
in delivery room, 181–182
fears of men during, 175–177
and preparation for, 174–175
stages of labor, and, 179–182
early labor, 179–180
pushing, 180–181
transition, 178–182
tasks of
breathing coach, 172
concentration, helping wife, 172–173
encouraging wife, 173
physical presence of coach, 173–174
timing contractions, 171
types of coaches, 175
and wife's needs, 170–171
Colic, 219, 265, 270–271
coping with, 271
evening colic, 270, 271
theories about, 270

Colman, Libby, 88
Complete Book of Breastfeeding, The (Eiger and Olds), 224
Complete Book of Pregnancy and Childbirth, The (Kitzinger), 131, 165
Complications in delivery, 193–206
  back labor, 203–205
    relief for, 204–205
    and rotation of baby, 204
  cesarean delivery, 198–203
    father's attendance, 201–202
    increases in, 198–199, 200
    planned cesareans, 199
    post-birth, mother during, 202–203
    reasons for, 199
    surgical procedure in, 201
  forceps delivery, 205–206
    problems related to, 205, 206
  postterm birth, 196–198
    coping with, 198
    inducing labor, 197
    signs of distress, 196
    tests given, 197
  premature birth, 194–196
    at-risk factors, 194
    care of preemies, 195–196
    drugs used, 195
    incidence of, 194
    prevention of, 194–195
Complications in pregnancy
  detection methods, 113–116
    amniocentesis, 114–116
    ultrasound, 113–114
  diabetes, 108–109
    gestational diabetes, 108–109
    insulin-dependent mother-to-be, 109
  ectopic pregnancy, 101–103
  high blood pressure complications, 103–105
    eclampsia, 105
    high-risk factors, 104
    preeclampsia, 104–105
  miscarriage, 95–101
  pelvic inflammatory disease (PID), 107
  sexually transmitted diseases, 106–108
    gonorrhea, 107–108
    herpes simplex, 106
    syphilis, 107–108
  stillbirth, 109–112
    feelings related to, 111
    marital crisis and, 111
    sex life and, 111–112
    signs of, 110
    statistical information, 109, 110
    support groups for parents, 113
Conception, 25
  best position for, 27
  and chromosomal activity, 25
  fertility in women, signs of, 27
  timing for, 26–27
Consistency, parental, 354
Contractions, 162–163
  Braxton Hicks contractions, 162
  purpose of, 162
  timing of, 171
Cost factors, having children, 17
Couvade syndrome, 70–71
  basis of, 70
  time for, 71
Cowper's glands, 22
Creasy, Robert K., 94
Crisis handling
  counseling and, 285
  crying, 267–271
  exhaustion, 271–273
  marital relationship, post-birth, 273–280
  pressures of new father, 280–284
  See also individual topics.
Crying of newborn, 267–271
  calming techniques

Index

physical security, 268
rhythmic movements/sounds, 268
colic, 270–271
  coping with, 271
  evening colic, 270, 271
  theories about, 170
effect on adults, 267, 269
needs related to, 267–268, 269
Cry reflex, 227

Day-by-Day Baby Care (Stoppard), 246, 251
Day-care, 304, 308–312
  evaluation of, 310–311
  finding facility, 309, 311
  licensing issue, 309–310
  pros/cons, 304–305
Decision to have children, 7–19
  age factors, 13–15
    biological clock, 14
    second families, 15
  components of, 7–10, 15
  delaying parenthood, 16–19
    advantages of, 18
    baby boomers and, 16–17
    cost factors, 17
  freedom issues, 11
  self-assessment and, 15
  timing for fatherhood, 10–11, 13
Delivery
  complications in delivery, 193–206
    back labor, 203–205
    cesarean delivery, 198–203
    forceps delivery, 205–206
    postterm birth, 196–198
    premature birth, 194–196
  emergency delivery, 190—192
    after-birth guidelines, 191–192
    cord, handling of, 192–193
    guidelines for, 190–191
    information sources on, 193
See also specific complications.
Delivery options
  alternative birth centers, 121
  birthing centers, 120
  birthing room in hospital, 119–120
  home birth, 121
  hospital delivery, 119
Delivery room, 141–142, 181–182
  delivery table, 141
Demerol, 152, 170
Denial, of impending fatherhood, 64–66
Detachment, from fetus, 64–66
Detection methods, 113–116
  amniocentesis, 114–116
  ultrasound, 113–114
Diabetes, 108–109
  gestational diabetes, 108–109
  insulin-dependent mother-to-be, 109
Diapering newborn, 247–251
  and boy's circumcision, 248–249
  cloth diapers, 249, 251
  diaper rash, 249
  disposable diapers, 249
  equipment for, 231, 248
  frequency of, 247–248
  powder issue, 249
  wiping, girls/boys, 248
Dick-Read, Grantly, 127, 128
Dick-Read methods, 127, 128–129
Discipline, 353–356
  consistency in, 354
  distracting baby, 354–355
  normal behavior versus misbehavior, 353–354
  physical punishment, 355–356
  setting limits, 355
Disposable diapers, 249
Divorce. *See* Single fathers.
Doering, S.G., 66
Down's syndrome
  amniocentesis and, 114–116

incidence of, 114
Dressing newborn, 251–253
  changing stretchie, 251–253
  overdressing, testing for, 253
Drug/alcohol use, and infertility, 35
Dual-career couples, 276–277, 301–303
  alternate schedules, 313–315
    flex-time, 314
    job sharing, 314–315
    part-time work, 315
  competition for baby, 290
  See also Child-care arrangements.

Eclampsia, 105
Ectopic pregnancy, 101–103
Education and Counseling for Childbirth (Kitzinger), 131
Eiger, Marvin S., 224
Electronic fetal monitor
  external monitor, 137, 138
  and hospital birth, 137–139
  internal monitor, 137, 138
  pros/cons, 138–139
Embryo freezing, 42
Embryonic development, 25, 29–32
  embryo to fetus development, 31–32
  implantation, 30
  morula, 30
  zygote, 29–30
Emergency Childbirth Handbook (Anderson and Shapiro), 193
Emergency Childbirth (White), 193
Emergency delivery, 190–193
  after-birth guidelines, 191–192
  cord, handling of, 192–193
  guidelines for, 190–191
  information sources on, 193
Endocrine disorders, and infertility, 35

Entwisle, D.R., 66
Epididymis, 22
Epidural, 153
Episiotomy
  criticisms of, 142–143
  and hospital birth, 142–143
  local anesthesia for, 142, 154
Equipment for newborn
  bathing/hygiene, 231–232
  changing diapers, 231
  clothing, 230
  eating, 229
  furniture, 234
  sleeping, 228
  toys, 234
  transporting baby, 233–234
Ernst, Kitty, 144
Exhaustion of parents, 271–273
  coping with exhaustion, 272
  mother as martyr role, 273
Expectant Fathers (Bittmen and Zalk), 56, 62
Experience of Childbirth, The (Kitzinger), 128, 131

Fallopian tube, sperm and, 23–25
False labor, 162
Family life
  caregiving, 297–301
  child-care arrangements, 304–322
  father-baby togetherness, 289–291, 294–296
  love, 356–359
  relationship, revival of, 292–294
  See also specific topics.
Fantasies/dreams, of father-to-be, 61–62, 66, 90, 91
Father-baby togetherness, 341–345
  age factors, 341–344
  alone with baby, 289, 294–295
  father-baby programs, 295
  hanging-out, 342–343, 360

Index

play activities, 290–291, 343
weekends, 289–290
Father Focus, 207, 213, 216
Fatherhood
  adoptive fathers, 324–332
  baby's firsts, 359–362
  and birth experience, 183–190
  change in, 3
  childbirth preparation, 117–157
  coaching during labor, 170–182
  crisis-handling, 265–284
  decision to have children, 7–19
  discipline, 353–356
  family life, 289–294
  feelings about pregnancy, 54–93
  joys/trials of, father's responses, 346–350
  love, 356–359
  men's conceptions of, 88–92
  and newborn, 207–234
  New Fatherhood, 1–4
  role modeling, 351–353
  single fathers, 332–338
  See also specific topics.
Fatherhood Project, 2
Fatherhood U.S.A., First National Guide to Programs, Services, and Resources for and about Fathers (Klinman and Kohl), 295
Father Power (Biller and Meredith), 335
Father's Book, The (Rossman), 84
Fathers (Parke), 320
"Father's Role in Infancy: A Reevaluation" (Parke and Sawin), 211
Feeding newborn, 242–247
  bottle-feeding tips, 243–247
    burping baby, 245–247
    holding baby, 244–245
    nipple opening, 243
    preparing formula, 243
    sterilizing equipment, 243
    warming bottle, 243–244
  frequency of, 247
  night feedings, 242
  See also Breastfeeding.
Feelings about pregnancy
  acknowledgment/acceptance of, 69, 74
  alienation from mother-to-be, 77
  couvade syndrome, 70–71
  feelings about fetus, 58–66
    detachment from fetus, 64–66
    fantasies/dreams, 61–62, 66, 90, 91
    and fetal movement, 59–61
    making contact with fetus, 62–63
    and sex of fetus, 60
    and sonogram, 58, 59, 60–61
    turning point in feelings, 59, 60–61
  fighting during pregnancy, 75–76
  first reactions, 54, 55–58
  jealousy toward mother-to-be, 74–75
  positive aspects, 72, 81–82, 90, 92, 93
  relationship concerns, 71–72
  resentment toward mother-to-be, 73
  sex, 82–88
  thoughts about father's father, 91
  and wife's happiness, 72
  worries of father, 66–69
    medical complications, 68, 69
    money, 67
    practical problems, 67–68, 69
    superstitions, 69
Fein, Robert, 210–211

Index

Fertility, *see* Infertility; Male infertility
Fertilization, 23–25
Fetal development, 44–53
  four weeks, 44
  eight weeks, 44–45
  twelve weeks, 45–47
  sixteen weeks, 47–48
  twenty weeks, 48
  twenty-four weeks, 48–49
  twenty-eight weeks, 50
  thirty-two weeks, 50–51
  thirty-six weeks, 51–52
  forty weeks, 52–53
  Financial pressures, 67, 280–283
  and full-time mothers, 316–317
Fink, Lois, 124
First Birth, The (Doering and Entwisle), 66
First Three Years of Life, The (White), 225, 291
Flex-time, 314
Forceps delivery, 205–206
  problems related to, 205, 206
Formula
  preparing, 243
  See also Bottle-feeding tips.
Full-time fathers, 318–322
  dealing with role, 321
  father-raised infants, characteristics of, 320
  reasons for nurturing father, 319–320
  societal feelings about, 319
  statistical information, 322
Full-time mothers, 315–318
  dividing responsibilities, 317–318
  emotional aspects, 316
  father's feeling toward, 315–317
  financial aspects, 316–317

Gag reflex, 226
Gamete intrafallopian transfer (GIFT), 42

Gentle Birth Book, The (Berezin), 133
Gestational diabetes, 108–109
Gilgoff, Alice, 150
Gonorrhea, 107–108
Greenberg, Martin, 188, 282

Hales, Dianne, 94
Hanging-out, father-baby togetherness, 342–343, 360
Hansen, Ron, 15
Herpes simplex, 106
High blood pressure complications, 103–105
  eclampsia, 105
  high-risk factors, 104
  preeclampsia, 104–105
Hillard, Dr. Paula Adams, 107
History of Women's Bodies, A (Shorter), 147
Holding newborn, 236–240
  for bottle feeding, 244–245
  favorite position of baby, 238, 239
  frequency issue, 236–237
  supporting head, 237
  talking and, 238
  wrapping newborn, 239
Home birth, 121, 147–150
  birth attendants, 148
  legality of, 148
  organizations for, 148–149
  planning for emergencies, 149
  preparation for, 149–150
  safety factors, 147–148
Home Birth Book (Ward and Ward), 150
Home Birth (Gilgoff), 150
Hospital delivery, 119, 119–120
  admission to hospital, 168–170
  birthing room, 119–120
  newborn in nursery, 187
  pre-birth tour, 135–136
  rooming in, 187
  typical birth, 136–143
    bonding time, 143

Index

delivery room/table,
140–141
electronic fetal monitor,
137–139
episiotomy, 142–143
intravenous (IV), 139–140
labor room, 140
prep, 136–137
Hot-line for parents, 285
Househusbands. *See* Full-time
fathers
Hoyt, Michael, 278
Husband-Coached Childbirth
(Bradley), 127
Hypospadias, and infertility, 36

Implantation, of zygote, 30
Inch, Sally, 143
Infant and Mothers (Brazelton),
262–263
Infection, and infertility, 35
Infertility
alternate fertilization methods
artificial embryonation,
42–43
artificial insemination,
40–41
embryo freezing, 42
gamete intrafallopian
transfer (GIFT), 42
sperm/egg donation, 43
surrogate mothering, 43
in vitro fertilization, 41–42
See also Male infertility.
In-laws
and breastfeeding, 222–223
new father dealing with, 209
pre-birth worries about, 69
Insulin-dependent mother-to-be,
109
Intravenous (IV), and hospital
birth, 139–140
In vitro fertilization, 41–42
costs, 42

Jealousy of father,
toward mother-to-be, 74–75
toward new mother, 275
Job sharing, 314–315

Karmel, Marjorie, 129
Kitzinger, Sheila, 128, 131,
150, 165
Kitzinger method, 131–132
Klinman, Debra G., 295
Kohl, Rhiana, 295

Labor, 158–206
admission to hospital,
168–170
negative aspects, 168, 169
coaching, 170–182
contractions, 162–163
getting to hospital, 166
going to hospital too soon,
165–166
inducing, 197
necessities for hospital,
167–168
for father-to-be, 167
for mother-to-be, 167–168
preparation, value of, 164
signs of
bloody show, 160–161
breaking waters, 161–162
contractions begin,
162–163
stages of, 163, 177
active labor, 178
afterbirth, 184–185
early labor, 164, 178,
179–180
transition, 178–182
See also Coaching.
Labor room, and hospital birth,
140
Lamaze, Fernand, 127, 129
Lamaze method, 127, 129–130
Leach, Penelope, 227, 238, 271
Leboyer method, 132–133
Leisure time pressures, 283–284
La Leche League, 221
Levine, James, 3, 297, 319
Local anesthesia, 153–154
paracervical block, 153–154

perineal block, 154
pudendal block, 154
Loneliness problem, single fathers, 335–336
Love, 356–359
  marital, during pregnancy, 72–74

McCall, Robert, 281, 284
Making Love During Pregnancy (Bing and Colman), 88
"Male Clock, The" (Hansen), 15
Male infertility, 32–40
  alternate fertilization methods
    artificial embryonation, 42–43
    artificial insemination, 40–41
    embryo freezing, 42
    gamete intrafallopian transfer (GIFT), 42
    sperm/egg donation, 43
    surrogate mothering, 43
    in vitro fertilization, 41–42
  alternative conception methods, 40–44
  incidence, 33, 37
  medical work-up for, 37–39
    organizations to contact, 39
    semen analysis, 37–38
    treatments used, 38
  production problems, 34–36
    aspermia, 34
    drug/alcohol use, 35
    endocrine disorders, 35
    infection, 35
    stress, 35
    undescended testes, 36
    varicocele, 34–35
  transport problems, 36–37
    hypospadias, 36
    obstructions, 36
    retrograde ejaculation, 36
    sexual problems, 37
Marital relationship
  post-birth, 273–280
    challenge to passion, 358
    chores, tension about, 275–276
    dual-career couples, 276–277
    going out, 258, 278–279
    hiding feelings, 275
    jealousy of father, 275
    love in, 356–359
    settling down of, 292–294
    sex, 277–278
    "stuck with baby" scenario, 276
    time squeeze, 274
  pre-birth
    alienation of husband, 77
    concerns about, 71–72
    entering new phase, 81–82
    fighting during pregnancy, 75–76
    jealousy of husband, 74–75
    positive aspects of pregnancy, 72, 81–82, 90, 92, 93
    resentment of husband, 73
    sex, 82–88
Masculinity, teaching to child, 353
Maternity Source Book (Lesko and Lesko), 134
May, Katharyn, 67
Maynard, Fredelle, 304
"Men's Entrance to Parenthood" (Fein), 210–211
Meredith, Dennis, 335
Midwives
  certified nurse midwives, 122
  lay midwives, 122
  source for locating, 123
  versus obstetrician, 122
Miscarriage, 95–101
Money worries, 67
Moro reflex, 226
Mother Care/Other Care (Scarr), 304, 305
Mothers (new), 218–224
  breastfeeding, 221–224
    advocates of, 221–222
    and alienation of father, 221

Index

and bonding, 221
difficulties of, 223
father's support and, 224
opponents of, 222–223
full-time mothers, 315–318
  dividing responsibilities, 317–318
  emotional aspects, 316
  father's feeling toward, 315–317
  financial aspects, 316–317
post-birth, physical aspects, 218
postpartum depression, 219–220
  counseling for, 220
  father's role in, 219
Mouth-to-mouth resuscitation, emergency delivery, 192
Movement of fetus, and feelings of father, 59, 60–61

Natural Childbirth (Dick-Read), 127
Newborn, 207–234
  caregiving routines, 236–264
    bathing newborn, 253–258
    diapering newborn, 247–251
    dressing newborn, 251–253
    feeding newborn, 242–247
    holding newborn, 236–240
    playing with newborn, 240–242
    sleeping, 258–261
  coping/adjustments of parents, 265–267
  crisis-handling, 265–284
    crying, 267–271
    exhaustion, 271–273
    marital relationship, post-birth, 273–280
    pressures of new father, 280–284
  developmental stages
    birth to six weeks, 363–365
    six months to one year, 370–375
    six weeks to three months, 365–367
    three months to six months, 367–370
  development of, examples, 262–263
  equipment needed for, 228–234
  father's feelings, 207–208, 210
  father's role
    breadwinners, 210, 214, 217
    learning method for, 213, 221, 264
    mother as expert problem, 212–213
    and needs of father, 211
    nontraditional fathers, 210, 214
  life of newborn, 224–228
    capabilities of newborn, 225–226
    reflexes, 226–227
    sleep needs, 227
  physical appearance at birth, 185–186
  women and, 218–224
    breastfeeding, 221–224
    physical aspects, post-birth, 218
    postpartum depression, 219–220
  work issue, 214–218
    dilemma for men, 216
    getting ahead at work, 217
    paternity leave, 215–216, 217–218
    societal pressures and, 217
  See also individual topics.
New Hope for Problem Pregnancies (Hales and Creasy), 94
Nontraditional fathers, father's role, 210, 214
Nurturing Father, The (Pruett), 2, 319, 352

Index

Obstetrician, versus midwives, 122
Obstructions, and infertility, 36
Olds, Sally Wendkos, 224
Ovulation, 26–27
  and menstrual cycle, 26
  mittelschmerz, 27
  signs of fertility, 26–27

Pacifier, 268
Painkillers
  anesthesia, 152–154
    epidural, 153
    local anesthetics, 153–154
    spinal, 153
  Demerol, 152
  disadvantages of, 151
  prepared childbirth, views of, 128, 130, 131
  Valium, 152
Painless Childbirth (Lamaze), 127, 129
Palkovitz, Rob, 155, 156
Paracervical block, 153–154
Parke, Ross D., 211, 320
Part-time work, 315
Paternity leave, 215–216, 217–218
Pelvic inflammatory disease (PID), 107
Perineal block, 154
Physical punishment, 355–356
Pitocin, 170, 197
Place for birth. *See* Delivery options.
Placenta
  afterbirth, 184–185
  development of, 30
  handling in emergency delivery, 192–193
Playing with newborn, 240–242
  activities for, 241–242, 291
  mothers *versus* fathers, 240–241, 290
  reading, 241–242, 291
  source books for, 242
Postpartum depression, 219–220
  counseling for, 220

  father's role in, 219
Postterm birth, 196–198
  coping with, 198
  inducing labor, 197
  signs of distress, 196
  tests given, 197
Preeclampsia, 104–105
Pregnancy
  father's feelings about, 54–93
  fetal development, 44–53
  problems in
    detection methods, 113–116
    diabetes, 108–109
    ectopic pregnancy, 101–103
    high blood pressure complications, 103–105
    miscarriage, 95–101
    sexually transmitted diseases, 106–108
    stillbirth, 109–112
  See also Complications of pregnancy.
Premature birth, 194–196
  at-risk factors, 194
  care of preemies, 195–196
  drugs used, 195
  incidence of, 194
  prevention of, 194–195
Prep
  and hospital birth, 136–137
  mini prep, 137
Prepared childbirth methods, 127–135
  biofeedback, use in childbirth, 134
  birth works, 133–134
  Bradley method, 130–131
  Dick-Read methods, 127, 128–129
  Kitzinger method, 131–132
  Lamaze method, 127, 129–130
  Leboyer method, 132–133
  sources of information, organizations, 135
  underwater birth method, 133

Index

yoga birth, 133
Preparing for birth. *See* Childbirth preparation.
Pressures of new father
  feelings of responsibility, 284
  financial pressures, 280–283
  leisure time pressures, 283–284
Prostate, 22
Pruett, Kyle D., 2, 319, 352
Pudendal block, 154
Pushing, 180–181

Reading to baby, 241–242, 291
Reflexes of newborn, 226–227
  cry reflex, 226
  gag reflex, 226
  Moro reflex, 226
  swimming reflex, 226
  tonic neck reflex, 226
  walking reflex, 226
Relatives, child-care by, 312–313
Resentment toward mother-to-be, 73
Respiratory distress syndrome (RDS), 109
Responsibility of fatherhood, fear of, 68–69
Retrograde ejaculation, and infertility, 36
Ritodrine, 195
Role modeling, 351–353
  sex roles, 351–353
Rooming in, 187
Rorvick, D.M., 28
Rossman, M., 84

Sachs, Jerry, 207, 213, 216, 217
Sawin, Douglas B., 211
Scarr, Sandra, 304
Schroeder, Pat, 215
Segal, Marilyn, 242
Semen analysis, for infertility, 37–38
Seminal vesicle, 22
Setting limits, discipline, 355
Sex, 82–88

alternative to intercourse, 88
experimentation during pregnancy, 87
post-birth, 277–278, 293
  breastfeeding and, 278
  emotional aspects, 277–278
  physical aspects, 277, 278
pre-birth, 82–88
  fear of hurting fetus, 85
  lack of desire, 86
  women's desire during pregnancy, 86, 87
Sex of child
  choosing sex
    dietary theory, 28
    Shettles theory related to, 28
    Whelan theory, 28
  conception and, 25
  and feelings of father, 60
Sex roles
  fathers with sons *versus* daughters, 351–352
  learning of, 352
  masculinity, teaching of, 353
Sexually transmitted diseases, 106–108
  gonorrhea, 107–108
  herpes simplex, 106
  syphilis, 107–108
Sexual problems, and infertility, 37
Shampoo, 255, 257
Shapiro, Pamela, 193
Shettles, Landrum B., 28
Shorter, Edward, 147
Siegel-Gorelick, Bryna, 311
Silver nitrate in eyes, 187
Simkin, Diana, 65, 125, 126, 175
Single fathers, 332–338
  joint custody fathers, 333
  loneliness problem, 335–336
  resources for, 337–338
  scheduling/planning, value of, 335
  shortcuts, making use of, 334
  statistical information, 332

stress of beginning phase, 334
time-alone, need for, 335
Six Practical Lessons for an Easier Childbirth (Bing), 129
Sleeping of newborn, 258–261
  characteristics of newborn sleep, 258–259
  encouraging acceptable sleep cycle, 258, 259–261
  feedings and, 260
  nighttime routines, 260–261
  position for, 241
  in own room, 260
Social life, going out, 278–279
Sonogram, 113–114
  explanation of procedure, 113–114
  and feelings of father, 58, 59, 60–61
Sousa, Marion, 150
Spanking, 356
Sperm
  and conception, 25
  and fertilization, 23–25
    and Fallopian tubes, 24–25
  number ejaculated, 23
Sperm/egg donation, 43
Sperm production, 21–22
  and frequency of sex, 22
  problems related to, 34–36
    aspermia, 34
    drug/alcohol use, 35
    endocrine disorders, 35
    infection, 35
    stress, 35
    transport problems, 36–37
    undescended testes, 36
    varicocele, 34–35
  semen analysis, 37–38
  testes and heat, 22
Spinal, 153
Spock, Dr., 253
Sponge bath, 255
Stillbirth, 109–112
  feelings related to, 111
  marital crisis and, 111
  sex life and, 111–112
  signs of, 110
  statistical information, 109, 110
  support groups for parents, 113
Stoppard, Miriam, 246, 251
Stress, and infertility, 35
Stretchies, dressing baby, 251–253
Superstitions, about childbirth, 69
Surrogate mothering, 43
Swaddling newborn, 239, 268
Swimming reflex, 226
Syphilis, 107–108

Talking to fetus, 62–63
Talking to newborn, 238
Testes, 22
  heat sensitivity, 22
  undescended, 36
Thank You Doctor Lamaze (Karmel), 129
Tonic neck reflex, 226
Touch relaxation, 131
Transition, labor, 178–182
Tub bath, 255

Ultrasound, 113–114
Underwater birth method, 133
Undescended testes, and infertility, 36
Urethra, 22

Vaginal birth after cesarean (VBAC), 134
Valium, 152
Varicocele, and infertility, 34–35

Walking reflex, 226
Ward, Charlotte, 150
Ward, Fred, 150
Whelan, Dr. Elizabeth, 28
White, Burton, 225, 291
White, Dr. Gregory J., 193
Whole Birth Catalog, 131

Index

Who Will Raise the Children? (Levine), 2, 297, 319
Womanly Art of Breastfeeding, The (La Leche League), 224
Women
  body changes in pregnancy, 84
  hormonal changes in pregnancy, 79–80
  husband's fears about, 78–81
  stresses of pregnancy, 78–79
  See also Mothers (new).
Working Parents' Guide to Child Care (Siegel-Gorelick), 311
Work issues, 214–218
  for new father
    dilemma for men, 216
    getting ahead at work, 217
    societal pressures and, 217
    paternity leave, 215–216, 217–218
  See also Dual-career couples; Full-time fathers; Full-time mothers.

Yoga birth, 133
Your Baby & Child: From Birth to Age Five (Leach), 227
Your Baby's Sex: Now You Can Choose (Shettles and Rorvick), 28
Your Child at Play (Segal and Adcock), 242

Zalk, Sue R., 56, 62
Zeus envy, 74–75
Zygote, 29–30

About the Author

David Laskin is the father of a daughter and twin baby girls, born while this book was going to press. He is the author of *The Esquire Wine and Liquor Handbook* (Avon, 1984) and *Getting into Advertising* (Ballantine, 1986). He has also written on infant development and a variety of articles on travel, home entertainment, and manners that have appeared in *Esquire* magazine, *Travel & Leisure*, and other publications. He lives outside of New York City with his wife, their growing family, and two large dogs.